NOTABLE NATURAL DISASTERS

NOTABLE NATURAL DISASTERS

Volume 3

Events 1970 to 2006

Edited by
Marlene Bradford, Ph.D.
Texas A&M University

Robert S. Carmichael, Ph.D.
University of Iowa

SALEM PRESS, INC.
Pasadena, California   Hackensack, New Jersey

∞ The paper used in these volumes conforms to the American National Standard for Permanence of Paper for Printed Library Materials, Z39.48-1992 (R1997).

These essays originally appeared in *Natural Disasters* (2001). New essays and other material have been added.

Library of Congress Cataloging-in-Publication Data

Notable natural disasters / edited by Marlene Bradford, Robert S. Carmichael.
    p. cm. — (Magill's choice)
    Includes bibliographical references and index.
    ISBN 978-1-58765-368-1 (set : alk. paper) — ISBN 978-1-58765-369-8 (vol. 1 : alk. paper) — ISBN 978-1-58765-370-4 (vol. 2 : alk. paper) — ISBN 978-1-58765-371-1 (vol. 3 : alk. paper) 1. Natural disasters. I. Bradford, Marlene. II. Carmichael, Robert S.

GB5014.N373 2007
904'.5—dc22

                                   2007001926

PRINTED IN CANADA

CONTENTS

■ APPENDIXES

■ INDEXES

COMPLETE LIST OF CONTENTS

Volume 1

Volume 2

Volume 3

NOTABLE NATURAL DISASTERS

■ 1970: THE BHOLA CYCLONE

CYCLONE

DATE: November 12-13, 1970
PLACE: Ganges Delta and East Pakistan (now Bangladesh)
SPEED: More than 100 miles per hour
RESULT: 300,000-500,000 dead, 600,000 homeless

On November 13, 1970, only minutes after midnight, after being tracked by satellite and radar from its birth a thousand miles to the south some two and a half days earlier, a massive cyclone struck the coastal region of East Pakistan (now Bangladesh). Laying waste to the delta formed by the Ganges and Brahmaputra Rivers, this cyclone wiped away entire villages, drowned an incalculable number of Bengalis, and compromised the agricultural production of the region. The response of the government of Pakistan, from its capital some 2,000 miles away, was perceived by the Bengalis of East Pakistan to be inadequate in substance and spirit. In addition to causing enormous physical damage, the cyclone and its aftermath contributed to the growing rift between the people of East Pakistan and the government that ruled them, thereby acting as a catalyst in the formation of the nation of Bangladesh the following year.

THE GEOGRAPHY. The particular geography of this delta, where the Ganges and Brahmaputra Rivers meet and pour out into the Bay of Bengal after their long journeys from the Himalayas in the north, is both a blessing and a curse. The geography both makes the delta extremely productive and leaves it susceptible to destructive and all-too-frequent cyclones. This is the largest delta in the world, composed of a broad, low-lying, alluvial plain—interlaced with a network of smaller rivers, canals, swamps, and marshes—and, further down-river, a jumble of alluvial islands lying barely above sea level. The soils of this region are renewed every year during monsoon season, when the rivers, swollen with meltwater from the Himalayas and excess rainwater, overflow their banks and spread their nutrient-rich sediment over the plains and islands. This process makes the delta soils rich enough to support three harvests per year, providing a large percentage of the foodstuffs necessary to feed the country, one of the most densely populated on earth. As an area of low-lying islands and plains it is entirely defenseless, however, against flooding, especially that brought from the south by cyclone-driven storm surges.

The Ganges Delta is frequently visited by some of the most destructive cyclones on earth. In 1737, for example, a cyclone took the lives of at least 300,000 people. In 1991 another killed 200,000 people in Bangladesh. In numerous other years (there were eight cyclones in the 1960's) lesser cyclones have caused tens of thousands of fatalities. These cyclones are spawned every late spring and autumn north of the equator in the warm tropical waters of the Indian Ocean. The cyclones produced there are inherently no more pow-

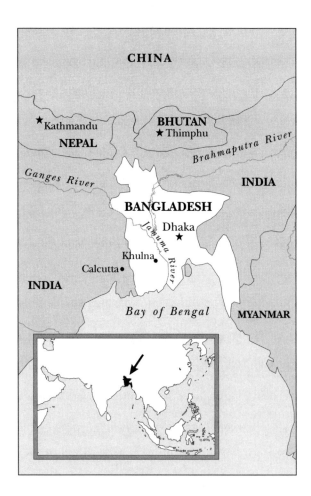

erful or intense than those produced in other regions of the world, but the geography of the Bay of Bengal in general, and of the Ganges Delta in particular, makes the cyclones especially destructive. The Bay of Bengal, shaped like a funnel, forces the cyclones, as they move north toward the Ganges Delta—which lies exactly at the northernmost point of the bay—into an increasingly narrower area, thereby concentrating the energy of the cyclone and the storm surge produced underneath.

THE CYCLONE. The cyclone that caused such havoc in East Pakistan in the autumn of 1970 was first identified by satellite at 9 A.M. on November 10 as a low-pressure area over the Indian Ocean, southeast of Madras, India, a coastal city on the western shores of the Bay of Bengal, and therefore some 1,000 miles to the south of East Pakistan. Moving northward, the low-pressure area evolved into a cyclonic storm with wind velocities of 55 miles per hour. The following morning the storm had reached a point some 650 miles south of Chittagong, East Pakistan's second-largest city and most important port, located just east of the Ganges Delta.

The storm progressed northward into the increasingly narrow, funnel-like Bay of Bengal, its winds now at hurricane force of 75 miles per hour. The accelerating winds and low-pressure area surrounding the eye of every cyclone tend to raise the water level of the ocean underneath by 1 or 2 feet, providing the basis of the storm surge associated with these storms. The approach of a cyclone to a coast forces the storm surge underneath into increasingly shallower water, thereby bringing it to ever-greater heights above normal sea level. This phenomenon is made worse at the top of the Bay of Bengal, where the coast nearly encircles the oncoming cyclone, concentrating, and hence raising, the storm surge even higher. Finally, as the cyclone strikes the very northern tip of the bay, its winds literally drive the storm surge into the extremely shallow water of the Ganges Delta and up and over its low-lying islands and plains.

As this particular hurricane made landfall just after midnight on November 13, 1970, it brought to the delta winds over 100 miles per hour and a storm surge with waves that measured up to 30 feet high. It did so at the worst possible moment: high tide, ensuring swift and sure destruction. The wind-driven storm surge literally flowed over the islands, removing everything in its path. Many islands were denuded of houses, crops, animals, and people. The storm surge, combined with the high tide and the quickly overflowing rivers—swollen with the torrents of rain delivered upriver by the cyclone—brought floodwaters up to 30 feet high in some places.

Fully half of the 242 square miles of Hatia Island remained under 20 feet of water for eight hours. In the trees, above the maximum floodwater line, clung many of the survivors, those delta residents fast enough and strong enough to latch onto trees and climb higher and higher as the waters continued to rise. Below them, at floodwater level, caught in the same trees, floated the corpses of drowned animals and individuals who did not reach safety.

The death toll of Bengalis was set officially at 300,000. Unofficially, it was thought to be much higher—500,000 or even 1 million. Observers attributed the higher death toll to three factors. Once the relief operations were underway, an untold number of corpses were cremated at the place and time they were found in order to lessen the possibility of epidemics. The cyclone struck at harvest time, when the population of this rich agricultural region swells with an influx of migrant workers helping to bring in the harvest. Uncounted and unknown, a large number of these people were assumed to be drowned. Finally, many of those who survived the immediate devastation died soon after of hunger, diseases, or injuries.

While the geographical characteristics and tidal circumstances made for an especially devastating cyclone, the particular socioeconomic characteristics of East Pakistan made it even worse. East Pakistan had one of the highest population densities in the world. At the time of the cyclone, it measured more than 1,300 people per square mile. Under the best of circumstances, evacuating such a large concentration of people under threat of imminent natural disaster would be enormously difficult. East Pakistan possessed, moreover, neither a transportation network nor, even more basic, a warning and evacuation system adequate to the task.

Soon after the disaster it was noted that while Calcutta Radio had reported from India about the cyclone and issued repeated emergency bulletins for hours before its arrival, Dhaka Radio—the only source of information for those living on the distant offshore islands of the Ganges Delta—had made only general reference to an arriving storm, failing to stress to its listeners the danger on the horizon. Having no radio at all, many other islands and villages received no news or warning whatsoever and were thus caught completely by surprise.

THE AFTERMATH. For those who did survive the cyclone and its aftermath, daily life and long-term reconstruction alike would be enormously difficult. It was estimated that the cyclone and its storm surge destroyed the houses of 85 percent of the families in the affected region, leaving some 600,000 survivors homeless. The storm also seriously damaged the agricultural sector of the region, depleting food supplies throughout the country. Hundreds of fishing and transport vessels, including one freighter weighing over 150 tons, were washed inland or otherwise destroyed. Over 1 million head of livestock were drowned. At least 1.1 million acres of rice paddies, holding an estimated 800,000 tons of grain, were destroyed. The storm also incapacitated some 65 percent of East Pakistan's coastal fisheries, thereby seriously compromising the country's most important source of protein for years to come.

A disaster of this magnitude visited upon a poor region such as East Pakistan required enormous immediate and long-term relief, necessitating both international aid and the concerted efforts of the Pakistani government. Within less than a month some $50 million of relief supplies had been delivered to East Pakistan, contributed by foreign governments, international organizations, and private volunteer agencies. The League of Red Cross Societies expected, however, that East Pakistan would need direct foreign assistance at least until April of 1971.

The World Bank had also devised a long-term reconstruction plan to the amount of $185 million, to be administered by governmental authorities with the advice of World Bank specialists. The delivery and distribution of such aid, especially emergency relief, was not without problems. The floodwaters, teeming with decaying corpses and excrement, made perfect breeding grounds for typhoid and cholera, thereby hindering the establishment and staffing of distribution stations.

The real relief problems were human-made and contributed to problems between East Pakistan and the central Pakistani government in Karachi. Before the end of the month of November, East Pakistani political and social leaders began to accuse the governing authorities of "gross neglect, callous inattention, and utter indifference" to the suffering of the survivors of the cyclone; this criticism was not unwarranted. Two days before that announcement the League of Red Cross Societies had decided to postpone further delivery of aid because of the increasingly large stockpiles of relief supplies that remained in Dhaka, the capital of East Pakistan, awaiting final distribution. A team of Norwegian doctors and nurses reported that it had been idle for two days, still waiting for instructions from the governmental authorities.

The relief effort of the government of Pakistan itself, from its capital in Karachi, over 2,000 miles away on the other side of India, was perceived to be slow and insufficient. Only after the embarrassment of international pressure and publicity did the government of Pakistan respond to the plight of the East Pakistanis. Meanwhile, people continued to die of starvation and disease by the tens of thousands, and refugees continued to stream across the border into the already overcrowded Indian city of Calcutta.

Two days after the disaster, General Agha Mohammad Yahya Khan, the commander in chief of the armed forces and effective ruler of Pakistan, which at the time was under martial law, visited Dhaka briefly after a visit to Beijing. He left the next day: The people of East Pakistan and their political leaders perceived this as evidence of official indifference to their suffering. Sheikh Mujibur Rahman, the father of modern Bangladesh, commented from jail, "West Pakistan has a bumper wheat crop, but the first shipment of food grain to reach us is from abroad. . . . We have a large army, but it is left to the British Marines to bury our dead."

On December 7, 1970, less than a month after the cyclone struck the Ganges Delta, elections for the Pakistani National Assembly were held; for the first time East and West Pakistanis would elect their representatives directly. The results were telling; the Awami League, the political party calling for the independence of East Pakistan, won 160 out of 162 seats allotted to East Pakistan. In April of 1971, East Pakistan would rename itself Bangladesh and declare independence. By December, after civil war and the defeat of the Pakistani army in Bangladesh by the army of India, Bangladesh became recognized as an independent nation.

Rosa Alvarez Ulloa

FOR FURTHER INFORMATION:

Cornell, James. "Cyclones: Hurricanes and Typhoons." *The Great International Disaster Book.* New York: Charles Scribner's Sons, 1976.

Frazier, Kendrick. "Hurricanes." In *The Violent Face of Nature: Severe Phenomena and Natural Disasters.* New York: William Morrow, 1979.

Heitzman, James, and Robert Worden. *Bangladesh: A Country Study.* 2d ed. Area Handbook Series DA Pam 550-175. Washington, D.C.: Government Printing Office, 1989.

Whittow, John. "High Winds." *Disasters: The Anatomy of Environmental Hazards.* Athens: University of Georgia Press, 1979.

■ 1974: THE JUMBO OUTBREAK

TORNADOES

ALSO KNOWN AS: The Super Outbreak
DATE: April 3-4, 1974
PLACE: 11 states in the U.S. South and Midwest, as well as Ontario, Canada
CLASSIFICATION: 6 tornadoes rated F5
RESULT: 316 dead, nearly 5,500 injured, $1 billion in damage

The largest tornado outbreak (several tornadoes in one day) to date in the United States resulted from the unusual collision of cold, dry air from the west upon warm, moist air extending east through the Ohio River Valley. The storm cell created was carried by strong, fast-moving winds common for systems in the early spring—a front moved from Colorado to Detroit in only a few hours, reaching the speed of 60 miles per hour near St. Louis. However, when the storm cell met the jet stream, events ceased to be common. Three parallel lines of squalls began to form shortly after noon on Wednesday, April 3, 1974. These squalls were more than 11 miles high and eventually a total of 2,598 miles long. They moved at an average rate of 50 miles per hour.

At 2:08 P.M. in Lincoln, Illinois, the squall line from St. Louis to Lake Michigan spawned the first of what would be 148 tornadoes in all before the activity ended at 5:20 A.M. on April 4. Meanwhile, a tornado in the second and more violent line from central Tennessee to southern Michigan touched down in Cleveland, Tennessee, at 2:10 P.M., with additional tornadoes in Jonesville and Depauw, Indiana, ten minutes later. The third line, along the Tennessee-North Carolina border, did not fully form until the early evening of April 3 but ultimately birthed just over one-third of the tornadoes in the outbreak and left 100 people dead.

The Jumbo Outbreak—or Super Outbreak, as a number of survivors have also termed it—was not only more extensive than all other known instances to date but also unusually intense, with tornado path lengths and widths one order of magnitude greater than those associated with average tornadoes. Natural barriers were thus no impediment to the powerful funnels. One of the worst storms moved continuously over 51 miles in Alabama, including across a lake. Among other damage, this tornado destroyed a mobile home park with its winds of 260 miles per hour. Another tornado climbed the 3,300-foot peak of Rich Knob in Georgia to ravage the valley below, while another of the Alabama funnels continued on after jumping a 200-foot cliff.

Yet the tornadoes did not form in any major population centers, while many people in the tornadoes' paths survived remarkably. For example, in Branchville, Indiana, a school bus rolled 400 feet off the road, killing the driver and his wife. Another bus driver nearby, though, evacuated the children on board and had them lie in a ditch. The bus blew over them, but no one else was seriously hurt. In another tornado, the winds caused the car of a man driving home from work to somersault twice and land in his neighbor's yard. Although he was badly cut by glass, the man found his family huddled safely in the basement beneath the rubble of his home. There were also the freakish stories typically created by tornadoes, such as that of the pet rabbit in a hutch behind a home in Dawson County, Georgia, that ended up safe in the kitchen while 3 of the 5 human members of the family perished.

Overall, 11 states—Alabama, Georgia, Illinois, Indiana, Kentucky, Michigan, North Carolina, Ohio, Tennessee, Virginia, and West Virginia—and over 50,000 people experienced the outbreak in the United States. Eight people also died and more than 10 were hurt in Windsor, Ontario, Canada. The National Guard was called out in Kentucky, Tennessee, and Ohio. All three states, as well as Indiana, Georgia, and Alabama, were later named federal disaster areas. Eight hundred Red Cross workers served the stricken communities. The power system of the Tennessee Valley Authority suffered the worst damage of its forty-year history, while 90 percent of Huntsville, Alabama, was left without electricity and nine towns in Indiana and Cincinnati, Ohio, were among municipalities that lost phone service.

At the height of activity, 15 tornadoes were on the ground simultaneously. Thirteen tornadoes were rated at an intensity of F1, 22 at F2, 30 at F3, 22 at F4, and 6 at F5 through a combination of decisions by local weather offices and aerial pictures. The strongest tornadoes occurred at Xenia, Ohio; Depauw, Indiana; Sayler Park, Ohio; Brandenburg, Kentucky; First Tanner, Alabama; and Guin, Alabama. Etowa, Tennessee; Cleveland, Tennessee; Tanner, Alabama; Harvest, Alabama; Huntsville, Alabama; and Livingston, Tennessee were all struck twice by funnels. In Huntsville, one injured man went to a church to wait for an ambulance, only to be killed by the second tornado ten minutes later. There were two cases of family tornadoes, or several tornadoes spawned from one funnel: near Monticello, Indiana, where 150 homes and 100 businesses valued at $100 million were destroyed, and along the Indiana-Kentucky border near Cincinnati, Ohio. During the outbreak, a moderate earthquake centered in Springfield, Illinois, occurred coincidentally. There were no injuries or damage caused by the tremor, though. The two communities hit hardest during the Jumbo Outbreak were Xenia, Ohio, and Brandenburg, Kentucky.

XENIA, OHIO. In Xenia, near Dayton, the storm began around 4:30 P.M. Eastern time on April 3 as two small funnels twisting around each other. These funnels intensified as they approached Xenia, creating suction vortices that spun over the city of 25,000 for the next forty-five minutes. One vortex moved from west to east at speeds nearing 200 miles per hour. As a whole, the Xenia tornado was composed of a dust column between 30 and 40 feet wide, probably spinning at 100 miles per hour.

There were no weather sirens in Xenia at the time, so many people had no idea the weather was deteriorating until the tornado was on top of them. By the time the tornado moved through Xenia, 35 people had died and 1 of every 25 residents (or 1,150 total) was injured. The dead included 2 National Guardsmen fighting a fire in the aftermath of the tornado and 5 people found at the A&W drive-in restaurant.

Fortunately, the elementary and secondary schools had all finished classes for the day, and students from Wilberforce College and Central State College were out of town on spring break, since there was almost no warning when the tornado first hit. Three schools were completely ruined, and three more were seriously damaged. At the high school, the drama troupe took refuge in a classroom outside the auditorium shortly before the roof collapsed and three school buses were tossed onto the stage. One family with 5 children miraculously

One of the tornadoes of the Jumbo Outbreak, this funnel cloud struck Xenia, Ohio, which suffered major damage. (AP/Wide World Photos)

survived despite having to take refuge in a glass shop, which exploded around them.

Half of the city's homes were damaged or destroyed. Typically, all the houses on one side of a street collapsed while the other side suffered less damage. This was because the wind blew in the garage doors on one side of the street, and the homes collapsed once the wind blew inside. All 3 power lines into Xenia were blown down, and 5 of the 7 supermarkets were demolished. Besides the National Guard, personnel from Wright-Patterson Air Force Base lent support to tornado cleanup efforts and supplied fresh water to Xenia. Damages in Xenia were estimated to be three-fourths of the $100 million total repair costs for Ohio. It took three months of 200 trucks per day to haul away the rubble.

BRANDENBURG, KENTUCKY. At 3:40 P.M., a tornado touched down near Hardinsburg, Kentucky. Half an hour later, it had grown to 500 yards across and struck Brandenburg in the most serious of the 26 tornado touchdowns in Kentucky during the Jumbo Outbreak.

Thirty-one of Brandenburg's 1,700 residents were killed when a tornado struck there, and 250 were hurt. This was a substantial percentage of the 71 dead and 280 injured reported in all of Kentucky as of April 4. Many tornado victims were apparently children playing outside after school. Soldiers from Fort Knox provided assistance with rescue and recovery, bringing searchlights the night of April 3 to search for the dead. Brandenburg's five-block downtown area was completely demolished. Total damages were estimated at $22 million.

LEARNING FROM THE JUMBO OUTBREAK. The spring of 1974 had already shown some penchant for storms. For example, 20 tornadoes were recorded on April 1, killing 2 and injuring 51 in ten states, while damaging or destroying 72 aircraft worth $1 million at North Metropolitan Airport in Nashville (now Nashville International Airport). Meteorologists knew that the weather patterns remained volatile, yet none of them could have predicted that within three days the United States would be on its way to suffering the most tornado deaths in one year since 1953. No one guessed that the previous record for tornadoes over a twenty-four-hour period would be smashed, either. That mark was the more than 60 funnels recorded on February 19, 1884, in Alabama, Indiana, Kentucky, Mississippi, North Carolina, South Carolina, and Tennessee. That tornado outbreak destroyed 10,000 buildings, killed 800, and injured 2,500.

However, tornado researcher Theodore Fujita was determined to use the events of April 3-4, 1974, to better understand tornadoes and to improve preparedness and safety. He flew over 10,000 miles after the outbreak in a joint survey with the University of Oklahoma and the National Severe Storms Laboratory, gathering a vast amount of useful data. In fact, nearly half of the tornadoes studied by Fujita and his assistants at the University of Chicago during his career were the ones from this outbreak.

Fujita accumulated evidence from the Jumbo Outbreak—a phrase he coined based on the 747 "jumbo jet" ("74" for 1974 and "7" from the sum of April 3 and 4)—to support two of his theories. First, in one forest, Fujita photographed a peculiar starburst pattern, where the fallen trees pointed out from one spot. This helped him argue for the existence of microbursts, phenomena that can push a tornado off its path. Second, Fujita was able to demonstrate the presence of suction vortices, small vortices within a tornado that seem to suck the debris together. Three motions coincide in the suction vortex—the motion of the tornado, the rotation of the suction spot around the tornado, and the spin of the vortex—and can result in a circular area of damage with a diameter of up to 20 feet. Because the Xenia tornado was transparent and its funnel did not extend all the way from the ground to the cloud, Fujita could show the motion of suction vortices by the movement of dust and debris in home movies from Xenia.

Fujita's research into the Jumbo Outbreak helped scientists distinguish between damage caused by tornadoes and by strong winds. They thus learned more about the conditions under which tornadoes occur so that the public can be warned earlier. In addition, the outbreak encouraged meteorologists to continue trying to improve their radar systems. By the late 1990's, tornadoes that were merely "green blobs" in 1974 could be seen clearly on Doppler screens. Meteorologists also urged towns to invest in weather sirens. For example, Xenia installed a system of ten alarms. Finally, many of the communities devastated by the outbreak took pride in rebuilding their homes and making them better than before.

Amy Ackerberg-Hastings

FOR FURTHER INFORMATION:

Ball, Jacqueline A. *Tornado! The 1974 Super Outbreak.* New York: Bearport, 2005.

Burt, Christopher C. *Extreme Weather: A Guide and Record Book.* New York: W. W. Norton, 2004.

Butler, William S., ed. *Tornado: A Look Back at Louisville's Dark Day, April 3, 1974.* Louisville, Ky.: Butler Books, 2004.

Fujita, T. Theodore. "Jumbo Tornado Outbreak of 3 April 1974." *Weatherwise* 27 (1974): 116-126.

Rosenfield, Jeffrey. *Eye of the Storm: Inside the World's Deadliest Hurricanes, Tornadoes, and Blizzards.* New York: Basic Books, 2003.

U.S. Department of Commerce. National Oceanic and Atmospheric Administration. *The Widespread Tornado Outbreak of April 3-4, 1974: A Report to the Administrator.* Rockville, Md.: Author, 1974.

Weems, John Edward. *The Tornado.* College Station: Texas A&M University Press, 1991.

■ 1976: EBOLA OUTBREAKS

EPIDEMICS

DATE: Late June-November 20, 1976, in Sudan and September 1-October 24, 1976, in Zaire

PLACE: Southern Sudan and northern Zaire (now Democratic Republic of Congo)

RESULT: 151 dead out of 284 cases (53 percent mortality), 280 dead out of 318 cases (88 percent mortality)

In 1967, 23 commercial laboratory workers were hospitalized in Marburg, Germany, for a hemorrhagic fever that was traced to the handling of vervets (African green monkeys) imported from Uganda. Six more medical workers in Frankfurt, Germany, who were involved in the treatment of these patients, also became sick. At the same time, a veterinarian who handled monkeys and his wife were infected in Belgrade, Yugoslavia. Electron microscopy work determined that the disease agent was an unusual-looking ribonucleic acid virus. It had a unique, slender filamentous comma shape or branched shape and caused 23 percent mortality. Relatively few detected recurrences of this disease have occurred since its discovery. However, a serologically distinct but related virus with similar effects, now known as Ebola hemorrhagic fever (EHF), was identified during two almost simultaneous epidemics during 1976.

The diseases begin four to sixteen days after infection as an increasingly severe influenza-like illness, with high fever, headaches, chest pains, and weakness for about two days. This is followed in the majority of cases by severe diarrhea, vomiting, dry throat, cough, and rash. Bleeding from body openings is very common, and patients can become aggressive and difficult to manage. The virus reaches high levels in the blood and other body fluids, and the resulting tissue infections are so extensive that organ damage can be widespread. Within seven to ten days the patient is severely exhausted and dehydrated and often dies of shock. The natural animal reservoir for this virus is not known, and human-to-human transmission mostly results from close, intimate contact. There is presently no known treatment.

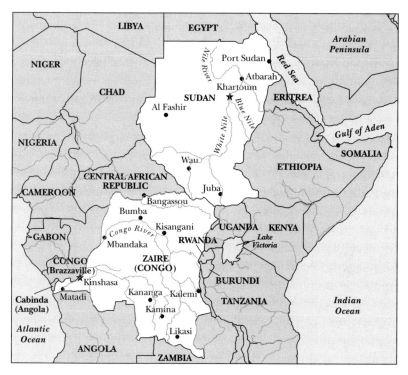

SUDAN. The epidemic started in Nzara township, where most residents live in mud-walled, thatched-roof houses in the thick woodlands adjacent to the African rain forest zone. The first persons infected with Ebola hemorrhagic fever are believed to be three employees of a cotton factory, part of an agricultural cooperative, in Nzara; local raw cotton is converted to cloth by the 455 employees of this factory. A factory storekeeper became ill on June 27, 1976, with a high fever, headache, and chest pains. He bled from the nose and mouth and had bloody diarrhea by the fifth day, was hospitalized in Nzara on June 30, and died on July 6. His brother nursed him and also became sick but recovered after two weeks.

Another storekeeper who worked with the deceased storekeeper entered the hospital on July 12 and died July 14. His wife took ill and died on July 19. Another factory worker employed in the cloth room next to the store where the two deceased employees worked became sick on July 18, entered the hospital on July 24, and died on July 27. None of the men lived near each other nor socialized together, and their lives were very different. Eventually associates of the third employee became ill, and one individual who managed the jazz club, a social center in Nzara, journeyed to the Maridi hospital, where he died. Forty-eight cases and 27 deaths in Nzara could be traced to the third employee. By July, September, and October, additional factory employees were getting sick but could not be tied directly to previously infected individuals. Most were cared for by family members in isolated homesteads. This helped limit the spread of the disease.

The individual who died in Maridi was cared for by close friends and several hospital employees, all of whom came down with the fever. They were cared for by others, who managed to spread the disease to various regions around the Maridi township. An additional source of infection arrived when a nurse from Nzara came in for treatment. Many of the hospital staff were also infected.

By the time the World Health Organization (WHO) team arrived in Maridi on October 29, the situation was dire there but improving in Nzara. The Maridi hospital was virtually emptied of patients; 33 of the 61 on the nursing staff had died, and 1 doctor had developed the disease. Eight additional people associated with hospital maintenance also died. Thus, the local community viewed the hospital as the source of their woes. Isolation measures were quickly adopted, and protective clothing was distributed within the hospital.

Five teams of 7 individuals each, including schoolteachers and older school boys led by a public health official, were to visit every homestead and identify infected individuals in the community, who were then requested to come to the hospital. If they preferred to stay at home, relatives were warned to restrict contact with the patient. Funeral rituals also hastened the spread of the disease because ritual called for the body being prepared for burial by removing all food and excreta by hand. Local leaders were apprised of the situation, and they encouraged people to bring their dead to Maridi, where medical personnel would cleanse the bodies. Their support accelerated the work of the surveillance teams, which expanded their efforts to include a 30-mile radius around Maridi by November 17.

The final count of 284 cases was distributed as 67 in Nzara, 213 in Maridi, 3 in Tembura, and 1 in Juba. Epidemiological analysis indicated that Nzara was the source of the epidemic, and the cotton factory was studied most intensively. Infections developed in the cloth room and nearby store, the weaving areas, and the drawing-in areas only. There were no infections in the spinning area, where most of the employees worked.

ZAIRE. The focus of the epidemic in Zaire was in a region where more than three-quarters of the 275,000 people of the Bumba zone live in villages with fewer than 5,000 people. This region is part of the middle Congo River basin and is largely a tropical rain forest. The Yambuku Catholic Mission was founded by Belgian missionaries in 1935 and provided medicines to a region of about 60,000 people in the Yandongi collectivity (county). In 1976 there were 120 beds supervised by a medical staff of seventeen, including a Zairean medical assistant and three Belgian nuns who worked as nurses and midwives. Around 6,000 to 12,000 people were treated monthly. Five syringes and needles were distributed to the nursing staff every morning for use at the outpatient, prenatal, and inpatient clinics. Unfortunately, they were only rinsed in warm water between uses, unlike in the surgical ward, which had its own equipment that was sterilized after every use.

The first person to exhibit definitive signs of the Ebola virus was a forty-four-year-old male teacher at the Mission School who had recently toured the most northern areas of Zaire, the Mobayi-Mbongo zone, by automobile with other Mission employees from August 10 to August 22. His fever was suggestive of malaria, so he was injected with chloroquine on August 26 at the outpatient clinic. His fever disappeared and then reappeared on September 1, along with other symptoms. He was admitted with gastrointestinal bleeding to the Yambuku Mission Hospital (YMH) on September 5. The medical staff gave him antibiotics, chloroquine, vitamins, and intravenous fluids but nothing worked. He died on September 8.

Records for the outpatient clinic were too incomplete to trace easily possible earlier cases, but there may have been one individual with EHF treated on August 28, who was described as having an odd combination of symptoms: nosebleeds and diarrhea. He may have been the source of the infection, but he left the clinic and was never found. Nine additional conclusive cases occurred in people who had received treatment for other diseases at the outpatient clinic at YMH. A sixteen-year-old female was given transfusions for her anemia. An adult woman was given vitamin injections so that she could care for her husband recovering from hernia surgery. Another adult woman was recovering from malaria, tended by her husband. All later succumbed and died of EHF, and soon those who had nursed these individuals or prepared their bodies for burial also came down with the disease. The disease struck 21 family members and friends of the first patient, and 18 died.

This new, mysterious disease that caused people to bleed to death and to go crazy was soon causing a panic in the local villages. On September 12 a nun became sick, and other nuns radioed for help. The provincial physician arrived on September 15 and, equally baffled, gathered as much information as he could and then returned to Bumba, where he requested help from administrators in Kinshasa. On September 19, the nun died; by then, the bleeding illness was responsible for deaths in more than 40 villages.

Two professors of epidemiology and microbiology from the National University of Zaire were sent to Yambuku. They arrived on September 23, expecting to study the situation for six days, but left after a day of collecting blood and tissue samples from cadavers and patients. The professors also took two nuns and a father back with them to Kinshasa for treatment. Thirteen of the 17 staff members at YMH had become infected and 11 had died, so the hospital was closed on October 3. At least 85 out of 288 cases, where transmission could be traced, had received injections at YMH. Another 149 patients had had close contact with infected patients, and 49 had been subject to injections and patient contact.

The former physician of Zairean president Mobutu Sese Seko, Dr. William Close, was contacted by the Minister of Health in order to gain assistance from the United States. He contacted the Centers for Disease Control (CDC) in Atlanta, Georgia, which provided laboratory support. By mid-October medical authorities had imposed a quarantine on the Bumba zone. Village elders requested their community members to stay in their homes, and all activities stopped. By now officials were aware that there was a similar epidemic in southern Sudan, and blood samples from both locales were shipped to the virus unit of the WHO in Geneva, which then forwarded them to the CDC. On October 15, the WHO reported the presence of a new virus, later named Ebola for a local river.

What followed was an internationally coordinated investigation of both Zaire and Sudan by at least eight nations, several international organizations, and Zaire's entire medical community. The most up-to-date isolation strategies were used, and patients were attended by personnel in protective suits. A complete epidemiological investigation was conducted, studying 550 villages and interviewing 34,000 families. Scientists took blood samples from 442 people in the communities where the infection was most prevalent. They also collected local insects and animals, with no success at finding the animal reservoir.

Although geographically and chronologically close, the two epidemics appear to have been independent events. There were relatively few travelers and no Ebola cases between the two locales. Molecular analyses also indicated the two strains of Ebola were different. The Nzara virus is relatively more infectious, and the Yambuku virus is more lethal. Both Ebola virus strains were placed in the new filovirus family.

It was not until 1995 that another major Ebola epidemic occurred, this time in Kikwit, Zaire. EHF outbreaks before 1995 were sporadic and small, including 1 death in Tandala, Zaire, in 1977; 34 cases and 22 dead in Nzara and Yambio, Zaire, in 1979; and 1 case in Tai, Ivory Coast. There may have been a near miss when macaque monkeys from the Philippines residing in a facility in Reston, Virginia, died from an Ebola-like filovirus in 1989. The virus did not affect humans. Scientists continued to search for a cure, knowing that the prevention of future epidemics hinges on identification of the animal reservoir and the presence of adequate health care facilities in some of the poorest regions of the world.

Joan C. Stevenson

FOR FURTHER INFORMATION:
Garrett, Laurie. *The Coming Plague: Newly Emerging Diseases in a World out of Balance.* New York: Penguin Books, 1994.

Klenk, Hans-Dieter, ed. *Marburg and Ebola Viruses.* New York: Springer, 1999.

Murphy, Frederick A., and Clarence J. Peters. "Ebola Virus: Where Does It Come from and Where Is It Going?" In *Emerging Infections,* edited by Richard M. Krause. San Diego, Calif.: Academic Press, 1998.

Preston, Richard. *The Hot Zone.* New York: Random House, 1994.

Simpson, D. I. H. *Marburg and Ebola Virus Infections: A Guide for Their Diagnosis, Management, and Control.* Geneva, Switzerland: World Health Organization, 1977.

Smith, Tara C. *Ebola.* Philadelphia: Chelsea House, 2006.

WHO/International Study Team. "Ebola Haemorrhagic Fever in Sudan, 1976. Ebola Haemorrhagic Fever in Zaire, 1976." *Bulletin of the World Health Organization* 56, no. 2 (1978): 247-293.

■ 1976: LEGIONNAIRES' DISEASE

EPIDEMIC

DATE: July 21-August 4, 1976
PLACE: Philadelphia, Pennsylvania
RESULT: 29 dead, 221 infected

Yearlong U.S. bicentennial celebrations reached a peak on July 4, 1976, in the city of Philadelphia. Philadelphians proudly displayed American flags on the porches of their row houses, welcoming the thousands of visitors who came to witness the United States celebration of the two hundredth anniversary of the signing of the Declaration of Independence. President Gerald Ford gave a speech at Independence Hall in Philadelphia to record the occasion for posterity. Later that afternoon, the historic Liberty Bell monument, which had been silent for many decades, was struck. Bells in towns across the country simultaneously echoed the toll of the Liberty Bell. By nightfall the excitement escalated. The light from red, white, and blue fireworks lit up skies from coast to coast.

Less than three weeks later, after so many jubilant festivities, Pennsylvanians were stunned and helpless when the city witnessed a major event in medical history and found it was again the focus of media attention. The stifling July heat and drizzling rain that fell during the legionnaires' parade added to the sticky humidity but did not offer much relief to spectators and legionnaire families lining the center city streets in Philadelphia. The veterans with the American Legion held parades to kick off their annual gatherings. The Bellvue-Stratford Hotel, a national and historic Philadelphia landmark built in the early 1900's, hosted the fifty-eighth Pennsylvania State American Legion Convention, where an outbreak of a pneumonia-like illness mysteriously occurred among a group of attendees. More than 4,000 delegates attended the four-day convention at the hotel, which lasted from July 21 to 24, 1976. One week after the convention, American Legion officials in Pennsylvania began receiving calls from members statewide: They reported several legionnaires had died and dozens of others were hospitalized with severe pneumonia. Leaders from the American Legion quickly alerted city and state health department personnel and media to the rapidly increasing number of legionnaires stricken by the mysterious illness.

The epidemic pneumonia that emerged following the American Legion convention was subsequently described as "one of the most publicized epidemics" in which the elite Centers for Disease Control (CDC) medical investigators had participated. State and national newspapers covering the story reported the link of the illness to legionnaire members, calling the mysterious pneumonia "Legionnaires' disease," and they constantly pressed researchers for information on the official death tolls and progress reports on the investigation of the outbreak. Ten days after the convention concluded, publishing a brief account in the *Morbidity and Mortality Weekly Report* of August 6, 1976, researchers from the CDC in Atlanta stated 22 people had died from pneumonia caused by Philadelphia Respiratory Disease. State and city physicians and epidemiologists investigating the cause of the illness that was later officially named Legionnaires' disease were not initially able to identify the agent responsible because it mimicked other illnesses and could not be cultured using standard laboratory techniques.

Four months passed before investigators were able to find the answers and to unlock the mystery that accompanied the sometimes-fatal infection. Then, on January 14, 1976, Joseph McDade, a CDC research microbiologist, isolated a bacterium that caused the epidemic. The bacteria responsible for the disease was named *Legionella pneumophila* (lung-loving). It was difficult to isolate and culture, and the patterns seen in chest X rays of the victims resembled patterns that had previously been associated with viral infections. Eventually, in this outbreak legionellosis caused 29 deaths (various sources list 29-34 deaths) and sickened 221 people, some of whom were not directly associated with the convention.

CLASSIFICATION AND DEFINITION. In 1999, scientists characterized *Legionella pneumophila* as a naturally occurring aquatic microorganism. *Legionella* species are now recognized as a leading cause of community-acquired pneumonia. The CDC has estimated that 17,000 to 23,000 cases of Legionnaires' disease occur annually in America, with less than 1,000 of these cases being confirmed and reported. The resulting mortality rate, which ranges up to 25 percent in untreated immunity-compromised patients, can be lowered if the disease is diagnosed rapidly and appropriate antimicrobial therapy instituted early. *Legionella pneumophila* is estimated to be responsible for 80 to 85 percent of reported cases of *Legionella* infections, with the majority of cases being caused specifically by *Legionella pneumophilia*.

RISK FACTORS, SYMPTOMS, AND TREATMENT. Those at risk for Legionnaires' disease include people fifty years of age and older, smokers, and those with pulmonary disease. People with weakened immune systems, such as organ transplant patients, kidney dialysis patients, and those suffering from cancer and AIDS, are also at risk, as are those who are exposed to water vapor containing *L. pneumophila*. Males are 2.5 times more likely to contract the disease than females.

People with legionellosis usually first display a mild cough and low fever and, if untreated, can quickly advance through progressive pneumonia and coma. The incubation period for *L. pneumophila* is two to ten days. Other early symptoms of this disease include malaise, muscle aches, and a slight headache. In later stages, victims have displayed high fevers (105 degrees Fahrenheit); dry, unproductive coughs; and shortness of breath. Gastrointestinal symptoms observed include vomiting, diarrhea, nausea, and abdominal pain. Since identification of *L. pneumophila*, clinicians have reported it is effectively treated with either erythromycin or a combination of erythromycin and rifampin.

RESERVOIRS AND AMPLIFIERS. Scientists sampling lakes, ponds, streams, marine and fresh waters, and soils have isolated the *L. pneumophila* bacterium in nature. Amplifiers are defined by scientists as any natural or human-made system that provides suitable conditions for the growth of the bacterium. Controversy still surrounds the exact location of the bacterial agent responsible for the Philadelphia outbreak; however, most articles list the hotel air conditioner water cooling tower as the source.

Scientific publications after 1978 reported the isolation of *L. pneumophila* from human-made plumbing systems, including showers, faucets, hot-water tanks, cooling towers, evaporative condensers, humidifiers, whirlpools, spas, decorative fountains, dental water units, grocery produce misters, and respiratory-therapy equipment. The plumbing systems of hotels, dental offices, hospitals, grocery stores, gymnasiums, and homes have also been documented as sources for the bacterium. Environmental factors associated with survival of this bacterium are water temperatures between 68 and 122 degrees Fahrenheit (20 and 50 degrees Celsius), stagnant water, pH ranges of 2.0-8.5, microbiotically nutrient sediments, and host microorganisms (algae, protozoa, flavobacteria, and *Pseudomonas* bacteria).

TRANSMISSION. In 1980, CDC investigators published six key events required for the transmission of *Legionella*. The first three events—survival in nature, amplification, and aerosolization—are influenced by environmental parameters (reservoir temperature and pH, microorganism populations, climate, humidity, and biocides). In contrast, the last three events—susceptible exposure, intracellular multiplication in human phagocytes, and diagnosis of Legionnaires' disease—are clinical parameters (patient risk factors, virulence, symptoms, laboratory testing, and diagnosis).

Anthony Newsome and Mary Etta Boulden

FOR FURTHER INFORMATION:

Fraser, David W., et al. "Legionnaires' Disease: Description of an Epidemic of Pneumonia." *New England Journal of Medicine* 297 (1977): 1189-1197.

Katz, Sheila Moriber, ed. *Legionellosis*. Boca Raton, Fla.: CRC Press, 1985.

McCoy, William F. *Preventing Legionellosis*. Seattle: IWA, 2005.

Shader, Laurel. *Legionnaire's Disease*. Philadelphia: Chelsea House, 2006.

Stout, Jane E., and Victor L. Yu. "Legionellosis." *The New England Journal of Medicine* 337 (1997): 682-687.

Thomas, Gordon, and Max Morgan-Witts. *Anatomy of an Epidemic*. New York: Doubleday, 1982.

Yu, Victor L. "Resolving the Controversy on Environmental Cultures for *Legionella*: A Modest Proposal." *Infection Control and Hospital Epidemiology* 19, no. 12 (1998): 893-897.

◼ 1976: THE TANGSHAN EARTHQUAKE

EARTHQUAKE

DATE: July 28, 1976
PLACE: Tangshan, northeastern China
MAGNITUDE: 8.0
RESULT: About 250,000 dead (the highest death toll for a natural disaster in the twentieth century), 160,000 seriously injured, almost the entire city of 1.1 million people destroyed

China has a long recorded history of earthquakes. Geologically, it is a region of complex tectonic relationships. The Indian Plate is pushing northward in the southwest, forming the Himalayas and elevated Tibetan Plateau, and oceanic plates are approaching and colliding in the southeast and east.

Historically, China is a vast region that has had a large population for millennia, as well as a relatively advanced culture, with recorded history extending back well over two thousand years. When the Communist Party took power in 1949 and the People's Republic of China began, a search was initiated by 130 historians to document the history of seismic activity. They found that there had been more than ten thousand earthquakes recorded in China in the previous three thousand years—over five hundred of them of disaster proportions.

SETTING. Tangshan is a large, thriving industrial city at 39.4 degrees north latitude and 118.1 degrees east longitude in Hebei Province of northeast China, 100 miles (160 kilometers) southeast of the capital of Beijing. It is about 25 miles (40 kilometers) from the Gulf of Chihli, on the Yellow Sea. Its name derives from the T'ang dynasty (618-907 C.E.) and the word for mountains, "shan." In the early 1970's it had a population of 1.1 million, much industrial production, and China's largest coal mine, at nearby Kailuan. There was little expectation that Tangshan was to become the site, in terms of death and destruction, of the worst natural disaster of the twentieth century, with the second highest death toll in the recorded history of earthquakes—exceeded only by a great earthquake in January, 1556, in Shaanxi (or Shensi), central China, in which 830,000 died when buildings and caves collapsed at night.

The important Beijing-Tianjin-Tangshan region of northeast China was being intensely studied for potential seismic risk. By the early 1970's the Chinese government had begun a major effort to investigate earthquake prediction, using the State Bureau of Seismology, other agencies, and an extensive network of field stations to monitor various geophysical and geological properties of the local earth, which were thought to be possible precursors that might herald an impending earthquake. This effort resulted in a spectacular success in 1975, when seismologists detected an increasing frequency of minor earthquakes in the region of Haicheng, northeast of Tangshan, along with some regional ground deformation. They thought this could indicate an upcoming, larger earthquake.

On February 4, 1975, their warning resulted in the evacuation of well over 1 million people from their homes, factories, and other workplaces—into the cold, without civil resistance. A few hours later, at 7:36 P.M., the Haicheng area was hit by a magnitude 7.3 earthquake, which destroyed 90 percent of the buildings of Haicheng as well as nearby towns and villages. There were only 1,328 deaths, however, compared to the doubtless tens of thousands who would have died without the advance warning and evacuation. A later report noted that the seismologists who had predicted the quake were "worshipped as saviours."

Unfortunately, nature would not easily yield its secrets and intentions. Despite much work in earthquake prediction in seismically active areas in the United States, Japan, Russia, and China, Haicheng remained the only major earthquake that had been predicted correctly—or with a short-term notice—by the year 2000. After the Haicheng event, various seismic stations in China issued their own predictions for local earthquakes, but none occurred.

The Tangshan area had likewise been monitored since 1974 for changes in such conditions as microseismicity (number and location of very small earthquakes), ground elevation, local sea level, gravity and magnetic fields, radon gas in groundwater, and even drought conditions. There was sufficient concern that on July 15, 1976, there was a meeting of technical experts in Tangshan. However, it was felt that there was no indication of potential seismic activity exceeding

magnitude 5, which was the threshold at which it would be reported to the civil authorities. Some thought an earthquake might be possible in the next few years, but there were no minor precursory foreshocks warning that a quake was imminent. There were also meetings in Beijing of the State Bureau of Seismology on July 24 and 26, regarding the possibility of a future earthquake in the Beijing-Tianjin-Tangshan area. While there was no technical reason for immediate concern, it was also true that an alert leading to evacuation would be very disruptive to life, production, and other economic activity in the large cities in the region.

Since the area is of intraplate nature, which is far away from the seismically and tectonically active margins of the crustal plates, earthquakes there are expected to be infrequent and of only moderate size. Human knowledge of crustal fracturing, stress, and potential for

713

faulting (slippage, which causes earthquakes) is imperfect. There had been major earthquakes in the general region of Tangshan in September, 1679, and in September, 1290 (with 100,000 deaths).

THE QUAKE. Without warning, at 3:42 A.M. on July 28, 1976, a massive earthquake struck the Tangshan area. There was a loud rumbling and roaring sound, followed by violent jerking back and forth. The earthquake (including subsequent aftershocks) leveled 20 square miles (50 square kilometers) of the densely populated industrial center of the city, flattened or severely damaged 97 percent of the buildings and three-quarters of Tangshan's 916 multistory structures (only 4 remained essentially intact), and left a ruin of crumbled buildings, fallen smokestacks, and rubble. Falling buildings, cement floor slabs, and beams immediately crushed thousands of people. Most of the disaster's victims survived the initial shock only to suffocate or succumb to injuries after hours and days trapped in the dusty wreckage.

There was no electrical power, no water, no telecommunication systems, no functioning hospital, no transport routes, and no imme-

The aftermath of the 1976 Tangshan earthquake. (National Oceanic and Atmospheric Administration)

diate search and rescue help. With 300 miles of railroad track ruined, 231 highway bridges damaged, and rivers without crossings, relief could not arrive quickly. It was over a day before the first of an eventual 100,000 army troops and 50,000 others could arrive. For ten days the workers did not have the necessary heavy equipment and cranes to clear the rubble and retrieve many people.

The city was initially shrouded in total darkness (it being nighttime) and a dense gray fog of soil, coal dust, and smoke. According to the local Chinese authorities, 242,769 people died and 164,851 were seriously injured. Other reports and international databases listed the official death toll as 250,000 to 255,000, and early estimates by visitors placed it even higher.

The earthquake had a magnitude of 7.8 as determined by Chinese seismologists, and 8.0 in the international database maintained by the U.S. Geological Survey/National Earthquake Information Center. Its focus, where rupture began, was at a relatively shallow depth of 14 miles (23 kilometers), and its epicenter was calculated at 39.5 degrees north and 117.9 east—virtually right under Tangshan. Later that same day, at 6:45 P.M. on July 28, there was a major aftershock, with magnitude 7.4 at the same focal region. It finished off most of the buildings that had survived the first shock. Within forty-eight hours of the initial earthquake, there were more than nine hundred aftershocks having magnitude of at least 3.0, including sixteen with magnitude at least 5.0.

AFTEREFFECTS. A second disaster was averted at the large Douhe River reservoir 9 miles (15 kilometers) northeast of Tangshan. The embankment dam was cracked and weakened, and if it collapsed it would have flooded the city. Furthermore, after the earthquake a heavy rain started, and the water level was rising. The floodgate could not be opened quickly to let out the reservoir water gradually and unstress the dam, because its electrical power was disabled. Fortunately, troops working manually for eight hours managed to get the floodgate open.

At the large coal mine complex, about 10,000 people were in the underground workings when the earthquake struck. The surface buildings were destroyed, but the large-amplitude surface wave vibrations—usually the most damaging of the seismic waves—became less intense with depth, and the deep workings were somewhat less affected. However, there was no electricity, no hoist cages for workers, and no water pumps to keep the workings from flooding with groundwater. Remarkably, only 17 mine workers died; the others managed to dig through the rubble and climb to safety or be rescued. Five men were brought up alive after fifteen days, having no food and only filthy water to drink.

RELIEF AND RECONSTRUCTION. The search and recovery of bodies was a slow and difficult task, with the stench of decaying bodies of people and animals, lack of clean water and sanitation, and increasing danger of an epidemic. Relief aid (clothing, tents, heavy equipment, and medical supplies) was offered by the United Nations, the United States, Great Britain, Japan, and others, but the Chinese government declined it. In retrospect, this denied timely and useful assistance. However, at the time, China was in its Cultural Revolution— a decade-long era which would last until September, 1976, when Chairman Mao Zedong died—and the Chinese wanted to display their self-reliance and not engender a dependent mentality and considered any outsiders and their assistance to be "interference by others."

It was also not an easy time for the State Bureau of Seismology and those engaged in earthquake monitoring and prediction. When the earthquake occurred, the recording seismographs in Beijing were driven off the scale by the large vibrations, and others around the country could not pinpoint the epicenter other than being somewhere around Beijing. So, with much of the telecommunication systems in the area disabled, scientists set out in vehicles in all directions to try to find the epicenter and greatest damage. After being credited with the success of predicting the Haicheng earthquake the previous year, the seismologists became ridiculed, and the failure to predict the devastating Tangshan event became blame for negligence. Anger and abuse were directed at those identified locally as earthquake experts, as if the inability to reliably predict one of nature's great uncertainties was somehow willful and deserving of punishment.

Within two years, a massive reconstruction effort had restored the city's industrial production to what it had been. By 1986, ten years after the earthquake, restoration was mostly complete, although some citizens were still in temporary shelters, and the population of Tangshan had increased to 1.4 million. Because it was now recognized that the city was on a major crustal fault, reconstruction was carried out to make structures more earthquake-resistant. Water pipes were made with flexible joints so they could withstand vibration, embankments were reinforced around nearby reservoirs, and hazardous industries were moved outside of town. One factory that had been destroyed in the great earthquake has been left as a memorial to the thousands lost.

Robert S. Carmichael

FOR FURTHER INFORMATION:

Chen, Yong, et al., eds. *The Great Tangshan Earthquake of 1976: An Anatomy of Disaster.* New York: Pergamon Press, 1988.

De Blij, H. J. *Nature on the Rampage.* Washington, D.C.: Smithsonian Institution, 1994.

Housner, George W., and He Duxin, eds. *The Great Tangshan Earthquake of 1976.* Pasadena: California Institute of Technology, 2004.

Qian Gang. *The Great China Earthquake.* Translated by Nicola Ellis and Cathy Silber. Beijing: Foreign Language Press, 1989.

Reese, Lori. "Tangshan: Earthquake, July 28, 1976—An Ominous Rumbling." *Time Asia* 154, no. 12 (September 27, 1999).

Sun, Youli. *Wrath of Heaven and Earth: Chinese Politics and the Tangshan Earthquake of 1976.* New York: St. Martin's Press, 2006.

■ 1980's: AIDS PANDEMIC

EPIDEMIC

DATE: Originating perhaps in the 1940's or 1950's, at pandemic levels by the 1980's
PLACE: Worldwide, especially Africa
RESULT: Millions dead and infected

At the beginning of the twenty-first century, human immunodeficiency virus (HIV) was infecting 6 million new individuals and killing about 2 million each year. Most of the 40 million infected during the 1990's were expected to die in the first decade of the new century. Prospects for a vaccine were poor, and chemotherapeutic drugs were too expensive for most.

SCIENCE. HIV causes the almost total destruction of CD4 helper T lymphocytes (CD4 lymphocytes). These cells are necessary for the development and maintenance of the immune response against myriad viruses and microorganisms. A person infected with HIV who has a very low CD4 lymphocyte count and one or more severe infectious diseases has acquired immunodeficiency syndrome (AIDS).

HIV, like all viruses, is unable to proliferate on its own. The only way it can reproduce is to get its hereditary information into an appropriate host cell. The hereditary information subsequently directs the synthesis of viral proteins and new hereditary information. New viruses "self-assemble" as they bud from the cell.

One of the proteins in the viral envelope, a glycoprotein called GP120, attaches the virus to an appropriate host cell. The viral attachment protein is designated GP120 because it has sugars attached to it and a molecular weight of 120 daltons. GP120 attaches the virus to the primary cellular receptor, CD4, embedded in the membranes of macrophages and CD4 lymphocytes. Cells are distinguished by cluster differentiation (CD) molecules in their membranes. After attaching the virus to CD4, the viral attachment protein binds a coreceptor, usually CCR5 on macrophages but CXCR4 on CD4 lymphocytes. Viral attachment to a coreceptor results in the subsequent fusion of the viral membrane with the host's membrane. Upon membrane fusion, the viral core diffuses into the host's cytoplasm, and a viral enzyme trapped inside the core converts the viral ribonucleic acid (RNA) into double-stranded deoxyribonucleic acid (DNA). The conversion of RNA into DNA is called reverse transcription and is carried out by the viral enzyme reverse transcriptase. The newly synthesized viral DNA is transported into the nucleus, where another viral enzyme called integrase modifies the DNA and promotes its integration into one of the host's chromosomes.

The integrated viral DNA, called the provirus, functions as a template for the synthesis of new viral RNA. Some of this viral RNA serves as messenger RNA (mRNA), which directs the synthesis of viral proteins. Full-length RNAs also serve as new hereditary information.

HIV is transmitted from one person to another in body fluids: blood, mothers' milk, semen, and vaginal secretions. Although the virus can be found in saliva and tears, it is present in such low concentrations that it is almost never transmitted through these fluids. Generally, in adults, HIV is transmitted during sexual intercourse. Viruses containing vaginal fluid deposit viruses on the mucous membranes of the mouth and genitals. Similarly, virus-laden semen may introduce viruses on the mucous membranes of the mouth, vagina, uterus, and colon. All these tissues are protected by macrophages that engulf the viruses and degrade them. If there are too many viruses, however, some of the macrophages become infected and the virus reproduces in them. Usually, CD4 lymphocytes are not infected until GP120 mutates to a form that binds the coreceptor on CD4 lymphocytes.

A fetus sometimes becomes infected when the virus passes through the placenta from infected mother to fetus; however, most infections in babies occur at birth because of exposure to contaminated blood or soon after birth because of drinking mother's milk. Viruses in the blood and milk are deposited on the mucous membranes of the mouth and throat, where they infect macrophages.

About one-quarter of the blood used for medical purposes (mostly transfusions) in nonindustrialized countries is contaminated with HIV. In Africa and Southeast Asia, medical quacks and unprofessional doctors may infect their patients with HIV by reusing contaminated needles. Transfused or contaminated blood releases viruses in the circulatory and lymphatic systems. Circulatory and lymphatic macrophages destroy most of the introduced viruses, but a few of the macrophages become infected. In some countries, as many as 50 percent of those who become infected with HIV have shared contaminated hypodermic needles when abusing cocaine, heroine, or opium.

Once HIV infects skin or circulatory and lymphatic system macrophages, it spreads rapidly to other macrophages in the lymph and blood. Four to six weeks after the initial infection, there may be as many as 1 million viruses per milliliter of blood produced each day. A person infected with this many viruses usually develops a headache, fever, enlarged lymph nodes, muscle aches, pharyngitis (sore throat), and a rash that may last a week or so. Some individuals experience an outbreak of oral candidiasis, caused by the yeast *Candida albicans.* CD4 lymphocytes sustain heavy casualties because of the high viral concentration. Typically, CD4 lymphocytes drop from about 1,000 cubic millimeters of blood to 500 cubic millimeters of blood, but in some cases the numbers may go as low as 250 cubic millimeters of blood.

The destruction of 50 to 75 percent of blood CD4 lymphocytes is caused by the massive binding of viruses or viral attachment proteins (GP120) to the lymphocyte receptors (CD4). This extensive binding of proteins to CD4 induces CD4 lymphocytes to commit suicide. Programmed suicide is used to eliminate cells that might be dangerous or that are no longer needed. This early in the infection, almost no CD4 lymphocytes are infected. Thus, their destruction is not caused by viruses infecting the cells or an immune system attack by CD8-cytotoxic T lymphocytes (CD8 lymphocytes). Macrophages are not significantly killed by viral or GP120 binding because they have very few CD4 molecules on their surface in comparison to CD4 lymphocytes.

About six weeks after the initial infection, the immune system begins to reduce the number of circulating viruses and the number of infected macrophages. Antibodies secreted by plasma cells into the lymph and blood link viruses together. Antibody-linked viruses are readily engulfed by macrophages and destroyed. CD8 lymphocytes, on the other hand, destroy infected macrophages. The number of circulating viruses goes from a high of about 1 million to as few as 1,000 per millileter of blood. This decline in viruses results in a partial recovery of CD4 lymphocytes. The number of CD4 lymphocytes may go from about 500 to 700 cubic millimeters of blood. The immune system is unable to eliminate all the viruses and infected macrophages. Proviruses are able to hide in Langerhans cells in the skin, glial cells and astrocytes in the brain, and dendrites in the testes and lymph nodes. Often, infected macrophages in these tissues fail to attract the attention of CD8 lymphocytes.

A balance between the immune system and the proliferating virus may exist anywhere from three years to fifteen years. During this period, the infected person may show little or no signs of disease and is said to be asymptomatic. Although a person may appear to be well, they are infective because viruses are produced by some infected Langerhans cells. During the asymptomatic phase of the disease, genetically diverse populations of the virus evolve. Some populations gain the ability to infect CD4 lymphocytes. As viral clones become increasingly more efficient at infecting CD4 lymphocytes, the viral populations gradually increase in number. The more viruses there are, the more binding of viruses (and/or GP120) to CD4 lymphocytes occurs. CD4 lymphocytes once again commit suicide at an increasing rate. Generally, the new clones of HIV able to infect CD4 lymphocytes cause these cells to fuse together and form giant multinucleated cells called syncytia. The efficiency of the immune system decreases drastically as syncytia-inducing HIV appear.

Although CD8 lymphocytes attack and destroy infected CD4 lymphocytes, this only accounts for about 1 percent of the CD4 cell loss each day. Most of the CD4 lymphocytes lost to viral (and/or GP120) binding and subsequent formation of syncytia are not infected. The destruction of uninfected CD4 lymphocytes increasingly weakens the immune system. The weakened immune system is no longer able to check HIV or fight off opportunistic pathogens. Thus, individuals infected with the new HIV clones begin to develop severe forms of common and less common diseases. HIV infected individuals that suffer from these various diseases are said to have AIDS. Without vigorous chemotherapy, death usually occurs within a year of an AIDS diagnosis.

The diseases most frequently seen in adults with AIDS are tuberculosis induced by *Mycobacterium avium* or *M. intracellulare* (10-68 percent); *Pneumocytis carinii* pneumonia (14-62 percent); *Candida albi-*

cans (yeast) infections of the mouth, pharynx, lungs, and vagina (10-50 percent); bacterial and viral diarrheas (45 percent); Kaposi's sarcoma, induced by human herpesvirus-8 (5-36 percent); cold sores, induced by human herpesvirus-1 and -2 (30 percent); HIV-associated central nervous system disease (15-30 percent), which includes HIV-associated dementia (15-20 percent) and cognitive/motor disorder (30 percent); *Toxoplasma gondii* infections of the central nervous system (3-27 percent); cytomegalovirus (CMV) infections of the intestines and eyes induced by human herpesvirus-5 (10-25 percent) and CMV pneumonia (6 percent); bacterial pneumonias (20 percent); shingles or varicella-zoster virus, induced by human herpesvirus-3 (15 percent); *Cryptosporidium*-caused diarrhea (10 percent); and *Cryptococcus neoformans*-induced meningitis (5 percent) and pneumonia (1 percent). The percent infected varies significantly when different populations are considered. For example, about 5 percent of persons who acquire HIV through intravenous drug abuse also become infected by human herpesvirus-8, whereas more than 30 percent of those who acquire HIV through sexual intercourse become infected with human herpesvirus-8. This accounts for the higher incidence of Kaposi's sarcoma in male homosexuals with AIDS as compared to intravenous drug abusers with the disease.

ORIGINS. A growing body of evidence suggests that the virus responsible for the AIDS pandemic appeared in the 1940's or 1950's in one of the African countries dominated by rain forests and chimpanzees: Cameroon, Gabon, Congo, or Zaire (now Democratic Republic of Congo). HIV-1 arose when a chimpanzee retrovirus, simian immunodeficiency virus (SIVcpz), infected a human. As HIV-1 spread, it evolved into ten distinct subtypes, designated MA through MJ. The viruses responsible for the AIDS pandemic belong to the "major" group of HIV-1, designated HIV-1:M. One of twelve hundred frozen blood samples taken in 1959 from a native of Zaire was positive for antibodies against HIV-1 and contained a portion of the viral hereditary information. Analysis of this information suggests that the virus existed just after HIV-1 began to diverge into distinct subtypes. The 1959 virus is most closely related to HIV-1:MD subtype but is also very closely related to HIV-1:MB and HIV-1:MF.

During the early 1970's, some of the evolving subtypes became established in prostitutes along the highways that link Zaire to East African countries. Truckers and military personnel spread HIV-1:MA, HIV-1:MB, HIV-1:MC, and other subtypes from Zaire into Uganda, Rwanda, Burundi, Tanzania, and Kenya. The HIV-1:MC subtype spread north from Kenya into Ethiopia and south from Tanzania into Zambia. In the 1990's, HIV-1:MC was most frequently detected in heterosexuals of South Africa. At about the same time, subtype HIV-1:MD spread from Zaire as far west as Senegal.

In the early 1970's, subtype HIV-1:MB spread from central Africa to Europe and to the United States, where it became the predominant subtype in homosexual and bisexual men. Thousands of men from America and Europe visited Kinshasa, Zaire, in late 1974 to view the heavyweight boxing championship bout between Muhammad Ali and George Foreman. Because of this event, HIV-1:MA and HIV-1:MB had many chances to spread to America and Europe. The first two deaths from AIDS in homosexual men were reported in the United States in 1978; a four-year incubation period is not unusual. In North America and in Europe, HIV-1:MB became associated with homosexual and bisexual males and their sex partners. On the other hand, in South America and in the Caribbean, HIV-1:MB became dominant in heterosexuals.

In the 1980's, various subtypes of HIV-1:M spread throughout the world. HIV-1:MA from East Africa, HIV-1:MB from North America and Europe, HIV-1:MC from South Africa, and HIV-2 from West Africa entered India to begin at least four separate AIDS epidemics. From India, HIV-1:MC spread north into China and south into Malaysia. From America and Europe, HIV-1:MB and HIV-1:MBs spread to Japan, Taiwan, the Philippines, Indonesia, and Australia. HIV-1:MB became the subtype associated with homosexual and bisexual men, whereas the HIV-1:Bs became the subtype associated with intravenous drug abuse. A number of epidemics raged in Southeast Asia during the 1990's. In this region of the world, HIV-1:MC and HIV-1:ME were dominant in heterosexuals, whereas HIV-1:MB and HIV-1:MBs were dominant in homosexual men and intravenous drug abusers.

Two strains of HIV-1 were discovered in central Africa during the 1990's which were so different from pandemic HIV-1:M that they could not be detected by the standard antibody tests. HIV-1:O circulated in Zaire, Congo, Gabon, and Cameroon but infected only a few thousand individuals. This virus originated from another chimpanzee virus very similar to the one that gave rise to pandemic HIV-1:M. The small number of individuals infected with HIV-1:O suggested that it might have appeared in the 1980's, but its great evolutionary distance from SIVcpz indicated that it has been around much longer than pandemic HIV-1:M (the "major" group). Possibly, HIV-1:O (the "old" group) first infected humans at the beginning of the twentieth century. HIV-1:N (the "new" group), designated YBF30, was found in Congo and Gabon. The small number of infections by HIV-1:N and the short evolutionary distance from SIVcpz suggested that this virus may first have infected humans just a little bit later than pandemic HIV-1:M.

HIV-2 is closely related to monkey retroviruses that infect macaque monkeys (SIVmac) and sooty mangabey monkeys (SIVsm). It is distantly related to the retroviruses that infect African green monkeys (SIVagm) and those that infect mandrill baboons of West Africa (SIVmnd). In the 1990's, HIV-2 was found predominantly in West Africa, from Ghana to Senegal. The variability of HIV-2 subtypes is nearly as great as that seen for HIV-1:M subtypes. This indicates that HIV-2 jumped from monkeys to humans in the late 1940's or 1950's. By the 1980's HIV-2 had spread to Western Europe; it was responsible for about 10 percent of the AIDS cases in Portugal. HIV-2 also managed to reach India a few years later.

Although AIDS induced by HIV-2 usually does not develop for ten to twenty years after the initial infection, it eventually kills. HIV-2 does not spread as efficiently as HIV-1:M through heterosexual intercourse or through mother's milk. Clearly, the infectivity of HIV-2 is much less than pandemic HIV-1:M. Nevertheless, approximately 200,000 West Africans were infected with HIV-2 during the 1990's. In fact, HIV-2 infections out numbered HIV-1 infections in Guinea Bissau, Senegal, and Gambia. In 1992, more people were infected with HIV-2 in Guinea Bissau than in any other country. Up to 13 percent of young men between fifteen and thirty-five years of age were infected. Many people in West Africa were infected with both HIV-1 and HIV-2.

AIDS came into prominence quietly in the United States. In 1978, AIDS was reported in two homosexual men who were suffering from multiple infections, extreme loss of weight, swollen lymph nodes, and malaise. It is estimated that these individuals were infected sometime in the early 1970's. This was the beginning of the AIDS epidemic in the United States. By 1985, 72 percent of the AIDS cases were in homosexual or bisexual men, and 17 percent were heterosexual intravenous drug abusers. These two risk groups accounted for 89 percent of the AIDS cases. In addition, about 4 percent were transfusion recipients and hemophilia patients. Approximately 4 percent of the cases were in heterosexual men and women, and 2 percent were in heterosexuals of African descent, mostly from Haiti.

The AIDS epidemic continued to expand in the United States. By 1995, AIDS cases totaled more than 400,000, whereas deaths added to more than 200,000. The numbers were getting so high that new AIDS cases and deaths per year were being reported instead of totals. In 1995, there were approximately 60,000 new cases and 50,000 deaths. The risk groups for contracting AIDS were changing. Many more heterosexuals were developing AIDS. In 1995, homosexual and bisexual men accounted for 50 percent of the AIDS cases, whereas heterosexual intravenous drug abusers accounted for 30 percent. Heterosexuals having sexual intercourse with HIV-infected persons became a major risk group, accounting for nearly 20 percent of the AIDS cases.

Although education, medical treatments, and new chemotherapies reduced the number of new cases of AIDS and the number of deaths by the late 1990's, most of this reduction occurred in Caucasians. The percent of white AIDS patients in 1986, 1996, and 2005 decreased—61 percent to 38 percent to 29 percent, respectively. However, the percent of black or Hispanic AIDS patients went up or stayed the same in 1986, 1996, and 2005—for blacks, 24 percent to 42 percent to 50 percent, respectively, and for Hispanics, 14 percent to 19 percent to 19 percent, respectively. The uninformed and poor were disproportionally developing AIDS and dying.

TREATMENT. By 1985, researchers in France and the United States developed a test for antibodies against HIV-1. All persons diagnosed with AIDS had antibodies against HIV-1 and were presumably infected with the virus. Persons not in high-risk categories were free of the antibodies and the virus. The antibody test for HIV-1 is important because it can be used to determine if asymptomatic people are infected many years before they develop AIDS. Early treatment prevents significant damage to the immune system, inhibits the spread of HIV-1, and delays the onset of AIDS. Nearly 100 percent of those infected with HIV-1 without aggressive chemotherapy die of AIDS.

A drug called azidothymidine (AZT), also called zidovudine, a nucleoside analog that blocks viral DNA synthesis, was introduced in the mid-1980's. In most cases, AZT was found to be useful for less than six months because of its toxicity and because of the rapid rate at which the viral reverse transcriptase becomes resistant to the drug. Beginning in 1996, AZT was used in conjunction with certain other nucleoside analogs (such as 3'sulfhydryl-2'deoxycytidine, abbreviated 3TC) that blocked viral reverse transcriptase. Resistance to the two-drug-combination therapy did not occur for a year or two. By 1997, there was a significant drop in the number of new AIDS cases and deaths in the United States. In 1998, the use of three-drug combinations (usually AZT, 3TC, and a protease inhibitor) effectively reduced HIV to undetectable levels in most people. The protease inhibitors blocked the viral protease needed for viral protein synthesis. The number of AIDS cases and deaths in the United States dropped more because of the three-drug therapy.

The first three-drug combinations had serious side effects. Some patients developed disfiguring fat deposits on their bodies (stomachs, chests, and neck) and lost excessive fat from their faces and limbs. The first protease inhibitors were also linked to an increase in diabetes. In some cases, patients with diabetes became sick, and their lives were threatened by continued use of the protease inhibitors.

IMPACT. Approximately 30 percent of babies born to HIV-infected mothers become infected. During the early 1990's, the number of babies infected per year in the United States amounted to more than 2,000. Treating infected mothers with AZT for a month before birth reduced the number of infected babies by 67 percent. In 1999, a study demonstrated that AZT treatment of the mother combined with cesarean delivery of the baby would reduce the number of babies born to HIV-infected mothers to less than 2 percent.

Worldwide at the beginning of the twenty-first century, more than 500,000 babies were infected each year. About 300,000 of these infections could have been prevented by treating the infected mothers with AZT for a month before birth and supplying the babies with a virus-free milk substitute. Almost all nonindustrialized countries failed to provide their poor with therapeutic drugs or milk substitutes.

A massive educational effort during the late 1980's and early

1990's alleviated the AIDS epidemics in the industrialized countries of North America and Western Europe, yet 100,000 new persons were infected during each of the last few years of the twentieth century. Male homosexual practices accounted for more than 25,000 of the new cases, whereas intravenous drug abuse was the cause of nearly 50,000. Although most older male homosexuals became monogamous and used condoms conscientiously, up to 50 percent of younger homosexuals had numerous sex partners and failed to use condoms regularly. More education might have convinced some of these young men to protect themselves by entering monogamous relationships with HIV-free partners and by using condoms conscientiously.

A number of studies demonstrated that education, drug rehabilitation programs, and the distribution of clean needles and bleach for sterilizing used needles reduced the number of persons infected by intravenous drug abuse. Education and services brought the death rates down in affluent communities in the United States; however, education, medical services, and chemotherapeutic drugs did not reach the poor blacks, Hispanics, whites, and Asians. Because these poor could not afford the $15,000-per-year treatment, their rates of infection, progression to AIDS, and death continued to increase as the twenty-first century began.

In the year 2000, four regions of the world accounted for more than 35 million (93 percent) HIV-infected persons: 25 million in sub-Saharan Africa, 8 million in Southeast Asia, 2 million in Latin America and the Caribbean, and 1 million in Asia). Each year, these four regions accounted for more than 5.5 million new infections and more than 2 million deaths.

The large number of persons infected and dying of AIDS at the beginning of the twenty-first century required massive worldwide intervention by the United Nations and the World Health Organization (WHO). However, these organizations were not up to the task of saving millions because they had myriad other agendas and lacked the tremendous amounts of money needed for education, medical services, and drugs to inhibit HIV.

THE FUTURE OF THE AIDS PANDEMIC. Greed and the struggle for power played an important role in the developing AIDS pandemic. Western governments, international corporations, politicians, drug lords, and rich profiteers backed dictators, civil wars, and attacks on indigenous peoples to gain control of cheap labor, markets, and natural resources (land, wood, water, and precious metals). Western governments and corporations are particularly interested in markets. For example, in the late 1990's, 41 international pharmaceutical companies blocked attempts by African countries to make or obtain inexpensive chemotherapeutic drugs to treat the growing number of HIV-infected persons. These companies were protecting their drug patents and royalties worth billions of dollars. The U.S. government, in support of these companies, gave South Africa a sample of what would happen if they violated U.S. intellectual property rights; the U.S. government denied preferential tariff treatment for a number of South African imports and restricted foreign aid to the country.

Nearly all the 40 million persons infected by HIV during the 1990's were expected to experience severe illnesses and painful deaths during the first ten years of the twenty-first century because they lacked the money for treatment. Secondary diseases from those dying of AIDS may spread and cause numerous localized epidemics that will further stress medical services. If anything substantial is to be done to save the uneducated and poor of the world from AIDS, everyone must realize how those in positions of power in the world are involved in the AIDS pandemic.

Jaime S. Colome

FOR FURTHER INFORMATION:

Barnett, Tony, and Alan Whiteside. *AIDS in the Twenty-first Century: Disease and Globalization.* 2d ed. New York: Palgrave Macmillan, 2006.

Goudsmit, Jaap. *Viral Sex: The Nature of AIDS.* New York: Oxford University Press, 1997.

Mann, Jonathan M., and Daniel J. M. Tarantola, eds. *AIDS in the World II.* New York: Oxford University Press, 1996.

Mayer, Kenneth H., and H. F. Pizer, eds. *The AIDS Pandemic: Impact on Science and Society.* San Diego, Calif.: Elsevier/Academic, 2005.

Piel, Jonathan, ed. *The Science of AIDS: Readings from "Scientific American."* New York: W. H. Freeman, 1989.

World Health Organization. Joint United Nations Programme on HIV/AIDS. *AIDS Epidemic Update: December, 2005.* Geneva, Switzerland: UNAIDS, 2005.

■ 1980: MOUNT ST. HELENS ERUPTION

VOLCANO

DATE: May 18, 1980
PLACE: Washington State
RESULT: 57 dead, estimated 7,000 big-game animals killed, nearly 200 homes and more than 185 miles of road damaged or destroyed, 4 billion board feet of timber blown down, detectable ashfall on 22,000 square miles

Although increased volcanic activity indicated an impending explosion, and in spite of intense efforts to anticipate its magnitude, scientists and government officials were unable to predict the catastrophic force of the 1980 eruption of Mount St. Helens. Before the eruption, the cone of the mountain had been so symmetrical that it had often been compared to Mount Fuji in Japan, but when the ash cloud cleared, only a hollowed-out, lopsided crater remained. The mountain had shrunk from the fifth highest in Washington State at 9,677 feet to the thirtieth highest at 8,364 feet, losing about 1,300 feet of its summit.

In the first seconds of the explosion, a magnitude 5.1 earthquake on the Richter scale caused by pressure from a magma intrusion triggered the collapse of one side of the mountain. This set off an enormous "debris avalanche" of large rocks and smaller particles, all moving at speeds of 70 to 150 miles per hour—the largest avalanche in recorded history. As the weight of the north face of the mountain slipped downward, the hardened rock cap over the "cryptodome," the hot magma intrusion, was pushed aside, releasing a huge lateral explosion. Within one minute a vertical eruption column developed, and within ten minutes the ash in the column had risen more than 12 miles into a mushroom cloud 45 miles across. The successive explosions equaled the force of 27,000 atomic bombs detonated in rapid sequence, at a rate of one per second for nine hours. Lava, rock fragments, and gases stripped off nearby layers of topsoil and leveled most vegetation within a 12-mile arc to the south, west, and north of the volcano.

FIRE IN THE CASCADES. Mount St. Helens is the youngest and most active volcano in the Cascade range, the only volcanic mountains to have erupted in the contiguous United States in recorded history. These mountains form the eastern side of the Pacific "Ring of Fire" series of volcanoes. Volcanologist Stephen Harris reports 14 ash or lava eruptions from eight different Cascade peaks in the two-hundred-year span between 1780 and 1980. Only Mount Baker and Mount Rainier showed as much activity as Mount St. Helens during these years.

Legends among the indigenous cultures of the Northwest often featured Mount St. Helens, which was known as Loo-wit ("keeper of the fire"), Lawelatla ("one from whom smoke comes"), or Tah-one-lat-clah ("fire mountain"). These names were descriptive of the volcano's continuing activity. George Vancouver became the first European to document an observation of the mountain in 1792, when he charted inlets of Puget Sound near what is now Seattle. He named the peak St. Helens after the title given a recently appointed ambassador to Spain. A major eruption occurred in 1800, between Vancouver's sighting and the Meriwether Lewis and William Clark expedition sighting in 1805. An 1847 painting by the artist Paul Kane known as *Mount St. Helens Erupting* conveys the active nature of the volcano during the middle of the nineteenth century.

Mount St. Helens has built up a symmetrical cone and then transformed it to rubble at least three times, the cone of 1980 being less than 2,000 years old. Geologists believe that the rounded summit dome formed about 330 years ago. Mount St. Helens is a strato-volcano, a volcano that repeatedly grows a composite cone made up of layers of lava, ash, and other materials. Through tree-ring dating, geologists are certain that Mount St. Helens has been dormant for only two long periods since 1480, several decades between the late 1700's and the 1800 eruption and a 123-year period between 1857 and 1980. During the dormant periods the growing silica content of the magma increased its viscosity, making it resistant to flowing and more active in dome building and fragmenting. Both activities contribute to eruptions of pyroclastic materials—combinations of incandescent rock fragments and hot gases.

Using modern techniques to map old mudflows and ash deposits, geologists established the active history of Mount St. Helens in 1960,

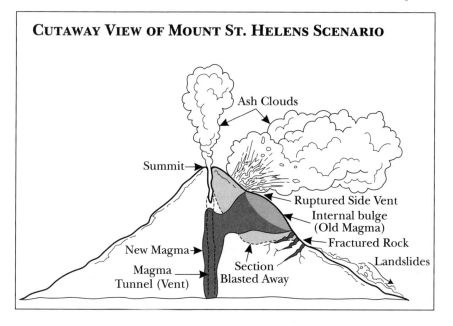

CUTAWAY VIEW OF MOUNT ST. HELENS SCENARIO

long after exploration and exploitation had begun. The first ascent of Mount St. Helens was led by Thomas J. Dryer in 1853. Timber cutting began in the Toutle River Valley in the 1880's, and mining claims were staked north of the volcano near Spirit Lake as early as 1892. Although most mining companies had ceased operations by 1929 because of declining profits, logging continued to increase and prosper. The Gifford Pinchot National Forest was established to augment logging and manage the forest.

Meanwhile, mountain-climbing enthusiasts and campers had discovered the beautiful recreation area. A Portland, Oregon, mountain-climbing group began regular ascents of Mount St. Helens shortly after 1900, and in 1909 the Portland YMCA built a summer camp on Spirit Lake, which lies at the base of the mountain on the north side. Use of the area continued to increase, so that by the 1970's as many as five hundred people might climb the summit of the volcano on a typical weekend. Spirit Lake itself offered fishing, swimming, canoeing, and other popular activities.

The mountain lies about 45 miles northeast of Vancouver, Washington, between Seattle and Portland, the two largest cities in the Northwest. Thus its symmetrical dome had been an inspiring feature of the landscape visible from many locales and observation points—including skyscrapers. After a March 20, 1980, magnitude 4.2 earthquake suggested that the sleeping volcano had awakened, officials were unable to discourage crowds of enthusiasts. Not only people who loved the mountain but also scientists, reporters, photographers, and others from all over the world wanted to witness the action. On May 18, 1980, 57 of them died.

POTENTIAL FOR DISASTER. Native American legend discouraged travel to Mount St. Helens and the other fire mountains. Tribes believed that the belching smoke, steam, and ashfalls were warning signals either of the Great Spirit's displeasure with human activities or evidence of wars between the gods. Male youths aspiring to become braves would climb to the tree line or slightly above and spend a tense night alone, subjecting themselves to the power of the Great Spirit. On their return to the tribe they would be accepted as men and braves. Few, if any, members of the public who visited or worked on or near the mountain, or in the surrounding area, regarded the peak as threatening to their lives or lifestyles.

After scientific confirmation of the dangerous patterns of volcanic activity in the Cascade Mountain Range in 1960, continued volcanic study focused on the volatility of Mount St. Helens. In a United States Geological Survey (USGS) pamphlet entitled *Potential Hazards from Future Eruption of Mount St. Helens* (1978), by Dwight R. Crandell and Donald R. Mullineaux, the authors warned of future volcanic eruptions. The work mapped out regions likely to be affected by pyroclastic flows, mudflows, floods, and ashfalls. Warning signs of eruptions were described in detail. The report was carefully evaluated before potential hazard warnings were issued, then a letter was sent to Washington State informing its government of the study's findings. Awareness of the USGS report spread among officials during 1979, but their planning efforts later proved to be inadequate to the size of the event to come.

INITIAL VOLCANIC ACTIVITY. Small earthquakes began in the Mount St. Helens area on March 16, 1980. On March 20 a magnitude 4.2 earthquake signaled that the mountain's 123-year dormancy had ended. Seismic activity slowly increased, then rose dramatically on March 25. There followed a two-day series of shocks, 174 with magnitudes greater than 2.6. On March 27 came a booming explosion of steam and ash. This, the first volcanic eruption since 1857, carried pulverized ash from old rock inside the volcano and opened a small oval vent about 250 feet across. Earthquake swarms continued as a series of steam explosions shot ash 10,000 to 11,000 feet above the summit. Many of the early eruptions were single, burstlike events, some of which carried ash as far south as Bend, Oregon, 150 miles away, and as far east as Spokane, 285 miles away.

In recognition of the danger signaled by the March 20 earthquake, officials initiated a hazard watch that took effect the same day as the first steam eruption, March 27. Two hundred copies of the 1978 USGS report were distributed to key personnel. In Vancouver, Washington, the United States Forest Service (USFS) headquarters for the Gifford Pinchot National Forest quickly became the Emergency Coordination Center (ECC). Arrangements were made to monitor the volcano, prepare for a possible eruption, and dispense information to the public.

The Mount St. Helens Contingency Plan, based on forest fire models, was developed by the USFS and others, including local officials. The Washington State Department of Emergency Services (DES), the Federal Aviation Administration (FAA), and the Washington National Guard were also involved in formulating plans for their roles in the action in the case of a major eruption. Throughout the preparations, officials believed that damage would probably be confined to the area within a 50-mile radius of the mountain.

Activity at the volcano continued, with some eruptions lasting for several hours. A graben, a depression in the ground, indicated that a large fault was opening below, nearly cutting in half the remaining snow and ice within the crater. A second crater had begun to appear by March 29, and a blue flame had been observed flickering and arching from one crater to the other. Ashes rolling down the sides of the mountain generated static electricity that flashed in lightning bolts, some of which were nearly 2 miles long. On March 30 ninety-three eruptions were recorded. On April 1 the first harmonic tremor further excited and alarmed scientists and other officials. Harmonic tremors, usually lasting from ten to thirty minutes, indicate that magma is moving or erupting underground.

These dynamic events electrified the public, and, as a result, members of the watch group in Vancouver found themselves involved in public relations efforts as well as in monitoring the volcano activity and evaluating the current hazard. The scientists most able to predict volcanic behavior were harried and tired, often working around the clock. The first hazard map of the danger zones around the mountain was drawn up between 1 and 5 A.M. because it was the only time the ECC office was quiet enough. Public Information Officers from the USFS held numerous press conferences, but phones continued to ring constantly. Everyone wanted what proved to be impossible—stating when a major eruption would occur, who would be affected by it, and how extensive the damage would be. Meanwhile, the ashfalls blackening the snow of the mountain provided constant reminders of the activity inside.

Public interest did not deter the essential work of monitoring the activity in the mountain. Instruments set up by University of Washington seismologist Steve Malone, USFS geologist Don Swanson, and other scientists contributed to making the Mount St. Helens event the best-recorded volcanic eruption in history. In addition to seismometers, tiltmeters and gravity meters tracked changes in size and shifts in position of portions of the mountain. Samples of gas from the summit were collected for sulfur-dioxide testing, while surveillance planes and satellites gauged temperatures with infrared photography. In addition to geologists and photographers, volunteer ham radio operators joined in the effort to track volcanic activity and were allowed into newly restricted areas.

The USFS exercised legal control over public access to federal lands, but its jurisdiction was shared with Burlington Northern, a company that owned most of the mountain itself, and Weyerhauser, owner of a large logging operation, on the nearby Toutle River. Agreements were reached, and public access to a "red zone"—all areas above timberline—was closed on March 25. A more extensive "blue zone" restricted access to an even larger area surrounding the red zone, beginning March 28. Neither zone was completely evacuated, and many individuals completely underestimated the dangers from floods, mudslides, and ash. Official warnings were discounted, and avoiding National Guard roadblocks became a game for curious or concerned spectators, especially after local residents began selling maps of the old logging roads that crisscrossed the area.

UNDER SIEGE. Mount St. Helens's normal runoff fills the tributaries of three river systems: the Kalama to the west, the Lewis to the south and east, and the Toutle with two forks on the north and northwest. The forks of the Toutle River join and flow into the Cowlitz River before it in turn enters the Columbia. Spirit Lake, north of the mountain, drains west into the North Fork of the Toutle. The road to Spirit Lake had been paved in 1946, and there were summer homes along the Toutle River road approaching the lake. Building had also taken place around the lake. After the public-access closure and evacuation, angry and persistent landowners demanded to be allowed into the area to bring out personal property. On the South Fork of the Toutle, Weyerhauser Company's 12-Road logging camp continued its operations, choosing to equip employees with ash-measuring devices as warning systems. Had the major eruption not occurred on a Sunday, 330 more workers would have been endangered.

Throughout April, monitors of the activity at the volcano observed a growing bulge caused by intrusions of magma on the north flank of the mountain. The deformation grew at a rate of about 5 feet per day. Scientists believed that it indicated a possible slope failure that could trigger a major eruption, but they had no way of knowing exactly when or even if the bulge would drop off or explode.

Geologists, worried that these observations might be in error and that instead the whole mountain could be tipping sideways, resorted to nailing yardsticks to tree stumps to verify their calculations. A bulge incident was clearly possible, perhaps likely, but without guarantees that were scientifically impossible, geologists were unable to persuade officials to enforce a complete evacuation. Debris avalanches, mudslides, and flooding increasingly threatened the Spirit Lake and Toutle River areas.

One resident who refused to leave the lake, eighty-four-year-old Harry Truman, drew national attention via the news media. He had lived at Spirit Lake for over fifty years and had buried his wife near the guest lodge he had built there. He claimed to communicate with the mountain and believed it would never hurt him, although he had stowed provisions in a nearby abandoned mine shaft, where he planned to wait out any unforeseen danger. Truman received thousands of letters expressing admiration or concern. A batch of letters from children at Clear Lake Elementary School near Salem, Oregon, did persuade him to take a helicopter trip to the school to explain

The 1980 eruption of Mount St. Helens blew off the top of the mountain. (National Oceanic and Atmospheric Administration)

that his place at Spirit Lake was as meaningful to him as life itself. Other local citizens, owners of vacation homes, had more pragmatic goals and continued to demand access to the restricted area.

On May 17, having persuaded then-governor and scientist Dixie Lee Ray to give them permission, twenty homeowners returned to their vacation homes near Spirit Lake to bring out their belongings. Reporters and photographers, with a Washington State Patrol airplane in the lead, accompanied them. Aware of the risks involved, the National Guard placed fifteen helicopters nearby in case rapid evacuation became necessary. A second trip was planned for the next morning.

CATASTROPHIC ERUPTION. On May 18, eleven seconds after 8:32 in the morning, the eruption began. No one had been able to predict either the incredible force or the actual timing of the history-making event.

Flying just east of the summit, geologists Keith and Dorothy Stoffel observed the earliest movement within the crater of the volcano from their Cessna. In the first ten to fifteen seconds of what would turn out to be a magnitude 5.1 earthquake, the entire north side of the mountain began to ripple and churn in eerie lateral movement. Then it began sliding further north. Ash clouds plumed above and burst from the fractures in the slide itself. Starting at nearly 220 miles per hour, the ash cloud accelerated to speeds near 670 miles per hour.

The Stoffels snapped photographs until they realized how the eruption had sent a huge cloud of ash blossoming above them. Only by using a full-throttle, steep dive did they manage to outrun the mushrooming cloud of gas, rock, ash, and hunks of glacial ice. A debris avalanche, with an area of 23 square miles, went crashing down the mountainside. The material spread out and split into several lobes, one raising waves up to 600 feet above Spirit Lake, another reaching the 4.5 miles to Coldwater Creek, and a third burying 14 miles of the North Fork of the Toutle River to an average depth of 150 feet.

Within fourteen seconds of the earthquake and avalanche, a lateral blast traveling at least 300 miles per hour blew out the north side of the mountain. The blast released 24 megatons of thermal energy, leveling everything in its path and creating a 230-square-mile fan-shaped area of complete devastation. At Coldwater II, the closest observation station set by the USGS, geologist Dave Johnson had just enough time to radio in, "Vancouver, Vancouver, this is it!" before he was pushed over a ridge, along with his Jeep and travel-trailer monitoring station.

Most of the erupting blast material, known as a pyroclastic surge, consisted of gas and ash. As the surge turned into pyroclastic flow, old rock exploding from the summit and north area of the cone came to predominate. Between one-third and one-half of the cubic mile of material was fresh magma. The flows covered 6 square miles adjoining the crater and extended as far as 5 miles north of the crater.

The composites of debris from the smashed dome and gases from the blast were incredibly hot—at least 1,300 degrees Fahrenheit. Superheated air at the leading edge of the blast traveled more than 17 miles and killed millions of trees in a "scorch zone" beyond the flattened forest of the "blow-down zone." Pyroclastic flows ranged as high as 660 degrees Fahrenheit.

The heat on the mountain melted 70 percent of its snow and glaciers. Loowit and Leschi Glaciers were completely destroyed, along with parts of 7 others. When the melted snow, melted glaciers, and groundwater combined with debris from the eruption, the mixture that resulted had the consistency of wet cement, yet it was traveling at speeds from 10 to 25 miles per hour. These mudflows or lahars continued down the Toutle River to the Cowlitz, destroying homes and bridges and reducing the carrying capacity of the river at Castle Rock from 76,000 cubic feet per second to less than 15,000, a reduction of about 80 percent. Reaching farther, the flow entered the Columbia River, about 70 miles away, reducing the shipping channel depth from 40 to 14 feet. Thirty-one ships in ports above the mouth of the Cowlitz River were stranded, and another 50 were unable to travel up the river until dredging operations were completed.

UP IN THE AIR. As if the devastation to the north and west of the volcano were not enough, the vertical eruption cloud and its contents created further havoc to the east. The volcano continued generating a plume of ash for over nine hours. Prevailing winds carried significant ashfall north and east across central and eastern Washington, northern Idaho, and western Montana. The ash reached Yakima, Washington, by 9:30 A.M., an hour after the eruption began. Residents, who had not been informed of the eruption, prepared for a thunderstorm. The magnitude of the eruption had caused so much confusion in the staff at ECC that a public announcement of the event did not come until 10:30 A.M.

When the ash began to fall in Yakima, townspeople did not know what it was, and many feared it would be harmful to their health.

Rapidly, the sky turned to a midnight gloom, earning May 18 the lasting nickname "Black Sunday." Yakima was reported to have received over 600,000 tons of ash before it stopped settling. (USGS figures were much lower, estimating the total ashfall for the entire eruption at 490 tons.)

Without doubt, the ash caused technological systems great problems. The ash was abrasive and electrically charged, affecting machinery. Air filters clogged, and carburetors failed. Across Washington, over 5,000 motorists were stranded; planes could not fly. One town, Ritzville, was inundated with talc-like ash that kept the highway closed for three days. The 1,800 residents of the town had no choice but to look after the 2,000 motorists stranded there when the highway closed. By 2:00 on the afternoon of the eruption, the ash plume hung 300 miles east over Spokane, Washington, and visibility decreased to 10 feet, closing the airport there. By 10:15 P.M. the ashfall reached West Yellowstone, Montana. On May 19 it fell visibly as far away as Denver and later in Minnesota and Oklahoma.

AFTERMATH. Following the catastrophic eruption on May 18, Mount St. Helens experienced five more explosive incidents, but the major damage had been done. After two years of searching and study, the official death count was fixed at 57. About 200 endangered individuals escaped the volcano's impact, including 25 tree planters who were on the east face of the volcano when it erupted. Autopsies of 25 of the dead revealed that most had suffocated, dying within minutes. Some burn victims walked several miles before dying. Other victims were found still clutching cameras, and, when developed, the film from one recorded the approaching blast that killed its owner. Searchers were unable to find 27 of the presumed dead, and some people believe that there were many more casualties than the official count. Visitors may view a memorial for Harry Truman near the site of the former guest lodge; Spirit Lake Memorial Highway also commemorates the victims. The Mount St. Helens Visitor Center near Silver Lake has made information on the eruption and its effects available.

Mount St. Helens continues to be an active volcano, and the risks of damage from another major eruption increase as human activities nearby also increase. Economic recovery from the May 18, 1980, eruption was successful due to rebuilding through disaster relief funds, insurance settlements, and renewed tourist trade. Weyerhauser harvested over 850 million board feet of lumber from downed trees. However, the volcano has produced ashfalls four times greater than the 1980 eruption several times in the past and may again. Winds blowing to the west would carry ash clouds to centers of population along the coast. Mudflows may once again rush downriver, destroying rebuilt dams and roads, filling river channels, and washing out seedling trees. Nearly $1 billion has been spent on efforts to reduce flood hazards. Scientists monitoring volcanic activity can measure and warn of new activity, but they must continue working to develop methods that will predict the time and magnitude of the next eruption.

Margaret A. Dodson

FOR FURTHER INFORMATION:

Carson, Rob. *Mount St. Helens: The Eruption and Recovery of a Volcano.* Seattle: Sasquatch Books, 2000.

Findley, Rowe. "Mount St. Helens: Mountain With a Death Wish." *National Geographic* 159, no. 1 (January, 1981): 3-33.

Harnly, Caroline D., and David A. Tyckoson. *Mount St. Helens: An Annotated Bibliography.* Metuchen, N.J.: Scarecrow Press, 1984.

Harris, Stephen L. "Mt. St. Helens: A Living 'Fire Mountain.'" In *Fire Mountains of the West: The Cascade and Mono Lake Volcanoes.* Missoula, Mont.: Mountain Press, 1988.

Parchman, Frank. *Echoes of Fury: The 1980 Eruption of Mount St. Helens and the Lives It Changed Forever.* Kenmore, Wash.: Epicenter Press, 2005.

Pringle, Patrick T. *Roadside Geology of Mount St. Helens National Volcanic Monument and Vicinity.* Rev. ed. Olympia: Washington State Department of Natural Resources, 2002.

Scarth, Alwyn. *Vulcan's Fury: Man Against the Volcano.* New ed. New Haven, Conn.: Yale University Press, 2001.

Tilling, Robert I., Lyn Topinka, and Donald A. Swanson. *Eruptions of Mount St. Helens: Past, Present, and Future.* Reston, Va.: U.S. Department of the Interior, U.S. Geological Survey, 1990.

■ 1982: El Chichón eruption

Volcano

Date: March 28-April 4, 1982
Place: Mexico
Volcanic Explosivity Index: 5
Result: About 2,000 dead, hundreds injured, hundreds left homeless, thousands evacuated, 9 villages destroyed, over 116 square miles of farmland ruined

An obscure and forgotten volcano erupted in 1982, becoming one of the most lethal eruptions to date. El Chichón (also known as Chinhónal) is located in the state of Chiapas in southern Mexico, about 416 miles east southeast of Mexico City. Prior to the eruptions in 1982, El Chichón was a heavily vegetated hill with an elevation of 4,429 feet and a height of about 1,640 feet. It had a shallow crater partly filled with water and a dome 1,312 feet high. After the eruption the elevation of the volcano was 3,478 feet with a height of 689 feet, making it now lower than the surrounding non-volcanic hills.

Although aware of the hot springs and steaming fumaroles (openings from which volcanic gases escape), the people living in villages at the base of the volcano did not consider it a hazard; the volcano had been quiet for at least 130 years. The fertile volcanic soil provided the farm families their only livelihood. They would not leave their land, especially when there was no indication of danger.

History. The volcano was "discovered" in 1928 during a geological survey by Fred Mullerried. The lush vegetation cover of the volcano indicated that there had been no eruptions for years, and the memories of the local inhabitants indicated that the most recent activity was a minor air deposition of volcanic debris around 1852. In his 1932 publication, Mullerried reported on solfataras (fumaroles that emit sulfurous gases) and seismic activity in the vicinity of the volcano in 1930. Considering these observations, he concluded that the volcano was capable of renewed activity. There was increased earthquake activity in 1964 and again in 1982 prior to the eruptions.

Two geologists of the Comisión Federal de Electricidad felt earth-quakes while investigating the geothermal potential of the area and correctly concluded that the volcano might be near eruption. Un-fortunately, the Comisión was not responsible for safety, and their report, released only a few months prior to the explosion of El Chichón, did not allow time for appropriate agencies to be made aware of the potential danger.

Radiocarbon age dates determined since 1982 indicate that El Chichón erupts about every six hundred years. Despite scientific ter-minology, one of the world's "extinct" volcanoes erupts about every five years, and these volcanoes, with repose intervals of hundreds of years, produce the most violent volcanic eruptions.

DESTRUCTION. It is estimated that 2,000 to 3,000 persons were killed and hundreds injured during the eruption of El Chichón. In terms of death, the 1982 eruption of El Chichón was the most de-structive volcanic explosion to take place in Mexico to date. In fact, this eruption was one of the thirteen most destructive eruptions worldwide to date and one of the two most destructive volcanic erup-tions in the twentieth century.

Early reports indicated that 153 people were killed by the collapse of house roofs and fires ignited by incandescent volcanic debris and that only 34 were killed by pyroclastic flows (flows of hot volcanic par-ticles and gases). Ultimately, probably 90 percent of the 2,000 to 3,000 fatalities were the result directly or indirectly of pyroclastic flows. Over 116 square miles of arable land was covered by volcanic debris, leaving it useless. As a result, the survivors lost not only their homes but also the means to sustain themselves. The land could not be farmed for years.

ERUPTION SIZE. There are several ways to describe the size of a vol-canic eruption: the amount of erupted material, the energy involved in the eruption, and the volcanic hazard. The 1982 eruptions of El Chichón produced enough pyroclastic material to cover nearly 6,000 American football fields to a depth of 328 feet (about 88,286 cubic feet). The energy released by the 1982 eruptions of El Chichón was about 8,000 times that liberated by a 1-kiloton atomic bomb.

The amount of energy released by a volcano is not necessarily di-rectly correlated with the degree of volcanic hazard. For example, enormous volumes of lava have flowed quietly from Hawaiian volca-

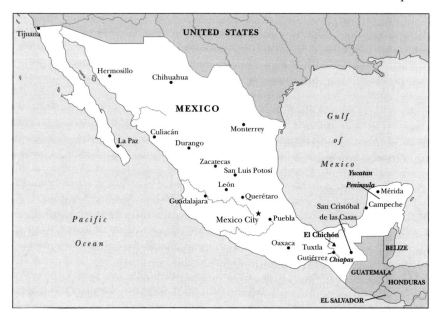

noes and have not been a major hazard despite releasing about one thousand times more energy than the eruption of El Chichón. A simple descriptive measure for volcanic hazard is provided by the Volcanic Explosivity Index (VEI). This index combines total volume of materials erupted, height of the eruption column, duration of the main eruptive phase, and several descriptive terms into a simple 0-8 scale of increasing explosivity. Most volcanoes have a VEI of 3 or greater, none has been assigned an 8, and only one has been assigned a 7 to date. In the light of these observations, El Chichón's VEI of 5 is a rather high value.

STAGE 1 ERUPTIONS. In the autumn of 1981, dogs became restless, earthquakes rattled dishes in the kitchens of the local inhabitants, and breezes occasionally wafted the rotten-egg odor of hydrogen sulfide gas. Although these were items for discussion in the village plazas, the villagers continued with life as usual, not knowing that the tremors and hydrogen sulfide were precursors to an eruption. After the eruption, study of seismograph records indicated that earthquake activity had increased in early 1982 and the centers of the earthquakes had risen from a depth of 3 miles to 1 mile.

The eruptions began near midnight on March 28, 1982, but on

March 29, at 5:15 A.M. local time, the morning quiet was shattered by an enormous roar and nearly continuous earthquakes. Massive explosions caused by hot gases ejected a huge ash cloud about 10,499 feet thick to a height of 59,054 to 68,241 feet, where the ash cloud was then driven northeastward by high-altitude winds. Volcanic particles deposited near the mouth of the crater were as large as 4 inches in diameter. This Plinian eruption continued for six hours, with lightning dancing in the ash cloud, accompanied by a deafening roar. (The term "Plinian" describes an explosive eruption caused by a tremendous uprushing of gas that results in a large eruption cloud.) The March 29 eruption of El Chichón removed much of the center of the volcano, converting the domed hill into a barren 0.6-mile-wide crater 984 feet deep. Rooftops were punctured by falling rocks and collapsed by layers of ash. The morning of March 31, 1982, automobiles in Austin, Texas, 994 miles away, were covered with a light coating of volcanic ash from El Chichón.

STAGE 2 ERUPTIONS. After minor explosions on March 30 and 31 and April 2, 1982, two additional major eruptions occurred on April 3 and 4 from the newly created crater. Volcanic dust from this eruption reached the height of 82,020 feet; however, the eruption column could not be maintained, and the column collapsed onto the volcano summit, dropping tons of volcanic debris from ash to block size (less than .0025 to greater than 2.5 inches in diameter, respectively). This material had great momentum and flowed downhill with hurricane speed toward the villages. Trees and buildings were ripped apart by the pyroclastic flows. What little of the villages remained was covered by ash. The flows followed the courses of stream valleys radiating from the volcano. One flow covered 38.6 square miles. The volcanic debris not only covered the land but also temporarily dammed streams. When these dams burst, the hot volcanic mud (lahars) moved down the streams, causing additional damage.

All the eruptions of El Chichón produced as much pyroclastic material (about 7 billion tons) as the 1980 eruption of Mount St. Helens in Washington State. The surge activity of April 4 resulted in the death of more than 2,000 people, and at least 9 villages within a 5-mile radius were destroyed. The villagers who had remained in their homes found some cover from the ashfall, but the homes were useless protection from the strong pyroclastic currents. Pyroclastic debris typically has a temperature between 392 and 1,472 degrees Fahrenheit (200 and 800 degrees Celsius). Two months after the eruption the pyroclastic flow deposits were still too hot to touch. Minor eruptions occurred on April 5, 6, 8, and 9.

EFFECT ON CLIMATE. Some especially cold years, for example 1783 and 1816, have been linked to major volcanic eruptions. Volcanic dust reflects solar radiation, resulting in cooler temperatures, but has a relatively short-lived impact on the earth's weather because these particles settle out of the atmosphere in less than two years. The dust cloud from the El Chichón eruptions circled the earth from south of the equator to as far north as Japan, producing brilliant red sunsets for months after the eruptions.

The greatest impact that volcanoes have on our weather results from the sulfur-dioxide gas they produce. In the lower atmosphere, solar energy converts the gas to sulfuric-acid aerosols, which can remain in the atmosphere for years. Sulfuric-acid aerosols reaching the stratosphere absorb infrared radiation, which cools the troposphere and scatters the solar radiation back into space, warming the stratosphere. These impacts were confirmed, in part, by data, which showed high concentrations of sulfur, collected after the eruption of El Chichón.

Compared to the Mount St. Helens 1980 eruption, the El Chichón eruptions were more gas-rich—especially regarding sulfurous compounds—resulting in more spectacular pyroclastic eruptions and producing more sulfuric-acid aerosols. Any cooling caused by the El Chichón eruptions was apparently more than compensated for by the warming from a following El Niño. Some scientists think that El Niños may be triggered by explosive volcanic eruptions such as El Chichón.

1996-1998 OBSERVATIONS. In 1998 fumaroles surrounded the yellow, sulfur beaches of El Chichón's shallow crater lake. Investigation of the site from 1996 to 1998 reported changes in hydrothermal activity. The surface temperature of the lake (average depth 4.3 feet) is very uniform, and even above submerged fumaroles it did not exceed 95 degrees Fahrenheit (35 degrees Celsius). This uniformity of temperature suggests that the lake water is not significantly influenced by underlying magma and is highly affected by seasonal variations in precipitation and ambient air temperature. Temperatures of water from springs on the slope of the volcano ranged from 124 to 160 degrees Fahrenheit (51 to 71 degrees Celsius), whereas water discharging from a boiling spring called Soap Pool inside the crater had a temperature of 208 degrees Fahrenheit (98 degrees Celsius). From 1997 to 1998 the flow of very saline water from Soap Pool decreased from about 44 to 13 pounds per second.

FUTURE. Although El Chichón appears to be entering a six-hundred-year cycle of repose, this may not be the situation because of poor accuracy in the determination of the eruption cycle. Also, there is an indication that at least a minor eruption occurred as recently as 1852. Monitoring of the volcano's seismic records, changes in fumaroles for release of hydrogen sulfide, and hydrothermal activity should provide a means of predicting future eruptions, regardless of the repose cycle. It is tragic that the scientific reports by Mullerried and the Comisión Federal de Electricidad were not available to the appropriate government agencies so that evacuations could have been made before the eruptions. It is difficult to say how many of the people would have responded to encouragement to evacuate since no one would have expected such a violent explosive eruption. Nonetheless, even with incomplete data and understanding, a warning could have saved hundreds of lives.

Kenneth F. Steele, Jr.

FOR FURTHER INFORMATION:

Bullard, Fred M. *Volcanoes of the Earth.* 2d rev. ed. Austin: University of Texas Press, 1984.

Chester, David. *Volcanoes and Society.* New York: Routledge, Chapman and Hall, 1993.

Duffield, W. D., R. I. Tilling, and R. Canul. "Geology of El Chichón Volcano, Chiapas, Mexico." *Journal of Volcanology and Geothermal Research* 20 (1984).

Fisher, Richard V., Grant Heiken, and Jeffrey B. Hulen. *Volcanoes: Crucibles of Change.* Princeton, N.J.: Princeton University Press, 1997.

Sigurdsson, Haraldur, ed. *Encyclopedia of Volcanoes.* San Diego, Calif.: Academic Press, 2000.

Tilling, R. I. "The 1982 Eruption of El Chichón, Southeastern Mexico." *Earthquake Information Bulletin* 14 (1982).

■ 1982: PACIFIC OCEAN
EL NIÑO

DATE: June, 1982-August, 1983
PLACE: Equatorial Pacific Ocean and bordering continents
RESULT: More than 2,000 dead, $13 billion in damage

Before 1982, "El Niño" was a term known almost exclusively to scientists studying the ocean, atmosphere, and weather. After 1983, so widespread and serious were El Niño's destructive consequences that the phenomenon became known worldwide as the largest force disrupting world weather patterns.

The El Niño of 1982 developed anomalously. Previous El Niños had begun in April with waters warming off the Peruvian coast and spreading westward. In this case the temperature rise started in the central Pacific and flowed eastward in June and August, and the barometric pressure increased in the western Pacific. Moreover, while the warm water moved slowly eastward toward South America, the westerly trade winds continued blowing unabated; normally they weaken. Volcanic dust lofted into the atmosphere from the eruption of El Chichón in Mexico masked some of these developments from satellites, and partly because of this, the beginning of a full-blown El Niño in November took observers by surprise. Before it ended in August, 1983, five continents had suffered its devastating effects.

Its intensity was unheralded. The Southern Oscillation—indicated by the difference in air pressure between Darwin, Australia, and Tahiti—was never before so great. Sea surface temperatures off the South American coast soared to almost 8 degrees Celsius above normal, another record. The mass of warm water increased evaporation, which fueled storms that lashed the coasts and Pacific islands near the equator.

Six hurricanes swept over Tahiti and nearby Tuamotu archipelago in the central Pacific; the area had not seen a hurricane for seventy-five years. More than 7,500 houses were flattened or lost their roofs, and 15 people died. The destruction ended tourism for the season, a main source of income. A hurricane also hit the Hawaiian Islands, which otherwise had a drought. Elsewhere in the Pacific scientists noticed that millions of seabirds deserted their nests and the warm water damaged reefs.

Ecuador and Peru were first hurt economically, then physically. The planktonic nutrients that normally rise from the seafloor with upwelling cold currents dwindled when El Niño's warm water arrived. Schools of commercial fish vanished. Fishermen were idled, as were industries dependent upon fishing, such as fishmeal production. Because the coast of both countries is very arid, when El Niño-spawned storms arrived, their torrential rains turned into floods that swelled rivers and raged through canyons. As a result, thousands of houses, mostly in rural towns or urban slums, were washed away, along with sections of roads and more than a dozen major bridges. At least 600 people were killed in the process. Important export crops—particularly rice, cacao, and bananas—also were heavily damaged, further crippling the national economies.

The west coasts of Central and North America soon experienced similar conditions. California was especially hard hit. Salmon and other cold-water fish departed north, hurting the local fishing industry, while seabirds died and tropical fish, such as barracuda, invaded the coastal waters. High sea levels, as much as 8 inches above normal, combined with storm-propelled waves, battered the coast. Wind gusts damaged houses, and a tornado even tore the roof off the Los Angeles Convention Center before ravaging the Watts district. Rain fell until rivers overflowed and hillsides were so soaked that mudslides occurred at record rates. In the Sierra Nevada and Rocky Mountains, snowpacks reached record depths. Altogether, more than 10,000 buildings were damaged or destroyed, and the economic toll on the West Coast, which included extensive damage to roads and agriculture, was estimated at $1.8 billion. Meanwhile, in the American South, heavy rains fell, nearly pushing the Mississippi River over its levees. The Atlantic hurricane season, however, was short and mild.

Across the Pacific, under the abnormally high pressure over the Indonesia-Australia region, conditions were dry. The drought in Australia starved thousands of livestock and wild animals and turned brushland parched and dusty. Immense dust storms dumped tons of dirt on cities, Melbourne most spectacularly, and brush fires raced out of control. At least 8,000 people were made homeless in the fires, and there were 75 fatalities. Late in the El Niño, downpours in eastern Australia led to flooding that drowned yet more livestock. Indonesia saw crops fail in the drought. In one area 340 people starved because of it. On the island of Borneo, forest fires, spread from land burned off by farmers, expanded unchecked. The smoke fouled cities, endangered air traffic, and caused one port to close temporarily. The fires were called one of the worst environmental disasters of the century.

Record drought also came to Africa, hurting the southern and Sahelian regions most. In some areas of South Africa 90 percent of cattle died as the grassland turned to barren hardpan. Tens of thousands of wild animals, from rodents to elephants, perished. To escape famine, the poor countries of the region had to rely on food shipments from North America. Many other effects, such as delayed monsoons in southern India and droughts in Brazil and Mexico, were teleconnections to El Niño. Scientists suspect that a cold snap in Europe and droughts in the Midwest, northern China, and central Russia might also have occurred because of El Niño, at least in part.

In addition to bringing the El Niño phenomenon forcefully to public awareness, the 1982-1983 event had three consequences. It spurred much scientific research aimed at making predictions of future El Niños reliable. It encouraged farmers in affected areas to reconsider how they manage their crops and livestock. Finally, it demonstrated dramatically that coastal cities, which are growing increasingly crowded, are vulnerable to El Niño-related natural disasters.

Roger Smith

FOR FURTHER INFORMATION:

Babkina, A. M., ed. *El Niño: Overview and Bibliography.* Hauppauge, N.Y.: Nova Science, 2003.

Canby, Thomas Y. "El Niño's Ill Wind." *National Geographic*, February, 1984, 144.

D'Aleo, Joseph S. *The Oryx Resource Guide to El Niño and La Niña.* Westport, Conn.: Oryx Press, 2002.

Fagan, Brian. "El Niños That Shook the World." In *Floods, Famines, and Emperors: El Niño and the Fate of Civilization.* New York: Basic Books, 1999.

Nash, J. Madeleine. *El Niño: Unlocking the Secrets of the Master Weather-Maker.* New York: Warner Books, 2002.

■ 1984: AFRICA

FAMINE

DATE: 1984-1985
PLACE: Ethiopia, Chad, Mozambique, Mali, Niger, Burkina Faso, and the Sudan
RESULT: 2 million dead, millions more displaced

When four-year-old Mamush Mekitew reached the American aid camp at Gehowa, Ethiopia, he weighed only 15 pounds. He suffered from acute diarrhea and vomiting and was so weak that he had to be given liquid through a nasal drip. His blind, widowed mother and an elderly uncle crooned to him day and night until he died. "He should not have been alive at all," said a nurse. "It was a miracle he held out for so long."

In many areas, the famine reduced the birthrate, as hungry adult women simply stopped ovulating. A United Nations Children's Fund (UNICEF) relief expedition mounted on camels toured the Sudan's remote Red Sea province and found that childbearing was almost a thing of the past. In a settlement called Bet Utr, not one of the women in thirteen families had given birth during the past year. Three women had died in childbirth, and one had miscarried. In a society where most women give birth every year, Bet Utr should have been teeming with children. In this time of troubles, however, only eight youngsters were left.

At a relief station in the southern town of Doba, Chad, a procession of mothers, their breasts dry and withered, their bodies caked with trail dust, pleaded for food and medicine for the children slung around their shoulders and backs. Doba was in the middle of a war zone, however, and there were few supplies. Two hundred children died from malnutrition in only two weeks. In the harsh semidesert wastes of eastern Chad, hardy desert nomads were reduced to eating the leaves of savonnier trees. Some died because they could not digest the leaves properly.

Like outcasts from the Bible, they trudged out of Tigre, Ethiopia (now a province of Eritria), escaping a parched, rebel-controlled province that was starved of food supplies by the Ethiopian government. Nearly 200,000 Tigreans fled to camps in neighboring Sudan. There were women too weak to finish the journey on foot, children who listened for water on makeshift hose lines, and children who arrived only to die.

IMPACT. The famine had two "belts" across sub-Saharan Africa. One belt ran from Mali, Mauritania, and Senegal in the west to Ethiopia in the east. The other belt ran from Somalia on the horn of Africa to Angola, Botswana, and Zambia in southern Africa. As of November, 1984, 50,000 people were dead from famine in Senegal, and 50,000 more were at risk. More than 150,000 cattle had been lost in the previous two years. In Mali, more than 1 million children were suffering from malnutrition, cholera, and measles. A total of 2.5 million people were at risk from famine. In Chad, at least 4,000 people, mostly women and children, had died from famine during the three months preceding December, 1984. Half a million more had been displaced by drought, and relief efforts were hampered by a civil war. In the Sudan, more than 1 million people were threatened by the famine. There had been a great influx of refugees from Chad and Ethiopia, which added to the civil strife already existing in the southern Sudan.

Like much of Africa, Ethiopia has always been subject to ecological disaster. Droughts and famines were reported as early as 253 B.C.E. In the great drought of 1888, a third of the population was said to have died from malnourishment and disease. This calamity in 1984-1985 was part of a thirty-year pattern. The rains have repeatedly failed along the Sahel, the wide swath of land that lies just below the Sahara Desert. As a result, this time there had already been at least 300,000 famine deaths in Ethiopia. A million more people may have been at risk and as many as 6 million people were facing food shortages. In Mozambique, perhaps 200,000 people may have already died from famine. Four million more were in danger largely due to a severe drought and a civil war.

ROOT CAUSES. Aside from the lack of rain, these peoples' greatest enemies have been deforestation, booming population, primitive agricultural methods, war, and governmental mismanagement. Black Africa is the world's poorest area, and it is the only region in which the population is growing faster than the food supply. Agriculture never fully recovered from the devastating drought of the early and mid-1970's. In 1982, Ethiopia's per capita food production was only 81 percent of what it was in 1969-1971. In Mozambique, the figure was at 68 percent. Chad's food harvest in 1983 was a disaster. Cereal production plummeted to 315,000 tons, well short of the 654,000 tons needed for minimum living needs. On average, African governments spend four times as much on armaments as they do on agriculture. Primitive farming, in turn, has devastated the environment.

Under increasing pressure for production, traditional fallow periods have been shortened, wearing out the soil. Most farmers have no chemical fertilizers, and the animal dung that they once used to enrich the soil is being burned for fuel, because so many trees have been cut down. In the mid-1960's, 16 percent of Ethiopia's land area was covered by forest. In the mid-1980's, the figure was just 3 percent. "With deforestation, the soil loses much of its capacity to retain moisture and consequently its productivity and resistance to drought," said a U.N. environmentalist. In the twenty years leading up to the mid-1980's, Mauritania lost more than three-quarters of its grazing land to the encroaching sands of the Sahara. Rainfall became another forgotten luxury. The rainfall in 1983 was the lowest in seventy years, and most of the grain crop failed. In some areas, 90 percent of the livestock died.

Ethiopia's leader at the time, Lieutenant Colonel Mengistu Haile Mariam, was warned of impending famine in 1982, in a report from a group of experts headed by Keith Griffin, an Oxford University economist. The Griffin team recommended immediate food rationing and heavy emphasis on rural development. Mengistu ignored the advice. Instead, Mengistu poured 46 percent of Ethiopia's gross national product into military spending, buying at least $2.5 billion worth of arms from the Soviet Union. What investment he did make in agriculture was concentrated on building Soviet-style state farms. Meanwhile, as hundreds of thousands starved in 1984 and 1985, Ethiopian officials spent more than $100 million sprucing up their capital, Addis Ababa, and erecting triumphal arches. This expenditure and construction were for the September, 1985, tenth anniversary of the military coup that overthrew Emperor Haile Selassie I.

In Chad before and during the famine, Libya occupied the entire northern half of the country. Meanwhile, a guerrilla conflict in the south rendered that area impervious to relief efforts. At that time, the country had only 60 miles of paved road. The rest of the roads were mostly impassable dirt tracks. The 1984 cotton harvest was the largest in sub-Saharan Africa. Much of the cotton was planted, however, at the expense of food crops. Since no one anticipated the severity of the drought, little of the profit from the abundant cotton crop was saved for emergency food aid. So the cotton money was gone, providing no relief from the killer famine.

THE LONG-TERM EFFECTS. The long-range damage of the famine was the potential effects upon the children who survived. An American child of four to six years old typically consumes 1,600 to 1,800 calories in a daily diet. In the African famine belts, a child the same age took in less than 800 calories per day, a starvation diet. At refugee camps, the basic ration consisted of gruel made from wheat, plus beans, other grains, and vegetable oil. That was not a balanced diet but was far better than anything outside the camps. After months or even years of malnutrition, African children were prey to a host of ailments. Iron-deficiency anemia was prevalent, and in some places a shortage of iodine in the diet caused a mini-epidemic of goiter, an enlargement of the thyroid gland.

For children born and raised at the peak of the famine, blindness was one of the more severe consequences. A lack of vitamin A—which comes from butterfat, eggs, liver, carrots, and leafy vegetables—leads to a condition called xerophthalmia (literally, "dry eye"). Night blindness is an early symptom. Later, sunlight becomes painful. The eyes stop lubricating themselves with tears, and their protective mucous cells dry out. The corneas are scarred and pitted until the victim becomes blind.

Physicians working in famine areas predicted that countless thousands of African children would emerge from the famine with some kind of damage to their mental capacities. Malnutrition can stop the growth of brain tissue, a loss that cannot be made up later in life. The belief was expressed that the thousands of orphans created by the famine would pour into towns and cities to scratch out a living as beggars or thieves. Whatever their work would be, many believed that these children would be so handicapped by the famine's effects that they would not be able to compete or make a living for their families.

RELIEF. Although the rains did eventually arrive in the spring of 1985, the more pressing matter was to get food and medical supplies to relief areas and refugee camps. Getting food into Ethiopia was only half the problem. A moonscape scarred with treacherous canyons and inhospitable mountains, the country is a logistical difficulty. Half its people normally lived a two-day walk from the nearest road. In 1985 there were only about 6,000 trucks in the entire country. At that time only a few hundred of the trucks had been used for relief. Relief supplies did finally begin to show up in quantity. The first food trucks reached the northern town of Korem in a military convoy, for protection against rebels. More than 50,000 people were waiting at the camp for food, and there was not enough to go around. Before the convoy came in, about 100 people were dying every day. Afterward the average dropped to somewhere between 30 and 50 a day. Doctors were forced to perform a gruesome act of triage, selecting only the hardiest refugees to receive food and clothing. The physicians would work their way through crowds. They used pencils to place marks on the foreheads of those who seemed most likely to survive. Aid was not to be wasted on the weak.

A Cooperative for American Relief to Everywhere (CARE) official once described Chad as having nightmarish logistical problems, even worse than Ethiopia's. Chad is a landlocked nation in which the nearest ports are 1,200 miles away, in Cameroon and Nigeria. At that time, food trains took at least three weeks to travel from the seacoast to Chad, and the transport depended on the cooperation of foreign governments. Also, the civil war and the Libyan occupation of Chad continued.

The rains themselves brought a new flood of trouble. Thousands of people in Ethiopia may have died of cold and disease in the rain and hail. Roads and bridges were destroyed, delaying food shipments to many of the country's 8 million famine victims. The rains ruined about 5,500 tons of precious grain at the port of Aseb in Ethiopia. Twenty thousand famine victims in Ethiopia lost their homes to the flooding Shebelle River. Storms also destroyed flimsy shelters in many feeding centers, increasing the threat of epidemics; thousands of people had already died of cholera in Ethiopia. The rains in Mozambique in southeastern Africa destroyed vital food crops, aggravating an already grim situation. By the beginning of May, 1985, more than 200,000 people had died in Mozambique, and 2.5 million people were still in urgent need of food.

Dana P. McDermott

FOR FURTHER INFORMATION:

Curtis, Donald, Michael Hubbard, and Andrew Shepherd. *Preventing Famine: Policies and Prospects for Africa.* London: Routledge, 1988.

Scott, Michael, and Mutombo Mpanya. *We Are the World: An Evaluation of Pop Aid for Africa.* Washington, D.C.: InterAction, 1994.

Tekolla, Y. *The Puzzling Paradox of the African Food Crisis: Searching for the Truth and Facing the Challenge.* Addis Ababa, Ethiopia: UNECA, 1997.

Varnis, Stephen. *Reluctant Aid or Aiding the Reluctant: U.S. Food Aid Policy and Ethiopian Famine Relief.* New Brunswick, N.J.: Transaction, 1990.

Von Braun, Joachim, Tesfaye Teklu, and Patrick Webb. *Famine in Africa: Causes, Responses, and Prevention.* Baltimore: Johns Hopkins University Press, 1999.

Webb, Patrick, and Joachim von Braun. *Famine and Food Security in Ethiopia: Lessons for Africa.* New York: John Wiley, 1994.

■ 1985: THE MEXICO CITY EARTHQUAKE

EARTHQUAKE

DATE: September 19, 1985
PLACE: Mexico City, Mexico
MAGNITUDE: 8.1
RESULT: 10,000 estimated dead, 30,000 injured, 2,850 buildings destroyed, 100,000 units damaged

Mexico City, the nation's capital, is located in the Valley of Mexico, situated between two towering mountain ranges, the Sierra Madre Occidental and the Sierra Madre Oriental, in the south central part of the country. The city itself is situated on a plateau surrounded by a series of mountains that include a string of volcanoes. The valley proper has an altitude ranging from 6,800 to 7,900 feet above sea level. Its floor, on which the modern city has been built gradually over the past five hundred years, is not geologically stable. Beneath the massive concentration of high-rise buildings, extensive freeways, and the marginal dwellings of the poor lies a weak foundation of watery shale rather than a firm base of bedrock, for the city was extended over areas that in precolonial times were lakes.

Contributing to the lack of stability has been the continuous pumping of water from the city's subterranean underpinnings, resulting in a constant shifting and weakening of its buildings' foundations. Structural engineers have developed techniques utilizing permanent hydraulic jacks to keep new high-rises level, but much of the older construction must be subjected to constant adjustment and realignment of its foundations in order to keep buildings from sustaining serious damage. The same is true for transportation and communication facilities—the freeways and the power and water lines.

Hundreds of earthquakes have been recorded in the past five centuries, since the Spaniards first entered Mexico. However, many of the low-lying edifices, built during the colonial era, have managed to survive the recurrent quakes better than the multistory buildings constructed in later times. In the case of relatively new construction, only the high-rises built in accordance with the latest scientific knowledge on quake resistance have weathered the tremors to which the city is constantly exposed.

THE PEOPLE. Archaeologists state that primitive tribes lived in the Valley of Mexico as early as fifteen thousand years ago. The area's appeal can be traced to the availability of fresh water, attracting humans and animals alike. The surrounding mountains also acted as a natural trap for game, making their capture less difficult to the prehistoric hunter. As the number of humans increased, the availability of this wild game dwindled. The shortage led ultimately to the evolution of an agricultural society, one that grew its sustenance from planned crops rather than depending entirely on the vagaries of the hunt.

The area's rich soil, combined with regular rainfall, led to the development of a substantial society, capable of building impressive stone structures for use as palaces, temples, and granaries. Civilizations such as the Teotihuacán and Toltec empires flourished for centuries, followed by that of the Aztecs, who held sway throughout central Mexico until the arrival of the Spanish conquistadores. The precolonial city constructed by the indigenous peoples dazzled the Spaniards on their arrival in the Valley of Mexico. The Aztecs had organized the city's functions in a manner superior to that which the Europeans had experienced at home. The treatment of sewage, for example, far exceeded in sophistication that found in European cities at the time.

In the process of their conquest of the Aztecs, the Spaniards laid waste to much of what was precolonial Mexico City, but they retained the location as the capital of what they called New Spain. A European-styled city rose from the ashes of the Aztec empire. Despite frequent fires and earthquakes—more than 340 quakes had been registered in the capital since the beginning of the colonial era—many examples of the initial Spanish colonial architecture can still be found throughout the city.

The Spaniards intermingled with the indigenous population from the beginning of their occupation. The conquistadores married into the noble families of the native peoples or made the Indian women their concubines. Today Mexico City's population is an amalgamation of European and Amerindian strains, giving the society a heterogeneous character.

More than 20 million people lived in greater Mexico City as early as 1986. This area includes the city itself and also the surrounding federal district. More than a quarter of the country's total population is crammed into the Valley of Mexico and its environs. Because the capital contains Mexico's economic and political seats of power, a constant influx of citizens seeking political advantage and employment opportunities pours into Mexico City in a continuous stream, many condemned to eke out a precarious existence.

During the second half of the twentieth century, Mexico's society became more urban than rural. Living in the cities became the goal of the country's rural poor. As a result, virtually any open space within greater Mexico City became home to economic refugees. These poverty-stricken families from the countryside seized small plots of land wherever they could, built shacks from any material they could find, and fought the local authorities to retain custody of them. The new arrivals sought work of any type in order to sustain themselves; thus, factories throughout the crowded city and its surrounding area often employ workers under illegal and unsafe conditions. These poorly paid workers are crowded into poorly constructed commercial buildings that constantly threaten their health and well-being. Congestive traffic conditions and the accompanying pollution have made the capital a poor-quality residential area for many, if not most, of its inhabitants. Moreover, only roughly one-third of its citizens can afford to rent or own homes in its formal real-estate market.

THE QUAKE. At 7:18 on the morning of September 19, 1985, Mexico City experienced a devastating earthquake. Technical experts described the event as a clash between two opposing seismic forces, the Cocos and the North American tectonic plates. The epicenter was determined to be deep in the Pacific Ocean, approximately 250 miles west of the Mexican coastline. Mexico City sits on what has been termed the "Ring of Fire" surrounding the Pacific Ocean and extending to Australia, Japan, Alaska, the western United States, Central America, and the western coasts of the countries of South America.

While some general damage occurred throughout Mexico's smaller southern cities and its rural areas, the capital itself experienced the greatest destruction. The quake measured 8.1 on the Richter scale. The tremor itself lasted over three minutes, shaking the city to its core. The damage was concentrated in the north, central, and eastern parts of the city.

The very nature of the ground beneath the city, with its lack of a solid rock base, resulted in extensive damage throughout its many districts, but especially in its very center. Dozens of the older hotels that lacked earthquake protection in the city's center collapsed, killing and injuring thousands of visitors. The Regis, the Diplomático, the Versailles, the Romano (all of its occupants were killed), and the De Carlo were among those most seriously affected. While the upscale Del Prado survived the quake itself, it was rendered uninhabitable.

The Regis, formerly a luxury hotel but over time one that had deteriorated to second-class status, was 90 percent occupied when the quake struck. A few guests managed to jump to safety from the second floor. The stairway between the first and second floor as well as the front of the building had collapsed in the initial tremor. A few minutes later the rest of the edifice blew up as a result of accumulated gas within its ruins.

Both the Navy ministry nearby, as well as a secondary school, the National College of Professional Education, suffered major damage. Navy personnel dug with their hands to try to free their fellow sailors. Several hundred students at the school were entombed in the ruins of their classrooms. They had been in class for only twenty minutes.

The poorly constructed, overcrowded factories in the city suffered major damage as well. Four hundred production centers were destroyed, over 800 garment workers were killed, and thousands were left without work once the tremors had ceased. The factories proved to be particularly vulnerable to quakes for two reasons: the poor construction of the buildings in which they were housed, and the fact that the floors of the buildings themselves were stressed by the heavy loads of machinery and rolls of material that they bore.

Several major high-rises in the Tlatelolco complex failed to survive the first tremors. In 1968 Tlatelolco had been the scene of the massacre of an estimated 300 students by the army at the instigation of the government. This 103-building housing development, containing the living quarters of many government workers, suffered major damage, leaving the hundreds that survived the initial quake without shelter. Forty-three of the 103 buildings were rendered immediately uninhabitable.

The development's thirteen-story Nuevo León Building ended up in ruins, with more than half of its 3,000 residents trapped in the wreckage. The remaining rubble alone stood four stories high. Prior to the quake, many of its occupants had complained to authorities about the poor condition of the building. Some of the accusers claimed that the builders had paid bribes to government inspectors to overlook the inferior quality of the materials used in its construction. Survivors from the surrounding buildings dug with their hands in an effort to free the Nuevo León's victims.

Famous tenor Placido Domingo had relatives trapped on the sixth floor in one of Tlatelolco's high-rises. He led a brigade of volunteers that banded together to pull people from the rubble and provide food and water for survivors and volunteers.

When aid workers using public and private vehicles took the victims of the Tlatelolco disaster to the National Medical Center they were turned back. All of its major buildings had been devastated. Seventy of the center's physicians, nurses, and other employees had been killed. Several hundred patients had been crushed at the site as well. Some experts maintained that the medical buildings themselves were of substandard construction and that building regulations had been ignored during their erection. Five major hospitals within the city were destroyed, and an additional 22 were heavily damaged. The loss of hospital beds alone numbered 4,200, about 30 percent of the city's existing capacity. Following the quake, a number of complaints arose about the marginal construction of many of the recently built government structures. The material used proved to be inferior to what had been specified in the contracts between the government and the builders.

The headquarters of the television station Televisa suffered immense damage. More than 77 of its employees perished in the building's collapse. Nevertheless, the station managed to get back on the air after five hours of broadcast suspension. The station could not send filming units into the streets since many were blocked by debris, but the station did manage to report on the quake utilizing helicopters flying over the city.

A second—less severe, but still powerful—earthquake occurred

The Mexico City earthquake reduced many buildings to rubble. (National Oceanic and Atmospheric Administration)

less than thirty-six hours after the initial temblor. Technicians rated this subsequent quake 5.6 on the Richter scale. The tremor resulted in the postponement of rescue efforts. Further loss of life occurred among injured and trapped victims from the first disaster. The Pino Suárez high-rise building at Tlatelolco, damaged in the earlier quake, collapsed in the second, killing many rescue workers.

The statistics at the end of the first day showed the following: The quake had contaminated the city's water supply, and it had severed both electrical and telephone service. The telephone center on Victory Street was destroyed, effectively closing down telephone communications from and to Mexico City. Initially, news concerning the quake could be transmitted only by some of the city's 1,800 licensed ham-radio operators. More than 250,000 citizens found themselves temporarily without shelter. Adequate food supplies still existed, but getting them to the needed areas presented serious logistical problems. However, groups of citizen volunteers set up kitchens and tents in the streets next to excavation sites and began preparing food and drink for both victims and volunteers.

Five days after the initial quake, officials at Mexico's national university began to assemble a list of the missing, because the computers there were more sophisticated than those available to the government. Nevertheless, the delay in initiating a program seeking to identify the missing, dead, and injured led to a great deal of confusion for friends and relatives trying to locate those whose whereabouts were unknown. No program had been prepared for the government's computer facilities to be utilized in such an emergency.

THE GOVERNMENT. After 1929 Mexico's federal, state, and regional governments were controlled by a single political entity, the Partido Revolucionario Institucional (PRI). The party has been accused of maintaining continuous control of the government by engineering elections, not only at the federal level but also in state and regional political contests. At the time of the 1985 earthquake, it was left to the country's president to personally appoint Mexico City's mayor, who was also named to the presidential cabinet. The responsibility for governing the city and providing for the welfare of its citizens lay with the office of the president.

Despite its claim to have a disaster plan for Mexico City to be implemented in the event of an emergency, when the earthquake struck, the Mexican government officials, initially at least, seemed to be helpless in the face of the tragedy. The extensive nature of the damage rendered previous planning inoperable. The city had an insufficient number of firefighters to meet the emergency. It also lacked the heavy construction equipment needed to begin removal of the thousands of tons of masonry rubble. The police and the army did little more than cordon off the damaged areas; they did not respond to the plight of the injured or aid in the removal of the dead. Some police were accused by onlookers of looting the damaged structures or taking bribes to allow businessmen to recover their records without addressing the need for first aid for injured employees. The police expelled a reporter on the scene who had observed the pilferage and who planned to expose the corruption.

More scandals involving the police surfaced with the unscheduled release of some prisoners held in local jails damaged by the quakes. They testified to the use of torture by their captors during interrogations. Corpses of prisoners killed by the quake also bore evidence of systematic brutalization after the rescuers exhumed the bodies from a building occupied by the office of the attorney general.

When the manual laborers assigned by the government to aid in rescue efforts arrived on the scene, their equipment proved to be totally inadequate to meet the formidable task of removing the huge piles of debris resulting from the demolished buildings. Only when private contractors moved their own bulldozers and tractors to the sites could any meaningful shifting of the debris be accomplished.

Immediately following the quake, Mexican president Miguel de la Madrid announced publicly that Mexico had adequate resources to meet the emergency and that foreign aid would not be needed. In one instance, a team of French rescue workers with trained dogs was prevented by Mexican officials from beginning search operations at a devastated building. The president reversed his decision two days later; the delay cost the lives of many of the trapped and injured who could have been rescued by the many teams of foreign workers who then entered the country. President de la Madrid, essentially a bureaucrat, lacked the necessary leadership characteristics needed in the president of a stricken country facing this type of catastrophe.

Ultimately, 60 foreign countries aided in the rescue effort. Thirteen specialty brigades from outside the country, with tools and bloodhounds, worked tirelessly at the sites of devastation to find both the injured and the dead. The Israelis sent a team of 25 along with 17 tons of equipment. Because of the constant threat of quakes in their own country, they had developed special equipment for locating and recovering those who had been trapped. In total, some 250 foreign governments, international relief agencies, and nongovernmental organizations of various types offered their services to Mexico. To complement these high-profile efforts, a group of young students from El Salvador drove several hundred miles from their Central American country in a battered passenger car, seeking to help in whatever capacity they could. Airplanes from the United States, the Soviet Union, France, Argentina, the Dominican Republic, Algeria, Switzerland, Colombia, Canada, Peru, Italy, Cuba, Spain, and Panama brought in tons of relief supplies for distribution to the injured and homeless.

RESCUE. The citizens of Mexico City themselves became the major participants in the rescue effort. Forming brigades of volunteers similar to the one led by Placido Domingo, working with a modicum of tools acquired from local hardware stores, and sometimes with only their bare hands, the teams sought to save the lives of their trapped and injured fellow citizens. They formed human chains and passed debris and broken concrete from hand to hand. In most cases the brigades consisted of friends or coworkers. Some slightly built rescuers, nicknamed moles, crawled through tiny openings in the ruins, risking their own lives, in an effort to aid the living and to recover the bodies of the dead. One of these heroes, Marcos Efrén Zariñana, slightly over 5 feet in height, became known as "the Flea." Observers credited him with personally saving a number of lives. The diminutive rescuer edged his way through tunnels too small for other workers to enter in order to pull out victims.

Citizens formed their own committees to distribute food, clothing, and blankets directly to the survivors. They did not trust government officials to carry out even these tasks. They continued to upbraid the police and the soldiers for failing to take a positive role in the rescue efforts. The army defended itself vociferously, maintaining that it had been given orders only to secure the afflicted areas and to prevent looting.

CONSEQUENCES. There were many economic and political consequences of the 1985 Mexico City earthquake. The government immediately began a rapid updating of building codes. It established for the first time a centralized national civil defense system. Nongovernmental organizations such as the Mexican Red Cross and the Catholic Church began to coordinate with one another their plans for addressing major emergencies such as the Mexico City earthquake.

The quake dealt Mexico a serious economic blow. The final estimate of the country's financial loss amounted to the equivalent of at least 4 billion U.S. dollars, possibly as much as $10 billion. The city lost hundreds of thousands of dollars in its normally lucrative tourist revenue. Moreover, hundreds of millions of dollars in wages literally disappeared when local businesses ceased to function. Reconstruction and rehabilitation costs were equivalent to 6 percent of the whole country's annual gross national product. The World Bank alone provided over half a billion dollars in reconstruction loans. The paid insurance losses exceeded any previous earthquake catastrophe except for those occurring in San Francisco in 1906 and Tokyo in 1923. The heavy concentration of industry in the capital further demonstrated that the nation's economic structure was ill served by allowing the bulk of its industry to locate in such narrow confines.

Some events developed after the catastrophe that the government had not foreseen. The PRI, although still the foremost political organization throughout Mexico, lost the support of many citizens of Mexico City. The general public saw the party as closely aligned with the government itself. Initially at least, the two together were seen as to have failed to contribute effectively to the rescue effort.

Eventually a citywide organization of ordinary citizens was formed to protest the manner in which the country's political leadership responded to the quake. Named the United Victim Network, its leaders pressured the office of the president to meet the needs of the homeless. The government, in an effort to regain support, and faced with a series of street demonstrations by this disaffected group of citizens, sometimes numbering in the thousands, took over some 600 acres of downtown real estate and, with the financial help of the World Bank, constructed dwellings for some 70,000 local citizens who were without housing. It added some small parks and playgrounds as well. Despite this highly publicized program, the government failed to win back the allegiance of most of the city's population.

The PRI's presidential candidate, Carlos Salinas de Gortari, barely won the national election held in 1988, three years following the quake. The opposition accused the government of fraud in tallying the votes. No questions of closeness arose in the case of the Mexico City vote, however—75 percent of the capital's voters backed his two opponents, Cuauhtémoc Cárdenas of the leftist Partido Democratico Revolucionario (PDR) and Manuel Clouthier of the Partido Acción Nacional (PAN).

In the years immediately following the quake, Mexico City's citizens continued to demonstrate their opposition to the existing political system. They had come to resent the country's president unilaterally selecting their mayor, a resentment kindled by the ineffectual handling of quake relief by the mayor's office. Finally, under pressure from an aroused and increasingly vociferous citizenry, the federal government capitulated and acquiesced to legislation enfranchising the city's residents.

Over a decade later, a further example of the rejection of the government's direct control of the reins of city government occurred when, in 1997, its citizens elected Cárdenas of the PDR its first popularly elected mayor over Alfredo del Mazo, the candidate chosen by the government and the PRI. The 1985 earthquake had changed forever the way that Mexico City was to be governed.

Carl Henry Marcoux

FOR FURTHER INFORMATION:

Centeno, Miguel Angel. *Democracy Within Reason: Technical Revolution in Mexico.* University Park: Pennsylvania State University Press, 1994.

Díaz Cervantes, Emilio. *The Placido Domingo Brigade: A Manual Against Disaster.* Mexico City: Ediciones Castillo, 1995.

Foweraker, Joe, and Ann L. Craig. *Popular Movements and Political Change in Mexico.* Boulder, Colo.: Lynne Rienner, 1990.

Gil, Carlos B., ed. *Hope and Frustration: Interviews with Leaders of Mexico's Political Opposition.* Wilmington, Del.: Scholarly Resources, 1992.

Kandell, Jonathan. *La Capital: The Biography of Mexico City.* New York: Random House, 1988.

Morris, Stephen D. *Political Reformism in Mexico: An Overview of Contemporary Mexican Politics.* Boulder, Colo.: Lynne Rienner, 1995.

Poniatowska, Elena. *Nothing, Nobody: The Voices of the Mexico City Earthquake.* Philadelphia: Temple University Press, 1995.

Quarantelli, E. L. *Organizational Response to the Mexico City Earthquake of 1985: Characteristics and Implications.* Newark: University of Delaware Disaster Research Center, 1992.

■ 1986: The Lake Nyos Disaster

Volcano

Date: August 21, 1986
Place: Cameroon
Result: 1,734 dead, 3,000 cattle dead, 4,000-5,000 people evacuated, 4 villages destroyed

The eruption of Lake Nyos in 1986 was the second time lethal gas released from a lake has claimed human lives. The first was on August 15, 1984, at Lake Monoun, another lake in Cameroon, when 37 people died. As the government had just put down an attempted coup at the time and was worried about the political overtones of the incident, the Monoun eruption received little public attention, but the eruption of Lake Nyos was so catastrophic that immediate international aid was needed.

History of Lake Nyos. Both lakes lie in the northwestern part of Cameroon, a tropical, West African country about the size of California. The lakes are located on the so-called Cameroon volcanic line, a zone of crustal weakness extending 1,000 miles northeast from Annobón Island in the south Atlantic through northwestern Cameroon and into northeastern Nigeria. Young cinder cones and basaltic lava flows appear along this line, as well as flat-floored explosion craters known as maars. The maars formed when rising, gas-charged magma came into explosive contact with near-surface groundwater. More than thirty of the Cameroon maars, filled by deep crater lakes, are strung out like jewels along the volcanic trend as it stretches across the nation.

The crater in which Lake Nyos lies is rimmed by vertical, bedrock fault scarps on the west, a partially collapsed volcanic cone on the east, a delta plain to the south, and an outlet spillway across the flank of an ash cone to the north. Because the ash deposits around the lake are unweathered and little eroded, geologists believe the crater in which Lake Nyos lies is only a few hundred years old. The lake itself is shaped like a lemon, with a maximum length of 1.2 miles and a maximum width of 0.7 miles. It is shallow at the south end, near the delta plain, but drops off steeply to a flat bottom about 680 feet deep. Prior to the eruption, the inhabitants called Lake Nyos "the good lake." It shimmered like a fallen piece of blue sky amidst the jutting rock cliffs and lush, green vegetation.

The part of Cameroon in which Lake Nyos lies is a remote, mountainous region reached only by crude dirt roads. Before the eruption, some 5,000 people lived in the 4-square-mile area surrounding the lake. They were drawn here by the deeply weathered volcanic rocks that provided rich soils for their crops of cassava, maize, and yams, as well as prime grazing land for their herds of cattle. In the villages, which were little more than a row of houses strung out along the roads, people lived in thatched huts or two-room, mud-brick homes with corrugated tin roofs. Family groups lived in clusters up in the hills. None of the inhabitants had telephones or electricity.

THE ERUPTION. The fatal eruption came without warning about 9:30 on the evening of Thursday, August 21, 1986. Although this was the rainy season, the eruption came during a lull between thunderstorms. As a result, people looked out in surprise when they heard a loud, rumbling noise, which lasted perhaps fifteen or twenty seconds, coming from the direction of the lake. One observer reported hearing a bubbling sound, and from his vantage point he saw a ghostly column of vapor rising from the lake's surface. The vapor then poured down the valley to the north, like a smoking river. He also saw a surge of water in the lake and felt a blast of air that had the odor of rotten eggs.

The people who lived in the valley north of the lake bore the brunt of the tragedy. The cloud of smoking vapor, which may have been as high as 150 feet, first struck the village of Lower Nyos, which lies about 0.3 mile beyond the lake. Thursday had been market day, and many people were still eating dinner when the cloud arrived, choking them in their homes. Those who tried to flee the cloud collapsed on the muddy roads leading out of town. Others died peacefully in their sleep. In all, some 1,200 people died in Lower Nyos that evening, with only one woman and a child known to have survived.

An additional 500 people perished in the villages of Cha, Subum, and Fang, which lay farther down valley as the toxic cloud rolled on for 5 more miles. A survivor from Subum said he had feelings of warmth and drunkenness before he lost consciousness, and he re-

membered an odor like that of cooking gas. Family members acted drunk and were coughing and crying as they fell to the floor, where some lay screaming or spitting up blood. Another Subum resident awoke gasping for air but managed to drag himself into a windowless shed behind the house, where he survived.

A few victims revived six to thirty-six hours later. They described feelings of dizziness, warmth, and confusion before losing consciousness, as well as shortness of breath. Only the people living in localities more than 2 miles from the lake reported an odor of rotten eggs or of gunpowder. When morning came, survivors of the eruption found the bodies of their cattle strewn about in the fields, and the bodies of their friends and relatives where they had fallen in their homes or along the roads.

It seemed as though a neutron bomb had struck. Everyone was dead, but the buildings remained untouched. Some of the victims had even stripped off their clothes, as if in a desperate attempt to escape the feelings of heat. Others lay amid scattered pots and furniture, where they writhed as the vapors strangled them. Oil lamps were snuffed out too, although they still contained oil. The animals were dead—goats, pigs, birds, small mammals, and insects down to the smallest ant. Later that day, when the bodies of the cattle began to bloat in the hot sun, they remained untouched by flies or vultures because the scavengers were dead too. Strangely enough, plant life seemed to have been unaffected.

The survivors hurriedly began burying the dead, with attention to their relatives first, and no one made any attempt to inform the outside world of what had happened, because of the lack of telephones and the poor roads. Thus the first word people had of the tragedy was from a government worker who headed into the area from the city of Wum on his motorcycle the afternoon of Friday, August 22. As he approached Lower Nyos, he first saw a dead antelope lying beside the road. Congratulating himself upon his good luck, he stopped to strap the animal to his motorcycle before continuing. Soon he encountered dead cattle and then the bodies of people. Now, beginning to feel ill himself, he turned his motorcycle around and hurried back to Wum, where he alerted the authorities. Full-scale relief efforts began on Sunday, August 24, when the president of Cameroon arrived by helicopter to inspect the scene, bringing with him doctors from Israel and a disaster team from France.

SCIENTIFIC ANALYSIS. Scientists came too, and, after the injured had been taken care of, they turned their attention to the lake. Just one glance revealed that the appearance of Lake Nyos had changed radically. Although the waters remained calm, the lake no longer looked like a fallen piece of clear blue sky, but rather an angry red eye festering in its crater socket. The water was stained a muddy, reddish brown by iron compounds that rose with the escaping gas, and mats of floating vegetation littered the lake's surface. The lake level had dropped by nearly 4 feet as well, and water had sloshed up on the south shore to a height of 80 feet and splashed over a 250-foot-high rock promontory on the southwest. The 20-foot high outlet spillway on the north had been overtopped as well, and downstream from the spillway, brush was flattened and several large fig trees lay uprooted, presumably by the blast of vapor coming from the lake.

The earliest newspaper accounts of the eruption reported that the gas expelled by the lake was hydrogen sulfide, an identification based on reports of the odor of rotten eggs. Scientists pointed out that carbon dioxide, not hydrogen sulfide, had been the culprit at Lake Monoun, and when water samples from Lake Nyos were analyzed, 98 to 99 percent of the gas still dissolved in the lake proved to be carbon dioxide. The amount of gas released by the lake during the eruption was estimated to have totaled about 1.3 billion cubic yards, based on a drop in lake level of nearly 4 feet. Because carbon dioxide weighs one and a half times as much as air, it would have hugged the ground as it moved down valley, asphyxiating its victims by forcing the breathable air aside.

Scientists considered three possible sources for this gas: volcanic, magmatic, or biogenic. If the origin were volcanic, the gas would have come from a near-surface eruption and should have had a high temperature. However, if the gas had a magmatic origin, it would have come from molten rock deep within the earth and consequently been cool by the time it reached the surface; it would also have lost its reactive constituents, such as sulfur and chlorine compounds and carbon monoxide. Temperature measurements made after the eruption indicated that the lake was still cool, so a magmatic origin was favored. Biogenic gas would have been cool too, having originated from the decomposition of organic matter on the lake's bottom, but carbon-14 tests dated the lake's gas as more than thirty-five thousand years old. This meant that the gas expelled by the lake was magmatic, for organic decomposition on the bottom of a lake only a few hundred years old could hardly account for such gas.

Springs around Lake Nyos contain high concentrations of carbon dioxide, so scientists believe the magmatic gas came into Lake Nyos with the groundwater. Once in the lake, the gas would have remained dissolved due to the weight of the overlying water. Because the lake was stratified, the gas would have concentrated in the cold, lowermost layers, gradually turning the lake into a time bomb waiting to go off. Any event that made the gas-rich water start to rise would have reduced the pressure on it and allowed carbon dioxide to bubble to the surface, just as a soda bottle fizzes when the cap is removed. Scientists could not be certain what made the water rise and initiate the eruption. Possibilities that were suggested include a rockfall into the lake, an earth tremor, a volcanic eruption, storm winds, or even seasonal cooling of the lake's upper surface, which would have caused the lake's water to overturn.

Carbon dioxide gas continued to leak into the lake after the eruption was over, and scientists predicted that in another twenty or thirty years the lake could be ready to erupt again. As a result they alerted Cameroon authorities that their crater lakes were potential hazards that would have to be monitored carefully. They also pointed out that the weak, natural dam forming the outlet spillway of Lake Nyos represented a hazard as well. Failure of this dam could cause a sudden lowering of the lake's level, triggering another explosive release of gas.

As a remedy for Cameroon's crater lakes scientists recommended reducing the gas content by controlled pumping. For an example of this, they cited an experimental project that began at Lake Monoun in 1992. Gas-rich deep water was pumped to the lake's surface, where the carbon dioxide was harmlessly released into the atmosphere, and then the degassed water was permitted to return to the lake.

Donald W. Lovejoy

FOR FURTHER INFORMATION:

Decker, Robert, and Barbara Decker. *Volcanoes.* 4th ed. New York: W. H. Freeman, 2006.

Eno Belinga, Samuel-M., and Isaac Konfor Njilah. *From Mount Cameroon to Lake Nyos.* Yaoundé, Cameroon: Classiques Camerounais, 2001.

Kling, George W., et al. "The 1986 Lake Nyos Gas Disaster in Cameroon, West Africa." *Science* 236 (April 10, 1987): 169-175.

Scarth, Alwyn. *Vulcan's Fury: Man Against the Volcano.* New ed. New Haven, Conn.: Yale University Press, 2001.

Stager, Curt. "Silent Death from Cameroon's Killer Lake." *National Geographic* 172, no. 3 (September, 1987): 404-420.

Tuttle, Michele, et al. *The 21 August 1986 Lake Nyos Gas Disaster, Cameroon: Final Report of the United States Scientific Team to the Office of U.S. Foreign Disaster Assistance.* Reston, Va.: U.S. Department of the Interior, U.S. Geological Survey, 1987.

■ 1988: YELLOWSTONE NATIONAL PARK FIRES

FIRE

DATE: Summer, 1988

PLACE: Mainly Yellowstone National Park, located predominantly in northwestern Wyoming and partly in southern Montana and eastern Idaho; also, surrounding national forests in the northern Rocky Mountains

RESULT: 2 dead; approximately 1.2 million acres burned, 793,000 in Yellowstone National Park itself; more than $3 million estimated in damage

The summer of 1988 saw the largest forest fire complex ever recorded for the Greater Yellowstone area, the largest in the northern Rocky Mountains for decades, and one of the most severe in U.S. history. The fires, which burned 36 percent of the more than 2.2-million-acre Yellowstone National Park and a total of 11 percent of the Greater Yellowstone Area, triggered the nation's most expensive fire-suppression effort and a heated debate about national park fire management policy.

Over the millennia, many conflagrations as large as the 1988 fires have swept across the vast volcanic plateaus of Yellowstone National Park. The fires have affected mostly the large stands of lodgepole pine, which dominate the high-elevation areas. These stands constitute 80 percent of the park's forests and cover nearly 60 percent of the park. The recurring, major fires are responsible for the mosaic landscape of different-aged pines. Tree-ring research shows that fires of this magnitude last struck in the early 1700's.

CRESCENDO OF FIRES. The 1988 fire season in the Greater Yellowstone Area began on May 24, when lightning ignited a blaze that rain quickly extinguished. Over the next six months, lightning and careless people triggered 247 more fires in the area. Early in the season, officials in Yellowstone National Park stuck to their policy, begun in 1972, of allowing lightning-ignited fires to burn in the backcountry, under certain guidelines. From 1972 through 1987, such fires had burned only 33,759 acres, and all these blazes had died naturally. Park staff did not foresee the extreme weather conditions that would develop in the summer of 1988.

The previous six summers had all been wetter than average, and rainfall in April and May of 1988 had been above average. However, the winters since 1982 had been consistently dry, and it is mainly the snowpacks in the mountains that moisten the park's plateaus. Weather experts were saying that the period leading up to 1988 was becoming the driest since the 1930's Dust Bowl. The summer of 1988 proved to be the driest in the park's history. Precipitation in June, July, and August was 20 percent, 79 percent, and 10 percent, respectively, of normal.

The failure of the usual June and July rains amplified the early fires. By July 15, 8,600 acres had burned; by July 21, more than 17,000 acres were ruined. The fires drew the attention of park visitors and the national media. On July 21, in a departure from policy, park officials decided to suppress all fires, whether caused by lightning or by humans. Nevertheless, within a week, fires in the park covered nearly 99,000 acres. By the end of July, dry fuels and high winds made the larger fires nearly uncontrollable.

In August, with almost no rain, temperatures remaining high, and a series of dry, cold fronts bringing strong, persistent winds, there was a marked decrease in moisture in forest debris. This dry fuel engendered near-firestorm conditions. By August 15, a total of 260,000 acres had burned. On August 20, the single worst day—dubbed "Black Saturday"—winds as high as 70 miles per hour pushed fire across more than 150,000 acres in and around the park. Walls of flame reached 100 to 300 feet high. More acreage burned in a single twenty-four-hour period than had burned during any previous decade in the park's history.

Firefighters and soldiers poured into Yellowstone National Park. Aircraft, both for transporting firefighters and supplies and for dropping water and fire retardant on the flames, arrived from around the nation, and dozens of trucks were brought in. Firefighters cleared firebreaks and set backfires. National news reporters also arrived in force. Local businesses became alarmed at the prospect of lost tourist income. The park's fire-management policy came under heated debate, from park border towns to the U.S. Congress, as the conflagrations raged on despite the firefighting effort.

Spot fires, caused by burning embers carried up in the smoke, were breaking out up to a mile and a half ahead of the fires, mocking firebreaks. Even marshes and swamps burned, as well as young, green forests, which park ecologists had not expected to ignite. Some days, the seven major fire complexes, which in the end were responsible for more than 95 percent of the burned acreage, advanced as much as 10 or 12 miles. Of these seven, three had been started by human beings, and park staff had attempted to suppress them from the outset. These three were ultimately responsible for more than half the area burned.

By August 31, 550,000 acres had burned. At that point, park officials abandoned traditional, direct attacks on the fires and withdrew firefighters to developed areas, to try to protect only life and property. On September 7, 100,000 acres burned. On September 10, park authorities evacuated several towns, including Mammoth Hot Springs, the park's headquarters. That night the wind turned north, and by morning it was snowing. The fires lost their strength, although they did not die out completely until the onset of winter, in November. After September 11, firefighters were gradually sent home.

A total of more than 25,000 firefighters, as many as 9,000 at one time, fought the fires in the Greater Yellowstone Area, at a total cost of about $120 million. They hand-cut a total of 665 miles of fireline and cut 137 miles of bulldozer lines, including 32 miles in Yellowstone National Park itself. Two of the firefighters were killed outside the park, one by a falling tree and the other while piloting a plane transporting other personnel.

EFFECTS AND THE RECOVERY PROCESS. After the fires, Congress funded the restoration of fire-damaged facilities, which included 67 destroyed structures, and studies of the long-term impact of the fires. Although the 1988 tourist season was cut short by the blazes, visitors returned in 1989.

Scientists, eager to study the ecological effects of severe fire in a natural laboratory, set to work examining the impact on wildlife and plants. From the start it was clear that the 1988 Yellowstone fires burned in a heterogeneous pattern, owing to variations in fuels, winds, and terrain. Substantial areas were untouched by fire or only lightly burned by fast-moving ground fires that left most of the trees alive. Other areas were completely blackened by fierce fires that reached into the canopy and burned the treetops.

Most of the severely burned land, however, defied theories that fires of this magnitude would "sterilize" the soil by killing root systems and seeds, opening the way for invading weeds. Although flames consumed the aboveground parts of grasses and other herbaceous plants, even the hottest fires rarely burned more than the top inch of soil, leaving viable seeds, bulbs, roots, and rhizomes below that depth. By the spring of 1989, grasses and flowers were growing abundantly.

The heaviest fires were in the huge stands of aging, diseased, highly combustible lodgepole pine. These fires promoted new growth by releasing nutrients long locked up in the old trees, by opening the forest canopy and permitting sunlight to reach the young plants, and by clearing deadfall. Unlike many of the park's herbaceous plants, most trees do not regenerate by sprouting from their roots. Rather, they depend on seeds, and lodgepole pine is a master at this method in fire-affected landscapes. The cones of many, though not all, lodgepole pines are sealed by resin until the intense heat of fire melts the resin and releases seeds that have been stored in the cones for many years. This produces a large crop of young pines to take advantage of the abundant water, nutrients, and space that become available after a fire. This cone adaptation, called "serotiny," resulted in the development of the even-aged pine stands covering much of the Rocky Mountains, where fires are frequent. By the spring of 1989, lodgepole pine seedlings were establishing themselves abundantly. Ten years after the fires, many of them were knee- to shoulder-high.

Fire also affected the park's lower elevation areas, characterized by sagebrush grasslands interspersed with forests of Douglas fir and aspen. The Douglas firs, which dominate only a small percentage of the landscape, came back more slowly than the lodgepole pines but, a decade after the fires, were emerging above the shrubs. The park's scattered groves of aspen, the only deciduous tree common in the park and declining there for decades, sprouted profusely from the roots, but the new shoots were grazed by elk. Regeneration of willows, which typically line the streambanks, and sagebrush also may have been fire-stimulated. Ten years after the fires, grasslands had recovered to prefire conditions.

As new plants of many kinds became established, the populations and kinds of insects and larger animals feeding on the abundant new food supplies increased. The rapid rebound of plants and animals throughout the park surprised many ecologists.

The fires' toll on large animals was relatively small. Many animals survived by moving away from the flames. Postfire searchers found, both within and outside the park, carcasses of 335 elk (of a herd estimated at more than 30,000), 36 deer, 12 moose, 6 black bears, and 9 bison, mainly in areas where fast-moving flames prevented escape.

Fires in the sagebrush grasslands on the park's northern range, which supplies critical winter forage for the park's largest herds of elk and buffalo, diminished these animals' food supply for the winter of 1988-1989. Many of the animals starved, but their deaths were attributed more to the severe winter and to the 1988 summer drought's effects on forage than to fire.

Some birds and many small mammals were killed by the fires. A few small fish kills occurred as a result of heated water or fire retardant dropped on the streams. The fires caused physical and food-web changes in the streams, but these did not seem to affect fish adversely.

CAUSES AND FIRE POLICY. After much debate, many scientists concluded that the most significant factor causing the 1988 Yellowstone fires was the combination of drought and sustained, strong winds. Their position was bolstered by the dating of charcoal in park lakebeds, which indicated that, over the past fourteen thousand years, the recurrence interval of major fires is fifty to five hundred years and is related mainly to drought. According to this view, abundant fuel, in the form of accumulated deadwood and old, diseased pines, would exacerbate, but not cause, the fires.

In contrast, a more traditional hypothesis holds that fuel buildup is a major factor leading to severe fires. Some scientists argued that Yellowstone National Park's fire-suppression policy, in force from 1872 until 1972, augmented the forest fuel buildup and thus made a severe conflagration more likely. However, most think that suppression, which was effectively carried out for only some thirty years, had little effect, especially at the higher elevations.

Many scientists concluded that the origin of the fires—natural or human-made—was less important than weather and fuel in determining overall fire severity. Fire experts also concluded that the massive firefighting effort probably did not significantly reduce the acreage burned, although it saved many buildings.

As a result of the controversy over federal fire policy touched off by the 1988 Yellowstone fires, national parks and forests suspended and updated their fire-management plans. In 1992, Yellowstone National Park again had a wildland fire-management plan, but with stricter guidelines for allowing naturally occurring fires to burn.

Jane F. Hill

FOR FURTHER INFORMATION:

Baskin, Yvonne. "Yellowstone Fires: A Decade Later—Ecological Lessons Learned in the Wake of the Conflagration." *BioScience*, February, 1999, 93-97.

Carrier, Jim. *Summer of Fire: The Great Yellowstone Fires of 1988.* Salt Lake City: Gibbs-Smith, 1989.

Despain, Don G. F. "The Yellowstone Fires: Ecological History of the Region Helps Explain the Damage Caused by the Fires of the Summer of 1988." *Scientific American*, November, 1989, 36-45.

Franke, Mary Ann. *Yellowstone in the Afterglow: Lessons from the Fires.* Mammoth Hot Springs, Wyo.: Yellowstone Center for Resources, Yellowstone National Park, 2000.

Lauber, Patricia. *Summer of Fire: Yellowstone 1988.* New York: Orchard Books, 1991.

Sholly, Dan R., with Steven M. Newman. *Guardians of Yellowstone: An Intimate Look at the Challenges of Protecting America's Foremost Wilderness Park.* New York: William Morrow, 1991.

Vogt, Gregory. *Forests on Fire: The Fight to Save Our Trees.* New York: Franklin Watts, 1990.

Wallace, Linda L. *After the Fires: The Ecology of Change in Yellowstone National Park.* New Haven, Conn.: Yale University Press, 2004.

■ 1988: The Leninakan Earthquake

Earthquake

Also known as: The Spitak earthquake
Date: December 7, 1988
Place: Armenia, then part of the Soviet Union
Magnitude: 6.9 and 5.8
Result: More than 60,000 dead, 15,000 injured, 500,000 homeless, at least 450,000 buildings destroyed, including 7,600 historical monuments, estimated $30 billion in damage

On December 7, 1988, devastation struck Soviet Armenia. Between 11:41 and 11:45 A.M. two tremors measuring 6.9 and 5.8 on the Richter scale destroyed or severely damaged the cities of Spitak, Leninakan (now Gyumri), Kirovakan (now Vanadzor), and Stepanakert and more than 100 villages. Erivan (now Yerevan), the capital, suffered damage, and the shock waves spread out some 150 miles into neighboring Georgia, Azerbaijan, Turkey, and Iran. The quakes were shallow, the most destructive kind. The point on the fault between two massive subterranean tectonic plates where enough pressure was exerted to create the focus of the earthquake was approximately 13 miles below the surface. The corresponding mark of the focus on the surface of the earth, the epicenter, was about 20 miles northwest of Kirovakan, 26 miles northeast of Leninakan, and 3.25 miles from Spitak, a city of 30,000 that was virtually erased from the face of the earth. Approximately 99 percent of its population vanished, buried under the rubble. About 80 percent of Leninakan, Armenia's second largest city, with a population of 290,000, was destroyed; 80 percent of Stepanakert, a city of 16,000, was destroyed.

The quakes occurred at the worst possible time, just before noon on a working weekday. In addition, the damaged or destroyed areas had more than 150,000 unregistered refugees from neighboring Nagorno-Karabakh, a small, predominantly Armenian province in Azerbaijan that was forcibly attempting to oust the Armenians. The quakes caused a rupture 8 miles long and 2 feet wide; the force of the subterranean shock could be compared to the explosion of 100 nuclear bombs.

Devastating as the quakes were, in intensity they were relatively mild. In comparison, the 1985 Mexico City earthquake registered 8.1 on the Richter scale, the 1964 Alaskan earthquake was 9.2, and the 1939 Chile quake was 8.3. On the Richter scale, a magnitude 7.0 quake is ten times more powerful than a magnitude 6.0 quake and one hundred times more powerful than a magnitude 5.0 quake. Although all of these earthquakes were of greater intensity than that of Armenia, none were as costly in terms of human life. What set the Armenian earthquakes apart is the large number of buildings the quakes either damaged or destroyed.

REASONS FOR THE SCOPE OF THE DESTRUCTION. The first reason was the nature of the quakes. Usually, major earthquakes are pre-

ceded by a series of foreshocks, mild tremors that give authorities time to prepare and potential victims time to seek safety. The Armenian quakes came without warning, although some people had noted beforehand peculiar animal and bird behavior. The two tremors were of about equal intensity. This meant that whereas the first tremor badly damaged buildings, the second, or aftershock, four minutes later, caused them to collapse, often on their occupants.

Soviet seismologists defended their lack of preparedness, maintaining that there had been no major earthquake in the area since 1046, when the ancient Armenian capital of Arni was destroyed by a quake. However, the area had experienced a series of quakes over the years. In 1667, a quake had taken 80,000 lives. The fault at the heart of the 1988 earthquake appears on a geological map dated 1971. The Caucasus Mountain range, in which Armenia is located, is a seismic area crisscrossed by fault lines and filled with extinct volcanoes. Soviet scientists were known to have acknowledged that a major quake in the area was long overdue.

A second reason was poor urban planning. In earthquake-prone areas provisions should be made for "areas of survival," or free space to which people can escape from the danger of collapsing buildings. There was no such provision in the Armenian cities. Buildings were placed close together so that the areas between them, including the streets, were filled with debris from the earthquakes. This not only failed to afford escape but also did not provide the firm, cleared ground the Caterpillar carriages of the moveable cranes needed to lift the heavy debris.

Inappropriate building design and faulty construction also contributed greatly. Substandard construction was probably the major reason for the scope of the Armenian catastrophe. Most of the newer buildings, both offices and apartment houses, eight or nine stories high, were prefabricated. Slabs of concrete rested on cement-block walls. When the quakes occurred, the unconnected elements toppled. The quality of the concrete was also inferior, unable to withstand strain and prone to crumbling. When the supports were destroyed, the slabs collapsed together like gigantic millstones, trapping many of the occupants of the buildings between them. After the quakes, lifting these huge slabs was beyond human efforts; the much-needed cranes and other heavy equipment arrived too late to save many victims. In rural areas, many of the houses were made of mud brick, with stone roofs that collapsed on the occupants. In rebuilding the decision was made to limit the height of buildings to three or five stories and to pour concrete on the site.

Another reason was ineffective assistance. The sheer scope of the tragedy, involving nearly 19 percent of the country's population, was beyond the capability of the Armenian authorities; help was needed from outside the country. With thousands of badly injured people trapped beneath the wreckage, every hour of delay meant additional loss of life. It was only because of glasnost, or the open-discussion policy of Soviet president Mikhail Gorbachev, that the outside world became aware of the disaster. (The 1948 earthquake in the Soviet republic of Turkmen that killed 110,000 was concealed for forty years.) Also, Soviet acceptance of outside help was unprecedented.

When the outside world did become aware of the disaster, the extent of the support, especially from the 6 million Armenians scattered throughout the world, was unparalleled. The total value of aid, estimated at $500 million, was the largest international response ever to a national disaster. The day after the quakes a French team of doctors, anesthesiologists, and medical technicians—together with supplies—was ready to leave for Erivan. However, they had to wait two days before permission was given to land—two days in which thousands died. President Gorbachev was in New York at the time but canceled his trip to fly back to the Soviet Union. He visited Armenia on December 10, ostensibly to take charge of the rescue operation, which had suffered from lack of leadership. The position of landlocked Armenia surrounded by alienated states made a desperate situation even worse because the necessary heavy equipment had to come by land. The only working rail line was from Erivan to Baku, the capital of Armenia-hostile Azerbaijan. Supplies came by air in such quantities that the Erivan and Leninakan airports became bottlenecks.

Meanwhile, aid workers desperately tried to free the victims whose cries and groans became ever fainter. In the end only 5,000 of as many as 80,000 were pulled from the wreckage. Most tragic was the death of more than 15,000 children, particularly in a country with a negative growth rate. By December 14, the Red Army wanted to clear all people from the damaged areas and to level the sites with bulldozers and sow them with lime and other disinfectants to halt the possible spread of disease from the decomposing bodies beneath the ruins. Desperate intervention by survivors still searching for possible living victims delayed the decision a few more days. As late as December 15, a living person was pulled from the wreckage. By December 17, foreign relief workers were ordered to leave; by December 23, efforts to locate more survivors ceased.

The injured who did survive faced another ordeal: inferior medical treatment. Relief doctors estimated Soviet medicine lagged a half-century behind that of the West. Not only were basic medications either in short supply or lacking but there was also a lack of sophisticated equipment, such as dialysis machines. One of the more urgent problems was to deal with "crush syndrome." When subjected to great external pressure, the kidneys shut down and toxemia or poisoning begins. Only the use of dialysis machines that serve to cleanse the blood can keep the victim alive. At Erivan's central hospital, 80 percent of the 600 survivors suffered from crush syndrome. Several dialysis machines were brought in by air, but not enough to save all who needed their use.

There were also psychological problems to solve. In a society such as Armenia's, where the extended family and clan take precedence over the individual, the loss of such support is emotionally devastating. There was scarcely a person in the entire republic that had not lost a relative; entire families disappeared. Hundreds wandered aimlessly with blank eyes through the ruins, clearly in need of counseling or psychiatric services, which were not readily available.

The poor health of the victims was a factor in the death rate. Relief workers, especially those trained in nutrition, noted that low resistance caused by poor dietary habits raised the mortality rate among the earthquake victims. Further undermining their health was frequent evidence of alcohol and tobacco abuse.

Lack of authority was also to blame. Despite its officially being called a "union" of quasi-independent republics, the Soviet Union was a dictatorship, with authority tightly controlled by Moscow. Despite Gorbachev's pledge to "take charge" in Armenia, centralized authority to direct the complicated relief operation, especially in the distribution of supplies, was sporadic and ineffective. Relief workers often did not know where to go or what to do, and there was much duplication of effort and plundering and disappearance of supplies. A number of the bureaucrats who normally would have been available for administrative duties lay dead beneath the rubble. Units of the Red Army that had been sent to the disaster area did not participate in the relief efforts; they merely enforced curfews and blocked access to the ruined sites.

ASSESSING THE DAMAGE. Given the secretive nature of the Soviet system it was impossible to arrive at accurate figures for the cost of the earthquakes. The Soviets estimated that 55,000 people had been killed. Relief workers estimated far more—possibly as many as three times that number. Especially devastating to Armenia was the loss of trained professionals and of children—a loss impossible to evaluate in monetary terms.

More than 500,000 were left homeless; Soviet authorities indicated a wish to resettle about 70,000 in other parts of the Soviet Union. Gorbachev pledged $8.5 billion for restoration purposes, the same amount of money that was allocated to repair the nuclear disaster at Chernobyl two years before. Authorities estimated that at least triple that amount would be needed to restore the cities, using earthquake-resistant and more expensive building techniques. In addition to the buildings, extensive damage was done to the infrastructure—to light, sewer, water, and gas lines and to the transportation system.

Help from Moscow never arrived. The Soviet Union was dissolved December 4, 1991. Armenia had declared its independence on September 21, 1991, to face the formidable task of rebuilding a shattered land.

Nis Petersen

FOR FURTHER INFORMATION:
Brand, D. "When the Earth Shook." *Time*, December 19, 1988, 34-36.
Coleman, Fred. "A Land of the Dead." *Newsweek*, December 19, 1988, 19-23.
Kerr, Richard A. "How the Armenian Quake Became a Killer." *Science* 243 (January 13, 1989): 170-171.
Novosti Press Agency. *The Armenian Earthquake Disaster.* Translated by Elliott B. Urdang. Madison, Conn.: Sphinx Press, 1989.
Verluise, Pierre. *Armenia in Crisis: The 1988 Earthquake.* Translated by Levon Chorbajian. Detroit: Wayne State University Press, 1995.

■ 1989: Hurricane Hugo

Hurricane

DATE: September 13-22, 1989
PLACE: The Caribbean, North Carolina, and South Carolina
CLASSIFICATION: Category 4-5
SPEED: 136 miles per hour with gusts over 150 miles per hour
RESULT: At least 75 dead (41 in the United States), $10 billion in damage

Hurricane Hugo belongs to a class of major hurricanes called Cape Verde storms. These hurricanes usually originate from strong African disturbances that intensify as they move off the West African coast and produce a tropical depression as they pass close to the Cape Verde Islands. Other hurricanes that were Cape Verde storms include Hurricane Donna in 1960 and Hurricanes David and Frederic in 1979.

Hurricane Hugo began on September 9, 1989, as a cluster of thunderstorms off the coast of Africa. On September 10, 1989, it became a tropical depression when it was located approximately 125 miles south of the Cape Verde Islands. The depression continued on a due-west course over the eastern Atlantic Ocean for several days. By September 13 Hugo was located 1,200 miles east of the Leeward Islands and was moving westward at 20 miles per hour. The storm had gained sufficient strength and organization by this time to be classified as a hurricane by the National Hurricane Center, and its wind speeds were clocked in excess of 74 miles per hour. A day later, Hugo's winds had increased to 115 miles per hour.

By September 15, sustained winds of 190 miles per hour were measured by reconnaissance aircraft at 1,500 feet. This made the hurricane a Category 5 storm on the Saffir-Simpson Hurricane Scale, the most intense category on the scale. Its central pressure was measured as low as 27.1 inches, which tied for the record minimum pressure in the Atlantic Ocean.

THE CARIBBEAN. Hurricane Hugo first reached land on September 16, when its eye passed over Guadeloupe. At that time its winds were estimated at 140 miles per hour. Its surface pressure was measured at 27.8 inches when its eye passed over the island. Approximately half of Pointe-Pitre, the capital city of Guadeloupe, was destroyed by the storm. In addition, 11 people were killed and 84 were injured. The neighboring island of Montserrat was also severely damaged. There, 10 people were killed and damages to property totaled $100 million.

Hurricane Hugo's next target was the Virgin Islands. On September 18, the eye of Hugo crossed the southwestern coastline of St. Croix. With maximum winds of 140 miles per hour the storm destroyed or damaged over 90 percent of the buildings on the island and left it without power, telephone service, or water. While the eye of the storm missed St. Thomas, the island still experienced extensive damage to buildings, utilities, and vegetation. Damage to the U.S. Virgin Islands totaled $500 million, while damage to the British Virgin Islands was estimated at another $200 million. Three people were killed by the storm, and another 7 died from storm-related causes. The damage was so extensive that in some areas of the Virgin Islands telephone service was not restored until March of 1990.

After hitting the Virgin Islands, Hurricane Hugo shifted slightly northward. It passed through Vieques Sound between the islands of Culebra and Vieques. The island of Culebra experienced sustained winds of 105 miles per hour and wind gusts of 150 miles per hour. Hurricane Hugo then moved over Puerto Rico on September 18. In the capital city of San Juan there were sustained winds of 77 miles per hour and peak gusts of 92 miles per hour. In Puerto Rico tens of thousands of people lost their homes, including 60 percent of the residents of Culebra. The most severe damage was to the electrical system, especially along the northeast coast of the island. All together, 35 municipalities were without power. A week after the storm an estimated 47,500 homes and businesses were still without power; as late as September 28, 10 days after the storm, electrical service was still only 40 percent restored.

Water service to the residents was also disrupted. One week after the storm, 25 percent of the island's residents were without water. In the first 10 days following the storm the U.S. Army Corps of Engineers distributed more than 2 million gallons of water from 33 tank trucks on the island. On Puerto Rico itself damage was estimated at

$1 billion. In addition, there were 2 deaths directly caused by the storm and 22 hurricane-related deaths.

Other islands in the Carribean affected by Hurricane Hugo were St. Kitts-Nevis and Antigua and Barbuda. Together these islands reported 2 people killed and $160 million in damages. All together it is estimated that Hurricane Hugo did a total of $3 billion in damages before it targeted the southeastern coast of the United States.

THE UNITED STATES. Following its passage through the Caribbean, Hurricane Hugo weakened from a Category 4 to a Category 2 storm on the Saffir-Simpson Hurricane Scale. On the morning of September 19, the eye of the storm had become poorly defined, and its strongest sustained winds were 100 miles per hour. As Hugo moved toward the South Carolina coast it strengthened once again to a Category 4 storm. When it came ashore near Charleston, the Charleston navy shipyard recorded gusts as high as 137 miles per hour. After hitting land, Hugo's sustained surface winds were clocked at 87 miles per hour at the customs house in downtown Charleston. Farther north, at Bull Bay, sustained winds were estimated to be as high as 121 miles per hour. When it hit the mainland, Hugo became the first Category 4 or higher storm to strike the United States coast since Hurricane Camille hit the Mississippi Gulf Coast in 1969.

In South Carolina thousands of people voluntarily began moving inland more than twenty-four hours before Hugo made landfall. At 6 A.M. on September 21, South Carolina governor Carroll Campbell issued a mandatory evacuation order for the barrier islands and the coast of South Carolina. A subsequent mandatory evacuation of all one-story buildings in Charleston was issued by Mayor Joseph P. Riley, Jr., because of the fear of a tremendous storm surge. It was estimated that more than 186,000 people left their homes, from Myrtle Beach to Hilton Head, South Carolina. The early warnings and evacuations were credited with saving thousands of lives.

Hurricane Hugo struck the South Carolina coast on the night of September 21. The center of the storm passed over Sullivan's Island, just north of Charleston. Sullivan's Island had a storm surge of 13 feet above mean sea level. At Bull Bay the storm surge was 20 feet, the highest ever reported on the East Coast of the United States. The death and destruction caused by Hurricane Hugo along the immediate coast and inland were extensive. However, because of evacuations and because the right side of the eyewall crossed the coast in one of the least populated reaches of South Carolina's coast, there were only 13 deaths in the state directly attributed to the storm. Of these, 6 deaths were from drowning and 7 were wind-related. Only 2 of the drowning deaths occurred in homes. Another 14 people died of storm-related causes.

THE DAMAGE. Property damage caused by Hugo was extensive. In Charleston an estimated 43 percent of the homes had at least $10,000 in damages. The roofs of Charleston city hall and the Charleston County courthouse were partially destroyed, causing significant damage to the contents of each. Several historical churches also lost their steeples. One week after Hugo only 25 percent of Charleston had electricity. The Charleston airport was closed to commercial traffic for a week due to damage to facilities and the lack of off-site power; full commercial service was not restored for eighteen days.

A survey by the Red Cross showed that 9,302 homes in the state were completely destroyed, over half of which were mobile homes. Another 26,772 homes suffered major damage, and 75,702 houses had minor damage. Major structural damage included loss of roofs, collapse of single-story masonry buildings, and complete destruction of mobile homes. The majority of inland wind damage was caused by falling trees, and along the coast major damage was caused by flooding. Approximately 65 percent of the houses on Sullivan's Island were structurally unsafe. On the barrier island to the north, the Isle of Palms, between 55 and 60 percent of the homes were deemed structurally unsafe. In addition, the Ben Sawyer Bridge, which provided the only access to the mainland from these islands, was blown out of position and tilted at a 30-degree angle. During this time the Red Cross served over 1 million meals to people. Between 1 and 1.5 million customers were without electrical power for two to three weeks; damage to power supply systems alone totaled more than $400 million.

Hurricane Hugo also caused extensive beach erosion and landward transport of sand from the beach. In some coastal areas Hugo did restore a more natural profile to beaches on which steep slopes had been artificially maintained. Beachfronts that lacked natural dune systems and natural vegetation were the most heavily damaged—residents in those areas suffered significant water damage.

In addition to damages to homes and government property, the timber, fishing, and tourism industries sustained heavy losses. For example, Hurricane Hugo destroyed more than 6 billion board feet of timber, more than three times the total lost in the Mount St. Helens volcanic eruption in 1980. The 150,000-acre Francis Marion National Forest, north of Charleston, had 70 percent of its trees damaged or destroyed. The value of the lost timber alone was estimated at over $1 billion. In North Carolina Hugo damaged more than 2.7 million acres of forest in twenty-six counties. Timber losses were valued at $250 million.

Hurricane Hugo had a faster forward movement than most storms. This resulted in higher-than-normal inland wind speeds. Columbia, South Carolina, which is over 100 miles from the coast, had sustained winds of 67 miles per hour, while Charlotte, North Carolina, recorded sustained winds of 60 miles per hour. As a result, Hugo caused destruction as far as 180 miles inland. In Charlotte, Hugo caused an estimated $366 million in damages. In the North Carolina counties of Mecklenburg, Gastonia, and Union, damage was estimated at $883 million. In North and South Carolina over 1.5 million people lost power because of the storm; Duke Power estimated that at least 700,000 of its customers lost service. In the weeks following Hugo, Duke Power had 9,000 workers replacing 8,800 poles, 700 miles of cable and wire, 6,300 transformers, and 1,700 electric meters. In some parts of North Carolina power was not restored for two weeks. Property losses in North Carolina totaled over $1 billion, while South Carolina had an estimated $4 billion loss. In addition, there was 1 death in North Carolina directly attributed to Hugo and 6 other storm-related deaths.

Additional death and destruction occurred as the remnants of Hurricane Hugo moved north. Virginia reported 6 storm-related deaths and damage estimated at $50 million, while 1 person died in New York.

At the time Hurricane Hugo struck in 1989, it was the most expensive hurricane in United States history. While figures vary, damages caused by the storm have been estimated as high as $7 billion in the United States, $2 billion in Puerto Rico, and $1 billion elsewhere. The total number of deaths linked to the storm, directly or storm-related, has been estimated at 75. Hugo remains one of the most destructive hurricanes ever to hit the Caribbean and the East Coast of the United States.

William V. Moore

FOR FURTHER INFORMATION:

Barnes, Jay. *North Carolina's Hurricane History.* Rev. ed. Chapel Hill: University of North Carolina Press, 1998.

Committee on Natural Disaster Studies. *Hurricane Hugo: Puerto Rico, the Virgin Islands, and Charleston, South Carolina, September 17-22, 1989.* Vol. 6. Washington D.C.: National Academy of Science, 1994.

Federal Insurance Administration. Federal Emergency Management Agency. *Learning from Hurricane Hugo: Implications for Public Policy.* Washington, D.C.: Author, 1992.

Fox, William Price. *Lunatic Wind: Surviving the Storm of the Century.* Chapel Hill, N.C.: Algonquin Books, 1992.

Joseph, Gloria I., and Hortense M. Rowe, with Audre Lorde. *Hell Under God's Orders: Hurricane Hugo in St. Croix—Disaster and Survival.* St. Croix, V.I.: Winds of Change Press, 1990.

U.S. Department of Commerce, National Oceanic and Atmospheric Administration. *Natural Disaster Survey Report: Hurricane Hugo September 10-22, 1989.* Washington D.C.: U.S. Department of Commerce, 1990.

■ 1989: The Loma Prieta
EARTHQUAKE

EARTHQUAKE

DATE: October 17, 1989

PLACE: Northern California, in an area extending from Watsonville and Santa Cruz in the south to San Francisco and Oakland in the north

MAGNITUDE: 7.0 or 7.1 on the Richter scale (U.S. Geological Survey recorded this earthquake at 7.1, but other geologists recorded it at 7.0)

RESULT: 67 dead, more than 3,000 injured, more than $5 billion in damage

The worst earthquake in American history did not take place in the West, where there are many fault lines, but rather in Missouri. Although the February 7, 1812, New Madrid earthquake (one of a series in the region) took place long before the development of the Richter scale in 1935, contemporary reports by witnesses led seismologists to conclude that the New Madrid earthquake was in the range of 8.8 to 11 on the Richter scale. The 1812 earthquake caused the earth to shake over an area of 5 million square miles. Two later destructive American earthquakes were the San Francisco earthquake of April 18, 1906, and the Good Friday earthquake of March 27, 1964, in Alaska. Although these two earthquakes resulted in extensive property damage and many deaths, they extended over smaller areas than the New Madrid quake. The Alaska earthquake was recorded at 9.2 on the Richter scale and caused shaking of the earth over approximately 500 square miles, whereas the San Francisco earthquake caused shaking of the earth over an area of 300 square miles and was estimated between 8.2 and 8.3 on the Richter scale.

The populations of San Francisco and Los Angeles are now much larger than they were in the first decade of the twentieth century. Were an earthquake of the magnitude of the New Madrid earthquake of 1812 or of the Good Friday earthquake of 1964 to occur near Los Angeles or San Francisco, it is probable that the number of deaths would be in the hundreds of thousands. It is not impossible that similar earthquakes might occur in California, which has the largest population of any American state.

After the terrible destruction and loss of life caused by the San Francisco earthquake, governmental officials and architects began to ask themselves what could be done to make buildings and bridges more resistant to seismic shocks caused by earthquakes, but few changes in building practices and codes were implemented until after the 1971 Sylmar earthquake near Los Angeles.

In 1972, the California legislature created a Seismic Safety Commission and instructed its members to make recommendations to make California buildings and bridges more earthquake-resistant. This commission concluded that the major destruction caused by earthquakes is not generated by the shaking itself but by the aftereffects, when improperly constructed buildings, dams, and bridges collapse. The collapse of these structures and fires caused by the bursting of underground gas lines contribute significantly to property damage and the loss of life right after earthquakes. The commission demonstrated that buildings built with reinforced bricks were more quake-resistant than those built with regular bricks.

The commission also demonstrated that wood-frame houses, even when constructed in conformity with existing building codes, were much more prone to quake damage than were houses built with reinforced brick. This had been known for a long period of time, but it was not financially feasible to ask people to tear down their wood-frame houses and to replace them with houses built with reinforced bricks. Also, the installation of additional steel rods tends to make dams and bridges more stable. The California Seismic Safety Commission pointed out that bridges and dams built before 1972 were not sufficiently reinforced, and it recommended that the government of California begin retrofitting, or reinforcing, these structures.

In addition, this commission pointed out that construction should be discouraged in areas that were highly susceptible to damage from earthquakes. This recommendation was impractical because far too much construction had already occurred in areas such

Part of the upper level of the San Francisco-Oakland Bay Bridge failed during the Loma Prieta earthquake. It had been scheduled for reinforcement the following week. (National Oceanic and Atmospheric Administration)

as the Marina District in San Francisco, which was created by filling in the land with sand, mud, and rocks. The foundation on which such construction was built was very susceptible to earthquakes—the ground tends to liquefy during severe seismic shocks. In addition, houses and businesses were built in very hilly areas, such as the Oakland Hills, during the first seven decades of the twentieth century. By 1972 it would have been impossible to move people and businesses from such areas. The government of California decided to create new building codes designed to make houses and public structures more quake-resistant and to undertake the retrofitting of existing dams, bridges, roads, and public buildings.

The reinforcement of existing structures was, however, a very expensive undertaking, and large tax decreases implemented in California in the 1970's and 1980's left the state government with insufficient means to complete this work in a timely manner. Ironically, the Bay Bridge, which connects San Francisco and Oakland, was scheduled to be reinforced just one week after the Loma Prieta earthquake. A portion of the upper level of this bridge collapsed during the Loma Prieta earthquake.

THE QUAKE. Northern Californians expected October 17, 1989, to be a joyous day for the region of San Francisco and Oakland. The Oakland Athletics and the San Francisco Giants, the two major-league baseball teams from Northern California, had qualified for the World Series, and a game was scheduled to begin around 5:30 P.M. local time in San Francisco's Candlestick Park. The game was being broadcast live on American television. As camera operators were filming pregame activities, the transmission of images to television screens around the world was interrupted. Television viewers were not sure what was happening until reporters outside Candlestick Park began to inform the world that an earthquake had occurred.

The quake occurred on a sunny day during rush hour. The roads and bridges from Watsonville to San Francisco were filled with cars and people, and others were in their homes waiting for the World Series game to begin. The epicenter of the earthquake was located on the San Andreas fault in the Santa Cruz Mountains, to the east of the cities of Santa Cruz and Watsonville. The nearest landmark to the epicenter was Loma Prieta Mountain, which is why seismologists refer to this quake as the Loma Prieta earthquake.

Television reporters were already in San Francisco to cover the World Series game, so news traveled quickly. Initial reports stressed the damage done to the cities of San Francisco and Oakland, but extensive damage also occurred on the campus of Stanford University, in the nearby city of Palo Alto, in Santa Cruz, and especially in the largely Hispanic town of Watsonville, which was the closest city to the epicenter itself. Although authorities from the state and federal governments and volunteers from the Red Cross thought they were sufficiently prepared for a natural disaster, each earthquake results in unexpected problems. The situation in Watsonville illustrates this point.

EFFECTS IN WATSONVILLE. Since the San Francisco earthquake of 1906, the demographics of California have changed greatly. California is a much more ethnically and linguistically diverse state than it was during the first decade of the twentieth century. Like many cities throughout California, Watsonville has a large Latino population, and it is surrounded by wealthier cities such as those in the Silicon Valley and in the suburbs of Santa Cruz, where the population is largely Anglo-American. Watsonville was 60 percent Latino in 1989, and most houses were of older wood-frame construction, built long before the implementation in the 1970's of stricter building codes. Since it was located close to the epicenter of this accident, structural damage in Watsonville was very significant.

The major industries near Watsonville are farming and food production. These labor-intense industries pay poorly, but they attract large numbers of emigrants from Mexico and Central America, who often receive even lower salaries in their native countries. Between 1984 and 1989, the population of Watsonville had increased by 38 percent, but non-Latinos still dominated the municipal government of Watsonville, since many of the recently arrived Latinos were not yet American citizens. This earthquake destroyed almost 10 percent of all apartments and houses in Watsonville, but the property damage affected the Latino neighborhoods more than the Anglo neighborhoods, largely because the structures in the Latino communities had been completed decades before and were of wood-frame construction and therefore not very resistant to seismic shocks.

When soldiers in the California National Guard and representatives from the Federal Emergency Management Agency (FEMA), the Red Cross, and the state of California arrived in Watsonville, an immediate problem became evident to almost everyone. Those who wanted to help the survivors did not speak Spanish and could not communicate with the Latino majority in Watsonville. Since so much housing in Watsonville had been destroyed, the Red Cross had no choice but to create makeshift disaster centers and housing enclosures located far from the Latino neighborhoods in Watsonville. The threat of aftershocks in the communities of Watsonville was simply too great for people to be allowed to stay near their severely damaged homes and apartment houses, but many Spanish-speaking residents did not understand why they were being forced to leave their neighborhoods for distant regions of Watsonville; they believed that this represented yet another example of Anglo bias against Latinos. Recent antagonism between Anglo and Latino communities in Watsonville only exacerbated relationships between these two groups in the days immediately following the Loma Prieta earthquake.

The various emergency organizations dealt with the problem by bringing in bilingual workers who could communicate with the Latino majority in Watsonville. The presence of bilingual workers who understood Latino culture helped to diffuse a volatile situation. The events in Watsonville helped the Red Cross, the California National Guard, and FEMA to understand that preparation for natural disasters required them to take into account not only problems related to health and housing but also the changing linguistic and cultural fabric of states such as California. Something positive, however, did result from the traumatic events in Watsonville. Anglos and Latinos learned to cooperate with each other in order to create a more unified city and to reduce political and cultural divisiveness.

In Watsonville, as in other cities affected by this earthquake, people discovered that their regular homeowner's insurance policies did not cover earthquakes. Earthquake insurance is extremely expensive, and it often includes very high deductibles and limits on the maximum liability for insurance companies. Individuals whose homes were destroyed by this earthquake had no choice but to turn to the federal government for loans to help them rebuild their residences. Such loans had to be repaid, and this created major financial crises for affected Californians. Companies and universities also suffered financially as a result of the Loma Prieta earthquake.

STANFORD UNIVERSITY. The case of Stanford University clearly indicates the gravity of the problems faced by universities and businesses. Stanford University was founded in 1885, and its campus is located near the San Andreas fault. Many of its older buildings were constructed with unreinforced bricks and are thus less quake resistant than buildings constructed with reinforced bricks. For many years Stanford University paid for earthquake insurance, but by 1985 the annual premiums became so prohibitively expensive and the coverage so limited that the trustees of Stanford University concluded that it would be inadvisable to continue coverage against earthquakes.

In his book *Magnitude 8*, Philip L. Fradkin explains that Stanford University was offered earthquake coverage for an annual premium of $3 million, with a deductible of $100 million and coverage for a mere $125 million worth of damage above the deductible. Although Stanford University suffered damages that amounted to $160 million as a result of the Loma Prieta earthquake, the decision not to renew earthquake insurance coverage in 1985 was perfectly understandable. Universities, private businesses, and homeowners often cannot afford such extremely expensive policies that offer such limited coverage. A typical homeowner's policy comes with a deductible of $250 to $500 and frequently includes full-replacement coverage. With earthquake insurance, the deductible is usually at least $6,000, and full-replacement coverage is not offered.

DALY CITY, SAN FRANCISCO, AND OAKLAND. Located almost 60 miles north of the Loma Prieta epicenter is Daly City, a bedroom community south of San Francisco. In Daly City, many people chose to live on the palisades, which offer exquisite views of the Pacific Ocean. Many houses were built on the cliffs in Daly City and appreciated greatly in value during the 1970's and 1980's. People were oblivious to the dangers involved in building houses on cliffs near the San Andreas fault. Many houses built on the palisades in Daly City were forced from their foundations during the Loma Prieta earthquake and were structurally destroyed. These houses had been built on an old garbage dump that had been covered with sand. The ground on which these beautiful and expensive houses had been built in Daly City was of insufficient strength to resist seismic shocks, and the ground liquefied during the Loma Prieta earthquake.

Houses on the cliffs in Daly City should never have been built there because the ground was not strong enough to resist earthquakes, contributing significantly to the property damage. Those who filled in the land in Daly City did not realize that they were creating a very dangerous situation for future residents. A similar error was made in San Francisco during the late nineteenth century and especially right after the 1906 earthquake.

Just north of Daly City are San Francisco and Oakland. They both suffered extensive damage during the Loma Prieta earthquake, although not because the two cities had failed to enforce new building codes or to prepare for earthquakes. Office buildings and public structures constructed with reinforced bricks and additional steel rods in both cities did not suffer structural damage during the Loma Prieta earthquake; large buildings did not collapse as they had during the 1906 San Francisco earthquake. The San Andreas fault runs through these two cities, and the danger of earthquakes is extremely high. Athough property damage in both Oakland and San Francisco was very extensive, especially in the Oakland Hills, the three places that suffered the greatest damage were the Marina District of San Francisco, the Nimitz Expressway in Oakland, and the Bay Bridge.

Municipal officials and developers concluded that filling in the lagoon in San Francisco would be financially advantageous because it would permit extensive growth in both housing and economic development. The area filled in was called the Marina District, which includes such famous places as Fisherman's Wharf, Market Street, Embarcadero Street, and Candlestick Park. At first, the lagoon area was filled in with sand and rocks, but starting in 1912 municipal officials used a mixture of 30 percent mud and 70 percent sand to fill in the area. In 1915, a world's fair was held in San Francisco's new Marina District; afterward, the wooden buildings were taken down and buried in the mixture of mud and sand. The wood deteriorated and made the land even less earthquake-resistant.

Unlike the residents of Watsonville, those who lived in San Francisco's Marina District were mostly wealthy and Anglo. Many of the structures in the Marina District were also built well before the stringent building codes of the 1970's. The combination of a poor ground foundation and inadequately reinforced buildings created conditions favorable for disaster. On October 17, 1989, wood frame houses

A building in the Marina District is shored up next to rubble from a collapsed apartment. (FEMA)

in the Marina District collapsed in large numbers, and gas mains and pipes burst because the ground of mud and sand was too weak to protect them. When the natural gas was released into the air, it provoked a series of dangerous fires. Although the gas supply was quickly cut off to the Marina District by the utility companies, the damage had already been done. Many houses collapsed as a result of the earthquake, but many more houses and commercial structures were destroyed by the numerous fires.

Although San Francisco had a professionally trained fire department and established procedures for dealing with emergencies, their ability to deal with so many fires at the same time was severely limited. Television cameras transmitted to viewers around the world images of the fires, which lasted throughout most of the night of October 17-18. Geologists determined that the way in which the Marina District ground was filled significantly increased the liquefaction of the land and made the effect of the sesimic shocks much worse in the Marina District. Sections of San Francisco that had not been developed on filled land were much more quake-resistant than the Marina District. Even after the Loma Prieta earthquake, construction continued in the Marina District, because the land there is so valuable. Builders were required to reinforce buildings and to respect stringent building codes, but there is no guarantee that the Marina District will not suffer extensive damage when the next earthquake takes place near San Francisco. Had people known in the late nineteenth century and the early twentieth century what geologists know today, the Marina District might never have been developed, and Stanford, near the San Andreas fault, and houses in hilly regions in Oakland and Daly City might not have been constructed.

FREEWAY COLLAPSES. Two other major catastrophes in the San Francisco region were the collapse of the Nimitz Expressway and a section on the upper level of the Bay Bridge. The Nimitz Expressway in Oakland was built between 1954 and 1957. It did meet construction codes in effect at that time, and its engineers thought that it was safe, but it was not sufficiently reinforced to cope with an earthquake of the magnitude of 7.0 or 7.1. A total of 41 people died, either on the two levels of the freeway or below the freeway. Many people driving on the lower level were crushed to death when the upper level collapsed on their cars. The death toll would most certainly have been much higher had the earthquake occurred even a few minutes later. The earthquake took place at 5:04 P.M., and by that time most commuters had not yet reached the Nimitz Expressway for their trip home from work. Had this freeway collapsed even fifteen minutes later, hundreds would probably have been killed.

The two major bridges into San Francisco, the Golden Gate Bridge and the Bay Bridge, were constructed in the 1930's. Although the Golden Gate is the more famous of the two bridges, the Bay Bridge is used more heavily because it connects Oakland and San Francisco. In 1989, the Bay Bridge was double-deck, and people thought that it was safe. During the Loma Prieta earthquake, however, bolts that connected the east and west ends of supports came apart, causing a portion of the upper level to collapse. Amazingly, only one driver was killed, when his car fell from the upper level to the lower level. Luck and effective defensive driving by people on the upper and lower levels of the Bay Bridge prevented a large loss of life.

It took a full month to restore this bridge to regular service. The damage to bridges between Watsonville and San Francisco could have been much worse: Only 18 of the more than 4,000 bridges had to be closed for repairs after the Loma Prieta earthquake.

RESULTS. The impact of the Loma Prieta earthquake on Northern California was quite significant. Economists have estimated that between $5.6 and $5.8 billion had to be spent to repair houses, roads, public and commercial buildings, and bridges damaged or destroyed by the Loma Prieta earthquake. At least 67 people were killed as the direct result of this earthquake, but it is difficult to determine how many fatal heart attacks were caused by the trauma of the event. Between 3,000 and 4,000 people were seriously injured, putting a strain on medical personnel between Watsonville and San Francisco. It is impossible to describe the psychological damage experienced by people who survived this temblor. When the Loma Prieta earthquake occurred, California was already suffering from a national economic downturn, which affected the Golden State more severely than other American states. The temporary or permanent closing of businesses in an economically important region of Northern California exacerbated an already bad economic situation.

Edmund J. Campion

FOR FURTHER INFORMATION:

Bolt, Bruce A. *Earthquakes.* 5th ed. New York: W. H. Freeman, 2006.

Chameau, J. L., et al. "Liquefaction Response of San Francisco Bayshore Fills." *Bulletin of the Seismological Society of America* 81, no. 5 (October, 1991): 1998-2018.

Fradkin, Philip L. *Magnitude 8.* New York: Henry Holt, 1998.

Hanks, Thomas C., and Gerald Brady. "The Loma Prieta Earthquake, Ground Motion, and Damage in Oakland, Treasure Island, and San Francisco." *Bulletin of the Seismological Society of America* 81, no. 5 (October, 1991): 2019-2047.

Newsweek, October 30, 1989, 22-48.

Reti, Irene, ed. *The Loma Prieta Earthquake of October 17, 1989.* Santa Cruz: University of California, Santa Cruz, 2006.

Schiff, Anshel J., ed. *The Loma Prieta, California, Earthquake of October 17, 1989: Lifelines.* Washington, D.C.: U.S. Government Post Office, 1998.

Time, October 30, 1989, 30-51.

Wells, Ray E., ed. *The Loma Prieta, California, Earthquake of October 17, 1989—Geologic Setting and Crustal Structure.* Reston, Va.: U.S. Geological Survey, 2004.

■ 1991: PINATUBO ERUPTION

VOLCANO

DATE: June 12-16, 1991

PLACE: Luzon, Philippines

RESULT: About 350 dead (mostly from collapsed roofs); extensive damage to homes, bridges, irrigation-canal dikes, and cropland; 20 million tons of sulfur dioxide spewed into the stratosphere up to an elevation of 15.5 miles

As early as April 2, 1991, people from a small village named Patal Pinto, on the Philippine island of Luzon, observed steam and gases smelling of rotten eggs (indicating hydrogen sulfide) emanating from near the crest of Mount Pinatubo, along with intermittent minor explosions. Within ten weeks, these early ominous activities culminated in a volcanic eruption that has come to be regarded among the largest that occurred in the twentieth century.

Pinatubo, located about 62 miles (100 kilometers) northwest of Manila, belongs to a chain of composite volcanoes constituting a volcanic arc in the Philippines. It is believed to have been the result of a lava dome that formed about five hundred to six hundred years ago during the last-known eruption. Its lower slopes and foothills were composed primarily of pyroclastic and lahar (volcanic mudflow) deposits from voluminous eruptions that occurred in prehistoric times.

More than 30,000 people inhabited the foothills of the volcano before the 1991 eruption. Cities and villages surrounding the base of the volcano on gently sloping alluvial plains were populated by as many as 500,000 inhabitants. Located about 15.5 miles (25 kilometers) to the east of the volcano was Clark Air Base, and 25 miles (40 kilometers) to the southwest was Subic Bay Naval Station, both belonging to the United States.

Prior to the 1991 eruption, Pinatubo had the appearance of a steep, domelike spheroid that rose about 2,297 feet (700 meters) above a gently sloping apron made of pyroclastic and epiclastic materials. Such a volcano belongs to the class of stratocones, of which such well-known exemplars as Fuji and Mayon are considerably larger than Pinatubo. The extensive pyroclastic apron of Pinatubo, however, indicated that the volcano was extremely active in prehistoric times. Until the collapse of the summit in the 1991 eruption, Pinatubo rose 5,725 feet (1,745 meters) above sea level, surrounded by older volcanic centers, including an ancestral Pinatubo due south, east, and northeast.

THE ONSET OF ERUPTION. Following the emission of hydrogen sulfide gas and steam together with a few minor, phreatic (steam-charged) explosions along a 1-mile-long chain of vents on the north side of the volcano around April 2, 1991, the Philippine Institute of Volcanology and Seismology (PHIVOLCS) installed seismometers near the mountain, which immediately began recording several hun-

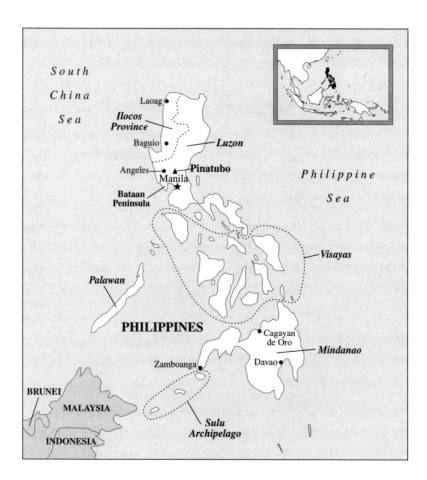

dred earthquakes a day. By April 5, nontelemetered seismographs installed on the northwest side of Pinatubo about 6 to 9 miles (10 to 15 kilometers) from the summit recorded between 40 and 140 seismic events (of magnitude less than 1.0 on the Richter scale) each day.

On April 23, a team of volcanologists from the United States Geological Survey (USGS) arrived at the scene following a request by PHIVOLCS to assist in the monitoring of the seismic activities near the mountain. Together, the Philippine and American experts installed a radio-telemetered seismic network and tiltmeters. These devices could locate the earthquakes and detect any new ground movement, respectively. They also measured fractures that opened during the early steam and vapor emissions from the chain of vents near the summit of the mountain.

Between May 13 and May 28, the geologists, with the help of the U.S. Air Force, measured a tenfold rise in the sulfur dioxide gas content of the steam plumes emanating from the summit. These and other measurements indicated that magma was rising within the volcano, and immediate preventive measures were necessary for the safety of people living in surrounding communities. The geologists established a set of alert levels ranging from 1 (implying low-level unrest) to 5 (indicating that eruption had started). On May 13, the alert level was set at 2, which meant that the seismic unrest probably involved magma.

Before April 2, 1991, the available geologic information on Pinatubo was quite limited. It was known to be a dacite dome complex about 2 miles (3 kilometers) in diameter, with voluminous fans of ash-flow deposits that were geologically young (less than ten thousand years old). The volcano was known to be thermally active, however, and had previously been explored as a potential geothermal energy source by the Philippine National Oil Company.

Anticipating that an eruption might be imminent, the geologists went to work designing a hazard map, in preparation for the worst-case scenario. This was an urgent matter, especially since a large number of small villages lay scattered on the northwest slope of the volcano and part of Clark Air Base and several urban communities (such as the city of Angeles, with a population of 300,000) lay within the potential range of pyroclastic and debris flows extending well beyond the volcano. Based on knowledge of the best-known distribution of each type of volcanic deposit from past eruptions, a joint USGS-PHIVOLCS team rapidly compiled a worst-case hazard map showing areas most susceptible to ash flows, mudflows, and ashfall.

Around May 23, the hazard map was distributed to officials of the Philippine civil defense organization, the local governments in neighboring communities, and the U.S. military. Based on data obtained following the actual eruption on June 15, the predictions by the hazard map vis-à-vis areas where the impact would be most severe were proven to be fairly accurate.

Near the end of May, the number of seismic events per day was fluctuating in a random fashion, and measurements of key seismic parameters such as earthquake hypocenter locations proved quite inconclusive. The likelihood of an actual eruption, though highly plausible, could not be precisely forecast. From late May until early June, indicators such as relatively long earthquake periods interspersed with periods of tremor, as well as the location of hypocenters beneath the steam vents, were clear precursors of imminent eruption. It was also observed that the emission rate of sulfur dioxide, which had dramatically increased during the preceding two weeks, had suddenly decreased. This finding was consistent with the escape vents of the gas being sealed off by magma rising within the volcano.

THE ERUPTION AND ITS AFTERMATH. During the second week of June, the east flank of the mountain became tilted by inflation, and a small lava dome extruded near the most vigorous steam vent. The tectonic earthquakes became progressively shallower and weaker, while the emission of low-level ash became continuous.

PHIVOLCS raised the alert level to 3 on June 5, indicating that eruption was likely within two weeks. On June 7, the extrusion of a small dome on the north flank, accompanied by numerous small earthquakes, triggered a level 4 alert, signifying eruption within twenty-four hours. Residents of Zambales, Tarlac, and Pampanga Provinces, within 12.4 miles (20 kilometers) of the volcano, were evacuated. As the dome continued to grow and ash emissions increased to alarming levels, alert level 5 (signifying eruption had begun) was declared on June 9. On June 10, a total of 14,500 nonessential personnel and dependents were moved by road from Clark Air Base to Subic Bay Naval Station. Most of the aircraft had already been removed from Clark Air Base at this time.

On June 12, the first of several major explosions occurred at 8:51 A.M., spewing airborne ash to the west of the mountain and sending pyroclastic flows down its northwest slope. The ash column reached a height of 62,335 feet (19,000 meters) above sea level, according to measurements by the weather radar at Clark Air Base. Explosions continued through the night of June 12 and the morning of June 13. Part of the dome was destroyed, and a small crater was formed adjacent to it. There was intense seismic activity, with buildup periods lasting as long as several hours prior to the explosions during June 12 through 14. The long buildup periods permitted short-term notification to Philippine civil authorities and U.S. military authorities regarding impending eruptions. The city of Angeles was placed on evacuation alert.

The climactic eruptive phase began around 1:09 P.M. on June 14, following an eight-hour episode of vigorous seismic activity. Explosive eruptions continued through the night and into the morning of June 15. Around 5:55 A.M., a massive lateral blast spread north, west, southwest, and northwest from the volcano, sending a broad column of ash 39,370 feet (12,000 meters) above sea level. This climactic blast was followed by six more eruptive pulses, after which the eruption became essentially continuous, lasting between the afternoon of June 15 through the early hours of June 16.

Coincidentally, Typhoon Yunya approached Pinatubo around the same time. The extreme combination of hazards, including the explosive eruption, a complete loss of telemetry between the summit and the observatories, and uncertainty regarding the effect of Yunya on the flow of volcanic debris, made it necessary to rapidly evacuate all remaining USGS, Air Force, and PHIVOLCS personnel from Clark Air Base. This task was accomplished by around 2:30 P.M. on June 15.

The volcano continued to erupt a column of ash rising 32,808 feet (10,000 meters) above sea level for several weeks, even though the overall seismic activity started to decline by late June 15. When the weather cleared on June 16, it was observed that the top of the volcano had been replaced by a 1-mile-wide caldera, and vast areas surrounding the volcano were covered by around 6,540 or 7,847 cubic yards (5 or 6 cubic kilometers) of pyroclastic deposits.

The presence of Yunya exacerbated the volcanic mudflows and

the dispersal of water-saturated ash across a large number of cities and villages. Cyclonic winds spread tephra over at least 7,722 square miles (20,000 square kilometers) surrounding the volcano. The weight of the wet, heavy ash led to the collapse of many buildings, which turned out to be the leading cause of the loss of 350 or so lives from the eruption. Mudflows triggered by the typhoon and heavy rainfall destroyed homes, bridges, and irrigation-canal dikes and buried vast areas of cropland.

The Pinatubo eruption was one of the largest in the twentieth century (being about ten times larger than the eruption of Mount St. Helens in the United States in 1980) and potentially threatened 1 million lives. Overall, it must be concluded that the evacuation and safety procedures followed jointly by the USGS, PHIVOLCS, and the various military and civil defense organizations via effective communication and timely, responsible action, helped avert disaster of a far higher magnitude. In fact, it is estimated that timely and effective intervention saved many thousands of lives (the actual casualty figure would be much lower had it not been for the presence of the typhoon), and at least $1 billion in property which might otherwise have been lost. In terms of accurate eruption prediction and highly effective response, the 1991 Pinatubo eruption provides an important model for future volcanic eruptions and other geological cataclysms.

Monish R. Chatterjee

FOR FURTHER INFORMATION:

Fiocco, Giorgio, Daniele Fuá, and Guido Visconti, eds. *The Mount Pinatubo Eruption: Effects on the Atmosphere and Climate.* New York: Springer, 1996.

Newhall, Christopher G., James W. Hendley II, and Peter H. Stauffer. *The Cataclysmic 1991 Eruption of Mount Pinatubo, Philippines.* Vancouver, Wash.: U.S. Geological Survey, 1997.

Newhall, Christopher G., and Raymundo S. Punongbayan, eds. *Fire and Mud: Eruptions and Lahars of Mount Pinatubo, Philippines.* Seattle: University of Washington Press, 1996.

Pinatubo Volcano Observatory Team. "Lessons from a Major Eruption: Mount Pinatubo, Philippines." *EOS/Transactions of the American Geophysical Union* 72 (1991): 554-555.

Scarth, Alwyn. *Vulcan's Fury: Man Against the Volcano.* New ed. New Haven, Conn.: Yale University Press, 2001.

Shimizu, Hiromu. *The Orphans of Pinatubo.* Manila, Philippines: Solidaridad, 2001.

Wolfe, Edward. "The 1991 Eruptions of Mount Pinatubo, Philippines." *Earthquakes and Volcanoes* 23, no. 1 (1992): 5-37.

■ 1991: THE OAKLAND HILLS FIRE

FIRE

ALSO KNOWN AS: The East Bay Hills fire, the Tunnel fire
DATE: October 19-21, 1991
PLACE: Oakland Hills, California, and vicinity
RESULT: 25 dead, 150 injured, 2,843 single-family homes destroyed, 433 apartment units destroyed, $1.5 billion in damage, 1,520 acres burned

The area of Oakland Hills is extremely susceptible to fires for many reasons. Oakland Hills is a small community near San Francisco located between Berkeley and Oakland and the hills that surround them. The houses located there are sheltered by trees, with narrow roads leading up steep hillsides to different subdivisions. Most of the houses in the Oakland Hills area in the 1990's were million-dollar dwellings that people had worked a lifetime to afford.

The Oakland Hills area is known as a wildland-urban interface. This is where human-made developments and wildland fuels meet at a boundary that is susceptible to wildfires because of the accumulation of dense fuels. In the late twentieth century, the number of people moving to the wildlands increased dramatically. Wildfires are actually beneficial to the natural cycles of many types of ecosystems, when they are not close to human settlements. They remove the weak and dead vegetation that are potential fuels for larger fires if they are allowed to accumulate and allow for a chance for renewal in the forest. The cleansing effects of the fires present dangers when homes are built in these wild areas, however.

In wildland-urban interface areas, city services such as fire protection and water supply are not always fully provided. Procedures for controlling wildfires often include sacrificing some areas in order to set up a perimeter firebreak. This procedure requires sacrificing some homes and property to save others.

It is essential for communities to prohibit dangerous building practices; mandate regular inspections to ensure adequate clearing of plants, shrubs, and trees away from homes; and seek support to implement these policies to protect people living in the wildland-urban interface. California has a law that designates hazardous fire areas as places covered by grass, grain, brush, or forest, whether publicly or privately owned, and regions that are so inaccessible that a fire would be difficult to suppress. The area of Oakland Hills was not considered hazardous because all the residences were accessible by paved roads, even though they were narrow and winding.

The Oakland Hills area was well known for fires in the past. In September of 1923 a wildfire started northeast of Berkeley and spread quickly. It burned 130 acres, consuming 584 buildings and causing $10 million worth of damage. After the fire, the city council passed legislation requiring fire-resistant wood coverings for roofs but rescinded the legislation before it could take effect. Another fire started in September of 1970 southeast of the University of California Berkeley campus. It destroyed 38 homes and damaged 7 others. The total cost of damage was $3.5 million. Yet another fire began in December of 1980 just north of where the Oakland Hills fire started. This fire destroyed 6 homes and injured 3 people in only twenty minutes.

In 1982, Berkeley designated a section of the city as the Hazardous Hill Fire Area after an extensive inspection program. Four months before the fire, in June of 1991, Berkeley passed an ordinance that required all houses in this area to have Class-A roofs. This ordinance did not include the area of the Oakland Hills fire.

THE OAKLAND HILLS FIRE. The story of the Oakland Hills fire actually begins the day before the fire started. On October 19, 1991, a fire of suspicious origin started near 7151 Buckingham Boulevard. The wind was not strong enough that day to push the fire very far. Firefighters were able to keep the blaze under control and thought they had extinguished it. The heat from the fire on October 19 that had been extinguished caused pine needles to drop from the trees, laying down a fresh layer of kindling. A type of debris called duff fell around and inside the area of the first burn. Duff is the pine needles, often up to a foot thick, that have accumulated under the trees; it is highly flammable. The water used by the firefighters extinguished the flames that burned on top of the duff, but the duff combined with ash and dust to form a crust. The fire continued to smolder under the crust. Firefighters followed prudent procedures by leaving their hoses in place overnight and returning periodically to the fire scene to check for signs of renewed fire.

At approximately 10:45 the next morning, as 25 firefighters were finishing up after the fire of the previous day, sparks burst out of the duff. They were carried by winds ranging from 16 to 25 miles per hour, with some observers estimating winds up to 65 miles per hour. The wind brought them to a tree that instantly burst into flames. Convective currents and strong winds allowed the fire to move out of the northeast region and spread to nearby vegetation. By 11:15 in the morning, the fire was raging out of control. The fire went uphill from the place of origin. The winds changed suddenly and blew the fire in many directions at once. A warm, dry wind blowing in the valleys of a mountain, called a foehn, pushed the fire back downhill just as fast as the fire was spreading uphill.

Minutes later, the winds changed again. This time the fire started spreading eastward, toward the Parkwood Apartments and the Caldecott Tunnel. Another change in the wind direction sent the fire to the southwest. Many pine trees and other shrubs burst into flames. Homes were becoming threatened, and firefighters struggled to contain the fire. The fire spread across Highway 24 and headed toward Lake Temescal. At the same time, another flame front started moving northwest, toward the Claremont Hotel and the city of Berkeley. The fire turned into numerous large fires because of spotting. Firebrands were carried by the fire to areas remote from the original fire. The winds caused the fire to descend along the ridge between Marlborough Terrace and Hiller Highlands. The winds accelerated the motion of the fire down the ridge, causing it to consume everything in its path.

Within one hour the fire had consumed 790 structures. The area south of Highway 24 and the area near the Caldecott Tunnel caught fire. An area called Upper Rockridge caught fire because of winds and spotting. By noon, 40 percent of the total affected area was burned. As the fire began spreading south and west, it reached flatter, more open ground and started slowing. The fire reached temperatures as high as 2,000 degrees Fahrenheit. Although this temperature can boil asphalt, this fire was not as fierce or hot as most wildfires.

ATTEMPTS AT EXTINGUISHING THE FIRE. Weather conditions and the rapid spread of the fire in many directions at once made it extremely difficult to extinguish the blaze. The fire hoses were mostly ineffective because the wind was so strong that it bent the water streams 90 degrees on 500-gallon-per-minute hoses. For the first three hours, air attacks were also ineffective because of strong winds, heavy smoke that obscured vision, and the continuous fuel chain available to the fire.

Fire units ran out of water during the fire owing to five primary factors. Large quantities of water were used by firefighters suppressing the fire; homeowners were wetting their roofs and vegetation with large quantities of water as well. Water pipes had burst, and water was freely flowing in destroyed homes. Tanks and reservoirs could not be refilled due to electrical power failures caused by the fire. There was also a problem with matching hoses to the fire hydrants. Some of the hoses from out-of-town fire brigades did not fit on the hydrants. Some had adapters that could be put on the hydrants, but many of the adapters were left on the hydrants as the fire overtook the perimeters.

Many of the homes had roofs covered with wooden shingles or shakes. Flaming embers were blown by the wind from houses that were already on fire onto the roofs of nearby homes, which then caught on fire. According to observers, homes burned to their foundations in ten minutes or less. The steep hillsides presented difficulties to the firefighters. Hoses and other equipment had to be dragged up the hills. The streets were very narrow. As firefighters were moving large trucks up the streets toward the fire, homeowners were moving away from the fire to evacuate the area, causing bottlenecks.

The first tactics the firefighters used were to retreat to the perimeter, attack the fire, and summon help. The fire was spreading so fast that the firefighters could not establish an effective perimeter. The units coming to assist the initial crew found other areas burning, so they stopped to fight those fires. However, they were overrun eventually by the fire. The fire departments had a difficult time communicating with other fire departments around the state because there were too many units trying to use the same radio channel and too few channels were available. The hilly terrain also caused interference with the radio signals, making it difficult to coordinate the attack.

The coordination of the firefighters improved as time passed. It was possible to establish good perimeter areas as the weather conditions became better and the fire reached areas where water was available. The firefighters were able to suppress the ignition of homes by breaking the chain of combustibles that was responsible for the earlier destruction of houses, allowing the firefighters to save many homes.

The Oakland Hills fire developed firestorm conditions within fifteen minutes. Firestorms are produced when the gases, heat, and motion of a fire build up to a point that they begin to create their own convection currents independent of external conditions. Oxygen is pulled into the base of the fire in great quantities, producing large convection columns when the air is heated at the fire. When the intensity of a fire reaches firestorm levels, a fire front can develop that is able to move away from the direction the wind is blowing.

The Oakland Hills and Berkeley fire departments were not the only ones to assist in extinguishing the fire. They were joined by 88 engine strike teams, 6 air tankers, 16 heliac units, 8 communications units, 2 management teams, 2 mechanics, and more than 700 search-and-rescue personnel from other municipalities. In addition, 767 law enforcement officers assisted.

EFFECTS OF THE FIRE. As a result of the fire, Assemblyman Tom Bates introduced a bill, later known as the Bates Bill, requiring the California Department of Forestry and Fire Protection, along with local fire authorities, to identify places in the Local Responsibility Areas that were considered to be "very high fire hazard severity zones." Terrain, foliage, building construction, and lack of adequate access were among the factors considered in establishing these zones. Once the hazardous areas were identified, the local authorities either adopted the state fire marshal's model ordinance, adding or subtracting areas from the identified zones; indicated that they already met or exceeded the Bates minimum; or a combination of these responses.

Most of the ordinances that were adopted required that all the dwellings in endangered areas must have at least a Class-B roof. A defensible perimeter around the home was also required. This included a 100-foot-wide area around the building where grass and ground cover could not exceed 3 inches in height. Specimen trees were allowed as long as they were at least 15 feet apart and no closer than 15 feet from the house. Access roads must be at least 10 feet wide and have 13 feet, 6 inches vertical clearance to allow passage for firefighting apparatus. In 1994, more legislation was passed, which raised the roofing requirement to a Class-A roof. Other directives included planting "fire-resistant" vegetation, requiring sprinklers in new homes where access is limited, providing standard hydrant connections, and improving communication systems for emergency workers.

Gary W. Siebein

FOR FURTHER INFORMATION:

Darlington, David. "After the Firestorm." *Audubon* 95, no. 2 (March/ April, 1993): 2-12.

Morales, Tony, and Maria Morales, eds. *Proceedings of the California's 2001 Wildfire Conference: 10 Years After the 1991 East Bay Hills Fire.* Richmond: University of California, Forest Products Laboratory, 2001.

Oakland Fire Department. *The Oakland Tunnel Fire, October 20, 1991: A Comprehensive Report.* Oakland, Calif.: Author, 1992.

Report of the Operation Urban Wildfire Task Force. Washington, D.C.: Federal Emergency Management Agency, United States Fire Administration, FA-115, 1992.

Steckler, Kenneth D., David D. Evans, and Jack E. Snell. *Preliminary Study of the 1991 Oakland Hills Fire and Its Relevance to Wood-Frame, Multi-family Building Construction.* Gaithersburg, Md.: National Institute of Standards and Technology, Building and Fire Research Laboratory, 1991.

Sullivan, Margaret. *Firestorm! The Story of the 1991 East Bay Fire in Berkeley.* Berkeley, Calif.: City of Berkeley, 1993.

■ 1992: Hurricane Andrew

Hurricane

Date: August 22-26, 1992
Place: Florida, Louisiana, and the Bahamas
Classification: Category 4
Result: 50 dead, $26 billion in damage

Although relatively small in size, Hurricane Andrew was a storm of enormous intensity that left a mammoth trail of destruction along its path across the Bahamas, south Florida, and Louisiana. Its final toll was an estimated $26 billion in damage in the United States alone, ranking it at the time as the most expensive natural disaster in the nation's history.

Andrew's Beginnings. Hurricane Andrew began as a tropical wave off the west coast of Africa and passed south of the Cape Verde Islands on August 15, 1992, at a speed of 18 miles per hour. As it continued its west-northwest movement, the storm picked up its pace to 23 miles per hour, nearly twice the speed of an average hurricane. Over the next few days, the storm passed to the south of a high-pressure system as steering winds began to move it closer to a strong upper-level, low-pressure system located near Bermuda. The currents gradually changed, and Andrew turned slowly to a northwesterly course. On August 20, the storm weakened to the point of almost disintegrating. The lower section of the storm was moving to the northwest, while the upper part of it was steered by strong upper-level winds to the northeast.

However, significant changes in the overall weather environment began to occur the following day. Satellite imagery indicated that the upper-level, low-pressure system near Bermuda had broken up, which decreased the wind-shear effect on Andrew. It enabled the storm to gather its pieces together, regain strength, and resume its movement. As it migrated further into the Atlantic, the storm increased in intensity and was designated the first tropical storm of the 1992 hurricane season. Simultaneously, a strong high-pressure system began to build along the U.S. southeast coast, which helped steer the storm directly west into warm tropical waters.

With winds measuring over 75 miles per hour, Andrew reached hurricane status at a point 800 miles east of Miami on August 22 and rapidly strengthened to a Category 4 storm. As it approached a point approximately 330 miles east of the Florida coast, a hurricane watch was posted from Titusville south to Vero Beach, south through the Florida Keys and over to the West Coast to Fort Myers.

Andrew maintained a due-west course and crossed Eleuthera Island and the southern Berry Islands in the Bahamas on August 23. Eleuthera Island suffered extensive damage when a 23-foot storm surge, one of the largest on record, washed ashore, leaving coastal areas in ruin. Government Harbour, Hatchet Bay, and Upper and Lower Bogue were among the communities severely damaged. Nearly every house on Current Island was destroyed.

Andrew weakened somewhat following its passage over the Bahamas but quickly regained its strength as it moved through the Florida Straits. At this stage weather forecasters noted a decreasing diameter and corresponding strengthening of the storm's "eyewall" convection. Measurements indicated a more vigorous counterclockwise rotation with the radius of maximum wind in the eyewall reaching 12 miles. Meteorologists believed the storm was undergoing a phenomenon called "eyewall replacement," in which the inner wall disintegrates and is replaced by the outer wall. During the replacement cycle, the storm would weaken, then immediately regain its strength as the new outer wall replaced the older inner one.

As the storm churned in the direction of Florida's east coast, Governor Lawton Chiles declared a state of emergency and alerted the National Guard for duty. Nearly 1 million people were ordered to evacuate the coastal areas of Broward County, Dade County, and the northern Florida Keys in Monroe County. Because Andrew had a smaller diameter than most hurricanes, the stronger winds did not become apparent to residents until the storm was almost on top of land. This served to hamper evacuation efforts, as many boaters waited until the final hours to move their craft inland, creating delays for land traffic as drawbridges were raised to allow the boats entrance to safer waters.

The potential for a natural disaster of epic proportions was apparent to officials, given the lay of the land in south Florida. The highest natural land elevation in the entire state is only 345 feet above sea level, and elevations in the southern portion of the state are even lower, with few rising above 20 feet. In addition, the state's coastal regions are low and flat and marked by numerous small bays, inlets, and a continuous series of barrier islands.

Throughout southern Florida residents made preparations for Andrew's arrival. Merchants and homeowners boarded up their properties and stocked up on water, groceries, gasoline, batteries, and candles in the event of a blackout or shortage. The rapid intensification of the storm came unexpectedly to local officials. In an advisory issued on Saturday, August 22, the National Hurricane Center (NHC) forecast that tropical storm winds would arrive in Miami at about 9 P.M. Monday. In its next advisory, issued six hours later, the NHC warned residents that the tropical storm winds would arrive around 5 A.M. Monday.

Hurricane Andrew slammed into south Florida around 5:05 A.M. on August 24, 1992, near Florida City, about 19 miles south of downtown Miami, and was accompanied by sustained winds estimated at 140 miles per hour with gusts up to 175 miles per hour and a storm surge of close to 16 feet. The surge pushed the waters of Biscayne Bay inland for several hundred yards. Due to the eyewall's contraction, hurricane-force winds extended out only about 30 miles around the wall. Officials considered it fortunate that the storm did not carry the heavy amounts of precipitation normally associated with a hurricane of Andrew's size.

THE DAMAGE. Immediately after its rapid passage over south Florida, the extent of damage and casualties could not be readily determined. National media reports initially indicated it was not as severe as expected and that downtown Miami and Miami Beach were relatively intact. As additional information began to filter in, the complete magnitude of the storm's impact became apparent.

The worst damage inflicted by Andrew was in southern Dade County, from the Miami suburb of Kendall, south through Homestead and Florida City, to the Florida Keys. Scores of neighborhoods lost all of their trees, with many crashing into homes and parked cars. Few homes were left standing as the gusting winds reached sufficient strength to strip the paint and roofs off houses and topple telephone and power lines, leaving nearly all of Dade County without electricity. The powerful winds were able to hurl concrete beams more than 150

The category 4 winds of Hurricane Andrew embedded this plank in the trunk of a royal palm. (National Oceanic and Atmospheric Administration)

feet, lift large trucks into the air, and disintegrate mobile homes. Air-conditioning units were torn from roofs, leaving gaping holes for the torrential rains to pour through, flooding floors below. In some areas the sustained winds unofficially reached 175 miles per hour, with some gusts reaching as high as 212 miles per hour. Barometric pressure registered a low at 27.23 inches.

Andrew heavily damaged offshore structures, including the artificial reef system off the southeast coast. One measure of its strength was its impact on the *Belzona Barge*, a 350-ton barge that prior to the hurricane was sitting in 68 feet of water on the ocean floor. A thousand tons of concrete from an old bridge lay on its deck. Andrew shoved the barge 700 feet to the west and stripped it of several large sections of steel-plate siding. Only 50 to 100 tons of concrete remained on the barge's deck. Another ship, the 210-ton freighter *Seaward Explorer,* moored off Elliot Key, was separated from its anchor by the surge and carried over the submerged key and across Biscayne Bay, where it finally was washed ashore.

WIND SPEEDS. According to a report issued by the National Oceanic and Atmospheric Administration, measuring the storm's sustained wind speeds became problematic once it reached land. Weather experts noted that the estimates were for those winds occurring primarily within the northern eyewall over an open environment, such as at an airport and at a standard 33-foot (10-meter) height. The winds occurring at other locations were subject to their complex interactions with buildings, trees, and other obstacles in their path. Such obstructions generate a drag that generally reduces the wind speeds. However, they are also capable of producing brief accelerations of winds in areas approximate to the structures. As a result, the wind gusts experienced at a given location, such as a building situated in the core region of the hurricane, can vary significantly and cannot be precisely measured.

The National Hurricane Center in Coral Gables noted the unfortunate circumstance of not having official measurements of surface winds near the area of landfall where maximum winds were likely to have occurred. The strongest sustained wind, registered at 141 miles per hour with a gust up to 169 miles per hour, occurred close to 1 nautical mile east of the shoreline. Many transmissions of wind speeds were interrupted when instruments presumably were disabled by the storm. A subsequent inspection revealed that one anemometer situated near the eye's path was bent 90 degrees from its normal vertical position. Wind measurements taken by aircraft at about 10,000 feet, when adjusted, support the estimate of sustained surface winds of 145 miles per hour.

There were no confirmed reports of tornadoes associated with Andrew as it passed over the Bahamas or Florida. A few unconfirmed funnel sightings were reported over the Florida counties of Glades, Collier, and Highlands. A number of weather observers did note the similarities in damage patterns between Hurricane Andrew and a tornado. While countless houses deep inland were leveled by Andrew, low-lying beachfront condominiums went unscathed. In Naranja Lakes, a south Dade County suburb, buildings whose tops were blown off stood across from others that were left undamaged. Scientists believe the random pattern of damage caused by Andrew was the result of small thunderstorms packed within the hurricane. The storms created vertical columns of air that opened vents in the eye's wall of clouds, which allowed the hurricane's most powerful winds to rush to the ground nearly 2,000 feet below with the concentrated fury of a tornado. Traveling west at 20 miles per hour the storm cut a swath of destruction that was easily discernible and unique to hurricane activity.

FURTHER DAMAGE. Throughout the region power lines and traffic lights dangled to windshield levels. Shredded shrubs and downed trees made driving through streets a hazardous chore. Numerous side streets were rendered impassable because of the debris. In addition, close to 3,000 water mains were damaged, along with 1,900 traffic lights, 100,000 traffic signs, and 2,200 street lights. Damage was also inflicted on 59 hospitals and health facilities, 7 post offices, 278 schools, Florida International University, Dade Community College, and the University of Miami.

In the fashionable seaside community of Coconut Grove, dozens of recreational boats were washed up into the streets and parking lots. At suburban airports, hangars were ripped apart and small planes piled atop one another. Homestead Air Force Base, located at the southern tip of the state between Everglades National Park and Miami, took a direct hit. Most of the air base's 200 buildings, including hangars, communication equipment, offices, housing, and other facilities, received damage. Nearly all of Homestead's 70 aircraft and 5,000 active-duty personnel had been evacuated; however, two F-16 fighters that remained were destroyed when a hangar door swung onto them. The base was home to two F-16 fighter wings and a U.S. Customs Service antidrug operation.

One of the hardest hit areas was Coral Gables in south Miami, where the National Hurricane Center is located and where gusts of wind up to 164 miles per hour were recorded. The storm blew the radar off the center's roof and shattered the building's windows. On the other hand, Miami Beach's Art Deco district escaped the brunt of the storm, though the plush Fontainebleau Hilton hotel was left with several feet of water in its lobby.

Nearly 90 percent of Florida City's 1,900 homes were either destroyed, severely damaged, or marginally damaged, including 1,475 mobile homes, 1,041 single-family homes, and 470 apartment units. In addition, a majority of its businesses fell victim to the storm, leaving residents both homeless and jobless. The city's entire infrastructure was also crippled severely. The city hall, police station, water and sewer system, and all of the city's parks were damaged, along with an elementary school, 9 churches, a museum, a community center, and a football field.

The story was similar in Homestead, where 85 to 90 percent of the housing units were destroyed or damaged. Among them were 1,167 manufactured housing units, 9,059 single-family dwelling units, and 7,580 multifamily units. Eight public schools and 22 parks in the city received severe damage, as did the Homestead branch of Metro Dade Community College.

The personal testimony of many residents reflects the fury of Andrew. Many recalled how their ears popped and sinuses ached as the barometric pressure plunged. Some heard the popping of automobiles while other claimed that the water was sucked from their toilets. Above all, it was the sound of the winds, described as akin to the blast of jet engines or the roar of a freight train, that many found most terrifying.

All together, nearly 25,000 homes were destroyed and close to 100,000 others were damaged in the region. Also destroyed or damaged were an estimated 8,000 businesses, putting over 80,000 people out of work. The National Guard provided tent cities for the homeless, but many chose to stay in what remained of their homes to protect them from looters. Nearly 43 deaths in Dade County alone were attributed directly or indirectly to the storm. Law enforcement officials, using police dogs, conducted searches immediately after the storm through the remnants of mobile-home parks. With communication outlets severely crippled, some local jurisdictions took to dropping leaflets from helicopters and sending automobiles mounted with loudspeakers through the most devastated areas to announce the latest information. In Miami authorities declared a curfew from 7 P.M. to 7 A.M., and police cordoned off many sections of the town.

As the wind diminished and the water receded, U.S. Army combat troops joined National Guard forces and police in setting up barricades around the major commercial centers in downtown Miami and Coconut Grove to prevent looting.

Andrew also took a heavy toll on animals. Hundreds of horses were killed and many other injured by flying debris. Thousands of pets roamed free as their confines collapsed around them. Although few, if any, animals escaped from local zoos, hundreds of monkeys and baboons fled from area research facilities, and countless numbers of exotic birds were reported missing. Agricultural damage in Dade County exceeded $1 billion, including an approximate $128 million loss in tropical orchards, a $349 million loss in crop production, and a $12.5 million loss in aqua culture and livestock.

An estimated 15,000 pleasure boats were victimized by Andrew's winds. The boat damage for the entire region approached $20 million. Only a handful of deaths were attributed to boaters who elected to ride out the storm in their boats, an unusually low death count for a storm of Andrew's magnitude.

Though the storm roiled the shallow waters of Biscayne Bay, 8 miles wide and only 12 feet deep, its major sediment deposits and grass beds were left relatively intact. The shallow waters had the effect of amplifying the storm surge so that the tide rose an estimated 12 to 16 feet above normal by the time it reached the western shore. The waters in the western portion of the bay were noticeably brackish following the storm. Freshwater extended out several hundred yards from the shoreline, and salinity was measured at 11 parts per 1,000 compared with the normal 34 parts per 1,000 up to a mile and a half out. Much of this effect was attributed to the decision of the state's water-management agencies to lower the level of Lake Okeechobee in anticipation of the storm to prevent excessive overflows.

The highest recorded high-water mark was 16.88 feet, at the Burger King Corporate Headquarters in south Dade County. High-water marks diminished from this point north to Broad Causeway, where they reached to 5.17 feet, and south to Key Largo, where they reached up to 5.49 feet. On the west coast of Florida, high-water marks ranged from 4.38 feet at Everglades City to 6.85 feet at West Goodland. The farthest the tidal surge extended inland was an estimated 3 miles from the eastern coastline. The surge's north-south range extended nearly 33 miles along the eastern coast.

Despite the massive devastation, civil defense officials estimated the damage could have been far worse if the hurricane had crossed the Florida peninsula a few miles farther north, through more densely populated regions. The relatively small diameter of the storm had the effect of reducing its exposure to more vulnerable coastal communities and thus was a major contributing factor in limiting overall damage and loss of life. According to officials, an additional factor in reducing fatalities was the evacuation and hurricane preparedness programs that were in force prior to the storm's arrival.

Florida's substantial natural resource base felt the full fury of Andrew. The storm's eye crossed three National Park Service sites: Biscayne National Park, Everglades National Park, and Big Cypress National Preserve. Artificial reefs along the coastline were severely damaged, as were thousands of acres of mangrove forest. Shorelines were littered with tons of marine debris as the strong currents tore away sea fans, sponges, and coral in areas of Biscayne Bay. The fragile Everglades region was damaged as entire groves of trees were flattened and exotic plants and wildlife habitats were destroyed. Virtually all large trees located in islands of dense undergrowth were defoliated. However, the storm had little effect on the interior freshwater lands of the Everglades, which are composed mainly of sawgrass. Samplings by the South Florida Water Management District following the storm indicate nearly all poststorm water-quality properties, including turbidity, color, ammonia, and dissolved phosphate, were within the range of pre-storm values.

The most prominent inhabitants of the marshlands, the alligators, appeared to have weathered the storm, though some of their nests were destroyed. All the radio-tagged Florida panthers, radio-tagged black bears, and white-tailed deer survived the hurricane. Egrets, herons, and ibis also came through the storm relatively unscathed. The largest concentration of dead birds discovered was at a roost in Biscayne Bay, where the corpses of approximately 200 white ibis were found.

One of the reasons for the relatively small damage to animals and plants was the nature of the storm. Unlike previous hurricane storm surges that inundated large areas of the marshlands with saltwater, Andrew's was unable to push deep inland owing to its direct westerly path that took it over Florida's relatively high east coast. In retrospect, the fact that Hurricane Andrew was a rapidly moving, compact, relatively dry storm rather than a larger, slower, or wetter system spared Florida an even greater natural disaster.

MOVING ON. Andrew moved quickly in an almost direct line across the extreme southern section of Florida in about four hours, entering the Gulf of Mexico south of Marco Island in a somewhat weakened state but with its eye still intact. As it plowed across the southern peninsula, it left a swath of destruction 25 miles wide and 60 miles long, though the impact of its storm surge on the southwest coast of the state was minimal.

Once again over warm waters, the storm began to intensify as it turned northwest toward the Louisiana coast. As it churned through the Gulf waters, Andrew continued to wreak damage estimated at a half billion dollars. Its winds toppled platforms, blew 5 drilling wells off location, caused 2 fires, and created 7 incidents of pollution.

Fearing a repeat of the scenes of devastation in southern Florida, officials and residents launched a massive evacuation effort along the Mississippi Delta region. An estimated 1.25 million people were evacuated from parishes in southeastern and south-central Louisiana. The eye of the storm skirted the Louisiana coast about 85 miles southwest of New Orleans. It finally made landfall approximately 20 miles west-southwest of Morgan City on the morning of August 26, leaving Grand Isle, the state's only inhabited barrier island, completely underwater. The storm struck with a Category 3 force as sustained winds of 140 miles per hour buffeted the sparsely populated marshlands.

Louisiana is known for its many bayous and waterways, which constitute much of the state's topography. Numerous barrier islands dot the coastline but generally are used as game preserves. A large portion of the southeastern section of the state rests at or below sea level and is not conducive to rapid runoff, thus making overflows potentially protracted and severe.

As it slid along the Louisiana coast, Andrew dealt a severe blow to the state's fishing industry, inflicting nearly $160 million in damage to freshwater fisheries. The state did fare much better than Florida in damage to boats, as Andrew missed the major shipping areas north and east of New Orleans. Many boat owners had enough advance warning to move their vessels into one of the numerous bayous, where they had more protection from the storm.

The storm continued to move west across southern Louisiana toward the cities of Lafayette and New Iberia. It spawned numerous tornadoes that caused widespread damage in several Mississippi, Alabama, and Georgia communities. One tornado occurred in the city of Laplace, Louisiana, killing 2 people and injuring 32 others. Tornadoes also were reported in the parishes of Ascension, Iberville, Baton Rouge, Pointe Coupe, and Avoyelles, though no casualties were reported.

Numerous reports of funnel clouds were received by officials in Mississippi and were believed to have caused damage in several of the state's counties. In Alabama, two tornadoes struck the mainland, while another hit Dauphin Island. Several destructive tornadoes that roared through Georgia were attributed to Andrew. Although rainfall was heavy throughout the region, it resulted in little significant flooding because of the dry conditions along the coast. Rivers were at midsummer stages, and soils were parched from lack of rain. An estimated 25 percent or less of the rain generated by Andrew ended up in the rivers as runoff. The remaining portion either was absorbed by the soils and plants or evaporated.

On August 26, Andrew was downgraded to a tropical storm as it moved northeast through Mississippi. The remnants of Andrew continued to produce heavy downpours that often exceeded 10 inches. On August 28, Andrew merged with a frontal system over the mid-Atlantic states, ending its trail of destruction.

William Hoffman

FOR FURTHER INFORMATION:

Barnes, Jay. *Florida's Hurricane History.* Chapel Hill: University of North Carolina Press, 1998.

Fyerdam, Rick. *When Natural Disaster Strikes: Lessons from Hurricane Andrew.* Miami Beach, Fla.: Hospice Foundation of America, 1994.

Peacock, Walter Gillis, Betty Hearn Morrow, and Hugh Gladwin, eds. *Hurricane Andrew: Ethnicity, Gender, and the Sociology of Disasters.* New York: Routledge, 1997.

Pielke, Roger A., Jr., and Roger A. Pielke, Sr. *Hurricanes: Their Nature and Impacts on Society.* New York: John Wiley & Sons, 1997.

Provenzo, Eugene F., Jr., and Asterie Baker Provenzo. *In the Eye of Hurricane Andrew.* Gainesville: University Press of Florida, 2002.

U.S. Department of Commerce. *Hurricane Andrew: South Florida and Louisiana, August 23-26, 1992*. Silver Springs, Md.: National Weather Service, 1993.

U.S. Park Service. *Hurricane Andrew, 1992*. Denver: U.S. Department of the Interior, 1994.

Williams, John M., and Iver W. Duedall. *Florida Hurricanes and Tropical Storms, 1871-2001*. Gainesville: University of Florida Press, 2002.

■ 1993: THE GREAT MISSISSIPPI RIVER FLOOD OF 1993

FLOOD

DATE: June-August, 1993
PLACE: Primarily Minnesota, Wisconsin, Iowa, Illinois, and Missouri
RESULT: 52 dead, 74,000 homeless, $18 billion in damage

Unlike other natural disasters, it is extremely difficult to pinpoint the actual starting point of the Great Mississippi River Flood of 1993. The river's upper basin experienced above-normal rainfall levels in the spring that resulted in some earlier flooding, and fall weather produced subsequent flooding as well. Yet since the greatest carnage occurred during the heavy rains from June through August, 1993, most experts use these parameters as the official beginning and end of the great flood of 1993.

CAUSES. The flood of 1993 can be attributed to the record rainfall that dominated the Midwest's weather during the summer of 1993. Other surface meteorological conditions, however, also played a pivotal role. Prior to the flood, the ground was already saturated, as soil moisture levels remained exceptionally high. Heavy winter snowmelt and spring rains further increased the dangers of flooding as the Mississippi River's vast tributary system began emptying its excess into the river. This water, moreover, substantially increased the chances of daily precipitation, since evaporation tends to be recirculated in the form of rainfall. From June through August, the Upper Mississippi River basin rainfall was 200 percent above normal, and the 20 inches of rain was the highest recorded total dating back to 1895. Along the Iowa shores alone it exceeded 36 inches. This problem was further exacerbated by the unusual number of cloudy days that not only inhibited the sun's ability to dry the land but also increased the likelihood of daily showers.

HUMAN AND PROPERTY COSTS. The flood primarily affected the Upper Mississippi River basin in the area located north of Cairo, Illinois. While the damage affected commerce, industry, and housing in over one-third of the United States, the heaviest flooding occurred in various river towns in Minnesota, Wisconsin, Iowa, Illinois, and Missouri.

This event represented the most costly flood on record in American history. Although the flood of 1927 resulted in the loss of 313 lives, compared to 52 in 1993, the property damage in 1993 was much more extensive. Floodwaters significantly ruined various portions of the physical landscape, wreaked havoc on river ecosystems, and destroyed crops. Its impact on the transportation system and agricultural income ravaged the region. Barges were unable to travel on the river for eight weeks. Major roads and highways were closed, often forcing people to miss work. Millions of acres of prime farmland remained under water for weeks, significantly weakening the country's food production, and soil erosion destroyed some of the best farmland in the country. Homes, farms, industries, and entire towns were obliterated by the river's rising waters. Communities fought to stave off the flood by organizing sandbagging activities to reinforce and raise the capacity of levees, and while some succeeded, over 1,000 levees eventually ruptured. All this carnage compelled President Bill Clinton to declare the region a disaster area, but local, state, and national agencies struggled to meet the demands of unprecedented relief efforts. While some individuals eagerly accepted assistance and attempted to rebuild their lives, many simply relocated to higher ground, believing that an idyllic life along the river's banks was no longer possible.

INFRASTRUCTURE COSTS. This flood also produced dire consequences for the entire ecosystem along the Mississippi River. Herbicides from flooded farms were washed into the river and eventually threatened fisheries in the Gulf of Mexico. Deforestation occurred, and trees that survived remained highly vulnerable to disease, insect attack, and stress. Flooding provided various pest species, such as mosquitoes, with ample breeding grounds. When a fish farm flooded on one of the river's tributaries, the Asian black carp escaped and endangered mussels and clams. Finally, ducks, which traditionally migrated to the region just in time for hunting season, bypassed the region because all the natural habitats and food sources were destroyed in the flood.

Agricultural and livestock production significantly declined as well and generated almost $9 billion in losses. Minnesota farmers burned wheat fields because they were too saturated to harvest. Corn and soybean yields dropped by 30 percent. These losses aided farmers in Indiana, Ohio, and other states that remained dry, but overall the loss of agricultural income decimated many state economies and forced the federal government to assume responsibility for disaster relief.

Other record losses shattered the transportation network. Damages to the infrastructure and revenue losses totaled $2 billion and forced many people out of work. Barges carry approximately 15 percent of all freight in America, with most of this traffic taking place along the Mississippi River. With the flood, however, over 2,900 barges and 50 towboats were stranded. Once the river reached the flood stage in June, the U.S. Army Corps of Engineers halted all barge traffic, and by the end of July this industry was losing $3 million per day. This also caused widespread unemployment in St. Louis as over 3,200 dockworkers were laid off.

The railroad industry experienced similar problems; its losses amounted to $241 million. Tracks, bridges, and signals were decimated and forced companies to close or to seek alternate routes. In-

Two bridges over the Mississippi River were washed out during the 1993 flood. (FEMA)

dustry leaders such as Union Pacific and Canadian Pacific were forced to halt operations from Wisconsin to St. Louis. Amtrak's Memphis-to-Chicago run had to be diverted 900 miles off course in order to complete its journey.

States were also forced to close roads and highways. More than 100 flooded roads and 56 bridges were shut down in Wisconsin, and in Missouri, many workers faced hours of delay in their daily commute to work. Finally, and most threatening, bridge traffic came almost to a halt. In early July, bridges were closed in Hannibal, Missouri, and Keokuk, Iowa. When the Quincy, Illinois, levee broke on July 15, there was no way to cross the river for a 250-mile area north of St. Louis. Coupled with the inability of ferries to operate in this weather, trucks and buses were forced to add over 200 miles to traditional delivery and transportation routes. Damage in this sector alone spawned over $1 billion in repair costs.

PERSONAL LOSSES. Nothing, however, outweighed the personal tragedies. More than 74,000 people lost their homes, heirlooms, and belongings. As water levels swelled and levees ruptured, entire communities were eliminated, and for many the carnage was so immense that they decided to never return to the river's edge. While the flood claimed many victims, the river towns did not go down without a fight. Communities built temporary levees with sandbags, plywood, and concrete. As the river continued to rise, people risked their safety to remain on the levees checking for seepage, leaks, and sand boils. These attempts, however, were highly unsuccessful. Over 80 percent of all state and local levees failed, causing many towns to evacuate.

Other towns were decimated beyond repair. Residents of Grafton, Illinois, along one of the most scenic stretches of highway in America, the Great River Road, were forced to flee as water covered the rooftops of many two-story homes. Roads in Alton, Illinois, were impassable, and water virtually obliterated many of the town's historic landmarks. In Valmeyer, Illinois, the community labored to save the town, only to see it completely demolished by the flood. In fact, when the waters receded, Valmeyer residents decided to relocate their entire town to a bluff overlooking the river instead of rebuilding on the banks. The entire island of Kaskaskia, Illinois, was covered with over 20 feet of water after its 52-foot-high levee broke. Most residents felt confident that they could withstand this disaster, but their plight clearly reveals the power of the Mississippi. At 9:48 A.M. on July 22, the levee ruptured, and since the island's bridge had previously been flooded out, everyone was forced to flee on two Army Corps of Engineers barges. Many livestock could not get out and drowned. By 2 P.M. Kaskaskia Island was entirely covered by water.

EFFECTS ON TOWNS. Both the devastation and personal courage that the flood generated can be observed in the story of one community. As the water traveled south down the river, the historic town of St. Genevieve, Missouri, was directly threatened. The home of several historical landmarks, including a number of two-hundred-year-old French colonial buildings, this town was the first European settlement west of the Mississippi River. It had experienced tragic floods in the past and had responded by building an elaborate set of levees and flood walls. It had survived the flood of 1973 when the river crested at 43 feet, and it had already begun to recover from a brief period of flooding in April. Yet nothing in its history could prepare St. Genevieve for its upcoming battle with the river.

Largely a town filled with quaint bed-and-breakfast inns, restaurants, and antique shops, St. Genevieve depended upon tourism for its survival. While the flood eliminated this industry and virtually destroyed the town's economy, it did not diminish the community's energetic struggle to avoid disaster. By the middle of July, Governor Mel Carnahan ordered in the National Guard in an effort to save one of America's most valuable historic treasures. The media quickly flocked to Missouri to cover this event, and St. Genevieve was featured on every major news network. The governor also allowed local prison inmates to work on the levee, and volunteers flocked to Missouri to fill sandbags and offer relief help. For the rest of July, the nation watched as St. Genevieve fought for its survival.

The river, however, continued to rise. By the end of July, as the water level reached 48 feet, one levee ruptured, sending more than 8 feet of water over sections of the town, damaging a number of homes and businesses and knocking some buildings right off their foundation; the people continued to fight. Volunteers worked at a feverish pace to raise the main levee to 51 feet and staved off disaster when the river crested at a record level 49 feet on August 6. Employees at a local plastic plant saved their factory by volunteering their time to build a levee around their plant. Yet the flood claimed several casualties. Forty-one historic buildings were damaged, tourism became nonexistent, and all the levee work had significantly undermined the town's service infrastructure.

The city of St. Louis, on the other hand, was spared. Once the river exceeded the 30-foot flood level, water started to steadily creep up the steps of the Gateway Arch. Several barges, including one containing a Burger King restaurant, broke away and crashed into the Popular Street Bridge. Oil refineries and petroleum processing plants threatened to dump poisonous chemicals into the river. Yet despite springing several leaks, the 50-foot flood wall held. Cities such as Des Moines, Iowa, and Kansas City and St. Joseph, Missouri, suffered record losses, but St. Louis's riverfront property remained dry.

The Great Mississippi River Flood of 1993 was the most costly flood in recorded history to date. Some experts claim it represents a five-hundred-year-flood of unprecedented proportions due to its length, volume, and carnage. It permanently eliminated numerous small towns, obliterated historical treasures, and destroyed priceless memories such as wedding pictures, souvenirs, high school yearbooks, and family correspondence. While the Midwest's struggle with the raging river held the nation's attention for only a few months, the devastation it wrought will be forever remembered as one of the most costly natural disasters in history.

Robert D. Ubriaco, Jr.

FOR FURTHER INFORMATION:

"America Under Water: A Special Section." *USA Today* 123, no. 2590 (July, 1994).

Changnon, Stanley, ed. *The Great Flood of 1993: Causes, Impacts, and Responses.* Boulder, Colo.: Westview Press, 1996.

Guillory, Dan. *When the Waters Recede: Rescue and Recovery During the Great Flood.* Urbana, Ill.: Stormline Press, 1996.

Myers, Mary Fran, and Gilbert F. White. "The Challenge of the Mississippi Floods." In *Environmental Management,* edited by Lewis Owen and Tim Unwin. Malden, Mass.: Blackwell, 1997.

National Weather Service. *The Great Flood of 1993.* National Disaster Survey Report. Washington, D.C.: National Oceanic and Atmospheric Administration, 1994.

Pielke, Roger A., Jr. *Midwest Flood of 1993: Weather, Climate, and Societal Impacts.* Boulder, Colo.: National Center for Atmospheric Research, 1996.

Stevens, William K. *The Change in the Weather: People, Weather, and the Science of Climate.* New York: Delacorte Press, 1999.

■ 1994: THE NORTHRIDGE
EARTHQUAKE

EARTHQUAKE

DATE: January 17, 1994

PLACE: Southern California, in an area extending from the San Fernando Valley to Los Angeles and Santa Monica

MAGNITUDE: 6.7

RESULT: 57 dead, more than 9,000 injured, approximately $20 billion in damage

Several different faults extend from Alaska to Mexico, and earthquakes with magnitudes exceeding 5.0 on the Richter scale occur rather frequently in areas of North America located near the Pacific Ocean. However, the epicenters of most of these serious earthquakes have not been located near heavily populated regions. The worst American earthquake was centered in New Madrid, southeastern Missouri, on February 7, 1812. Although the Richter scale was not developed until 1935, contemporary reports have enabled seismologists to conclude that this earthquake had a magnitude between 8.4 and 8.8 and caused the earth to shake over 5 million square miles. That area of the United States was not then heavily populated, however, and only about 1,000 people died. On March 27, 1964, the Good Friday earthquake took place in Alaska; it was recorded at 9.2 on the Richter scale. It caused tsunamis, giant waves which drowned 120 people in relatively sparsely populated areas of Alaska such as Valdez, Seward, Kodiak Island, and the Kenai Peninsula. Only 131 people died as a result of this earthquake. An earthquake of magnitude 9.2, 10.0, or 11.0 in a heavily populated area of California, for example, would most certainly result in hundreds of thousands of deaths.

LESSONS FROM OTHER CALIFORNIA QUAKES. Before the Northridge earthquake of January 17, 1994, many earthquakes had occurred in California, but the three which affected the lives of large numbers of people were the San Francisco earthquake of April 18,

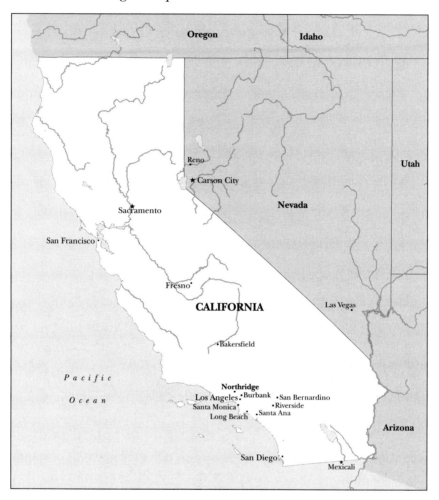

1906; the Sylmar earthquake of February 9, 1971; and the Loma Prieta earthquake of October 17, 1989. When the 1906 San Francisco earthquake took place, the population of San Francisco was around 400,000. This earthquake measured 8.2 or 8.3 on the Richter scale and shook the earth over an area of approximately 300 square miles. It caused numerous fires when gas mains burst, and approximately 700 people died.

Not many lessons were learned from the 1906 San Francisco earthquake. Developers and government officials did not then realize that it was extremely dangerous to build on hilly areas and land reclaimed from the sea by filling the water with a combination of sand, mud, and rocks. In both the greater San Francisco and the greater Los Angeles regions, houses, bridges, dams, and public buildings were constructed near faults and in areas where the ground was highly susceptible to seismic shocks.

During the 1971 Sylmar earthquake, centered just to the north of Los Angeles, 65 people died, 47 of them in the collapse of the San Fernando Veterans Administration Hospital. This hospital, completed in 1925, was not designed to resist seismic shocks. People did not realize that public buildings should be constructed with reinforced bricks or that installing additional steel rods and wrapping more of them around existing rods made buildings more resistant to seismic shocks.

The deaths of so many people in the San Fernando Veterans Administration Hospital persuaded the California legislature to act quickly. In 1972, it created a Seismic Safety Commission and instructed the members to make recommendations to the governor and state legislators so that houses, public buildings, and other structures could be made more earthquake-resistant. The commission recommended that strict building codes be implemented in California to improve the safety of buildings and public structures throughout California. New building codes approved in the 1970's required builders to install more steel rods than had been previously required in new construction and to use reinforced bricks. In addition, the Seismic Safety Commission strongly recommended that existing bridges, dams, and overhead highways be "retrofitted," or reinforced with additional steel rods.

The changes implemented after the Sylmar earthquake dramatically decreased the number of deaths and the amount of property damage caused by the 1989 Loma Prieta earthquake, which was recorded at 7.1 on the Richter scale. The result was 67 deaths, more than 3,000 injuries, and damage well in excess of $5 billion dollars. However, only 18 of the more than 4,000 bridges and overhead highways in the region between San Francisco to the north and Santa Cruz and Watsonville to the south had to be closed for repairs as a result of this earthquake. Had not so many bridges and highways been retrofitted during the 1970's and 1980's, the loss of life and the amount of property damage would have been much higher.

The number of deaths and the property loss caused by an earthquake depend on a variety of factors. The epicenter and the time of an earthquake play major roles in determining the number of fatalities and the amount of damage. The epicenter of the Loma Prieta earthquake was located 70 miles south of San Francisco and Oakland, in the middle of the Santa Cruz Mountains and several miles from the cities of Watsonville and Santa Cruz. This distance significantly decreased the effect of this earthquake on very heavily populated cities such as San Francisco and Oakland and their surrounding communities.

THE NORTHRIDGE EARTHQUAKE. In 1994, the residents of Southern California were not as fortunate as their neighbors in Northern California in terms of location. The Northridge earthquake on January 17 originated in the heavily populated San Fernando Valley of Los Angeles, just 20 miles northwest of the downtown area. (The epicenter was later determined to be not in Northridge but in Reseda, an adjoining community.) The focal point of the Northridge earthquake was 12 miles below the surface, and it caused the ground to shake over a wide area. Serious damage occurred as far west as Sherman Oaks and Fillmore; north to Santa Clarita; as far east as Glendale, Pasadena, and Los Angeles; and south to Santa Monica. It is fortunate, however, that this earthquake struck the greater Los Angeles area at 4:31 A.M. Had it struck during rush hour, the loss of life on Southern California highways would have been exceedingly high. Moreover, Southern Californians were fortunate indeed that the magnitude was not higher than 6.7. An earthquake of the magnitude of the 1964 Good Friday earthquake or the 1906 San Francisco earthquake would have killed far more people and resulted in property damage well in excess of the $20 billion caused by the Northridge earthquake.

When this earthquake took place, people were sleeping in their apartments, mobile homes, and houses. Sixteen were killed when the three-story Northridge Meadows apartment complex collapsed. The victims all lived on the first floor, which was flattened by the weight of the two floors above. Some of the victims died in their sleep, while others had been jolted awake moments before the collapse but had no means of escape. Many were crushed instantly, and some slowly suffocated in the rubble before help could reach them. Emergency personnel were able to rescue all those who lived on the second and third floors, but few were pulled out alive from the first floor.

This apartment complex was made of wood frame stucco, which is not very resistant to seismic shocks. To make matters worse, the carports on the first floor were supported by a series of single steel supports, which buckled and collapsed. Many wood frame stucco apartment complexes, like the Northridge Meadows apartment complex, were built in the 1950's and 1960's to accommodate the large influx of people who had moved to the greater Los Angeles region. Such apartment complexes were much cheaper to build than buildings constructed with reinforced bricks. It should be remembered, however, that people did not know at the time that such apartment houses would perform so poorly during earthquakes. Building codes in effect during the twenty years before the 1994 Northridge earthquake would have prohibited the construction of wood frame stucco apartment complexes with carports supported by single steel columns. Other similar apartment complexes collapsed in such widely separated cities or communities as Fillmore, Van Nuys, Los Angeles, and Sherman Oaks. In affected areas, apartment houses built with re-

A house is shifted from its foundation by the powerful Northridge earthquake. (FEMA)

inforced bricks and reinforced with more steel rods than had been required before the 1970's performed rather well during this earthquake and did not collapse.

Mobile home parks also suffered greatly either as a direct result of the seismic shocks or because of the fires that occurred when underground gas mains burst and ignited when the gas encountered a fire source. Over one hundred mobile homes were destroyed by fire, but quick and effective action by firefighters and other emergency officers resulted in the loss of just one life, an extraordinary figure because the fires began while almost all the residents were asleep. Fires of intensity equal to those seen in San Francisco's Marina District right after the 1989 Loma Prieta earthquake broke out in many different regions of the San Fernando Valley and the rest of Los Angeles.

DAMAGE IN THE SAN FERNANDO VALLEY. Since Northridge was very near the epicenter of this earthquake, it is not surprising that this community suffered such extensive damage on that Monday morning. Part of the precast concrete parking garage for the Northridge Fashion Center collapsed. Both this parking garage and the adjoining mall suffered major structural damage. No loss of life occurred, however, because there were no customers in the mall or garage at such an early hour of the morning. Only one employee was at the site—a man driving a steam cleaning truck in the parking garage was trapped for several hours before being rescued. Had the earthquake taken place a few hours later, when the mall would be open for business on the Martin Luther King, Jr., holiday, thousands might have been killed or seriously injured.

Seismic shocks also caused a similarly built precast concrete parking garage on the campus of California State University, Northridge (CSUN), to collapse, destroying the cars inside. Many other buildings there suffered major structural damage. However, there was no loss of life on the campus. It is fortunate that this earthquake took place on Martin Luther King, Jr., Day because all state and federal offices were closed, as were all schools and universities. More students would have been on campus had this disaster not occurred on the third day of a long weekend.

Both of these two parking garages and the Northridge mall had been constructed after the implementation of strict building codes in the 1970's, but these structures could not resist the seismic shocks since they were located so close to the epicenter of this 6.7 earthquake.

In other areas of the San Fernando Valley, office buildings, private homes, and public buildings constructed after 1972 performed generally quite well during the earthquake because they were in conformity to codes which required that buildings be relatively resistant to seismic shocks.

LIQUEFACTION. A common result of earthquakes is liquefaction of the ground. This phenomenon occurs when the ground upon which houses and structures have been built is primarily soft material such as sand or clay, not bedrock. When encountering seismic shocks, the ground itself weakens and behaves like water.

This effect had been noticed in 1989 in San Francisco's Marina District, which had been reclaimed from the sea by filling the area with massive amounts of mud, sand, and rocks. This combination appeared to make the ground stable, but liquefaction caused the collapse of many buildings and structures which had conformed to strict building codes. The buildings themselves were sound, but the ground on which they had been constructed was too weak to support structures during a major earthquake.

Geologists who studied the Northridge earthquake concluded that liquefaction caused major landslides in the Santa Susana Mountains, which literally changed the shape of the terrain, and in residential areas such as Pacific Palisades where houses built on cliffs overlooking the Pacific Ocean came loose from their foundations and slid down hills. The ground on which these expensive homes had been built was simply not solid enough to resist seismic shocks. In hindsight, it becomes clear that houses should not be built on cliffs located near faults.

The problem of liquefaction was by no means limited to mountain ranges and houses built on palisades. Much of what now appears to be stable ground in Southern California was, in fact, created by draining wetlands. Those who drained the wetlands thought that they were helping people by making more land available for housing and business, but ironically they had created a disaster waiting to happen. The Santa Monica Freeway was built over land reclaimed from marshes. The ground on which this heavily traveled expressway was built was not as earthquake-resistant as the architects and contractors had

The Interstate 5 and SR14 freeways collapsed during the quake. (National Oceanic and Atmospheric Administration)

thought. A portion of the Santa Monica Freeway collapsed not because of structural deficiencies but rather because some of the ground on which it was built liquefied during the Northridge earthquake and the ground itself was no longer strong enough to support the weight of the freeway.

Other overhead highways collapsed because even well-constructed and reinforced highways could not resist such strong shocks emanating from such a close epicenter. Amazingly, only one motorist died as a result of the collapse of a highway. In the darkness of the early morning and with the power out, police officer Clarence Dean could not see that a portion of Highway 14 on which he was driving had collapsed. He drove his motorcycle over the edge and was killed instantly. During the Loma Prieta earthquake, 41 people were killed when a portion of the Nimitz Expressway collapsed in Oakland; that earthquake took place at 5:05 P.M., when many people were driving on the highways and bridges of the San Francisco Bay area. There was very little traffic on the highways in and around Los Angeles when the Northridge earthquake struck at 4:31 A.M. on a national holiday. At another time of day, hundreds if not thousands of deaths could have occurred on the usually heavily traveled highways around Los Angeles.

FIRE AND FLOOD. Another serious problem faced by residents and emergency personnel following the Northridge earthquake was the extremely large numbers of fires which occurred throughout the affected areas. Fires were fought over an area extending 25 miles in all directions from the epicenter. The Los Angeles Fire Department had to extinguish 476 earthquake-related fires on January 17, 1994, in Los Angeles County alone, and the earthquake caused dangerous fires in surrounding counties as well.

The community of Granada Hills experienced simultaneous flooding and massive fires, when water mains and gas mains burst. A gas main explosion on Balboa Boulevard in Granada Hills was the worst fire caused by the Northridge earthquake. People living in that area had to flee their homes and apartments in their pajamas. firefighters brought water trucks with them because the water main had burst and they could not obtain water from fire hydrants. Another earthquake-related fire began when 40,000 gallons of gasoline spilled onto the street in Pacoima and caught fire. Emergency personnel managed to extinguish this inferno, and although there was extensive property damage in Pacoima, no one was killed.

There was also environmental damage when a pipeline burst and spilled 150,000 gallons of crude oil into the Santa Clara River. Toxic specialists were able to control this potentially dangerous situation, and the river itself did not catch fire. A chemical fire started in a science building of the campus of CSUN, and another potentially dangerous situation occurred when a train derailment resulted in the release of 8,000 gallons of sulfuric acid. In both cases, prompt response by representatives from various local, state, and federal environmental agencies permitted control of the situation and the prevention of an environmental disaster.

It is very fortunate that the federal government, the state of California, and hospital administrators learned a valuable lesson from the 1971 Sylmar earthquake. People realized that it was necessary to reinforce existing hospitals and to build new hospitals so that they would not collapse during earthquakes. Considerable money was spent between 1971 and 1994 in order to make the hospitals of Southern California more resistant to seismic shocks. It was expected that the hospitals might experience minor structural damage during severe earthquakes but that they would not collapse. These newly built or reinforced hospitals were designed to continue operating after a major earthquake. Although patients had to be evacuated from the Veterans Administration Hospital in Sepulveda and from St. John's Hospital in Santa Monica, no one was killed in either hospital, and most hospitals in the greater Los Angeles area continued normal operations despite the Northridge earthquake. Two other hospitals, Olive View Medical Center and Holy Cross Medical Center, both in Sylmar, had to cease operations temporarily because of flooding and the loss of electrical power, but neither hospital had very extensive structural damage. The systematic reinforcement of existing hospitals and the construction of new, quake-resistant ones enabled medical personnel to meet the needs of the thousands of people injured as a result of the Northridge earthquake.

EFFECTS. The effect of the Northridge earthquake on the greater Los Angeles region was profound. By early 1994, California, especially Southern California, was slowly beginning to recover from an economic downturn that had begun in the late 1980's.

The Northridge earthquake caused at least $13 billion in damage, but most estimates place the actual damage as close to $20 billion. In comparison, the Loma Prieta earthquake, which took place four years before the Northridge earthquake, caused property damage of between $5 billion and $6 billion. Massive assistance from the federal government helped the state of California restore the infrastructure in and around Los Angeles, and interest-free loans from the federal government made it possible for individuals to rebuild their homes and for business owners to rebuild their establishments. As was the case for the Loma Prieta earthquake, most property owners in the

Los Angeles region did not carry earthquake insurance because such insurance is almost prohibitively expensive and comes with very high deductibles and very limited coverage. Regular homeowner's insurance does not cover damage caused by earthquakes. Loans from the federal government remain the only real option for most people.

Emergency officials from local, state, and federal governments; members of the California National Guard; and volunteers from the Red Cross, the Salvation Army, and other nonprofit organizations met the immediate needs of the survivors. Makeshift housing was created for people whose homes and apartments had been destroyed. Food and bottled drinking water were distributed to those who had lost almost everything but their lives during this terrible earthquake. The federal government gave housing vouchers to survivors so that they could rent homes or apartments until they could return to their former places of residence. The Federal Emergency Management Agency (FEMA) coordinated relief operations. In the days after the Loma Prieta earthquake, emergency personnel realized that they had not hired enough Spanish-speaking people to assist Latino victims of that earthquake. Emergency organizations learned from this experience, and there were enough bilingual personnel from both government agencies and volunteer organizations to assist Spanish-speaking survivors of the Northridge earthquake.

It took several months to repair the many highways which had suffered serious damage. Traffic on the remaining highways and bridges in Southern California was even worse than usual because travelers could no longer use such frequently traveled highways as the Golden State Freeway and the Santa Monica Freeway. Using financial incentives, the federal government and the state of California had these damaged highways rebuilt in record time and made sure that they met strict building codes. By 1995, Southern California had basically recovered economically from the property damage caused by the Northridge earthquake, but it is difficult to assess the psychological damage experienced by survivors who had lost their homes and their personal possessions. Although property damage caused by the earthquake was very high, Southern Californians were thankful that no more than 57 people had died during this disaster. With a different set of circumstances, it could have been much worse.

Edmund J. Campion

FOR FURTHER INFORMATION:

Bolin, Robert. *The Northridge Earthquake: Vulnerability and Disaster.* New York: Routledge, 1998.

Bolt, Bruce A. *Earthquakes.* 5th ed. New York: W. H. Freeman, 2006.

Earthquakes and Volcanoes 25, nos. 1/2 (1994).

Fradkin, Philip L. *Magnitude 8.* New York: Henry Holt, 1998.

Hall, John F., ed. *Northridge Earthquake January 17, 1994. Preliminary Reconnaissance Report.* Oakland, Calif.: Earthquake Engineering Research Institute, 1994.

Newsweek, January 31, 1994, 16-37.

Sieh, Kerry, and Simon Le Vay. *The Earth in Turmoil: Earthquakes, Volcanoes, and Their Impact on Humankind.* New York: W. H. Freeman, 1998.

Woods, Mary C., and W. Ray Seiple, eds. *The Northridge, California, Earthquake of 17 January 1994.* Sacramento: California Department of Conservation, Division of Mines and Geology, 1995.

■ 1995: THE KOBE EARTHQUAKE

EARTHQUAKE

ALSO KNOWN AS: The Great Hanshin-Awaji Earthquake, the South Hyogo Prefecture earthquake

DATE: January 17, 1995

PLACE: Kobe, Japan

MAGNITUDE: 7.2

RESULT: 5,502 dead, 37,000 injured, 200,000 buildings destroyed or damaged, more than $50 billion in damage (the most financially costly natural disaster to that time)

The city of Kobe (pronounced koh-beh) lies on the southern coast of Japan's main island of Honshū. Situated on the Inland Sea between the islands of Honshū and Shikoku, it is Japan's second largest seaport and an important center for shipbuilding, steel-making, and other commerce and industry. Its population of 1.4 million is densely concentrated along the narrow coastal plain that fronts inland mountains.

Without warning, just before dawn on the wintry morning of January 17, 1995, the Kobe area was struck by an earthquake that would be the most devastating seismic event in earthquake-prone Japan since the Tokyo quake of 1923, and the most expensive natural disaster to that time. The epicenter was 20 miles (32 kilometers) southwest of downtown Kobe, at 34.6 degrees north latitude and longitude 135 degrees east. This was about 19 miles (30 kilometers) south of the coastline, near the tip of Awaji Island. Slippage occurred on the Nojima fault, including surface rupture along at least 6 miles (9 kilometers) with displacement (slip) up to 5 feet (1.5 meters), and perhaps 6.5 feet (2 meters) depth. The total length of the ruptured fault at depth was 19 to 31 miles (30 to 50 kilometers). The movement was lateral (strike-slip), with the fault oriented to the northeast toward the northern portion of the city of Kobe. The focus (zone of initial slip) was at a depth of 13 miles (21 kilometers) below the tip of Awaji Island.

This event has been called the Great Hanshin-Awaji Earthquake or the South Hyogo Prefecture earthquake, after the local province, but internationally it is more commonly known as the Kobe earthquake for that nearby city. While it was not a truly great earthquake in magnitude and energy release, it had devastating consequences for people and urban structures because of its proximity to Kobe and the densely populated corridor along the coast, because of the orientation of the rupture directly toward the city, and because of the shallowness of the rupture.

The magnitude of the main shock was 7.2 on the Richter scale, and 6.9 on the moment-magnitude scale. It occurred at 5:46 A.M. local time on January 17, which was 8:46 P.M. January 16, Universal time (Greenwich Mean Time). Aftershocks continued for many months after the initial major shock. In the seven days after, there were nineteen aftershocks having magnitudes of 4 to 5. People reported that the approaching seismic waves created a rumble, then a roar, followed by strong vibrations both vertically and horizontally. The wrenching vibrations lasted about twenty seconds.

AFTEREFFECTS. The casualties and destruction were staggering. At least 5,502 people were killed, mostly from immediate crushing or entrapment in the rubble. This figure included 28 who were killed in a landslide at Nishinomiya, a town just east of Kobe. Early reports revealed 27,000 injured, but this was later raised to 37,000. As many as 310,000 people had to be evacuated to temporary shelters, including school gymnasiums and city offices, and over 70,000 were still in those shelters two months later. Initially, many residents had to camp out in the freezing January weather, having lost their homes or being afraid of more damage and collapse from the continuing aftershocks. According to the international edition of *Newsweek* for January 30, 1995,

> Everything but misery was in short supply. Many people spent the nights in the open air because no one could provide them with shelter. One moment they were well-dressed, propertied, and secure; the next they were refugees shuffling through rubble-strewn streets fretted by flame, lugging possessions on their backs, surrounded by the corpses of loved ones and neighbors.

Approximately 200,000 buildings were destroyed or damaged. More than 50,000 were reduced to rubble or complete collapse, thousands of others were so damaged that they had to be torn down, and others were consumed in the subsequent fires. While some modern structures, especially those built to an earthquake-resistant code (with reinforcing and bracing) instituted in 1981, were relatively unscathed, many suffered damage. Some collapsed, tilted, or sank because of unstable or settling soil and sediment.

Superficial ground accelerations in Kobe and adjacent Nishinomiya were measured at up to 50 to 80 percent of the acceleration of gravity—too high for most unreinforced structures to withstand. When materials (soft soil, alluvial deposits, landfill) are unconsolidated, and especially when they are water-saturated as after rains and in coastal regions, they lose strength and absorb energy when vibrated by seismic waves. Ground motions are amplified, and damage is intensified. This behavior, termed liquefaction, causes much worse damage than that received by structures on firm bedrock. Some of the worst structural damage was thus along the Kobe waterfront, with its water-saturated landfill in place for port development and creation of habitable land for the expanding population.

Portions of the elevated Hanshin four-lane expressway, Japan's primary east-west traffic artery through coastal Kobe, collapsed. A section 656 yards (600 meters) long toppled over sideways to rest at a 45-degree angle. There was much ground failure, cracking, and sinking along the waterfront. The elevated rail line of the high-speed Shinkansen ("bullet") train, constructed to be almost indestructible, was snapped in eight places. Fortunately, the first train of the day had not yet left for Kobe.

Particularly vulnerable to the horizontal shaking of earthquake waves were the older two-story houses built of wood frames with heavy tile roofs. They collapsed, trapping their occupants, and were then burned in fires ignited by ruptured gas lines. There were over 300 fires in the area, and a dozen of them raged for twenty-four to forty-eight hours. Fire fighting was impossible, because major utilities—water mains, as well as electricity, gas, and telephone lines—were severed and disabled. Further, the roadways were congested with fallen buildings, rubble, and people fleeing, checking on relatives, or engaged in rescue efforts. Roads, bridges, and rail lines (for the public transportation electric trains) were cut. With the loss of utilities, there was no heat for the cold January weather and no water for drinking, plumbing, or bathing.

Factories and shops that did survive the earthquake had to shut down operations because of lack of power and other utilities, toppled equipment, and lack of employees. Despite the destruction and abandonment of homes, stores, and shops, there was virtually no looting or civil disturbance. The Japanese virtues of order and discipline, stoicism, and civility were evident and focused the citizenry on applying their perseverance and hard work to the tasks of survival and reconstructing their lives.

Damage and casualties occurred along the coast through Nishinomiya and as far as Osaka, Japan's second-largest city, which is 18 miles (30 kilometers) from Kobe. The latter had cracked walls, broken windows, and 11 earthquake-related deaths.

Japan is a nation with high cost of living and an elaborate urban infrastructure. Rebuilding costs, public and private, have been variously estimated from U.S. $40 to 100 billion—exceeding those of any other natural disaster to that time. This figure does not include indirect losses such as lost economic productivity and business activity. Little of the residential losses was covered by insurance—only 9 percent of Japan's population has home earthquake insurance, and only 3 percent in Kobe, which was thought to be in a region of low seismic risk.

RESCUE AND RELIEF. The rescue efforts and distribution of emergency relief materials—food, water, fuel, and blankets—were hampered by an initially slow response by local government authorities and uncharacteristic disorganization. Assistance was also slowed by the congested urban destruction and impassable roadways. Roads that could have been cleared for emergency vehicles—fire, police, and search and rescue—were not cordoned off and thus became clogged with residents with their vehicles and possessions. The officials also delayed in calling in the national armed forces for assistance.

The lack of civic preparedness for such an earthquake disaster was surprising, considering the generally high awareness in Japan of the prospect of such an event. Many people have an earthquake-emergency kit of supplies in their homes. Every September 1, Disaster Prevention Day, on the anniversary of the Great Kwanto Earthquake that hit Tokyo and Yokohama in 1923, there are nationwide community drills on disaster response, evacuation, mock rescues,

The Kobe earthquake toppled part of the Hanshin expressway. (AP/ Wide World Photos)

and protective measures. Ironically, Kobe rose to become a busy port and international trading city in 1923, when foreign merchants left the devastated port city of Yokohama after the earthquake there. In fact, some Japanese survivors of the 1923 earthquake had come to Kobe to settle and were still alive for the 1995 event—thus experiencing the two most devastating earthquakes in Japan in the twentieth century.

REASONS FOR THE SCOPE OF THE DESTRUCTION. Kobe was not well prepared, psychologically and organizationally, for a major earthquake. First, it was some distance back from the seismically active zone of earthquakes associated with the oceanic trenches off Japan's southern and eastern margins. It was thus believed to have less potential for suffering a major shock. Second, there was a belief that modern engineering and building design had made structures less susceptible to being damaged and disabled by an earthquake. This event, having a fairly large magnitude and being shallow and nearby, demonstrated the continuing vulnerability of an urban infrastructure.

Third, there was an expectation, or hope, that Japan's application of technology to the problems of understanding earthquake mechanisms, monitoring for precursory indications of an impending event, and public warnings issued to the citizenry would give advance warning of a likely event. Unfortunately, the earthquake struck on a then-unsuspected fault and without any obvious premonitory indicators such as minor foreshocks. However, there were reports of odd animal behavior near Kobe in the hours and days before the earthquake. These included fish near shore, birds, and sea lions at the zoo. The composition of well water used for local sake (rice wine) production varied unusually—especially for radon, a gas whose presence in deep groundwater has been linked to pre-earthquake straining.

Ironically, on the day the earthquake struck Kobe, the fourth Japan-United States Workshop on Urban Earthquake Hazard Reduction was beginning down the road in Osaka. After the earthquake, the meeting was canceled because the participants had gone to Kobe to assess and investigate the disaster and its consequences.

Three years after the earthquake, in April, 1998, the world's longest suspension bridge opened there. The Akashi Kaikyo bridge connects the mainland west of Kobe across the Akashi Strait to Awaji Island. Its total length is 15 miles (24 kilometers), and the center suspension span is 1.2 miles (2 kilometers) long. The bridge is designed to withstand a magnitude 8.0 earthquake. Each of the tall towers supporting the center span is equipped with 20 vibration-control pendulums to reduce bridge movement if buffeted by earthquake waves or high winds.

This was the biggest earthquake to hit a densely populated area of

Japan since June, 1948, when a magnitude 7.1 quake struck Fukui, on the north coast of Honshū island, killing about 5,000. With Kobe's death toll of 5,502, it was the deadliest seismic disaster since the September, 1923, Great Kwanto Earthquake of magnitude 8.3 that struck Tokyo and Yokohama and killed 143,000, mostly in the fires that raged after the shock.

The geological fact of life for Japan is that the beautiful island nation, the world's second-largest economic power, is constructed on vulnerable and unstable terrain. The inexorable movement and collision of tectonic plates—the Pacific and Philippine from the east, the Eurasian from the west, and the North American from the north—mean that faults will continue to rupture and cause earthquakes into the foreseeable future.

Robert S. Carmichael

FOR FURTHER INFORMATION:

Proceedings of the International Symposium on Earthquake Engineering Commemorating the Tenth Anniversary of the 1995 Kobe Earthquake: January 13-16, 2005, Kobe/Awaji, Japan. Tokyo: Japan Association for Earthquake Engineering, 2005.

Reid, T. R. "Kobe Wakes to a Nightmare." *National Geographic,* July, 1995, 112-136.

Schiff, Anshel J., ed. *Hyogoken-Nanbu (Kobe) Earthquake of January 17, 1995: Lifeline Performance.* Reston, Va.: American Society of Civil Engineers, 1999.

Shea, Gail Hynes, ed. *Lessons Learned Over Time.* Oakland, Calif.: Earthquake Engineering Research Institute, 2000.

Somerville, Paul. "Kobe Earthquake: An Urban Disaster." *EOS/Transactions of American Geophysical Union* 76, no. 6 (February 7, 1995): 49-51.

"Twenty Seconds of Terror." *Newsweek,* January 30, 1995, 19-30.

■ 1995: Ebola outbreak

Epidemic

DATE: April-May, 1995
PLACE: Kitwit, near Kinshasa, Zaire (now Democratic Republic of the Congo)
RESULT: 245 dead, 50 infected

Gaspard Menga died on January 13, 1995, in Kitwit General Hospital. For a week he struggled against some unknown enemy, suffering a soaring fever, headaches, horrible stomach pains, uncontrollable hiccups, and massive bleeding—blood in his vomit, diarrhea, nose, and ears. Bebe, Philemond, and Bibolo Menga all died in a similar manner within weeks of preparing Gaspard's body for burial, the preparation being a traditional procedure that involved washing the corpse. Philemond's nineteen-year-old daughter Veronique also died in the same manner, having helped care for her ailing father.

Of 23 members of the extended Menga-Nseke family, 13 perished because of the Ebola virus between January 6 and March 9, 1995. Four of them died in Kitwit General Hospital, which means the deadly virus probably lurked in the hospital for more than two months—perhaps mistaken for shigellosis, a common bacterial disease—before erupting in mid-April when surgery on an infected laboratory technician named Kimfumu spread Ebola to a dozen doctors and nurses. Kimfumu was a thirty-six-year-old laboratory technician who was responsible for collecting blood samples from suspected shigellosis cases. Kimfumu became ill, and his stomach was distended; the physicians thought he had an intestinal perforation caused by typhus. They operated twice. During the first operation, the physicians could not find any perforation, but they did remove Kimfumu's inflamed appendix on April 10, 1995. When Kimfumu's stomach remained severely distended, they operated again. This time when they opened the abdomen, they were horrified to see huge pools of blood—uncontrollable hemorrhaging from every organ. Kimfumu died, and soon, one after another, members of the two

854

surgical teams that had operated on the man also died. The dead included four anesthesiologists, four doctors, two nurses, and two Italian nuns.

SYMPTOMS AND SPREAD OF EBOLA VIRUS. Symptoms of Ebola hemorrhagic fever (EHF) begin four to sixteen days after infection. Victims develop fever, chills, headaches, muscle aches, and loss of appetite. As the disease progresses, vomiting, diarrhea, abdominal pain, sore throat, and chest pain can occur. The blood fails to clot, and patients may bleed from infection sites, as well as into the gastrointestinal tract, skin, and internal organs.

Ebola virus is spread through close personal contact with a person who is very ill with the disease. In previous outbreaks, person-to-person spread frequently occurred among hospital care workers or family members who were caring for an infected person. Transmission of the virus also has occurred as a result of hypodermic needles being reused in the treatment of patients. Reusing needles is a common practice in developing countries, such as Zaire and Sudan, where the health care system is underfinanced. "The major means of transmission appears to be close and unprotected patient contact or preparation of the dead for burial," said a World Health Organization (WHO) statement.

Ebola virus can also be spread from person to person through sexual contact. Close personal contact with persons who are infected but show no signs of active disease is very unlikely to result in infection. Patients who have recovered from an illness caused by Ebola virus do not pose a serious risk for spreading the infection. However, the virus may be present in the genital secretions of such persons for a brief period after their recovery, and therefore it is possible they can spread the virus through sexual contact.

EPIDEMIC SITE AND SANITARY CONDITIONS. Kitwit, a community of between 250,000 and 400,000 people, is located about 260 miles (400 kilometers) northeast of Kinshasa, the capitol of Zaire, now the Democratic Republic of the Congo. Kitwit, really no more than a huge village without running water, a sewage system, or electricity, became filled with fear. As of May 20, 1995, Ebola had infected 155 people and killed 97. Most of the fear in Kitwit was directed at the hospital, where the gruesome illness with mysterious origins spread slowly, doctors believed, unnoticed for months until magnified by nonsterile practices. These practices and conditions, including a lack of adequate medical supplies and the frequent reuse of needles and syringes, played a major role in the spread of disease. The outbreak was quickly controlled when appropriate medical supplies and equipment were made available and quarantine procedures were used. The same was true for earlier outbreaks of Ebola.

BIRTH OF THE EPIDEMIC. The Mengas' experience, like the other chains of transmission, seem to show that Ebola initially simmered in Kitwit, spreading within families for two to three months. It exploded into an epidemic in mid-April of 1995 in the hospital. In all chains of transmission the virus seems to have hit hardest in the first rounds of spreading, waning in transmissibility and virulence over time, eventually burning itself out.

Early in the epidemic a nurse at the Mosango Mission Hospital became infected tending a patient who had fled Kitwit, a ninety-minute drive from Mosango. The nurse died after particularly acute hemorrhaging. The terrified staff disinfected and scrubbed the room,

Hospital workers transport the body of an Italian nun who died after contracting the Ebola virus in Zaire. (AP/Wide World Photos)

burned the bed linens, and sealed the chamber for two weeks. Fifteen days after the nurse died, a young woman with an unrelated problem was placed in the room, Mosango physicians said. She contracted Ebola and died. Her only contact with the virus, scientists said, was the mattress upon which she had lain.

Physicians in Kitwit General Hospital were in a state of panic. Their patients were dying despite antibiotic therapy, and the medical staff and nuns were falling victim to the mysterious ailment as well. A tentative diagnosis of shigellosis—a bacterial disease that normally had a 30 percent fatality rate but should have been curable with antibiotics—was assigned to the crisis. The fatality rate from Ebola proved to be in the vicinity of 90 percent.

AID FROM BELGIUM AND ELSEWHERE. A Zairean doctor who arrived in Kitwit in mid-April radioed an urgent message to a contact in Brussels requesting ciproflaxin, one of the most powerful and expensive antibiotics on the market. The doctor also mentioned in his message to Brussels that the cases in Kitwit reminded him of an epidemic he had seen in 1976 in Yambuktu, Zaire, the country's first Ebola outbreak. Money was not available for the antibiotic, but the contact passed the message on to Antwerp's Institute of Tropical Medicine. The word Ebola stood out for an official of the Institute of Tropical Medicine who had been involved in the 1976 Ebola outbreak in Zaire. He told the Brussels contact to tell the Zairean doctor to send blood and tissue samples immediately. The samples arrived in Antwerp on May 6, 1995, but were quickly sent to the American Centers for Disease Control (CDC) in Atlanta. If it was Ebola, the official at the Institute of Tropical Medicine and officials from the World Health Organization (WHO) agreed, then it should be handled in the most secure facility available. Physicians from both the CDC and the WHO were dispatched to Kitwit, and a physician and a team of two volunteers arrived from Médecins sans Frontières (MSF, or Doctors Without Borders).

PHYSICIANS AND VOLUNTEERS ARRIVE. On May 10, 1995, the CDC physician, an American epidemiologist, arrived at the Kitwit General Hospital and surveyed the situation. He recalled that "[t]here was blood everywhere. Blood on the mattresses, the floors, the walls. Vomit, diarrhea . . . wards were full of Ebola cases. [Non-Ebola] patients and their families were milling around, wandering in and out. There was lots of exposure." The women mourners sat on a slab of concrete walkway that led from the wards, which were full of Ebola patients, to the morgue. Family after family sat on the walkway, rocking and wailing near the morgue.

Dr. Barbara Kierstein from MSF later said that the hospital was in a sorry state and the patients were in a sorrier state. The Kitwit General Hospital staff had no protection, and they had not been paid for risking their lives. So Kierstein and her team decided to focus on hospital sanitation and establishment of an isolation ward. On Thursday, May 11, 1995, Kierstein and her team began hooking up the hospital's ancient water system but gave up after realizing that all the pipes were blocked and rusted. Instead, they set up a plastic rainwater collection and filtration system. A thin, plastic wall was set up, isolating a ward for Ebola patients. The doctors dispensed gloves and masks to the hospital staff.

SUPPLIES AND THE END OF QUARANTINE. On Saturday, May 13, 1995, Kierstein decided that additional help was needed, and she and her team spent Saturday morning listing essential supplies, using a satellite telephone to pass the list to Brussels. The request was to send respirator masks, latex gloves, protective gowns, disinfectant, hospital linens and plastic mattress covers, plastic aprons, basic cleaning supplies, water pumps and filters, galoshes, and tents. Kierstein commented that she had seen many African countries, and, even compared to others, the conditions at Kitwit General Hospital were shocking. She further stated that the only thing the hospital staff had to work with was their brains. For twenty-six days, however, the brains and dedication of the on-site rescue teams—as well as the numerous Zairean volunteers and medical workers—continued to be their main weapon. The supplies did not begin arriving in suitable amounts until May 27, 1995.

Meanwhile, Zairean officials had quarantined the Kitwit area. The quarantine was lifted on Sunday, May 21, 1995, so as to allow long-awaited food deliveries to reach Kinshasa. The road between Kitwit and Kinshasa carries much of the capital's food, grown in the fertile Bandundu region where Kitwit is located. Compulsory health checks continued on road travelers from Kitwit to Kinshasa until the number of recorded deaths remained static at 245. The road health checks ceased on Tuesday, June 6, 1995. The final count was 245 deaths recorded out of 315 people known to have been infected.

Even as a long-term investigation strategy was being prepared that would reveal the entire history of Kitwit's epidemic, officials in Zaire said that bloody diarrhea had broken out elsewhere in Kitwit's province of Bandundu. In an area 470 miles north of Kitwit, in a town called Tendjuna, 25 people had died from the ailment. Experts initially assigned a diagnosis of shigellosis to the illness.

Researchers have begun to get a handle on the Ebola virus's high pathogenicity. Research work at the University of Michigan Medical Center in Ann Arbor reports results suggesting that the virus uses different versions of the same glycoprotein—a protein with sugar groups attached—to wage a two-pronged attack on the body. One glycoprotein, secreted by the virus, seems to paralyze the immune system response that should fight it off, while the other, which stays bound to Ebola, homes in on the endothelial cells lining the interior of blood vessels, helping the virus to infect and damage them.

It seems that as Ebola invades and subverts the cells' genetic machinery to make more of itself, it also damages the endothelial cells, making blood vessels leaky and weak. The patient first bleeds and then goes into shock as failing blood pressure leaves the circulatory systems unable to pump blood to vital organs. Long before their immune systems can mount an antibody response—a process that can take weeks—most Ebola victims bleed to death. If confirmed in infected animals and humans, the findings suggest that these glycoproteins could be targets for anti-Ebola vaccines as well as for drugs that treat Ebola infections. A vaccine has been developed that works in monkeys, but human trials have not yet proved successful.

Dana P. McDermott

FOR FURTHER INFORMATION:

Centers for Disease Control and Prevention. "Outbreak of Ebola Viral Hemorrhagic Fever—Zaire, 1995." *Morbidity and Mortality Weekly Report* 44 (1995): 381-382.

_____. "Update: Outbreak of Ebola Viral Hemorrhagic Fever—Zaire, 1995." *Morbidity and Mortality Weekly Report* 44 (1995): 399.

Cowley, Geoffrey. "Outbreak of Fear." *Newsweek* 125 (May 22, 1995): 48.

"Ebola's Lethal Secrets." *Discovery Magazine* 19, no. 1 (July 1, 1998): 24.

Klenk, Hans-Dieter, ed. *Marburg and Ebola Viruses.* New York: Springer, 1999.

Murphy, Frederick A., and Clarence J. Peters. "Ebola Virus: Where Does It Come from and Where Is It Going?" In *Emerging Infections,* edited by Richard M. Krause. San Diego, Calif.: Academic Press, 1998.

Regis, Ed. *Virus Ground Zero: Stalking the Killer Viruses with the Centers for Disease Control.* New York: Pocket Books, 1996.

Smith, Tara C. *Ebola.* Philadelphia: Chelsea House, 2006.

■ 1995: Chicago heat wave

Heat wave

DATE: July 12-17, 1995
PLACE: Midwest and Northeast, especially Chicago and Milwaukee
TEMPERATURE: Up to 106 degrees Fahrenheit
RESULT: More than 1,000 dead (465 in Chicago, 129 in Milwaukee)

In July of 1995 an unusually strong upper level ridge of high pressure slowly moved across the Great Plains and came into contact with exceptionally humid conditions at ground level. The slow progression of the air mass created good opportunities for daily heating and the accumulation of humidity. Working together, these two factors produced extraordinarily hot and humid weather in the Midwest and on the East Coast. When this air mass came into contact with the urban sprawl of Chicago, Milwaukee, and other cities, the results became particularly deadly. The concrete and steel buildings trapped the heat, while the lack of a breeze made for stifling conditions. Further, even the daily low temperatures remained unusually high, preventing nighttime cooling from helping to dissipate the daytime heat buildup.

THE TEMPERATURES CLIMB. Temperatures across the Midwest and East Coast soared during the record-breaking event. The National Weather Service (NWS) issued the first heat advisory for Chicago on July 12, 1995. By July 13 Chicago experienced temperatures of 104 degrees Fahrenheit at O'Hare airport and 106 degrees Fahrenheit at Midway. Both represented the highest daily temperatures ever recorded at those locations up to that point, and the city witnessed the second-highest summer temperatures in its history to that date, falling just one tenth of a percentage point short of the overall record. Taking into account the Heat Index, which reached 119 degrees Fahrenheit on July 12 and continued to climb, it became the worst summer on record for Chicago. The intense heat caused a section of Interstate 57 in downtown Chicago to buckle, closing an intersection for repairs.

Milwaukee also witnessed extreme temperatures, experiencing a high of 101 degrees Fahrenheit on July 14. As the air mass moved eastward, other cities reported record-breaking heat. Philadelphia hit 103 degrees Fahrenheit on July 15, while New York City hit 102 degrees the same day. Baltimore had a city record of 102 degrees, and Danbury, Connecticut, also set a city record with 106 degrees. Washington, D.C., had to close the Washington Monument for several days to prevent heat exhaustion in tourists.

THE DEATH TOLL. As the temperatures soared, people suffered physically from the heat, and the first injuries and deaths were soon reported. Because the heat came early in the summer, before people's bodies became acclimated to hotter temperatures, residents, especially of northern locations, suffered more from the heat, with some succumbing to death. Heat caused the heart to pump blood more forcefully, because of the expansion of blood vessels to cool the body. Hearts needed time to become fully acclimated to the extra exertion. When the heat wave happened suddenly, as in 1995, heart attacks and other physical distress resulted.

Dr. Edmund Donoghue, the Cook County medical examiner during the summer of 1995, established three specific criteria for determining if a fatality resulted at least in part from the heat. Donoghue maintained a death was attributable to the heat if one of the following factors was indicated at the time of death. If the body temperature had risen to at least 105 degrees at or shortly after the time of death, if there was evidence of elevated temperatures at the location where the victim was discovered, or if the victim was seen alive for the last time at the height of the heat wave and subsequently found in a decomposed state, then Donoghue called the death heat-inspired. His findings were later adopted by the NWS to establish the death toll for the heat wave of 1995.

Although people died in other locations, such as the 11 who died in New York City and the 21 in Philadelphia, the worst fatalities occurred in Chicago and Milwaukee. In Chicago, 435 people officially died as a result of the heat wave, with 162 being recorded on July 15 alone. Others were rushed to local hospitals. At one point, 18 hospitals in Chicago placed their emergency rooms on bypass status, as they were unable to handle any more patients because of the overwhelming numbers of victims from the heat wave. The Cook County coroner's office filled the 222-bay morgue and needed to use 7 refrigerated tractor trailers to store additional corpses awaiting autopsies. Everyone at the morgue worked overtime to clear the backlog of heat-related cases. In Milwaukee, 129 people officially died as a result of the event. Bodies were directed to local funeral homes when the medical examiner's office became full. Many of the dead had body temperatures in the range of 107-108 degrees. Emergency rooms in Milwaukee also experienced an upsurge in patients, with some closing for short periods of time because of the caseload.

Two of the dead were three-year-old boys left inside a locked van for an hour when their caregiver forgot about them when she took several other children into a mall on a field trip. Most of the people who died from the heat were senior citizens, especially those living alone or who had apartments on the second floor and higher. They often died with their windows closed and doors locked. A. D. and Willie May Gross of Chicago, both in their sixties, died together in their home, which did not have air-conditioning. Rescuers found the doors and windows bolted and shut, with the temperature inside the house at 125 degrees Fahrenheit. The Chicago Housing Authority never placed enough air-conditioning units into the public housing projects, even though managers asked for units in recreation rooms and common areas to provide a cool area for residents. Many residents, especially of public housing, feared the crime outside their apartments more than the heat and refused to open doors and windows to allow air circulation. The homes of many of the dead were in the range of 100 to 120 degrees Fahrenheit.

Other victims declined assistance even when it was offered to them. One eighty-seven-year-old casualty, Mabel Swanson, could have gone to stay at a neighbor's air-conditioned apartment in Chicago, but she preferred to stay in her own home. She died during the night from the heat and was discovered by a neighbor the next morning. Chicago established designated cooling stations where residents could enjoy air-conditioning and get relief from the oppressive conditions, but these centers went largely underused during the crisis. One center had room for 200 people but was empty during the heat of the day.

Most of the dead lacked air-conditioning in their homes and apartments and used fans instead. In Kansas City, Missouri, which also saw its share of deaths, Arthur Castlebery died at home with three fans blowing on him. When the mercury rose above 90 degrees and the humidity was above 35 percent, fans acted like a convection oven, heating the room further by circulating the hot air, rather than cooling it off. The temperature in the room was 110 degrees when Castlebery's body was discovered.

OTHER EFFECTS. Commonwealth Edison Company, the local electric company for Chicago, demonstrated an inability to handle the increased demand for electricity during the heat wave. Several substations caught fire or otherwise failed, and the company resorted to rolling blackouts to ration the power throughout the city without notifying consumers in advance. During these rolling blackouts, residents experienced two- to four-hour power outages over the course of the day. In other instances, substations failed entirely, leaving tens of thousands of residents without electricity for up to forty-eight hours. This critical situation contributed to some fatalities. Although eighty-nine-year-old Florentine Aquino had air-conditioning in his home, a rolling blackout halted his electric service. His wife awoke to discover him lying dead next to her in their bed the next morning. After the event, lawyers filed a class-action lawsuit against Commonwealth Edison because of the outages.

Most of the victims of the heat wave suffered from diseases exacerbated by the high temperatures. Diabetes, pulmonary heart disease, upper respiratory problems, and high blood pressure contributed to their deaths. Others had more unique problems. Eight-year-old Kyle Garcia from Kenosha, Wisconsin, died from dehydration. Garcia was in a full body cast, covering his chest to his feet, and his body could not process liquids, making it unable to prevent death. Mental illness also contributed to a number of deaths. An antipsychotic medication given to schizophrenics prevented perspiration and impaired their ability to dissipate heat, causing heat exhaustion and death for some. Twelve of the dead in Milwaukee took these psychotropic or mind-altering medications, with fatal consequences.

The heat wave of 1995 initiated a spate of research into deaths caused by heat exhaustion and related causes. The NWS conducted a study for later emergency disaster procedures in the event of future heat waves. It found that, although heat waves annually killed more Americans than hurricanes, tornadoes, or blizzards, the general public lacked awareness of the deadly potential. In particular, the NWS implemented a series of policies, such as better warning systems and the establishment of cooling stations, to handle heat waves and to prevent the high casualty rate of the summer of 1995.

James B. Seymour, Jr.

FOR FURTHER INFORMATION:

Changnon, S. A., K. E. Kunkel, and B. C. Reinke. "Impacts and Responses to the 1995 Heat Wave: A Call to Action." *Bulletin of the American Meteorological Society* 77, no. 7 (1996): 1497-1506.

Klinenberg, Eric. *Heat Wave: A Social Autopsy of Disaster in Chicago.* Chicago: University of Chicago Press, 2002.

Kunkel, K. E., S. A. Changnon, B. C. Reinke, and R. W. Arritt. "The July, 1995, Heat Wave in the Midwest: A Climatic Perspective and Critical Weather Factors." *Bulletin of the American Meteorological Society* 77, no. 7 (1996): 1507-1518.

U.S. Department of Commerce. *Natural Disaster Survey Report, July, 1995, Heat Wave.* Silver Springs, Md.: National Weather Service, 1995.

■ 1996: The Mount Everest Disaster

Blizzard

Date: May 10-11, 1996
Place: Mount Everest, Nepal
Wind Speed: 45 to 80 miles per hour
Temperature: With wind-chill factor, minus 94 to minus 148 degrees Fahrenheit
Result: 9 dead, 4 injured with severe frostbite

Extremes attract adventurers who seek to fly the fastest, descend the deepest, or climb the highest. Mount Everest, the Earth's highest peak at 29,108 feet, has long been considered the crowning goal for many mountaineers. Because of its location in the Himalayas between Tibet (where its name is Jomolungma) and Nepal (where its name is Sagarmatha), Mount Everest is often subject to extreme and unpredictable weather. The unexpected arrival of a savage blizzard on the high slopes of Everest during the spring of 1996, when the mountain was crowded with climbers, played an important role in the greatest tragedy in this mountain's long history of calamities.

By 1996, in the seventy-five years since the first attempt to climb Everest, more than 140 climbers had died. The largest single cause of death was avalanches, with falls into crevasses and from the mountain a distant second. Until the 1996 tragedy, there had been only 13 weather-related deaths. Furthermore, throughout most of the history of mountaineering on Everest, almost all deaths were of professional or highly skilled climbers. After 1985, however, climbing high mountains became a business, and populating the slopes of this dangerous mountain with amateurs of varying abilities was another factor that figured into the disastrous loss of life in 1996.

The leaders of the commercial companies that developed to meet the need of those who could pay $65,000 to reach the top of the world knew that their success depended on the vagaries of Everest's weather, and so clients were brought to the mountain in the spring to take advantage of the brief period of good weather between the decline of

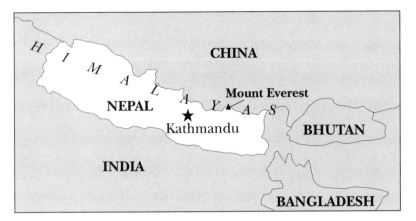

winter and the arrival of the summer monsoons. It was during this time period that, in 1953, Sir Edmund Hillary and his Sherpa guide, Tenzing Norgay, became the first people to reach the summit; their route, up the Khumbu Icefall and Glacier through the West Cwm and up the Southeast Ridge, became the standard way to the top. Because of the brief weather window, Everest's base camp at 17,600 feet was crowded with more than four hundred people in the spring of 1996.

THE EVEREST EXPEDITIONS. Some of these people had specific goals other than merely climbing Everest. For example, the film director David Breashears was shooting a $5.5 million giant-screen (IMAX) film about climbing the mountain. Others were part of commercial expeditions. For example, Rob Hall, who, like Hillary, was a skilled New Zealand climber, led the Adventure Consultants Guided Expedition. Among his clients was Jon Krakauer, an American journalist who had been assigned by *Outside* magazine to research an article on commercial climbing. Hall had already guided a record 39 climbers to the summit, but he was receiving competition from an American company, Mountain Madness Guided Expedition, led by Scott Fischer. Fischer was assisted by the guides Anatoli Boukreev, a Russian, and Neal Beidleman, an American. Among Fischer's clients was the millionaire socialite and journalist Sandy Hill Pittman, who was making daily reports of his trip on the World Wide Web.

As the clients acclimatized to the altitude, they also adapted to each other. Variations in economic backgrounds, states of health, and climbing ability did not make such adaptation easy. Nevertheless,

Hall and Fischer guided their groups through the Khumbu Icefall, a river of glacial ice, to Camp 1, at 20,000 feet. Later, their clients trekked 4 miles and 1,700 vertical feet from Camp 1 to Camp 2, in the West Cwm, the earth's highest box canyon. While more than 100 climbers were going through the Icefall and up the West Cwm, a storm hit on April 21, with winds of over 60 miles per hour. Another storm arrived on April 23, with very strong winds pummeling the upper slopes, delaying the establishment of Camp 3 (at 24,000 feet) and Camp 4 (at 26,000 feet). When the weather stabilized, toward the end of April, oxygen cylinders and other materials necessary for the summit climbs were carried to the higher camps.

By the first week in May, most clients had completed their acclimatization at the higher camps and were preparing for a summit bid. The IMAX climbers, who were higher on the mountain than the Hall and Fischer groups, decided against their attempt to reach the summit on May 9 because of a violent windstorm, which also hampered Sherpas setting up tents in the South Col (the plateau where Camp 4 was located).

THE ASCENT TO THE SUMMIT. Despite the storm, Hall and Fischer brought their guides and clients to Camp 4 for a possible ascent on Friday, May 10. When the climbers awoke late Thursday night, the winds had died down, and they left the Col around midnight. Mount Everest above the South Col is called the Death Zone because the combination of the lack of oxygen, low temperatures, and high winds can quickly amplify small mistakes into tragedies. Each climber carried two oxygen cylinders (a third was available on the South Summit in a cache stocked by the Sherpas). Within two or three hours after leaving the South Col, Fischer's Mountain Madness climbers began to overtake Hall's group, and by 4 A.M. both groups were commingled. Though the groups were mixed, the philosophies of their leaders differed. For example, Hall taught his clients the Two O'Clock Turnaround Rule: If you are not on the summit by 2 P.M., go back down the mountain, no matter how close you are to the top.

Because there were so many climbers on the Southeast Ridge, the pace was slow and traffic jams occurred, such as at the Hillary Step, a steeply sloped tower of rock not far from the summit. Guides rigged ropes up this 40-foot cliff to help their clients conquer Everest's final obstacle. Boukreev, Fischer's chief guide, reached the summit several minutes after 1 P.M. Krakauer arrived about five minutes later. During the next few hours clients and guides from both Hall's and Fischer's groups reached the summit, along with others, and the weather, though very cold, did not appear threatening. Most climbers were worried about their dwindling supplies of oxygen, not about a storm. However, some guides noticed that clouds were filling the valleys below, obscuring all but the highest peaks. Unknown to the climbers, these innocent-looking puffs were actually the tops of thunderheads gradually moving up the mountain's sides.

Rob Hall reached the top at 2:30 P.M., thus breaking his own Two O'Clock Turnaround Rule. More ominously, Scott Fischer did not reach the summit until 3:40 P.M., and others arrived still later. In fact, Hall had left the summit to help his client Doug Hansen up the final section of the Southeast Ridge. Why Hall encouraged Hansen to continue his ascent so late in the day is one of the perplexing questions of the Everest tragedy. In 1995 Hall had turned Hansen back when he was close to the summit, and it is reasonable to speculate that it would have been particularly difficult for Hall to deny Hansen the summit a second time. After Hansen reached the top, Hall and his client began their descent and quickly ran into trouble. Beginning at 4:30, Hall repeatedly sent radio messages that he and Hansen were in trouble high on the summit ridge and urgently needed oxygen. Fischer, too, was in difficulty. On the summit he had told a Sherpa that he was not feeling well, and he experienced debilitating problems during his descent.

THE BLIZZARD STRIKES. The situation of the many climbers descending the Southeast Ridge was made even more difficult by the storm clouds which, by 5:15, had blanketed Everest's heights. Between 6:30 and 6:45 P.M., as dim daylight turned to darkness, Krakauer stumbled into Camp 4. By this time the storm was a full-blown blizzard, and visibility had dropped to 20 feet. Ice and snow particles carried by 80-mile-per-hour gusts froze exposed flesh. Despite these conditions, Hall had managed to get Hansen down to the top of the Hillary Step, but their progress then stopped. Fischer, too, was stranded on the ridge, and several of the clients of Hall and Fischer were lost in the snow and ice as they tried to descend to Camp 4 (one later compared their plight to trying to find a path in a gigantic milk bottle).

When the Mountain Madness clients did not return to Camp 4 by 6 P.M., Boukreev decided to discover their whereabouts, but the high winds and whiteout conditions made his search fruitless, and he was forced to return to camp. Meanwhile, Beidleman, Boukreev's fellow guide, had managed to get his group off the ridge and onto the broad expanse of the South Col, but they were on its eastern edge, far from the tents of Camp 4 about 330 yards to the west (a fifteen-minute walk in good weather). The storm was so intense that they could not see the lights of Camp 4, and only a few people in their group had headlamps with functioning batteries. Since their oxygen supplies had been depleted, they were all at the point of physical collapse. Some in Beidleman's group were Hall's clients (Yasuko Namba and Beck Weathers), while others were part of Fischer's group (Tim Madsen, Charlotte Fox, and Sandy Pittman). Failing to find Camp 4, the group decided to huddle and wait for the storm to subside.

Fearing they would all die, Beidleman later gathered a small group of the ambulatory climbers to make another attempt to find their camp. Wobbling into the wind, which occasionally knocked them down, they eventually stumbled into Camp 4 sometime before midnight. They told Boukreev that those left behind needed help. After his attempts to find volunteers for a rescue team were frustrated, Boukreev, on his own, made two long forays into the furious storm to bring the stranded climbers to safety. He eventually saw the faint glow of Madsen's headlamp and was thus able to save his life, along with those of Fox and Pittman. (He assumed that Namba was dead, and he did not come across Weathers.)

During the night, Rob Hall, still on the ridge, was in radio contact with base camp. Without Hansen, who was presumed dead, Hall had managed to descend to the South Summit. At 5 A.M. on Saturday, May 11, base camp was able to arrange a telephone call from Hall to his wife in New Zealand. In this conversation and a later one at 6:20, she tried to get her husband to move down the mountain, but his legs were frozen, and he was too weak.

With daylight, there was a break in the storm, and a team was organized to locate the bodies of Beck Weathers and Yasuko Namba. The team found Namba partially buried in snow and, surprisingly, still breathing although judged to be near death. Namba did die, but Weathers was later able to rescue himself by walking directly into the wind and stumbling into Camp 4. He was bundled into two sleeping bags and given oxygen.

ANOTHER STORM. The gale that struck on Saturday evening was even more powerful than the one that had lashed the Col the night before. The storm collapsed Weathers's tent and blew his sleeping bags off him. With his badly frostbitten hands, he was unable to pull the bags back over his body. The storm was so intense that his anguished cries were unheard, and he had to suffer, unprotected, through yet another Everest blizzard. When the murderous winds abated and his condition became known to the other climbers, he was injected with dexamethasone, which helped him recover enough to stand and walk with assistance. He somehow managed to get to a lower camp, where a helicopter evacuated him to Kathmandu.

When the storm finally ended, the remaining members of Hall's and Fischer's groups descended the mountain, but the bodies of Rob Hall and Scott Fischer were left where they had died. By the time Krakauer reached base camp, 9 climbers from four expeditions were dead. Because all this drama on the high slopes of Everest had been closely followed by the world media, the tragedy generated great interest. Jon Krakauer's account of what happened appeared in the September, 1996, issue of *Outside* and in his book, *Into Thin Air*, which was published in April of 1997 and began its long run on the bestseller charts. In his book, Krakauer criticized some of Boukreev's decisions in the Death Zone. Boukreev defended his actions in his own book, *The Climb: Tragic Ambitions on Everest*, published in 1997. His views were given some sanction when, on December 6, 1997, the American Alpine Club honored him with their David A. Sowles Memorial Award for his courageous rescue of three climbers trapped in a storm on the South Col of Mount Everest. The controversy between Krakauer and Boukreev came to an end when Boukreev was killed in an avalanche on the slopes of Annapurna on Christmas Day of 1997.

Robert J. Paradowski

FOR FURTHER INFORMATION:

Boukreev, Anatoli, and G. Weston DeWalt. *The Climb: Tragic Ambitions on Everest.* New York: St. Martin's Press, 1997.

Coburn, Broughton. *Everest: Mountain Without Mercy.* Washington, D.C.: National Geographic Society, 1997.

Groom, Michael. *Sheer Will.* Milsons Point, New South Wales, Australia: Random House, 1997.

Jenkins, Steve. *The Top of the World: Clmbing Mount Everest.* Boston: Houghton Mifflin, 1999.

Krakauer, Jon. *Into Thin Air: A Personal Account of the Mount Everest Disaster.* New York: Villard, 1997.

■ 1997: THE JARRELL TORNADO

TORNADO

DATE: May 27, 1997
PLACE: Jarrell, Texas
CLASSIFICATION: F5
RESULT: 27 dead, 8 injured, 44 homes damaged or destroyed

During the last week of May, 1997, a cold front pushed through the central plains of Oklahoma and Kansas. The front caused severe thunderstorms and caught the attention of Dr. Charles Doswell, a research meteorologist at the National Severe Storms Laboratory (NSSL) in Norman, Oklahoma. Dr. Doswell recognized that the higher humidity near the Gulf of Mexico would add strength to the storms as the front plunged into Texas. In order to follow atmospheric developments, Doswell drove to the Fort Worth National Weather Service office on the morning of May 27.

As expected, the morning was typical of spring. It started with clear skies, high humidity, and rapidly warming temperatures. Initially, cooler temperatures aloft slowed vertical development of storm clouds. In the early afternoon, however, the sky grew darker near Waco, Texas, as a single towering cumulus erupted through the upper layers of the atmosphere to form a supercell, the strongest type of thunderstorm. Doswell's hunch of pending trouble proved correct as the cold front plowed into the rich humidity from the Gulf of Mexico. This collision of energetic air masses would sustain this individual supercell for the next six hours. However, instead of moving in the typical northeasterly direction, this supercell plunged southward, growing in strength along the intersection between the cold front and the warm moist air to the south. That uncommon southerly movement would cause one of the most devastating tornado effects ever recorded. Before the day was over, this supercell spawned 22 tornadoes, killing 30 in all.

The first of the tornadoes formed 10 miles south of Waco at 1:37 P.M. It was followed by a continuous succession of tornadoes forming one after another. Each tornado in turn traced a southerly course,

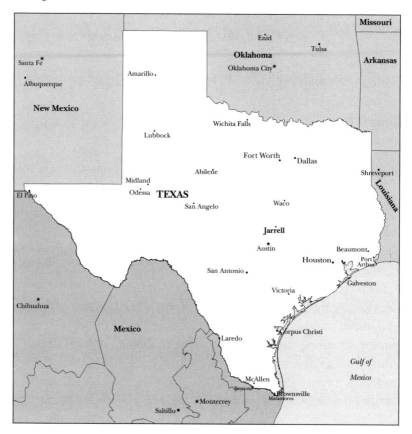

following the leisurely pace of the parent supercell. These tornadoes achieved F2-level strength, with winds approaching 150 miles per hour. One of the tornadoes in this series tracked across Lake Belton, briefly assuming the characteristics of a waterspout. A flotilla of cabin cruisers, ski boats, and party barges disappeared below the surface as this tornado sank the largest marina on the lake.

Word of the approaching tornadic thunderstorm had circulated from numerous radio and television sources during the first two hours of tornadic activity. Initially, only a small number of people were at risk. Forming just west of Interstate 35, these tornadoes spiraled through rural areas without nearing any population centers. By 3:50 P.M., a new tornado was just forming 3 miles north of Jarrell, Texas. Its forward motion was very slow, and many Jarrell residents, who had been watching the tornado for several minutes, escaped by driving south on the interstate at its approach. Unfortunately, school had let out for the day twenty minutes earlier. Many of the younger students were just reaching home either on foot or by bicycle. Aware of the danger, some of these students accompanied their friends to the new subdivision just west of town. In some instances, a few parents left work early to be with their children at home.

THE INITIAL TOUCHDOWN. The initial touchdown point was north of Jarrell in a cotton field. Green with maturing cotton plants, the 30-acre field was instantly defoliated. Although relatively weak, the wind force scoured away several acres of topsoil, exposing the limestone base a foot below the original surface. As a result, a great mud storm developed at the base of the tornado, plastering 4 inches of mud against fence posts, tree trunks, foundations, and farm equipment. Typical in an F2 tornado, with winds exceeding 100 miles per hour, the first farm home lost its roof.

The tornado rapidly grew in strength over the next 0.5 mile as the second home was flattened, with most of the debris strewn downwind. On this day the owner chose to drive away rather than stay in his underground storm shelter. The 4,000-pound concrete roof of the shelter was torn from its moorings, never to be found in subsequent searches. With winds now approaching 200 miles per hour, the tornado siphoned 25 vertical feet of water from the well nearby.

The track of the tornado was plainly evident in the grassland beyond the homestead. It was mostly defoliated, the few remaining blades of grass shredded and flattened to the ground. The tornado path, now 800 feet across, bore the spiraling marks characteristic of a multiple-vortex tornado. Sometimes called suction spots, these intense whirlwinds within the main funnel carved their spirals several inches into the soil.

In the field beyond, the tornado raked across a wheat field ready for harvest, sending millions of wheat shafts spiraling into the vortex. The wheat shafts, as rigid as ice picks at such high velocities, impaled the cattle in the adjoining field. Of a herd of 130 cattle, half a dozen survived, wheat stitched into their hides and underbellies. Film evidence taken at the time revealed that many of the animals were vaulted into the air and dropped to the ground repeatedly. Internal injuries were severe; most of the cattle had four broken legs.

Typically, hair was removed from the hide. In extreme examples, even the hide was stripped away, exposing muscle and bone.

DOUBLE CREEK ESTATES. For the next 2 miles, the rotational velocity and width of the tornado continued to increase. Its intensity was most apparent along the only road leading to Jarrell's newest housing addition. This is where the devastation of an F5 tornado first became apparent. Winds in excess of 300 miles per hour lifted steel, concrete, and rock as easily as a wind gust stirring a leaf pile. For example, steel posts that once supported barbed-wire fences were lashed back and forth by the strong winds, breaking them off at ground level. Many sections of roadway were destroyed by the intense pressure of wind that gripped the pavement, disintegrating the pieces as they vaulted into the air. The energy of the wind alone peeled bark from the few tree trunks still standing.

At 0.5 mile wide, the path of the tornado now curved westward, centering on Double Creek Estates. Perhaps because of its westward travel, the forward motion of the tornado had slowed to a walking speed. It would take seventeen minutes for the tornado to travel the next mile over Double Creek, pulverizing homes, appliances, and automobiles, and taking human life. One of the residents had a collection of nearly 75 vintage Chevrolets that was swept into the maelstrom. Only a handful of cars remained intact, while most were reduced to shrapnel. Even engine blocks and transmissions were shattered from the repeated blows. In the first seconds, the great wind swept entire homes from their foundations. The residents were also swept along in a torrent of wind, metal, and wood.

With the exception of shattered fragments of wood that had speared the ground, there was little debris remaining in the vicinity of Double Creek Estates. The house foundations left behind gave mute testimony to the sequence of destruction. Although most of these homes were solidly built of brick veneer construction, the force of the wind and flying debris instantly disintegrated roofs and walls. Even the bricks were launched into the air, to be shot out of the tornado in a great fusillade. Bricks were scattered across the countryside, disproportionately favoring the left side of the tornado path. Clearly, with the counterclockwise rotation of the funnel, these homes were destroyed at the first instant by the leading edge of the tornado.

In some houses, the vinyl flooring was glued to the concrete foundation in bathrooms and kitchen areas. Long slashes in the vinyl cutting from right to left also confirmed that these floors were entirely exposed in those first moments. Modern construction practices attach the lumber to the concrete slab by shooting nails through the wood into the concrete beneath. All lumber attached in this manner was removed from the slabs. Other attached objects, including door thresholds, carpet tacking strips, toilets, tubs, and brick veneer fireplaces, were also removed. Copper water lines, plastic fittings, and wires were sheared off at the surface level of each slab. Even the concrete slabs had great gashes on their surfaces, with chunks of concrete nicked away from the corners and edges. Apparently, the homes of Double Creek Estates were not simply flattened, with their debris accounted for nearby, but rather annihilated one hundred times over as the tornado ground away any object that extended above ground.

While at its maximum strength over the subdivision, even the distant surface winds plunging into the tornado created amazing effects. Round hay bales weighing 1,500 pounds were tumbled into the tornado from 0.25 mile away. About 1,000 feet south of the path, a home seemed undamaged on the side facing the tornado. However,

A tornado that struck Jarrell, Texas, on May 27, 1997. (AP/Wide World Photos)

the inbound winds shattered windows and removed shingles on the side facing away from the tornado. This homeowner also lost his tractor-trailer rig as the inflowing winds pulled it into the tornado.

THE WEAKENING TORNADO. The tornado would not lift for another 3 miles; however, the first signs of weakening began about 1 mile beyond the subdivision. Three great piles of debris spaced about 1,000 feet apart formed into a straight line near the centerline of the tornado footprint. At about 100 feet long, each streamlined hill was formed from the most massive objects available: automobile parts, appliances, trucks, and farm implements. Such objects apparently accumulated as flying debris slammed into the side of each pile. Smaller debris, perhaps transported higher in the tornado, rained down over a dozen square miles near the lift-off point. Consisting mostly of metal, plastic, and wood, these objects typically weighed just a few pounds. Finally, the lightest debris was transported by the supercell thunderstorm, later to fall to earth at great distances. Although most of this material could not be absolutely confirmed as originating from this event, a box of checks bearing the name of one of the victims was discovered 100 miles south of Jarrell.

THE AFTERMATH. The shattering intensity of this tornado is expressed in the statistics: 27 dead and 8 injured. Other great tornadoes have claimed more lives, but no other tornado event can claim a 75 percent mortality rate. The irresistible force of 300-mile-per-hour winds sitting in place for several minutes caused more complete damage than a rapidly moving tornado of similar force.

Despite all odds, there were survivors. A woman hid in her bathtub as her home was destroyed around her. Located just outside the path under weaker wind conditions, her house was carried several hundred feet away. She rode along with her house while in her tub. When she stood up at the end of her ride, the bathtub fell into pieces around her.

Even more amazing is the foresight of a family that survived beneath their house in the Double Creek subdivision. Having experienced a tornado ten years earlier, this family built a storm shelter by hand-digging a hole through the slab. Taking two years to complete, this unique structure built of solid concrete and encased beneath the original foundation may have been the only shelter that could survive the intensity and duration of the Jarrell tornado.

Don M. Greene

FOR FURTHER INFORMATION:

"Funnel Cloud of Death." *Newsweek,* June 9, 1997, 68.

Grazulis, Thomas P. *The Tornado: Nature's Ultimate Windstorm.* Norman: University of Oklahoma Press, 2003.

Lindell, Chuck. "Jarrell's Healing Year." *Austin-American Statesman,* May 24, 1998.

_____. "A New Day in Jarrell." *Austin-American Statesman,* January 4, 1998.

Phan, Long T., and Emil Simiu. *The Fujita Tornado Intensity Scale: A Critique Based on Observations of the Jarrell Tornado of May 27, 1997.* Gaithersburg, Md.: U.S. Department of Commerce, Technology Administration, National Institute of Standards and Technology, 1998.

■ 1997: SOUFRIÈRE HILLS ERUPTION

VOLCANO

DATE: June 25, 1997
PLACE: Montserrat, Caribbean
RESULT: 19 dead, 8,000 evacuated

When explorer Christopher Columbus sighted an eastern Caribbean island and named it Montserrat in 1493, no one then knew enough geography to understand what lands he could yet discover in the region, and no one yet knew—and would not know for another four and a half centuries—about plate tectonics and the geological reason for the island's existence. After permanent settlers arrived from England and Ireland in 1632, and then indentured servants and slaves from West Africa later in that century, they would be intermittently reminded of the dramatic power of volcanic activity and the evolution of such an island—a lesson that continues to this day.

GEOGRAPHY. Montserrat is an island of 39 square miles (102 square kilometers). It is one of an eastern Caribbean chain of islands, the Lesser Antilles, extending in a crescent 400 miles (650 kilometers) long, which connects the Virgin Islands in the north to Trinidad near Venezuela in the south. Montserrat is a dependent island governed by Great Britain. Some of the better-known islands in the chain are St. Kitts, Antigua, Montserrat, Guadeloupe, Dominica, Martinique, St. Lucia, St. Vincent, and Grenada. They owe their existence to the collision of tectonic plates moving slowly under the earth's surface.

While the American Plate is moving westward from the spreading Mid-Atlantic Ridge, the small Caribbean Plate (from Cuba and the West Indies south to South America) is moving relatively eastward at about 0.4 inch per year. The slow collision in the eastern Caribbean causes oceanic crust to be thrust downward, causing partial melting in the mantle, and magma (molten rock) erupts periodically to form volcanic islands.

Montserrat is, like the others in the Lesser Antilles, a typical stratovolcanic or composite-type volcano, built up of successive lava flows plus layers of ejecta (ash and larger rock fragments) erupted explosively. The process creates attractive conical-shaped volcanoes with dangerous capabilities for destruction. The magma in this crustal environment tends to be viscous, and it can congeal into a domed plug in the crater at the top of the vent of the volcano. The pressure in the subterranean magma, especially from its contained gases, can build up and produce periodic plumes of ash or, occasionally, a catastrophic and massive eruption with much ash and gas. Many of these islands have experienced volcanic activity in the past few thousand years.

The active volcano on Montserrat is called Soufrière Hills, and is about 3,000 feet (915 meters) high. The bottom of the volcano, and of the island, is on the seafloor, at a subsea depth of about 4,900 feet (1,500 meters). *La soufrière* is French for "sulfur pit," and in creole French it also refers to volcanic and sulfurous hot springs.

HISTORY OF ERUPTION. Soufrière began erupting, mostly ash and gas, on July 18, 1995, after having been dormant since the island's set-

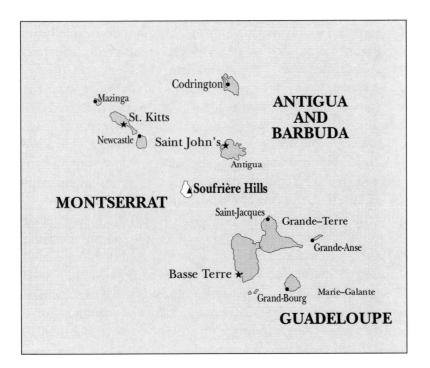

tlement. Unusual subterranean activity had been noted as early as 1989 by a local seismograph, which detects and records seismic wave vibrations from such behavior as magma cracking rock as it wells upward. The instrument was one of thirty-two seismographs situated in the Antilles Islands and operated by the Seismic Research Unit of the University of the West Indies, in Trinidad. With the active eruptive activity, an international team of geologists and geophysicists was gathered, from the Trinidad unit, the British Geological Survey, and the U.S. Geological Survey. They set up monitoring instruments on and around the volcano—seismographs and ground-deformation and gravity instruments—to try to monitor the pulse of the volcano to assess and possibly predict its future activity. This would be done at the Montserrat Volcano Observatory, which was recently established.

For several weeks, a series of earthquakes caused the volcano to tremble, and there were intermittent small phreatic (steam-charged) eruptions of fine gray ash and sulfurous gases. The ash showered the southern half of the island, including the main town and capital, Plymouth, on the southwest coast only 3 miles away.

The volcano crater began to fill with a viscous lava dome that plugged the vent. If this plug, like a cork in a bottle, could not contain the pressure, it and the underlying magma could explode up into a plume of ash and could generate fearsome pyroclastic flows down the volcano's slopes. Pyroclastic, from the Greek *pyro* for fire and *klastos* for broken, refers to the hot fragmental material being erupted, in this case as a flowing cloud of searing hot ash and gas, much of the latter poisonous. Such hot gaseous flows, or nuées ardentes, are one of the greatest hazards of eruptions. They are denser than air and thus hug the slopes, travel very fast—up to 70 to 120 miles per hour (110 to 190 kilometers per hour)—and kill people by scorching, roasting, and asphyxiating.

In late August, 1995, a series of eruptive ash events darkened the sky over Plymouth. The authorities recommended the evacuation of the south half of the island, either to the sparsely settled north end or to other islands or countries. Because no one could know when—if ever—the volcano might erupt massively, this was a wrenching development for the island society. There is uncertainty with a dome-building, slowly erupting volcano, because an end can come—after months or years—with a final catastrophic explosion or it can simply fizzle out.

Plymouth itself housed half the island's population of 11,000 as well as the nation's only port, only hospital, government, industries, and people's homes. Most of Plymouth had just been reconstructed from the effects of the devastating Hurricane Hugo of 1989. Tourism—the main economic activity, along with agriculture and a small but thriving music industry—would be decimated, unemployment would soar, and people would have to abandon their homes, schools, and farms for an indefinite time.

By the following April, 5,000 people had moved to the north end of the island, and 3,000 people had left the island. Of the latter, about 1,000 went to Great Britain, which was also providing funds on Montserrat for resettlement, social services, and maintenance of island life.

On September 17, 1996, the lava dome collapsed to produce a pyroclastic flow that moved quickly toward the sea to the east, as well as an ash plume over 32,000 feet (10 kilometers) high. The ashfall darkened the sky, and there was a sulfurous smell; the lava doming continued. By early June the following year, there were more earthquakes from the volcano and its subterranean magma chamber. A few farmers, disobeying the evacuation orders, still tended their crops on the fertile lower slopes of the volcano.

THE BIG ERUPTION. On June 25, 1997, there was a more persistent ash eruption, and at about 1 P.M. a major eruption began, finally, but as the volcanologists had feared. The crater's lava dome collapsed, and the pyroclastic ash and rubble cascaded down the volcanic slopes at more than 70 miles per hour and with a temperature of about 15,000 degrees Fahrenheit (8,000 degrees Celsius). Trees were flattened and scorched, and structures were devastated. Nineteen people were killed, by burning or asphyxiation, and many were entombed in the pyroclastic flow. Twenty-seven other people were rescued in time from the mountain region by helicopter.

In late August, 1997, there were more pyroclastic flows in all directions off the mountain. These covered the now-desolate and deserted southern half of the island and smothered Plymouth's structures that were still standing. More people left the island—many probably permanently—as life and the environment became progressively less hospitable and more uncertain. For two years, Soufrière Hills on Montserrat had been volcanically active and making the lands progressively more uninhabitable. However, some good things resulted from the eruptions: Once the activity subsided to dormancy again the ash would weather in the warm moist climate there to create new fertile soil. Also, the oceanic island was enlarged, in an age-old process, by the volcanic flows that reached and extended the shoreline.

OTHER ERUPTIONS. There are other notable eruptions in the Lesser Antilles that also involved the hazard of pyroclastic flows. In 1979, St. Vincent's volcanic peak, La Soufrière, erupted, but a prior evacuation of the area saved many lives. This was unlike May 7, 1902, there, when an explosive eruption created an ash and steam plume that rose over 30,000 feet (9 kilometers) and a pyroclastic flow that caused about 1,600 deaths. In 1976, some eruptive activity of another volcano named La Soufrière, on Guadeloupe just to the southeast of Montserrat, prompted an evacuation of 70,000 people for several months; however, in this case there were only minor explosions. The most devastating eruption was from Mount Pelée, on the island of Martinique farther to the south. On May 8, 1902, an explosion generated a pyroclastic flow that killed 30,000 people—virtually the entire town of St. Pierre.

Robert S. Carmichael

FOR FURTHER INFORMATION:
Davison, Phil. *Volcano in Paradise: The True Story of the Montserrat Eruptions.* London: Methuen, 2003.

Dittmer, Jason. "The Soufrière Hills Volcano and the Postmodern Landscapes of Montserrat." *FOCUS* 47, no. 4 (Spring, 2004): 1-7.

Druit, T.H., and B. P. Kokelaar, eds. *The Eruption of Soufrière Hills Volcano, Montserrat, from 1995 to 1999.* London: Geological Society, 2002.

Graham, Wade. "Getting to Know the Volcano." *The New Yorker* 73, no. 1 (February 17, 1997): 43-47.

Pulsipher, Lydia M. "Montserrat: The People, the Land, and the Volcano." *FOCUS* 44, no. 3 (Fall, 1997): 29-33.

Williams, A. R, and Vincent J. Musi. "Montserrat: Under the Volcano." *National Geographic* 192, no. 1 (July, 1997): 58-77.

■ 1998: Papua New Guinea tsunami

Tsunami

Date: July 17, 1998
Place: Northwestern Papua New Guinea
Result: 2,000 dead, 500 missing

On July 17, 1998, an undersea earthquake measuring 7.0 on the Richter scale struck about 18 miles (29 kilometers) off the northwest coast of Papua New Guinea. Although seismological stations in the South Pacific measured the tremor, the earthquake erupted under the seabed so close to the coast that there was no time to send warnings to villagers to evacuate.

Starting as long, silent ripples on the deep waters of the Bismarck Sea, the waves swept toward the shore at dusk. They gathered height and power as they neared the beaches around Sissano Lagoon in West Sepik Province. At that point, they were up to 33 feet (10 meters) high and sounding, some said, like a jet plane taking off. The waves crashed over the thatched wooden houses as villagers were preparing dinner. "We just saw the sea rise up and it came toward the village and we had to run for our lives," said a man who lost 8 members of his family.

The Death Toll. The population of the affected area, a strip of land about 25 miles (40 kilometers) long and 370 miles (590 kilometers) northwest of the capital Port Moresby, numbered between 8,000 and 10,000. At least 6,000 people were homeless after their houses were reduced to matchwood by the tsunami. The governor of West Sepik Province said, "I am looking at a very conservative figure of 3,000 people dead, based on the number of bodies recovered so far and the number of people seen hiding in the jungle. I've had a look and all there is are bodies. The stench is overpowering." A Roman Catholic priest echoed the governor's estimate. He said that many of those killed were children who had been too small to run away and too weak to climb coconut trees to safety before the waves engulfed them. The area disaster coordinator said that the village of Warapu alone had a death toll of 500, mostly elderly people and schoolchil-

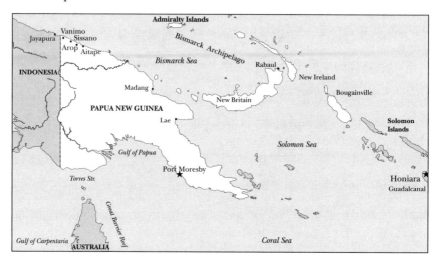

dren. "Schools in Arop, Sissano, and Warapu will be closed because we don't have the children. They're all dead," he said. The final count would be 2,500 dead or missing.

Papua New Guinea is the eastern half of the large island of New Guinea and a former British colony. It has been a member of the British Commonwealth since 1975, when Australia, which administered the country on Britain's behalf, granted it independence. Queen Elizabeth II sent a message of sympathy to the region. "She said she was shocked at the tidal wave and that her thoughts were with the families of the bereaved and injured," a Buckingham Palace spokesperson said.

RELIEF EFFORTS. A week after the disaster, the official death toll was 1,500, but thousands remained unaccounted for. Bodies, some partly eaten by crocodiles, dogs, and pigs, were still being spotted in the lagoon and nearby mangrove and bush areas. With many of the bodies quickly deteriorating because of the tropical heat, bereaved families dug makeshift graves in the rubble of their homes. There were no coffins. The dead were simply covered with straw matting. While 700 injured were being treated in local hospitals and by doctors and nurses flown in from Australia, Japan, and New Zealand, numbed survivors gathered in makeshift aid centers. Some parents had lost all of their children. Other victims had been unable to find a single family member alive. Approximately 200 children who were visiting one of the villages for a traditional festival were feared dead, swept away in an instant.

Many of the survivors, fearing more waves, took refuge on higher ground. Some walked for four hours through dense jungle to villages that lay inland. Devastation lay behind them. Village huts, some built on the sandy shoreline shaped by a 1935 tsunami, had been ripped from the ground. The region's lack of airstrips meant that Australian Army Hercules planes ferrying in medical supplies and a mobile field hospital had to land in Vanimo, the provincial capital, about 69 miles (110 kilometers) west of the disaster zone. Their cargo was then reloaded onto small planes and helicopters to be taken to the centers where aid workers and church officials cared for survivors.

Several days after the disaster, the Adventist Development and Relief Agency (ADRA) flew into the area sixteen water tanks that had been shipped from Australia the previous year for drought victims. Helicopters carried another twenty of the 317-gallon (1,200-liter) tanks into accessible areas of the rugged country. The area surrounding the lagoon and the worst-hit villages of Sissano, Warapu, and Arop were sealed off to stop the spread of disease from decaying corpses. However, some people from the vanished villages were already asking aid workers for axes and bush knives so they could rebuild their homes and vegetable plots on their traditional lands.

Dana P. McDermott

FOR FURTHER INFORMATION:

Geist, E. L. "Source Characteristics of the July 17, 1998, Papua New Guinea Tsunami." *EOS/Transactions of the American Geophysical Union* 79, supp. (1998): 571.

Monastersky, R. "How a Middling Quake Made a Giant Tsunami." *Science News* 154 (August 1, 1998): 69.

———. "Waves of Death." *Science News* 154 (October 3, 1998): 221.

Satake, Kenji, ed. *Tsunamis: Case Studies and Recent Developments.* Springer, 2006.

Tappin, David R. "Sediment Slump Likely Caused 1998 Papua New Guinea Tsunami. "*EOS/Transactions of the American Geophysical Union* 80 (July 27, 1999): 333.

■ 1998: Hurricane Mitch

Hurricane

Date: October 27, 1998
Place: Central America
Classification: Category 5
Result: More than 11,000 dead, 1 million homeless, $4 billion in damage

Hurricane Mitch began as a tropical wave that moved across West Africa beginning on October 8, 1998. For the next seven days it moved over the tropical Atlantic to the Caribbean Sea, entering that body of water on the 18th and 19th. Showers and thunderstorms developed at that time, coming to the attention of a United States Air Force Reserve reconnaissance plane patrolling the area. On October 22, the plane reported that the storm had become a tropical depression, a harbinger of the troublesome weather conditions ahead.

Mitch achieved hurricane strength on October 24, developing heavy winds and dumping enormous quantities of rain on Jamaica and the Cayman Islands. Damage to the Caribbean islands proved to be slight compared to what followed as the storm moved further west. Mitch reached the Central American coast on October 27. The hurricane turned out to be one of the most powerful Atlantic storms on record, with winds exceeding 180 miles per hour. As a result, Central America and southern Mexico experienced torrential rainfall for several days in a row, inundating some principal cities and much of the countryside as well. The U.S. National Hurricane Center classified Mitch as a Category 5 hurricane.

As it moved toward the mainland, the direction of the storm in its earliest stages proved to be unpredictable. Not knowing what to expect, most of the population of Belize City, estimated at 75,000 persons, fled inland. The refugees utilized both private transportation and government-commandeered buses. Mexico's southern state of Quintana Roo evacuated all of its villages in a 165-mile swath south of the city of Playa del Carmen. The tens of thousands of tourists staying in the resort cities of Cancún and Cozumel stood in long lines at airports seeking flights inland to any destination available that was considered outside the danger zone. Cancún had been hit in 1988 by Hurricane Gilbert, during which some 300 people were killed.

After moving briefly through the Caribbean on October 25, Mitch arrived off the coast of Honduras two days later, making landfall on the morning of the 29th. Because of the slow progress of the storm, the rainfall from it reached tremendous proportions, estimated at up to 35 inches initially, primarily in Honduras and Nicaragua. The resulting flash floods and mudslides pouring down from the isthmus's central mountain range killed thousands of people.

THE DAMAGE. The damage suffered by the areas reached by Mitch resulted primarily from the rainfall rather than the direct loss caused by the heavy winds themselves. Before it ended, the hurricane dumped a peak load of 50 inches of rain in some areas. The high waters that followed carved paths of destruction that destroyed entire neighborhoods, especially the low-lying communities exposed to raging rivers that had been only small streams prior to the hurricane.

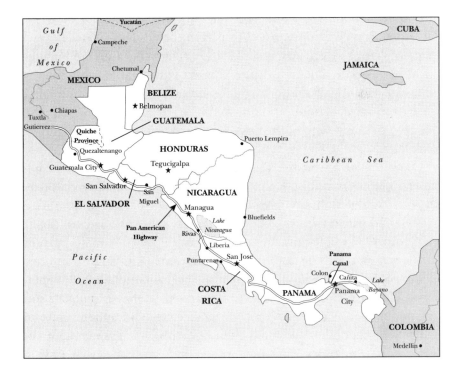

The storm not only destroyed homes but also wiped out roads, schools, and bridges, impeding any attempts to furnish aid to its victims. In addition to the destruction of the isthmus's commercial agriculture, many poor families lost the small plots of land from which they drew much of their basic diet, consisting of corn, beans, rice, and other vegetables. Fertile topsoil washed away in the heavy inundation. Chickens, pigs, and cattle also disappeared under the rising floodwaters. Military mines, souvenirs of the civil wars of the previous decade, washed down from the mountains, ending up in areas where survivors sought to start replanting. A number of deaths and serious injuries occurred after the storm was over as a result of this further threat to life and property.

Substantial damage to the commercial banana plantations along the Central American east coast also meant the loss of livelihood for hundreds of workers. Until the banana area could be replanted, estimated to take a full year at least, no work existed for the majority of the employees of such large concerns as the United Fruit Company and its numerous subsidiaries.

The contamination of local drinking water gave rise to the threat of dysentery and other waterborne communicable diseases for the survivors. People were exposed to respiratory illnesses. Wells caved in, debris clogged streams, and rotting garbage contaminated neighborhood cisterns. The authorities advised citizens that water had to be boiled before it could be used for either drinking or cooking. A large number of schools also fell victim to the storm, depriving the children in many areas of the opportunity to continue pursuing their education.

Once the storm hit the Central American mainland, it soon became apparent that the neighboring countries of Honduras and Nicaragua would sustain the most damage, with lesser problems arising in El Salvador and Guatemala. Mitch largely spared Belize, southern Mexico, and Costa Rica.

Nicaragua's most deadly loss occurred when a mudslide, triggered by the collapse of a wall of the volcano Casitas, wiped out whole villages. The onrushing mud and rain reached to the rooftops of the tiny pueblo of El Porvenir, close to the volcano, and buried many of its inhabitants before they had the opportunity to evacuate. Posoltega, another nearby village, met an equally horrendous fate. Only a few hundred of its 2,000 inhabitants survived the sea of mud that tore through the small hamlet.

In its initial assessment, the Honduran government estimated that the final death count in the country could reach 5,000. Honduras's president, Carlos Roberto Flores Facusse, said that the floods and landslides had wiped out many villages as well as whole neighborhoods in the larger cities. Two large rivers, the Ulúa and Chameleon, rose so high as to isolate Honduras's second major city, San Pedro Sula, and convert the valley surrounding it into a lake. The Choluteca River near the country's capital, Tegucigalpa, also flooded over its banks, pouring into the city at such a rapid rate that the water reached the second story of Tegucigalpa's major commercial buildings. The president estimated that the storm had destroyed over 70 percent of the nation's crops, the economic mainstay of this nation of 6 million people. The dollar crop loss amounted to $6 billion for the impoverished country. One million homes needed to be replaced.

El Salvador, on Central America's west coast, suffered mostly from the heavy runoff of rain from the mountains of its eastern highlands. The water poured into the country's principal river, the Lempa, so quickly that it destroyed a number of villages on its banks. Remote villages, such as Chicuma, El Salitre, Las Marías, and Hacienda Vieja, lost all of their subsistence crops.

While Guatemala did not experience the same degree of damage as did neighboring Honduras and Nicaragua, the Polochic River Valley and the southern coast lost over $1 million in vital food supplies as well as a substantial amount of housing and potable water. A plane carrying religious missionaries seeking to do relief work crashed, killing 10 passengers and injuring 7 others. The plane had sought to fly into San Andreas Xecul, 60 miles west of Guatemala City, during the downpour.

RELIEF EFFORTS. For Nicaragua and Honduras, the poorest of the Central American republics, Mitch created an economic disaster. Neither country possessed the resources to meet their immediate emergency requirements, much less the long-term essentials needed restore the countries to their pre-hurricane conditions. Their governments pleaded for outside assistance.

The destruction of the roads and bridges throughout Central America precluded any rapid response by surface vehicles to much of the damaged countryside. As a result, both foreign governments and private groups began massive airlifts, utilizing light planes and helicopters to ship emergency food and medical supplies into the more remote areas of both countries.

President Bill Clinton of the United States pledged $80 million for immediate emergency aid, then raised the total dollar commitment to $300 million by March, 1999. Former U.S. president Jimmy Carter urged that the $16 billion in foreign debt owed by Honduras and Nicaragua be forgiven by their First World creditors. Scores of nongovernmental organizations throughout Europe, including those from such small countries as Ireland, Finland, and Denmark, joined in the major effort. Mitch had set the economic development of Central America back by twenty years.

The United States government sent in Army engineers to reconstruct the key roads necessary to open the badly damaged backlands. The engineers built four pontoon bridges at critical junctures to replace key destroyed structures. These so-called temporary replacements were designed to be strong enough to support all but the heaviest of trucks, supplies, and equipment. Military helicopters from a number of countries continued to push far into the hinterland to deliver food and medical supplies and to establish bases from which the rescuers could operate. Medical teams from the U.S. Army, Navy, and Air Force, the reserves from all three, and the National Guard sent in medical teams to cope with respiratory and gastrointestinal diseases and cholera.

A major problem developed with the indiscriminate influx of various types of medicinal supplies into the beleaguered countries. Initially, the affected countries provided little direction for their transmittal. Finally, the Pan American Health Organization took over and established a priority list of critical medicines that the personnel on site felt were needed, seeking to end the shipment of unwanted or inappropriate drugs.

The response to requests for aid by Central Americans living abroad proved to be overwhelming. Southern California, home to many Central American immigrant families, responded with tons of medicines, food, and clothing. The American Red Cross alone received over 100,000 inquiries during the first five days following the commencement of the storm. Directed to deliver their contributions to the consulates representing Honduras and Nicaragua, those anxious to help found that these officials could not cope with the influx of aid packages. The sorting, boxing, and storage of the goods and their transportation to Central America were beyond the physical and financial capabilities of these small offices.

Confusion reigned when the goods arrived at their Central American destinations as well. Neither Honduras nor Nicaragua had organized distribution centers to process the materials received from various overseas sources. At the Honduran port of Puerto Cortés, by early January, over 1,000 huge containers of relief supplies lay unclaimed at the docks. Ships seeking to unload more supplies had a difficult time finding any adequate space ashore for their cargos.

In the case of Nicaragua, the Catholic Church had been designated initially to fulfill the distribution function. A change in government plans resulted when President Arnoldo Alemán assigned his Liberal Party to the task, seeking to take political advantage of the catastrophe. Not only did many of the contributions end up in hands for which they were not originally intended, but also a great deal of the material continued to remain stranded at the airport and seaport sites where it had been unloaded. Alemán, in a further gesture of defiance to the international community, refused to allow President Fidel Castro's Cuban medical teams and supplies to enter the country, despite the great shortage throughout the devastated areas of Nicaragua.

Faced with the backup of supplies, relief agencies asked the public to donate cash rather than goods. Unfortunately, those wishing to help preferred to collect canned goods and clothing in their own communities regardless of how appropriate such collected goods were. They continued to ship the accumulated commodities to the already-crowded port facilities. Once there, local relief organizations, hamstrung by local government red tape, quite often lacked the funds to pay for shipment of the goods into the interior.

Moreover, the fact that the major commercial fruit companies had to devise a recovery program before they could start producing for the export market exacerbated the problems for both Honduras and Nicaragua. The two countries characteristically suffer a high unemployment rate, but Mitch wiped out most of the jobs held by those agricultural workers with the big fruit producers. The number of laborers heading north to the United States to find work increased substantially. Often they were accompanied by young boys and girls of school age who could not continue their education because of the heavy destruction of the school plants throughout the isthmus. Moreover, rumors began to circulate among the unemployed that the U.S. government had approved the entry of immigrants into the country because of Mitch's damage. Such was not the case. The government had agreed only to suspend temporarily the deportation of illegals already residing in the United States. The new wave of illegal immigrants, when apprehended, were turned back by the American border patrol.

CONCLUSION. Hurricane Mitch precipitated a series of unmitigated disasters in Central America. Thousands of residents of the isthmus either died, suffered debilitating injuries, or simply disappeared as a result of the storm's ferocity. The infrastructure to all the countries in the area experienced extensive damage. Mitch destroyed roads, bridges, communications lines, and key public buildings, such as hospitals and schools. Critical crops and livestock were lost in the ensuing deluge. Long after the storm was over, corpses littered the paths of the torrents of water that had passed through inhabited areas.

Within a few days of the storm's inception it became apparent that both Honduras and Nicaragua would sustain the greatest long-term damage. Whole communities in both countries had disappeared under the heavy inundations that accompanied the fierce winds. The governments of the two nations could not cope with the immensity of the tragedy. The rest of the world community would have to respond to the emergency created by the hurricane.

During the decade prior to the 1998 debacle, the U.S. government gradually had reduced the aid it had provided to the fledgling democracies of the area. Having determined that Central America would not fall under the influence of the former Soviet Union and Cuba, the interests of American foreign policy turned elsewhere. U.S. aid had amounted to hundreds of millions of dollars to rightist elements in conflict with leftist governments and insurrections, but the American government stopped paying. By 1998, aid to El Salvador had diminished from $500 million annually to a mere $35 million. At one time in the 1980's the American government had spent over $300 million a year supporting Nicaragua's Contra movement. In 1998 the U.S. commitment to that country had dropped to $24 million.

Nevertheless, when Mitch hit the isthmus the United States quickly furnished emergency aid. Other countries, large and small, forwarded money and relief supplies as well. The World Bank provided emergency loans for the reconstruction of both housing and commercial buildings. Nongovernmental organizations, such as the American Red Cross, Cooperative for American Relief to Everywhere (CARE), and United Nations Children's Fund (UNICEF), responded promptly with goods and aid workers.

The work of the rehabilitation of Central America would continue for a long time, taking years for the area to recover from the effects of the storm. The vast majority of the region's poor still live below the poverty level. It has been argued that the United States could do some things to alleviate some of Central America's economic and social problems: canceling the outstanding debt owed to the United States by Honduras and Nicaragua, offering the same trade agreements to Central America as are presently enjoyed by Mexico and Canada under the North American Free Trade Agreement (NAFTA) treaty, and giving Central American immigrants currently residing and working in the United States at least temporary protection from deportation until the economic emergencies in their home countries are brought under control.

Suggested measures for improving the Central American economy from within included the affected governments launching social programs designed to alleviate the economic hardship facing the poorest segments of their societies. Restoration of the economies cannot be left to market conditions or to chance. Also, a common emergency policy in the region would ensure a cooperative effort to meet the threat of other natural disasters like Hurricane Mitch, which are likely to threaten Central America again in the future.

Carl Henry Marcoux

FOR FURTHER INFORMATION:

Carrier, Jim. *The Ship and the Storm: Hurricane Mitch and the Loss of the "Fantome."* New York: McGraw-Hill, 2002.

Gass, Vicki. *Democratizing Development: Lessons from Hurricane Mitch Re-*

construction. Washington, D.C.: Washington Office on Latin America, 2002.

Granby, Phil. "Hurricane Mitch Aftermath." *JAMA: Journal of the American Medical Association* 281 (April 7, 1999): 1162.

Lapp, Elam D. *Hurricane Mitch in Central America.* Millersburg, Pa.: Brookside, 1999.

LeoGrande, William M. "Central America's Agony." *The Nation,* January 25, 1999, 21.

Mastin, Mark C. *Flood-Hazard Mapping in Honduras in Response to Hurricane Mitch.* Tacoma, Wash.: U.S. Department of the Interior, U.S. Geological Survey, 2002.

Padgett, Tim. "The Catastrophe of Hurricane Mitch." *Time International,* November 16, 1998.

Zarembo, Alan. "Helping Honduras." *U.S. News & World Report,* December 21, 1998.

_____. "A Hurricane's Orphans." *Newsweek,* March 15, 1999, 43.

■ 1999: THE GALTÜR AVALANCHE

AVALANCHE

DATE: February 23-24, 1999
PLACE: Galtür and Valzur, Austria
RESULT: 38 dead, 10 houses destroyed, 2,000 trapped

The winter of 1998-1999 produced heavy snowfalls in the Alpine countries of Europe: Switzerland, Austria, southeastern France, and northern Italy. After several winters of little snowfall—and therefore poor skiing conditions—the snow was welcomed by skiers, hoteliers, tour operators, and local inhabitants involved in the tourist industry. Unfortunately, the snow produced a number of hazards and disasters, the worst of which befell the two neighboring Austrian villages of Galtür and Valzur.

These small but popular resorts, known as the Gem of the Tirol, lie almost at the end of the Paznaun Valley, which runs approximately 25 miles southwestward from Landeck, in the western Tirol. The valley nearly touches the neighboring Austrian province of the Vorarlberg and runs almost to the Swiss border. Conditions in the valley had been deteriorating for six days before the first avalanche struck Galtür. The previous Wednesday, February 17, a storm had broken. The villages had been whipped by high winds and heavy snow, closing the main road down the valley. A small slide hit Galtür, "a wall of white and black," as an eyewitness described it, but it went largely unreported. The temperature rose sharply over the weekend of February 20-21, but snow continued to fall. Tourists were being told, however, that it was still safe at Galtür, even though notices of high avalanche risk had been issued at the main resort of Ischgl.

Meanwhile, conditions were deteriorating elsewhere in the Alps. On February 20, 100 tourists, including Queen Beatrix of the Netherlands and Princess Caroline of Monaco, had been flown to safety by helicopter from the Austrian ski resort of Lech. By Monday, February 22, the Chamonix Valley in the French Alps had been closed off because of the risk of avalanches, and the melting snow was causing flooding along the Rhine and elsewhere. In Valais, Switzerland, an avalanche was being reported every twenty minutes, and in the worst of them, 9 chalets and a car were swept away, leaving 8 people missing and 2 dead.

In western Austria (the Vorarlberg and Tirol), some 30,000 tourists were trapped in various ski resorts because of heavy snowfall, maximum avalanche warnings having been issued. In Galtür itself, Monday, February 22, saw temperatures drop and the wind pick up again. On the same day, chamois (small goatlike antelope) were spotted coming down off the high mountains into the valley, an unusual event. The mood in the village was becoming uneasy.

THE AVALANCHE. On Tuesday, February 23, a traditional ski race had been arranged around the village streets to alleviate the boredom of the skiers who had, by now, been unable to ski for a week. Many people, fortunately, left their chalets and hotels to gather in the main square to watch, despite blizzard conditions that afternoon. Suddenly a great wall of snow, some 45 feet high, rushed down on the village, demolishing a boardinghouse, ripping off the two top floors of two houses, and filling many other houses completely with snow, trapping those inside. Nobody had heard the avalanche coming; they were suddenly plunged into a darkness created by a thick white cloud, like very dense fog. The avalanche did not reach the main square, however, stopping just short of the church. People were immediately dazed and shocked, but locals began digging into the snow at once, as it takes only fifteen minutes to be suffocated if buried within the snow.

The avalanche had, in fact, forked into two parts, with the other branch going around the western part of the village, causing serious damage to chalets on the outskirts. The maximum speed was esti-

mated at 180 miles per hour. The weather forecast continued to call for poor conditions, and new snow was expected. Because of this, relief efforts from the outside could not begin until early the next morning.

DIGGING OUT. On Wednesday, the skies were clear for the first time in a week. At 7 A.M., two hundred Austrian soldiers and firemen arrived by helicopter to take over the rescue operations. Using dogs and scanning equipment, they managed to recover 18 corpses, including 3 children and a pregnant mother, but by the end of the day 15 people were still missing. A serious effort was also being made to helicopter out some 2,000 villagers and tourists to Landeck, but even with helicopters landing and taking off every two minutes many were left waiting when bad weather closed in again. Some people had only blankets and tea, according to a local doctor.

Worse was to follow. A second avalanche hit the neighboring village of Valzur on February 24, destroying 4 houses and burying 6 people. The snowslide was 45 feet high and some 600 feet wide and traveled up to 180 miles per hour. Four bodies were immediately recovered, but 9 more remained missing.

Perhaps one of the most amazing rescues was at Valzur. A four-year-old boy, Alexander Walter, was found by rescue dogs after one hundred minutes; he was pronounced dead at first but was resuscitated in the helicopter and taken to the hospital at Zams, where he made a full recovery within six days. It was suggested that his young age had saved him, his body having closed down so as to need almost no oxygen.

The next day, Thursday, February 25, sunshine returned, but by then, the three-hundred-strong rescue team had begun to crumple with fatigue and the emotional strain of finding corpses. Counselors were helping them, parents who had lost children, and disoriented children. One German woman, for example, had survived, only to learn that her two children were dead. The Austrian helicopters had been joined by those from Italy and U.S. bases in Bavaria and were able to evacuate all those remaining who wished to leave.

Rescuers found 2 more bodies the next day at Galtür, bringing the total to 30, and 2 more in Valzur, bringing the final death toll there to 7. They were still looking for a girl believed to be in the ruins of the house where her parents' bodies had been discovered. The body of the fourteen-year-old German girl was finally found in the cellar on the 27th.

The victims were taken to St. Wilten monastery chapel, Innsbruck. Sunday, February 28, was declared a day of mourning by the Austrian prime minister, Viktor Klima. Thirty-eight bodies were buried that morning in a service attended by the prime minister and representatives from those countries affected—Germany, the Netherlands, and Denmark in particular. The disaster was the worst in Austria in nearly fifty years, when in 1954 more than 50 people had been killed at Blons in the Vorarlberg.

Amazingly, some one thousand tourists chose to stay in Galtür to complete their holiday or wait for the roads to reopen, even though local authorities, backed by the Austrian government, had decided to evacuate the whole valley. At Ischgl, many returned to skiing on the slopes, though they too were unable to get out of the village.

CONTROVERSY. By now, serious criticisms were being leveled against the Austrian tourist industry for ignoring avalanche warnings from meteorologists and against tour companies for bringing out yet more skiers. The largest British tour operator, Thomsons, did cancel vacations to Galtür and four other destinations (St. Anton and Ischgl in Austria, Zermatt and Grindelwald in Switzerland), offering full refunds, but most operators merely sent their clients to different resorts. It was estimated that another 15,000 Britons alone were heading for the Alps at the weekend, while tourists who were stuck there had to hire private helicopters to get out. One German lawyer trapped at Ischgl threatened to sue the authorities for negligence.

SCIENTIFIC QUESTIONS. The immediate scientific causes for the avalanche lie in the types of snowfall in the preceding months, although a very hot summer in 1998 had given rise to speculation that the winter would not be normal. In late January there were heavy snowfalls, but the snow was light and dry. This was followed by another snowfall in mid-February that was very wet and heavy, due to different temperatures. The snow base was therefore very unstable, the heavy snow not binding at all with the light snow, which in itself was not solid enough to act as a foundation. The second snowfall had been exceptionally heavy: 12.1 feet (3. 7 meters) of snow fell in February in the Galtür area, four times the average for the month.

This was not all, however. Gale-force winds at high altitudes, up to

Rescue workers uncover the body of a Galtür avalanche victim. (AP/ Wide World Photos)

95 miles per hour, had left some mountaintops bare, causing huge accumulations of snow on the sheltered slopes. The winds were then followed by rain, which made the snow even heavier and more unstable. These factors made the avalanche risk huge. Even so, Christian Weber, an Austrian avalanche expert, was quoted as saying, "With all

our predictive mechanisms, we were not able to forecast Galtür. Avalanches are coming and crashing down in areas where they never happened before."

In the longer term, the joint effects of increased road traffic through the Alps—both heavy trucks and tourist cars—with the resultant increase in pollution, and of global warming are creating new climatic conditions, whose effects are not yet certain. The summers seem to be longer, delaying the snowfall. Such changing environmental factors raise serious questions over the future safety of skiing in the Alpine region.

POLITICAL QUESTIONS. As indicated, both the Austrian authorities and the tourist industry were blamed for the loss of lives. Although it is difficult to know whether the number of tourists in Galtür had any significant effect on the force of the avalanche, it is possible to question both the building regulations and the early warning systems. In Switzerland, new chalets are banned in all areas likely to suffer from avalanches; this is not so in Austria.

The other questions, about the number of tourists allowed in and the problem of dissuading them from coming, are more complicated. On the Tuesday of the Galtür avalanche, Hansjorg Kroll, chief of tourism of the Austrian chamber of commerce, is quoted as saying, "We must thank the Lord God for sending us this snow." With bookings up 30 percent over several poor seasons, there seemed every justification for such a statement. However, it is not merely the number of skiers that is significant, it is also the areas to which they are allowed to go. Although this does not seem to have been significant at Galtür, elsewhere avalanches were set off by skiers going off the trails. Where some warnings were posted for the areas, no one seemed to want to pay attention. Officials concluded that there was thus an urgent need to reassess the demands of the tourist industry, which is much needed for the local economy, against the needs for safety.

David Barratt

FOR FURTHER INFORMATION:

BBC. *Horizon.* "Anatomy of an Avalanche." www.bbc.co.uk/science/horizon/1999/avalanche.shtml.

The Sunday Times (London), February 28, 1999.

The Times (London), February 23-March 1, 1999.

■ 1999: THE OKLAHOMA TORNADO OUTBREAK

TORNADOES

DATE: May 3, 1999
PLACE: Primarily central Oklahoma, especially near Oklahoma City, and Sedgwick County, Kansas
CLASSIFICATION: Up to F5
RESULT: 49 dead, more than 900 injured, more than 17,000 buildings damaged or destroyed, about $1.5 billion in damage

According to the weather forecast that the *Daily Oklahoman* published early in the morning of Monday, May 3, 1999, Oklahoma City was to have winds that day ranging from 10 to 20 miles an hour, but storms were possible in much of Oklahoma the following day. That forecast of storms, as events turned out, was off by a day.

At about 6:00 Monday morning in Norman, a short drive south of Oklahoma City, the Storm Prediction Center of the National Weather Service noted a dry line extending from south to north across the panhandles of Texas and Oklahoma and said there was a low possibility of severe thunderstorms and even tornadoes in Oklahoma as a result of this meeting of hot, dry air from the west and warm, wet air from the east. By 11:15 that morning, the possibility had become moderate. By 3:49 P.M., after having received weather-balloon readings indicating layers of winds in different directions and at different speeds, the Storm Prediction Center officially revised its forecast to include a high possibility of dangerous spring storms.

When, at 4:30 P.M., radar in Norman found a tornado in a supercell, the National Weather Service sent out a tornado warning for central Oklahoma, including metropolitan Oklahoma City. Fifteen minutes later, a tornado touched the ground near Lawton, in the southwestern part of the state. An evening of death and destruction had begun for both Oklahoma and Kansas.

STORMS. Of the 76 tornadoes that formed late in the afternoon and night of May 3, the worst was the 0.5-mile-wide one, which traveled about 90 miles in Oklahoma from the Lawton area northeast into the central part of the state. That long path included 19 miles through the Oklahoma City area only a little after the evening rush hour, from the unincorporated community of Bridge Creek in northeastern Grady County; through the big suburbs of Moore, Del City, and Midwest City; to the town of Choctaw in eastern Oklahoma County. According to meteorologists from the University of Oklahoma, the rotating wind in that tornado reached the very top of the F5 category of the Fujita scale—318 miles an hour—and may have set a record speed up to that date for any natural wind on earth. That monstrous tornado was one of from three to five produced along one storm path.

Among the other storm paths in Oklahoma, a second, northwest of the greatest one, reached from southern Blaine County well into Kingfisher County, where the little town of Dover endured an F4 tornado, with wind between 207 and 260 miles an hour. A third storm path, west and north of Oklahoma City, stretched from northern Grady County into Noble County; in Logan County, that storm path generated another F4 tornado. A fourth storm path, south and east of the metropolitan area, extended from eastern Cleveland County through Pottawatomie County and into Lincoln County. That same night, in Kansas, a severe thunderstorm generated tornadoes in Sedgwick County. Most notably, an F4 tornado passed through Haysville and the adjacent southern part of Wichita.

PROPERTY. In all, tornadoes in the Great Plains on May 3 caused such damage that President Bill Clinton declared Sedgwick County, Kansas, a disaster area, along with 11 counties in Oklahoma, from Caddo and Grady Counties, southeast of Oklahoma City, to Tulsa County, in the northeastern part of the state. Property damage in the two states was about $1.5 billion, and while people in the building trades found their work in high demand after the storms, many other people worried about how they would ever make a living again.

As in all tornadoes, motor vehicles and mobile homes were especially vulnerable. Whirling winds tossed cars many yards from where they had been and flipped them upside down; even huge tractor-trailer rigs fell victim to the winds. The big tornado in Sedgwick County shredded and knocked over trailers in the Lakeshore Mobile

Homes Resort and at Pacesetter Mobile Homes; earlier, the even more powerful tornado in central Oklahoma had devastated mobile homes in the Southern Hills section of Bridge Creek.

More surprising, for persons accustomed only to weak tornadoes, the most powerful of the tornadoes on May 3 virtually flattened solidly built, fairly new houses, as in the especially hard-hit Highland Park neighborhood in Moore, Oklahoma, where concrete slabs were the chief evidence after the storm of the sites of many families' homes. The devastation there and in other severely affected neighborhoods and towns resembled the devastation from wartime bombing, as one Oklahoma City survivor said. In some places, cars rested where houses had once stood, debris seemed to be everywhere, and returning citizens, deprived of landmarks, could hardly find where they had lived before the storm had struck.

Schools and businesses also sustained damage. In Moore, the F5 tornado wrecked part of Westmoore High School; not long afterward, in tiny Mulhall, Oklahoma, north of Oklahoma City, another tornado destroyed the elementary school. At Stroud, a town of 3,200 on Interstate 44, midway between Tulsa and Oklahoma City, the damage to businesses imperiled the town's economic life, because the tornado that passed through the town tore much of the roof off the Integris Stroud Municipal Hospital; devastated the headquarters of the Sygma Network, a distributor of restaurant supplies; badly damaged the Wendy's Restaurant, the Best Western Motel, and two mobile home parks; and in effect destroyed the large Tanger Outlet Mall that had for several years been a familiar sight to motorists between Oklahoma's two largest cities.

PEOPLE. Even more important than the indirect effects the tornadoes of May 3 had on people through the immense destruction of property were the direct effects the tornadoes had through injuries and death. Altogether, 49 people died because of the dangerous weather, 44 in Oklahoma and 5 in Kansas. More than 900 other persons in those states suffered injuries.

The scenes of horror were many. For instance, while the F5 tornado was ravaging Bridge Creek, Oklahoma, a mother and her six-year-old son raced toward a creek to take what meager shelter they could, but the child saw his mother fly away in the wind and looked for her in vain after the storm. After the tornadoes in the Wichita area, police officers saw the body of a young, bearded man lying with his face in storm water amid the wreckage at Pacesetter Mobile Homes. On May 12, nine days after the storm, two young women were searching together on their own for the last of the Oklahoma missing, Tram Thu Bui, in the hope of finding her alive. Instead, they found her dead, her shoulder exposed amid wreckage in a ditch in Moore, 50 yards from the overpass under which she, her husband, her daughter, her son, and other persons had tried to take refuge when the tornado had approached as they were traveling on Interstate 35.

Along with the horror, however, came heroism and generosity. Official storm chasers and law enforcement officers sometimes risked their lives as they tried to warn people of oncoming tornadoes. Rescue workers, paid and unpaid, roamed through debris looking for the dead and the living. Members of the National Guard patrolled ravaged neighborhoods, and nurses, doctors, and other medical professionals worked hour after hour to care for the wounded. Crews from utility companies labored to ensure public safety and eventually to restore water, electricity, gas, and telephone service. Charitable organizations sent their workers and opened their buildings to help. In Moore, the First Baptist Church, just east of Interstate 35 and adjacent to the Highland Park neighborhood, became a makeshift hospital soon after the F5 tornado had done enormous damage nearby.

Letting the tall, generator-lit cross at the front of the building serve as a beacon for the hurt and homeless, rescuers established a triage center in one part of the building, while the choir room became a temporary morgue.

A few of the heroes died while saving other persons. Ordinary people did extraordinary things. For example, to save her eleven-year-old son, Levi, Kathleen Walton released her grip on him as the giant tornado in metropolitan Oklahoma City sucked her out from under the overpass on Interstate 35 where they had sought shelter. Not far away, in Del City, Gustia Miller, seventy-six years old, and his wife, Dorothy, tried to use their bathtub as a tornado shelter when the same tornado approached their home. When the bathroom window broke, Mr. Miller put himself in extreme peril to hold a pillow to the opening in an effort to keep debris from hitting his wife. During the night, he died of his injuries.

Yet there were happy stories too. For days after the tornadoes, a British couple, John and Barbara Potten, were feared dead. They had been touring the United States in a motor home and had telephoned relatives in Britain around 3:00 in the afternoon of May 3 to report their arrival in south Oklahoma City. When, the next day, they failed to follow their standard practice of calling home, their relatives and Oklahoma law enforcement officers worried. In reality, however, the Pottens had quickly driven out of Oklahoma when they had learned of the possibility of tornadoes and, several days later, near the Canadian border, they called relatives in Australia. Amazingly, another person was found alive in a dramatic incident. Soon after the huge tornado had hit Bridge Creek, Oklahoma, Grady County deputy sheriff Robert Jolley, looking at rubble, spotted brown hair and realized that a silent baby was lying in the mud. When he had dug her out and started cleaning the mud from her eyes, she began crying, much to his relief; he took her to a school where emergency medical technicians were working. Thus, although her grandmother, Catherine Crago, died in the tornado, ten-month-old Aleah Crago survived without serious injury.

LESSONS. Besides lessons about courage and generosity, one of the lessons Oklahomans and Kansans learned from the tornadoes of May 3, 1999, was the importance of skillfully operated, technologically sophisticated equipment for the detection both of the weather conditions that produce tornadoes and of the tornadoes themselves. The expensive Next Generation Weather Radar (NEXRAD) used by the National Weather Service meteorologists in Norman led to early and accurate tornado warnings and therefore saved many lives. Had there been no radar at all, and had there been no warnings broadcast on radio and television, the death toll would have been enormous, especially in the Oklahoma City and Wichita metropolitan areas.

Another lesson is one that President Bill Clinton mentioned while touring a devastated neighborhood in Del City, Oklahoma, on Saturday, May 8. Looking at the ruins of homes, he noted how few of them had had basements or storm cellars and urged his audience to include safe rooms when they rebuilt their houses. Designed at Texas Tech University, safe rooms are closetlike shelters on the ground floor inside houses; indeed, interest in safe rooms greatly increased in the disaster areas after May 3, as did interest in old-fashioned storm cellars and in above-ground shelters standing outside the home. Thousands of victims, along with many thousands of others, realized in the aftermath of the tornadoes of May 3 how powerful those storms can be.

Victor Lindsey

FOR FURTHER INFORMATION:

Federal Emergency Management Agency. *Midwest Tornadoes of May 3, 1999: Observations, Recommendations, and Technical Guidance.* Washington, D.C.: Author, 1999.

Kavanaugh, Lee Hill. "'Slight' Chance of Storms, Then . . . Death Dropped from Sky." *Kansas City Star,* May 5, 1999, p. A1.

Riley, Michael A. *Reconnaissance Report on Damage to Engineered Structures During the May, 1999, Oklahoma City Tornado.* Gaithersburg, Md.: U.S. Department of Commerce, Technology Administration, National Institute of Standards and Technology, 2002.

Stevens, William K. "Winds of Change." *Tulsa World,* May 16, 1999.

U.S. National Weather Service. *Oklahoma/Southern Kansas Tornado Outbreak of May 3, 1999.* Silver Spring, Md.: U.S. Department of Commerce, National Oceanic and Atmospheric Administration, National Weather Service, 1999.

Zollo, Cathy. "Tornadoes Were in the Air." *Wichita Falls Times Record News,* May 5, 1999.

■ 1999: THE İZMIT EARTHQUAKE

EARTHQUAKE

ALSO KNOWN AS: The Kocaeli earthquake, the Marmara earthquake
DATE: August 17, 1999
PLACE: Northwestern Turkey
MAGNITUDE: 7.4
RESULT: More than 17,000 dead, 25,000 injured, more than 250,000 homeless, 17,000 buildings destroyed, 25,000 buildings badly damaged, total economic cost estimated at $15 billion

The Northern Anatolian fault, which is some 600 miles long, runs east to west through northern Turkey, paralleling the coastline of the Black Sea. It marks the division of the Eurasian Plate to the north and the Anatolian Plate to the south. The Anatolian Plate itself is a small plate, wedged between the north-thrusting Arabian and African Plates. It is highly unstable—both the Northern and Southern Anatolian faults have given rise to frequent earthquakes over the centuries. Like the San Andreas fault in California, the Anatolian fault is a right lateral strike-slip fault, about 10 miles deep. Also like the San Andreas fault, it moves about an eighth of an inch a year and has branches at either end.

Seismologists noted a steady east-to-west shift of earthquake epicenters along the North Anatolian fault in the twentieth century, thrusting the Anatolian Plate in a westward direction. An earthquake occurred in eastern Turkey, for example, with a magnitude of 7.9 on the Richter scale, followed by another, some 100 miles to the west, in 1942, with a magnitude of 7.1. Then, just two years later, in an area north of the capital Ankara, in central Turkey, another earthquake occurred, with a magnitude of 7.3.

Since then, earthquakes occurred along the fault in 1957 and 1967, each one moving further west, of approximately the same magnitude. Seismologists warned the Turkish government that the next earthquake along the fault could be in northwestern Turkey, and that suitable preparations needed to be made. More specifically, in 1997, Ross Stein, a geophysicist at the U.S. Geological Survey at

Menlo Park, California, suggested, together with two colleagues, that there was "an increased probability" that the next earthquake would be around İzmit, some 50 miles east of Istanbul, Turkey's largest city.

Northwestern Turkey is the most densely populated area in the country. With 20 million inhabitants, it contains nearly a third of Turkey's population. In it lies Istanbul, with 8 million inhabitants, growing at a rate of almost half a million a year; the new industrial areas around İzmit, with over half a million inhabitants; and Bursa, with nearly 1 million residents. Some new resort areas along the south coast of the Sea of Marmara, especially on the Gulf of İzmit around the town of Yalova, are also located in northwest Turkey. Half the nation's production takes place in the eleven provinces (or counties) surrounding Istanbul. Many migrants from the relatively poor areas of eastern Turkey come to these cities and towns to find work. A major oil refinery was constructed by the government-owned gas company just outside İzmit, as well as Honda and Toyota vehicle factories, a Pirelli tire factory, and several other multimillion-dollar construction projects largely financed by Western companies. Many small-scale businesses also sprang up. New hotels and apartment blocks were quickly constructed to deal with the sudden boom in workers and tourists. Swampland was drained around the Gulf of İzmit to create more building space.

To guard against earthquake hazards, the Turkish government laid down strict building codes, equal, it claimed, to those in force in other earthquake-prone areas, such as California and Japan. These included regulations of the height of buildings (a two-story maximum in many cases), quality of concrete, strength of steel rods, and depth of foundations. Unfortunately, the inspection and control of these regulations was left in the hands of local city and town officials, who were subject to political pressures, bribery, and lack of expertise. Enforcement procedures were generally weak.

Turkey itself is a centralized secular country, even though 99 percent of its population is Muslim. It has had a number of military regimes, and the army has always been large for the size of the country—some 800,000 personnel. Turkey's democratic structures have been considered weak and open to corruption. Nevertheless, respect for the country has been continuously inculcated into the population, particularly in an effort to keep the state secular—its ideal when the country became a republic after World War I. The economy grew during the 1990's at a rate of 7 to 8 percent yearly. At the time of the 1999 earthquake it was economically sound, despite some loss of tourist revenue over recent terrorist attacks by Kurdish rebels. Its annual gross national product stood at $200 billion.

THE EARTHQUAKE. At 3:02 A.M. on Tuesday, August 17, a temblor shook northwestern Turkey with its epicenter near İzmit. It lasted forty-five seconds. First estimates of its magnitude were put at 7.1 by the National Earthquake Information Center at Golden, Colorado, and at 6.8 by the Turkish authorities. Both figures were later revised to 7.4, making it one of the worst quakes to hit Turkey in the twentieth century. It was felt as far away as Ankara, 270 miles to the east.

At the time the quake hit, the population was asleep, so first reports were confused. A few deaths at Adama, Eskisehir, and Istanbul, 162 in total, were reported on Turkish television at daylight. One of the worst-hit areas was Bursa, the foreign press reported, where an oil refinery was blazing out of control. (In fact, the refinery was at İzmit.) As the day wore on, it became clear that the worst-hit areas were

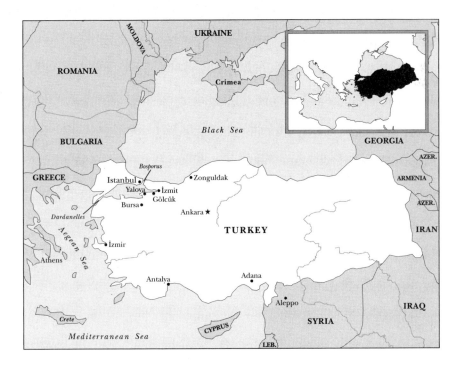

İzmit; Gölcük, where there was a naval base; and Yalova, where 90 percent of the houses had collapsed. At Gölcük 248 sailors and officers were reported trapped under collapsed buildings.

It soon became apparent that initial numbers were hopelessly underestimated. Large parts of many towns and cities had been totally devastated, many buildings had simply collapsed on their sleeping occupants, and many others that remained standing were in too perilous a condition for people to remain. A seawall had given way in the Bay of Haldere, and further along the coast, a mile of shoreline had sunk into the sea. Many places within an area of 100 miles east of Istanbul were without electricity and water. Road and rail communications were severely disrupted by fallen bridges and sunken pavements, although telephone communications between the main cities were quickly restored. So many aftershocks occurred (250 within the first twenty-four hours, 1,000 in the ensuing month) that people were afraid to stay indoors even when their houses stood secure.

RESCUE AND RELIEF EFFORTS. By the end of the first day, the Turkish government had reported 13,000 injured. Hospital beds were set up in the streets of İzmit. In one of the suburbs of Istanbul, reporters saw piles of debris 20 feet higher than the bulldozers that were working to rescue people from the collapsed buildings. In fact, bulldozers and other heavy moving equipment were in very short supply over the first few days, and most early rescue attempts were characterized by families and neighbors working by hand or with small-scale machinery—often borrowed or stolen—to rescue their kin. Many inhabitants seemed too shocked and dazed to do anything.

Soon, great tent cities sprang up for the homeless, whose numbers were constantly being revised upward, finally reaching half a million people. Some of the shortage of suitable vehicles could be explained by their being trapped or destroyed in collapsed buildings, as could the shortage of medical supplies. However, the biggest feature of the first few weeks after the quake was the complete lack of any large-scale local rescue plans. There were no militias or civil-defense personnel, no official rescue workers seen by the vast majority of inhabitants, nor any sign of the army becoming immediately involved.

In fact, it was the foreign rescue teams who were the first to reach many of the stricken areas. An Israeli team was the first to arrive, the morning after the quake. The Israeli rescue team was also the largest.

The Israelis sent 2 fire-fighting planes, teams of dogs, and 350 rescue workers. They also sent a field hospital and 200 medical workers. Eventually 80 countries and international organizations sent rescue teams or aid, with about 2,000 personnel directly involved. Besides the response from Israel, immediate responses were also made by Germany, the United States, France, Switzerland, and Great Britain, among others. The U.S. 70-person rescue team from Fairfax, Virginia, was typical of many. It naturally took several days to assemble and fly out, not reaching Turkey until two days after the quake. The unit was rushed to İzmit. A much larger U.S. relief effort was then promised, consisting of 3 naval vessels equipped with 80 beds, operating tables, doctors, dentists, and paramedics, as well as 22 rescue helicopters. This could not arrive until the weekend, however.

Those teams that were near at hand found movement difficult, with blocked roads and little direction or coordination from the Turkish government. Many foreign teams, as has been stated, found no local network at all and had to devise their own plans and organization. In the end, many rescue teams felt they had accomplished far less than they might have in better circumstances.

The government did slowly begin to make specific requests for help: body bags, tents, flashlights, blankets, garbage trucks, disinfectant, and tetanus vaccine. At the same time it imposed a blockage on aid by insisting that it be channeled through the Red Crescent (the Muslim equivalent of the Red Cross). National pride and religious feelings seemed to be the main cause for this demand. Indeed, the minister of health, Osman Durmus, declared Turks should not accept blood donated by Greece nor medical aid from the United States, and that foreigners should not actually deliver any relief aid. Aid from Islamic countries and groups was also blocked, the government fearing that any sympathy gained for political Muslims would undermine the secularity of the state.

The Turkish Red Crescent appealed to the International Red Cross for $6.92 million in aid. At the same time, the European Union sent $2.1 million, Britain $800,000, Germany $560,000, and other countries and charities smaller amounts for immediate help. The United States gave some $3 million. Most of these amounts were quickly increased as the scale of the disaster became apparent. A private German television appeal raised $7 million, a Dutch appeal raised $13 million. Even traditional foes of Turkey—Armenians, Kurds, and Greeks—sent gifts.

Turkish television broadcast graphic scenes of the devastation and early rescue attempts to drag people out of the wreckage. This caused an unorganized stream of Turkish volunteers from other parts of the country to make their way toward the devastated area. Some did sterling work in helping with the rescue efforts, especially groups of students from Istanbul, but many efforts were counterproductive, causing 20-mile traffic jams along already damaged highways, thus preventing heavy equipment and much-needed supplies from reaching their destination. Such volunteers often brought aid that was not actually needed, such as bottled water or bread. On the positive side, very little looting was reported.

As stated, the epicenter was near the industrial city of İzmit. One of the main dangers there was the oil refinery on the edge of the city, which had caught fire immediately and blazed uncontrollably for three days, despite aerial attempts to douse the flames. A nearby fertilizer plant with 8,000 tons of inflammable ammonia could have exploded easily, so all the nearby inhabitants had to be evacuated. At the hospital, medical supplies ran out, and nearby pharmacies were raided. An astonishing number of buildings less than five years old had collapsed, and the mayor declared he would need 250 teams to rescue everyone.

At Gölcük, the naval base and most of the town were flattened. One of the prominent features here, as elsewhere, was the haphazard nature of the building collapse. Some buildings were left standing; others appeared to be until it was clear that the first floor had sunk completely into the ground. Other buildings stood tilting sideways at 45-degree angles; many had cracks and fissures running through them. Each building had to be assessed separately for rescuing those still trapped inside, and it was often difficult to obtain the ground plans for the structures. It was feared that up to 10,000 people were trapped in the town.

Criticism was leveled against the government that its main rescue efforts, using Israeli as well as naval personnel, had been directed toward the army barracks, leaving individuals on their own. In fact, the navy did set up a crisis center, but it was in the town center and few trucks could reach it.

914

By Friday the death toll in Gölcük had reached 7,000, and bodies were being lined up in an ice rink for identification. Voices could still be heard in the rubble two and a half days after the quake, but lack of equipment or the wrong equipment continued to hinder the rescue teams. In other towns, the death toll also continued to rise: İzmit reported 3,242 dead and 8,759 injured; Adapazari 2,995 dead and 5,081 injured; Yalova 1,442 dead and 4,300 injured; and Istanbul, 984 dead and 9,541 injured. In Adapazari 963 bodies were interred in a mass grave. Not until Saturday, August 21, did soldiers appear, reaching a total of 50,000 eventually. Their first jobs were to pick up the rotting garbage, to spray disinfectant, and to set out lime. The stench of rotting bodies and garbage was giving rise to fears of an epidemic of cholera or typhoid, but in fact there was little medical evidence to support such fears. Nevertheless, dysentry and scabies were real threats to the tent-dwellers.

By the weekend, hope of pulling more survivors from the wreckage was fading. On Saturday the 21st, Austrian rescue workers pulled a ninety-five-year-old woman from a seaside complex at Yalova; on Sunday just two survivors were found. The last survivor to be pulled out was a small boy who had somehow survived for six days. At this stage, some foreign rescue teams began to pull out.

In some areas, it was reported that the army had intervened in these final rescue attempts, taking over from the foreign teams, but had only made a bad situation worse through their inexperience. However, the army's presence helped to stem the tide of volunteers and ease the massive traffic jams. Rain began falling the second week, keeping up for three straight days. To add to the misery of the homeless, many of the army-supplied tents were found not to be waterproof.

PUBLIC CRITICISM. After the initial shock of the quake, the severity of which affected the whole nation deeply, public criticism and anger quickly took over, on the part of both the survivors and the mass media. It was pointed in two directions: at the government for its inaction and lack of preparedness, and at the contractors and local officials who had allowed substandard buildings to be erected. Both criticisms point to the fact that the extent of the destruction was human-made—that a 7.4 earthquake should not have had such a deleterious effect.

The government tried to allay this criticism in a number of ways. On the evening of the quake Prime Minister Bülent Ecevit made a national broadcast. Parliament met in special session on Thursday, August 19, when Koray Aydin, minister of public works and housing, gave a report, stating that this was the greatest natural disaster in the history of Turkey. On the same day, the prime minister broadcast again, trying again to allay public anger, but the only positive step he took was to announce plans for more tents. The next day he ordered immediate burial of the dead and asked for more body bags. The much more robust response of the government and military to a November earthquake did lessen immediate criticism, even though confusion and delay were still very much in evidence.

The minister of the interior, Sadettin Tantan, promised harsh punishment for contractors, engineers, and building owners. In Duzce alone, magistrates arrested 33 very quickly. Three provincial governors were also dismissed for their failure to coordinate efforts, being replaced by cabinet ministers. However, some politicians were willing to avoid a cover-up. The minister of tourism, Erkan Mumcu, declared the lack of response was symptomatic of the Turkish political and economic system. By contrast, on August 25, Ecevit criticized the press for its "demoralizing" earthquake reporting and shut down one of the more outspoken private television stations under an anti-incitement law.

The case against contractors and local officials was overwhelming. For example, in Avcilar, the worst-hit suburb of Istanbul, a five-story building had collapsed in twenty-seven seconds, while a mosque standing nearby stood firm. The reasons the building collapsed were clear: cheap iron for support rods, too much sand mixed with the concrete, some buildings built without permits, and some with stories added without permission. In one case, local officials had ordered a halt three times to a building, but it had been completed just the same, demonstrating the weak enforcement laws, even when local inspectors were doing the job properly. A report by the Turkish Architects and Engineers Association suggested that 65 percent of new buildings put up in Istanbul were not in compliance with the building regulations. The strength of the quake by the time it had reached Istanbul was only 5.5, and all the buildings should theoretically have been able to withstand that magnitude quake. Other claims were made that of Turkey's forty thousand contractors, most were unqualified.

In Yalova, for example, survivors burned the car and stoned the house of one local contractor by the name of Veli Gocer. Seven of the 16 buildings he had constructed had collapsed. He quickly fled to Germany but is reported in an interview with the newspaper *Bild am Sonntaq* to have said that while he sympathized with the victims, he should not be made a scapegoat. His training was in literature, he said, not in civil engineering, and he had believed the builders when they had told him he could mix large quantities of beach sand with his concrete as a way of cutting costs.

THE GEOLOGICAL AFTERMATH. Besides the many small aftershocks, two major aftershocks caused panic and some further deaths and damage. The first of these was on August 31, lasting ten seconds, with a 5.2 magnitude and its epicenter east of İzmit. The second was on September 13, registering 5.8 on the Richter scale. The Anatolian fault had ruptured for at least 60 miles east of İzmit, and in some places the ground was offset by 12 feet. One possible reason for this was that the original quake may in fact have been caused by two fault segments splitting thirty seconds apart, thus causing such a large shock.

Mehmet Au Iskari, director of Turkey's leading observatory, observed continuing unusual seismic movements that could suggest another temblor soon. On Monday, November 15, a temblor of approximately 7.2 magnitude struck with its epicenter at Düzce, 90 miles east of Istanbul. At least 370 people were killed and 3,000 injured.

The U.S. government, aware of the similarities between the San Andreas fault and the Anatolian, quickly dispatched a team of experts from Menlo Park, California, and Golden, Colorado, as well as from the University of Southern California and San Diego State University. They were to investigate what lessons could be learned from a country where building regulations were, in theory, as strict as those in California, and especially the lessons from those buildings that were left standing and the type of soil they were built on.

Geologists and seismologists made a prediction that the next big quake on the fault will be in Istanbul itself, or a little to the south, in the Sea of Marmara, in perhaps thirty to fifty years. Istanbul is somewhat more secure than the İzmit area in that it is built on harder rock and is 6 to 10 miles from the fault line. However, if the standard of building construction is not improved, that will clearly be of little advantage in the next big quake.

THE ECONOMIC AFTERMATH. The northwest region of Turkey was the base for the country's economic growth during the late twentieth century, with many new industries creating new jobs. The destruction of much of this area was bound to have enormous economic consequences. Reconstruction of houses, apartments, shops, hotels, and factories, as well as the infrastructure of roads, railways, bridges, sewerage, and water supply, would cost billions of dollars. Added to this was the unemployment that followed the loss of workplaces and small businesses, the loss of stock and capital, and the loss of production. Worst hit were the small to medium-sized businesses that had fueled the economic progress of the 1990's. Fewer than 10 percent of houses were covered by insurance, adding to the financial loss.

Turkey's hopes of being in an economically sound position to apply for membership in the European Union (EU), whatever its democratic weaknesses, were thoroughly dashed. However, the EU did express sympathy for Turkey's plight. President Jacques Chirac of France wrote to each of the EU states asking for a "new strategy" for dealing with Turkey, after a two-year freeze in dialogue.

Turkey had also been in negotiation with the International Monetary Fund (IMF), especially since it had been in financial difficulties in 1999. It had been seeking to put the IMF's recommendations into practice. The loan originally requested had been $5 billion, but with the estimated $25 billion total loss, such a sum had clearly become too small. The government announced that it would endeavor to stick to the previously agreed fiscal measures. The government also immediately put aside $4 billion to repair businesses and $2 billion to $3 billion to repair the oil refinery. However, foreign aid would clearly be needed to supplement the long-term IMF loan. The World Bank pledged $200 million for emergency housing, and the EU gave $41.8 million. The future of Turkey's economy looked considerably bleaker than it had for many years, however.

THE POLITICAL AFTERMATH. Potentially the most damaging results of the quake were in the political arena. The country's disillusionment with the government went deeper than particular individual politicians. It reflected a questioning of the paternalistic state that hitherto had been trusted by its citizens to care for them. Such an attitude had been fostered to bring unity to a country whose secular basis lay counter to the traditionalism of many of its conservative Muslims, who would prefer an Islamic republic.

The exposure of corruption at a local level, although well known by the population before, added to public anger and frustration, as did the inept bureaucracy. Most of the country's residents had experienced this frustration daily in a minor way, but the earthquake brought years of simmering annoyances to the boil. In a country where the state was treated with great respect, the depth of such anger and criticism may well have permanently undermined such trust, making the job of future governments that much harder. Indeed, some politicians and academics took the opportunity to call for reform, even to the extent of rewriting the constitution.

Not all the political aftermath was negative, however. International relationships were improved in a wave of sympathy, however frustrated individual foreign relief and rescue teams were (the U.S. naval ships were barely used in the end, for example). Prime Minister Ecevit arranged a meeting with U.S. president Bill Clinton to ask for more U.S. aid. Turkish-Israeli relationships were also strengthened by the early and efficient arrival of Israeli rescue teams. Even the Kurdish rebels in the southeast of the country offered a temporary cease-fire.

Perhaps the most remarkable benefit politically was the blossoming of Turkish-Greek relationships. Enemies for centuries, these neighboring countries became antagonistic over the island of Cyprus, which was divided into Greek and Turkish sectors after a Turkish military invasion in the 1970's. The sending of a small Greek rescue team to the quake site was therefore an important symbolic gesture. This gesture was returned by the Turks when Athens was hit by an earthquake on September 9, 1999. A spontaneous response of reconciliation was released between the two populations and taken up by the media and politicians. The following month, President Clinton sought to seize on this goodwill by offering to broker talks over Cyprus. Rarely does an earthquake have such a profound effect politically and economically, as well as in terms of human tragedy.

David Barratt

FOR FURTHER INFORMATION:

The New York Times, August 17-September 14, 1999.

Tang, Alex K., ed. *Izmit (Kocaeli), Turkey, Earthquake of August 17, 1999, Including Duzce Earthquake of November 12, 1999: Lifeline Performance.* Reston, Va.: American Society of Civil Engineers, 2000.

U.S. Geological Survey. *USGS Scientific Expedition: Earthquake in Turkey—1999.* http://quake.wr.usgs.gov/research/geology/turkey/index.html.

Youd, T. Leslie, Jean-Pierre Bardet, and Jonathan D. Bray, eds. *1999 Kocaeli, Turkey, Earthquake Reconnaissance Report.* Oakland, Calif.: Earthquake Engineering Research Institute, 2001.

■ 2002: SARS EPIDEMIC

EPIDEMIC

DATE: November, 2002, to July, 2003
PLACE: Worldwide, but primarily Asia and Canada
RESULT: 8,422 reported cases and 916 known deaths

Severe acute respiratory syndrome (SARS) was the first major health crisis of the twenty-first century. SARS is one of the fastest spreading and most virulent diseases known. It occurs as a severe form of pneumonia and may result in death in patients with preexisting health issues or those who seek treatment too late. From November 27, 2002, to July 14, 2003, SARS infected 8,422 victims worldwide and caused 916 known deaths. In China alone, the source of the outbreak, there were 5,327 cases, with 349 people dying of the disease.

Prior to the identification of SARS, an occurrence of an atypical pneumonia was reported in Guangdong Province, China, in November, 2002. By February, 2003, 24 provinces in China reported cases of atypical pneumonia. A Guangdong physician treating patients suffering from this pneumonia traveled to Hong Kong and checked into a hotel in Kowloon on February 21, 2003. By March 4, he was dead, and 12 guests of the hotel housed on the same floor were infected even though they had had no direct contact with him. Hong Kong is a major transportation hub for all Asia. In a matter of days, these 12 people spread SARS throughout Hong Kong, Canada, Singapore, and Vietnam. By the end of March, 2003, cases of SARS were diagnosed in Italy, France, Ireland, Germany, Switzerland, Spain, Thailand, Malaysia, Taiwan, the United Kingdom, and Romania; by the end of April, cases appeared in the United States, Australia, Brazil, India, Mongolia, South Africa, Kuwait, the Philippines, Sweden, Indonesia, and South Korea. During May, cases appeared in New Zealand, Colombia, Finland, Macao, Russia, and Taiwan. It would take until midsummer 2003 to contain and control the SARS outbreak through quarantine, isolation, and travel restrictions. In an age of globalization and rapid transportation between nations—air travel to any location on the planet in less than 24 hours—the SARS outbreak demonstrated the severe threat of pandemic posed by new and rapidly emerging communicable diseases.

THE NATURE OF SARS. SARS is an infectious respiratory illness known as an atypical pneumonia. Typical pneumonia is primarily caused by bacteria such as streptococcus, while atypical pneumonia results from viruses such as influenza or specialized bacteria such as chlamydia or mycoplasma. All pneumonia results in stress to the respiratory system. In cases of SARS, however, not only is the respiratory system affected but other organs are involved in the infection as well, especially the liver.

The onset of SARS is marked by a rapidly raising fever and dry cough, followed by shivering, dizziness, lethargy, muscle ache, vomiting, skin rashes, diarrhea, sore throat, and upper respiratory distress. In some patients, these symptoms may be followed by difficulty in breathing and rapidly progress to a severe form of pneumonia resulting in death when the heart and other organs fail from oxygen deprivation. The causal virus of SARS is a unique coronavirus. Coronaviruses are one of the viruses responsible for influenza and about 20 percent of common colds. Coronaviruses can survive in an exposed environment for up to three hours and can infect humans as well as birds, cows, rabbits, dogs, cats, mice, and pigs.

The SARS virus is spread by direct person-to-person contact or contact with aerosolized respiratory secretions from coughing, sneezing, or breathing. In addition, droplets or respiratory secretions that end up on a victim's hands from rubbing the mouth or nose can also transfer the infection to touched objects. A vaccine for SARS is still in the experimental stage, but patients diagnosed and treated in the early stages of an infection usually recover. Treatment typically includes steroids and broad-spectrum antiviral drugs, and in some cases supplemental oxygen and assisted ventilation.

OUTBREAK AND CONTROL. Coronaviruses and influenza are widespread in the environment and exist in a range of animal hosts, especially birds and pigs. Certain avian strains of influenza have demonstrated the ability to mutate and cross species barriers to infect humans. Southern China is home to massive commercial-scale poultry and pig industries and has a history of spawning new, highly virulent strains of influenza. In the last four decades of the twentieth cen-

Workers in Beijing spray disinfectant at the National Library in an attempt to combat the spread of SARS. (AP/Wide World Photos)

tury, at least four new strains of influenza spread globally from China. The huge number of poultry and pigs contained on these commercial farms provides an easy opportunity for any virus, mutated or otherwise, to find an available host and multiply readily. Animal handlers, cooks, and fresh food market vendors may all have first-line contact with an infected animal. If a cross-species mutation of an animal virus occurs, these people are the first to be exposed.

On November 16, 2002, in Foshan, China, a chef specializing in the preparation of exotic meats was diagnosed and hospitalized with an atypical pneumonia. The patient was able to recover, but four members of the hospital staff who treated him soon showed signs of the same infection. In a matter of days, a number of food handlers and vendors from Guangdong Province's street markets were hospitalized with a similar pneumonia. Chinese medical authorities suspected that the patients were suffering from a new strain of influenza, but tests for influenza came back negative, as did tests for anthrax and plague. Tests did indicate several different respiratory pathogens present in lung secretions, including metapneumovirus and chlamydia.

By February, 2003, the World Health Organization (WHO) was notified of this unknown respiratory illness infecting 305 patients and resulting in at least 5 deaths in Guangdong, China. All reports of atypical pneumonia or other symptoms indicative of a new strain of influenza reported to WHO are given high-priority status for tracking and action. The outbreak of the illness remained localized around Guangdong, with the majority of victims being food handlers working in open-air markets or health professionals who dealt with infected patients. The epidemic seemed to reach its peak in early February, and then cases began to decline. This all changed on February 21, 2003, when a physician from Guangdong traveled to Hong Kong and checked into the Metropole Hotel. The physician had been treating patients with SARS, and at the time of his arrival in Hong Kong he was already symptomatic of the infection. The physician fell ill and was taken to Prince of Wales Hospital, where he eventually died after infecting many of the hospital's staff and patients.

Within days, 12 guests staying on the same floor of the hotel as the physician were diagnosed with the Guangdong respiratory illness. One of the infected guests, an American businessman, traveled to Hanoi, carrying the disease with him to Vietnam; he was asymptomatic at the time of his travel but on February 26, 2003, was admitted to a Hanoi hospital and put under the care of a WHO physician, Dr. Carlo Urbani. Another unknowingly infected guest traveled to Singapore; she was hospitalized soon after her arrival, where she infected medical staff and other patients. Two unknowingly infected guests flew to Canada, one to Vancouver and the another to Toronto. Guests in China who became symptomatic while still at the hotel were admitted to Hong Kong hospitals, where again many of the staff members and patients were exposed to the disease. The important fact of the Metropole Hotel outbreak is that none of the infected guests had any direct contact with the visiting Guangdong physician.

Because of SARS' incubation period of 2 to 14 days, Hong Kong's cosmopolitan setting, and the ability of unknowing carriers to serve as a vector in a matter of hours via air travel, infected travelers were able to seed local epidemics throughout the world. The disease carrier from Singapore was eventually linked to more than 100 SARS cases in Singapore; the Toronto carrier initiated an outbreak in a Toronto hospital resulting in 132 cases and 12 deaths.

On March 15, 2003, WHO issued a statement that severe acute respiratory syndrome was a global health threat because it was spreading so far and so quickly. On the same day, Air China Flight 112 flew from Hong Kong to Beijing, and 22 passengers and 2 flight attendants fell ill, beginning a SARS outbreak in Beijing. The Beijing outbreak resulted in the most cases and largest number of SARS-related deaths in China.

During the last week of March, 2003, a second outbreak of the illness in Hong Kong began when an infected victim with renal disease passed the disease throughout the Amoy Gardens apartments. The Amoy Gardens is a densely populated housing development. Many of the floor drain traps were not sealed, and many of the bathrooms were openly connected to the sewer pipes. Virus-heavy droplets coming from the infected apartment easily spread through the drains. Initially, SARS was thought to be transmitted only through direct person-to-person contact with respiratory secretions. Because many cases suggested no direct contact between victims, however, environmental transmission was suspected as an additional vector. The Amoy Gardens cases tended to confirm this conclusion, as 213 residents fell ill within the apartment complex. The Hong Kong government first isolated the complex and then relocated residents to two "holiday camps" for quarantine. That same week, a public housing complex across the street from Amoy Gardens reported a new outbreak of 30 cases and was immediately isolated.

Dr. Carlo Urbani, the Italian epidemiologist working with WHO in Hanoi who first named the disease "severe acute respiratory syndrome," became a victim of SARS and died on March 29. In memory of his research, WHO formally designated the disease "SARS" on April 16. By the end of April, 2003, SARS was identified in 14 countries around the globe, with more than 1,300 cases and 50 known deaths; by the end of the month, SARS was reported contained in Vietnam, and new cases in Singapore and Hong Kong were diminishing. Unfortunately, a new outbreak of SARS was reported in Taiwan, where a misdiagnosis resulted in the disease spreading widely throughout regional health care facilities. Random cases continued to appear in China, but the second largest outbreak was in Toronto. The traveler landing in Vancouver from Hong Kong arrived showing signs of infection, was quickly isolated, and recovered without infecting others. In Toronto, the carrier from Hong Kong was able to infect family members and eventually a number of health care providers. By mid-March, Toronto public health officials alerted the public to the outbreak of an atypical pneumonia. Before the end of May, nearly 7,000 cases of voluntary quarantine were imposed on suspected patients or carriers to stop the outbreak in and around Toronto.

Throughout the world, stringent control measures were taken to stop the spread of SARS. Most important, airport and border guards began screening travelers for fever, and strict isolation and quarantine protocols were instituted in areas reporting SARS symptoms. By mid-May 2003, the number of new cases of SARS diminished, and at that time researchers in Hong Kong discovered the genetic sequencing of a coronavirus found in civet cats to be 99 percent the same as the SARS virus. On May 24, 2003, the Chinese government temporarily banned importing exotic meat from civet cats, a popular Guangdong Province delicacy. It is likely that the original reported human infection of SARS, the exotic meat cook from Foshan, had contracted the disease from preparing civet cat.

Besides the human toll, SARS inflicted economic and political damage. During the months of outbreak, Asian countries saw an estimated financial loss of $28 billion. For the first time in its history, WHO issued an advisory suggesting that travelers avoid parts of the world infected with a disease. Airlines cut 10 percent of their flights from North America to Asia, and some countries saw a drop of more than 60 percent in tourism. In Canada, China, and the United States, sporting events, public gatherings, film productions, religious services, and parades were all canceled as a result of concerns about SARS. After the SARS outbreak was contained, public health officials and political leaders, especially in China, were accused of cover-ups and mismanaging the crisis to avoid economic disruption.

An interesting footnote to the SARS legacy occurred in June, 2006, when Chinese researchers revealed that at least one of the reported SARS deaths in China during 2003 was actually the result of H5N1 avian influenza, raising the possibility that other cases attributed to SARS may have actually been human cases of H5N1 bird flu and that the Chinese government covered up the possibility that two pathogens were experiencing simultaneous outbreaks in China.

Randall L. Milstein

FOR FURTHER INFORMATION:

Kleinman, Arthur, and James L. Watson, eds. *SARS in China: Prelude to Pandemic?* Stanford, Calif.: Stanford University Press, 2006.

Koh, Tommy, Aileen Plant, and Eng Hin Lee, eds. *The New Global Threat: Severe Acute Respiratory Syndrome and Its Impacts.* River Edge, N.J.: World Scientific, 2003.

Leung, Ping Chung, and Eng Eong Ooi, eds. *SARS War: Combating the Disease.* River Edge, N.J.: World Scientific, 2003.

Levy, Elinor, and Mark Fischetti. *The New Killer Diseases: How the Alarming Evolution of Mutant Germs Threatens Us All.* New York: Crown, 2003.

Schmidt, A., M. H. Wolff, and O. Weber, eds. *Coronaviruses, with Special Emphasis on First Insights Concerning SARS.* Boston: Birkhäuser Verlag, 2005.

■ 2003: EUROPE

HEAT WAVE AND DROUGHT

DATE: July-August, 2003
PLACE: Europe, especially France, Italy, Spain, and Portugal
TEMPERATURE: Up to 45 degrees Celsius (C) or 113 degrees Fahrenheit (F)
RESULT: As many as 40,000 dead, 32 million tons of grain harvest lost, 1.6 million acres of land burned

In July, 2003, an extreme buildup of high pressure in the upper atmosphere over Europe created a deadly heat wave that extended across the continent from northern Spain to the Czech Republic and from northern Germany to southern Italy. In early August, a second high pressure zone, existing both at surface levels and aloft, extended from Canada across the North Atlantic into western Russia and Central Europe. There it joined with amplified high pressure ridges to produce a massive formation that then shifted westward to cover all of Europe. In addition, hot and dry desert air from Africa, energized by sub-Saharan monsoons, swept into Europe from the south. The result was the worst natural disaster to affect the continent within the preceding 50 years, taking a toll of as many as 40,000 lives.

EXTREME WEATHER. In the spring of 2003, unseasonable high pressure ridges deflected the rain and cool air that the jet stream normally carries into Western Europe from the Atlantic Ocean, resulting in above-normal temperatures beginning in May. The situation worsened the following month. Switzerland experienced its hottest June in 250 years, and temperatures in Milan, Italy, hit a record of more than 40 degrees Celsius.

Measurements of the heat wave in July and August established average temperatures of approximately 3.5 degrees Celsius higher than seasonal averages. While these differences seem minimal, atmospheric scientists cited the period as perhaps the hottest in 500 years. Although Spain is subject to hot summers, its high temperature of 45 degrees Celsius may have set the record for the heat wave. Record temperatures were also noted in Germany, where highs reached 40.6 degrees Celsius on August 9, and in Switzerland, where thermometers recorded 41.1 degrees Celsius on August 11. Britain experienced its hottest day in history at 38.1 degrees Celsius on August 10. During the period from August 1 to August 12, Paris recorded average temperatures that were 11.8 degrees Celsius above normal, while average temperatures in Zurich, Switzerland, exceeded the norm by 9.5 degrees Celsius.

THE DEATH TOLL. Heat-related suffering and the risk of death escalate when normal or ambient temperatures are exceeded by as little as about 5.6 degrees Celsius for two or more consecutive days. In Europe, tens of thousands of deaths resulted from the unusually high temperatures combined with the extended duration of the heat wave.

Exacerbating the situation for city-dwellers was the phenomenon known as the "heat island" effect, the result of common features of the urban landscape such as dark surfaces that absorb heat, tall buildings that trap accumulations of stagnant air between them, and decreased vegetation. Waste heat from vehicles and machinery contribute to the situation, while heat-induced chemical reactions in automobile exhaust lead to dangerous levels of ozone concentration. In comparison to surrounding areas, cities retain heat through the night, allowing residents little relief. It is estimated that cities suffer temperatures higher than those in suburban and rural areas by a range of about 1.1 to 5.6 degrees Celsius. These factors contributed to the high death tolls in Europe's cities.

In France, an estimated 14,800 people died between August 1 and August 20. The central and eastern regions of France were especially hard hit, with high death rates in Dijon, Paris, Le Mans, and Lyon. On the nights of August 11 and 12, death rates more than doubled as Paris experienced its highest recorded nighttime temperature—25.5 degrees Celsius. In Paris, few doctors were available during the heat wave; hospitals and morgues filled to capacity, and overflow bodies had to be stored in refrigerated tents set up outside the city.

Not surprisingly, elderly city residents proved to be the most vulnerable to the heat wave, a result of both physical conditions and social customs. Air-conditioning was not used extensively or systematically in French residences, hospitals, or retirement homes, endangering those unable to bear extreme heat and humidity. Many older residents were without family to rely on because of summer holidays, which typically fall in August. While a significant number of the elderly died at home alone, many others died in institutions. More than 60 percent of the deaths in France during the heat wave took place in hospitals, private health care facilities, and retirement homes, with many of the deaths occurring among those aged 75 and over. This situation subsequently led French authorities to question their nation's overall efforts at care for the elderly.

Although the epidemic proportions of the death toll in France were the worst in all of Europe, death and suffering disrupted normal life across the continent. Several thousand casualties occurred in Italy's largest cities, with Rome reporting more than 1,000 deaths. Further heat-related deaths took place in Spain, Portugal, the United Kingdom, the Netherlands, Germany, Belgium, Austria, Bulgaria, the Czech Republic, the Slovak Republic, Hungary, and the Balkan nations.

Death toll figures rose in confusing proportions from country to country. Totals were compiled using a variety of methods, resulting in a perplexing series of estimates and revisions. The frequently quoted higher death toll figures were eventually arrived at by using statistics to compare the number of deaths during the heat wave to averages from previous years. These "excess" mortality figures were based on averages of "expected" mortality. Comparative mortality rates established that the heat wave had intensified chronic medical conditions such as heart disease and respiratory ailments, a factor that frequently led to what were categorized as heat-related deaths. In the years following the heat wave, reported death toll figures rose sharply as methods of calculation were refined and additional heat-related deaths were included in the totals. In 2006, Italy announced a death toll for the heat wave of 2003 of nearly 20,000, more than twice the country's previous estimate.

Even when bodies were counted, they were not always identified. In early September, for instance, 57 unclaimed victims of the Paris heat wave were interred following a closed ceremony attended only by city officials and the President of France.

ENVIRONMENTAL EFFECTS. Drought and wildfires heightened by the heat wave adversely affected the economy of Europe. Drought conditions in July and August of 2003 intensified as the days went by. The heat wave followed a dry spring in which below-normal amounts of rainfall left both Western and Eastern Europe in serious need of moisture. In Western Europe, the hot, dry spring accelerated crop growth; thus crops were in greater-than-normal need of moisture during July and August when high temperatures and solar radiation increased. The situation became so drastic in areas of Switzerland, where water is rarely lacking, that the use of river water for agricultural purposes was prohibited, causing losses of an estimated $230 million. Over all of Europe, the drought reduced crop yields and killed some kinds of vegetation. The yield of green fodder for livestock was particularly hard hit. The United States Department of Agriculture estimates that Europe lost 32 million tons of its projected grain harvest—a figure comparable to half of the entire United States wheat harvest. Such losses throughout Europe reached totals in the billions of dollars.

Surface levels of rivers shrunk to record lows. The Sava River in Croatia, for example, was at its lowest level in 160 years. The 1,800-mile-long Danube, which passes through or forms a border of 10 countries in Central Europe, fell so low that the river, famous for its beauty, seemed to be trickling away. Submerged tanks and ships from the World War II era were revealed for the first time. Managers of transportation on the international waterway attempted to keep river travel operating, but smaller vessels became necessary as larger ships and barges grounded out in shallows. When workers in Novi Sad, Serbia, were unable to raise a pontoon bridge on the Danube, river travel was halted for three weeks. An estimated 10 percent of the Danube delta wetlands dried out completely.

Surface water levels in lakes were depleted as well. Lake Balatan in Hungary, the largest lake in Central Europe and a popular resort area, shrank away from its shores by as much as 300 feet, forcing vacationers to trudge through wide expanses of mud in order to swim.

Forests were also affected by the drought, leading to concerns over increased incidence of tree diseases. However, a more immediate danger threatened as wildfires set forests ablaze. More than 25,000 fires were reported in Portugal, Spain, Italy, France Austria, Finland, Denmark, and Ireland, resulting in a loss of nearly 1.6 million acres. In Portugal alone, nearly 965,000 acres burned—nearly 6 percent of the country's forested lands. The fires were so difficult to control that Portugal requested assistance from the North Atlantic Treaty Organization (NATO). When this aid was denied, the country requested assistance from the European Commission to cover losses exceeding $1 billion.

RESPONSES TO THE HEAT WAVE. As water levels sank and fires raged, officials attempted to protect citizens from other heat-related dangers. The heat buckled roads in Germany and railroad tracks in Britain, resulting in lowered rail and automobile speed limits. Cities reduced speed limits to control ozone levels, and Portugal was forced to suspend rail traffic altogether. Adding to the problems of Swiss officials, glacial melting in the Alps resulted in increased climbing accidents as the ice became unstable. On a somewhat less serious note, residents of the Croatian island of Pag were forbidden to shower at the beach, while zoo officials in Austria sprayed ostriches with cold water and fed iced fruit to chimpanzees.

During the extreme heat, electricity-producing utilities requested that rules governing wastewater temperatures be relaxed so that nuclear reactors and coal-fired plants could continue operation. German and French nuclear plants continued to produce electricity, although a French coal-fired plant was shut down. Several nuclear reactors in France ran so hot during July that plant managers experimented with sprinkler systems, a situation that greatly concerned environmentalists. Normally a leading electrical power exporter, France cut sales to surrounding countries during the heat wave. Italy's electricity grid was subject to rolling blackouts, affecting millions of Italians.

In the aftermath of the ruinous summer, Europeans focused on preparations for future heat waves. Governmental entities throughout Europe reviewed data and developed plans to cope more effectively with extreme heat, often by expanding the roles of governmental health services. At least one scientific study found that global warming, believed by most authorities to be exacerbated by greenhouse gases and other pollutants created by human activity, had almost certainly doubled the risk of future heat waves.

Margaret A. Dodson

FOR FURTHER INFORMATION:

Larsen, Janet. "Are More Killer Heat Waves on the Horizon?" *USA Today* 132 (May, 2004): 56-58.

Le Comte, Douglas. "A Year of Extremes: 2003's Global Weather." *Weatherwise* 57, no. 2 (March/April, 2004): 22-29.

Stott, Peter. "Human Contribution to the European Heatwave of 2003." *Nature* 432 (December 2, 2004): 610-614.

Tagliabue, John. "Utilities in Europe Seek Relief from the Heat." *The New York Times*, August 12, 2003, p. A6.

United Nations Environmental Programme. "Impacts of Summer 2003 Heat Wave in Europe." *Early Warning on Emerging Environmental Threats.* http://www.grid.unep.ch/product/publication/download/ew_heat_wave.en.pdf.

Vandentorren, Stéphanie, et al. "Mortality in 13 French Cities During the August 2003 Heat Wave." *American Journal of Public Health* 94, no. 9 (September, 2004): 1518-1520.

◼ 2003: THE FIRE SIEGE OF 2003
FIRES

DATE: October 21-November 4, 2003
PLACE: Los Angeles, San Diego, Ventura, San Bernardino, and Riverside Counties, California
RESULT: 22 dead, 80,000 residents displaced, 3,500 homes destroyed, 743,000 acres burned; insurance losses estimated at $2 billion

A series of wildfires that first broke out on October 21, 2003, raged across the landscape in the vicinity of Los Angeles and San Diego in Southern California, collectively constituting the largest wildfire in California history. It came to be known as the Fire Siege of 2003.

THE WILDFIRES. In all, at least 12 separate wildfires burned during this time period: the Verdale and Grand Prix Fires in Los Angeles County; the Old Fire in San Bernardino County; the Cedar, Paradise, Otay, and Roblar 2 Fires in San Diego County; the Piru and Simi Incident Fires in Ventura County; and the Pass, Mountain, and Wellman Fires in Riverside County.

The first of these fires, the Grand Prix Fire, broke out on October 21 in the San Bernardino National Forest. Officials suspected that it had been deliberately set. On October 25, the Cedar Fire, which would become the largest of these blazes, broke out around San Diego. It was known to have been caused by a lost hunter who fired a flare. There was also a major outbreak in the Simi Valley to the northwest of Los Angeles. The hot foehn winds, called Santa Ana winds, that sometimes blow across Southern California had begun on October 23. They whipped up all the fires and made firefighting extremely dangerous, resulting in the death of a Canadian firefighter whose position was overwhelmed by flames.

Although some 16,000 firefighters were deployed in an effort to stop the blazes, their efforts were largely ineffectual. Protecting life became more important than protecting property, as 3,500 homes were destroyed. The fires moved quickly, and notice to evacuate sometimes came too late. Of the 22 individuals killed by the fires, 10

934

had been trapped in their cars as they tried to flee the Cedar Fire.

On October 26, officials in San Diego advised residents not directly threatened by the fire to stay home because the quantity of ash in the air had reached dangerous levels. Indeed, the smoke plumes were so high that they were visible on the International Space Station at the height of the wildfires. Conditions in the atmosphere were so bad that it was necessary to close the Southern California Radar Approach Control facility near San Diego, disrupting air traffic throughout the nation. An NFL game between the San Diego Chargers and the Miami Dolphins, scheduled to take place in San Diego on October 27, had to be moved to Tempe, Arizona, because the Chargers' regular stadium had been converted into an evacuation center.

A change in the weather on October 30 at last enabled fire officials to get control of the situation. The Santa Ana winds had died down on October 27, and light rain began to fall on October 30. By November 4, officials were at last able to get control of the fires. Although President George W. Bush and California governor Arnold Schwarzenegger toured the area on November 4, relatively little federal aid was available to cope with the destruction.

FACTORS IN THE OUTBREAK. Four factors played an important role in the outbreak of so many destructive wildfires within two weeks. They were topography, climate, vegetation, and demographics. All four played a role in creating a series of wildfires of unprecedented scale.

Los Angeles and San Diego Counties, located on the Pacific coast of Southern California, are fringed by the San Gabriel and San Bernardino Mountains that separate the areas from the Mojave Desert directly to the east. The areas are effectively a bowl that ensures continuity of weather and vegetative conditions in the land so embraced. The eastern edges of this bowl have been declared national forests, the Cleveland and the San Bernardino National Forests, which effectively transfers the maintenance of the vegetation to the U.S. Forest Service. Even before European settlement of the area, it was subject to periodic wildfires, as determined by the government investigators who have been seeking to understand the causes of the Fire Siege of 2003.

Besides topography, the climate that prevails in this basin is highly conducive to wildfires. It is called a Mediterranean climate, with limited precipitation occurring largely in the winter and high temperatures and very dry conditions in the summer. Rainfall in the winter months (November to April) is normally around 20 inches (500 millimeters), but in the summertime (May to October) it is less than 5 inches (125 millimeters). Moreover, the area is prone to Santa Ana winds, especially in the fall, that can reach 60 miles per hour (100 kilometers per hour), making firefighting both problematic and dangerous. The mountain ranges just inland concentrate these winds by funneling them through passes in the mountains.

The result of these two factors, topography and climate, is that most of the land does not produce trees but rather a semi-desert brush called chaparral, which is highly flammable. Of the area burned in the fires, only 5 percent had coniferous trees growing on it, the rest being covered in chaparral bushes. Such vegetation normally burns at intervals varying between 5 and 100 years; within 3 to 5 years of a burn, new chaparral growth appears and the cycle is repeated.

The remains of a house caught in a firestorm in San Bernardino, California. (FEMA)

Because both Los Angeles and San Diego are located at the sites of important seaports, they have experienced major population growth, especially in the latter half of the twentieth century. Further, that growth has been characterized by the expansion of housing into the open lands on the fringes of the city centers, creating what is called the intermix fire, one that occurs on land that is both wild and occupied. Between 1950 and 1990, 100 million people moved into this area. Between 1970 and 1980, counties that happened to adjoin wilderness areas increased their population by 13 percent; between 1980 and 1990, the increase was 24 percent. This explosive population growth has continued since 1990.

This exurban expansion took the form of wooden houses with wooden roofs, which are especially susceptible to fire. As population expanded into lands that had been occupied previously only by vegetation, the risk of fires being started expanded exponentially, even if they were not intended, as many of them were. Most of the fires in this great sequence of wildfires were attributed to arson, even though no one was caught.

LESSONS OF THE FIRE SIEGE. The Fire Siege of 2003 gave new fuel to a controversy that had been engaging land management agencies in the area for several decades: Were the fires the consequence of improper fire management, and could they have been prevented?

The fires provoked an intense debate among many officials as to the appropriate policy to follow in the Southern California region. The drought that characterized much of the western parts of the United States in the later decades of the twentieth century and that has lasted into the twenty-first century has made the question of fire control of vital concern, especially as the population of the western states continues to grow at a very rapid rate.

Early in the twentieth century, as the U.S. Forest Service took charge of many parts of the western United States with the creation of the national forests, the Forest Service became responsible for managing forest fires in the region as part of the obligation to maintain the forests in the areas that it controlled. Huge wildfires in the early years of the century, especially those that burned in many parts of the West in 1910, led the Forest Service to adopt a policy of fire suppression of all fires in the first hours in which they were detected.

The development of many new technologies during World War II, such as helicopters and large water balloons towed by airplanes, together with the substantial expansion of the road system in the national forests by the Civilian Conservation Corps in the 1930's, led the leaders of the Forest Service to believe that they had the situation under control. In the 1960's, however, the development of the environmental movement, which advocated returning to the "natural" conditions prevailing before settlement and in particular to the creation of "wilderness" forests, led to a policy in which fires in wilderness areas were allowed to burn until they burned out. However, the devastating fire that broke out in Yellowstone National Park in 1988 led to a reevaluation of this policy. Efforts were made to combine "controlled burns" (fires deliberately set by government officials) in strategic locations with the idea that deliberately burning lands containing considerable burnable material would create patches that would lack the fuels to support large fires.

At the same time, government officials began to realize that a uniform policy throughout the entire country was not practicable. Crafting a policy specifically for the chaparral lands in the vicinity of the major California cities became a high priority. Specialists in the U.S. Geological Service and at the University of California at Los Angeles (UCLA) began an intensive study of the history of fires in the region.

They discovered that fires recur on the topography and in the vegetation of the area every 30 to 40 years, although some particularly sensitive areas may burn more frequently. The rapid growth of the human population in the area has substantially raised the risk, because although many western fires are ignited by lightning, such events are rare in the Los Angeles-San Diego coastal area. Overwhelmingly, people are the cause, particularly fires that are deliberately set, and there is little likelihood that this situation will change in the future. They also realized that, although creating fire breaks may work in many areas, the very high flammability of the chaparral vegetation makes this an unworkable strategy in this area. The one advantage of periodic deliberate control of vegetation is that it can reduce the risk of soil loss that occurs after a fire.

Thought needs to be given by local officials to the pattern of human settlement and to the regulations that control it, such as zoning regulations. In addition, specific requirements governing exurban houses, such as nonflammable roofing and siding materials, can make it much easier to save houses in the path of a fire in this region. Basically, the chaparral region, given its topography and its climate, can be expected to burn at regular intervals, and there is not much that wildland fire officials can do about it. The best approach is to treat fires in this region as natural catastrophes much like earthquakes. Wildfire management would also benefit from the full development of evacuation plans, as moving people out of the path of danger must be given a very high priority.

Nancy M. Gordon

FOR FURTHER INFORMATION:

California Department of Forestry and Fire Protection. *California Fire Siege 2003: The Story.* Sacramento, Calif.: Author, 2003. Also at http://www.fire.ca.gov/php/fire_er_siege.php.

California Legislature. Joint Legislative Committee on Emergency Services and Homeland Security. *2003 Historic Southern California Fires: An Assessment One Year Later.* Sacramento, Calif.: Senate Publications, 2004.

Keeley, Jon E., and C. J. Fotheringham. "Historic Fire Regime in Southern California Shrublands." *Conservation Biology* 15, no. 6 (December, 2001): 1536-1548.

Keeley, Jon E., C. J. Fotheringham, and Max A. Moritz. "Lessons from the October 2003 Wildfires in Southern California." *Journal of Forestry* 102, no. 7 (October/November, 2004): 26-31.

Krauss, Erich. *Wall of Flame: The Heroic Battle to Save Southern California.* Hoboken, N.J.: John Wiley & Sons, 2006.

Pyne, Stephen J. *World Fire: The Culture of Fire on Earth.* Seattle: University of Washington Press, 1995.

■ 2003: THE BAM EARTHQUAKE

EARTHQUAKE

DATE: December 26, 2003
PLACE: Bam, Iran, and the surrounding area
MAGNITUDE: 6.5
RESULT: More than 26,000 killed, about 75,000 left homeless, including 30,000 injured; more than 85 percent of the buildings in Bam destroyed, including the historic Citadel

The Earth's crust is cracked and broken into large segments called plates. These plates may be 25 to 320 kilometers (15 to 200 miles) thick and a few hundred to thousands of kilometers wide. The plates dip into the mantle, a global layer of hot, dense rock that is generally not molten but plastic. In a simplified view, convection currents in the mantle rise, move across the top, and then cool and sink at the glacial speed of a few centimeters (1 or 2 inches) per year. The motion of the mantle carries the plates on chaotic journeys so that some plates slide by, pull away from, or crash into other plates. This movement is the source of earthquakes. Large quakes occur when one plate is locked against another, allowing stress to build for years or centuries until the weakest link gives way and that part of the plate lurches forward.

With about 130 major earthquakes during recorded history, Iran ranks among the most seismically active countries of the world. It is spanned by a network of faults at the boundary between the Arabian plate and the Eurasian plate. On Friday, December 26, 2003, a segment of the Arabian plate broke loose and ground northward. A small precursor quake struck at 4:00 A.M., and some residents of Bam, Iran, rushed out into the streets. Unfortunately, since small quakes occur there often and nothing further happened immediately, most went back to bed. The magnitude 6.5 quake struck at 5:26 A.M., releasing energy equivalent to 5.6 megatons of TNT. The quake's focal point was almost directly beneath Bam. Seen from above, the sand-colored houses, walls, towers, and arches gave Bam the look of a fantastically intricate sand castle. After the quake, it looked as if vandals

940

had kicked down the walls, stomped on the towers, and sat on the castle. Most of Bam was rubble.

AFTERMATH. The ancient city of Bam was built on a desert plateau in the southeastern region of Iran. The old city was made of adobe, bricks of mud mixed with straw or animal dung and dried in the sun. Thick walls were constructed with bricks plastered together with layers of clay, and roofs were decked with heavy tiles or more bricks built into cupolas and vaults. Adobe works well in a country where it rarely rains, and the thick walls helped to keep the interiors of the houses cooler during the heat of the day. During the quake, however, the adobe disintegrated, turning walls and roofs into tons of dirt that cascaded down onto the sleeping inhabitants. Those who freed themselves or were quickly pulled from the rubble by family members or neighbors had a good chance of survival, but after the first few hours, searchers found very few survivors. There were two miracle survivors: a 97-year-old woman, Sharbānou Māndarāī, was trapped for eight days in the airspace beneath a table near a ventilation pipe and was rescued in amazingly good condition, but a 56-year-old man pulled from the rubble after 13 days was in poor condition.

The final toll was 26,271 killed, more than 30,000 injured, and more than 75,000 left homeless. Approximately 85 percent of the buildings were completely destroyed. It made little difference if the buildings were ancient or modern, since building codes had not been followed. For example, two modern hospitals, supposedly built to withstand such quakes, collapsed in ruins. All of Bam's 131 schools were destroyed, and about a third of the teachers were killed. A prison at the edge of the city collapsed, setting the prisoners free. After standing guard for nearly 2000 years, the largest adobe building in the world, the Citadel, or Arg-e-Bam, a magnificent warren of ramparts, towers, arches, courtyards, and narrow passages, was now largely rubble. Most of the date palms that were claimed to have produced the world's best dates were lost.

Iranian president Mohammed Khatami announced that the disaster was more than one nation could handle, and he appealed for international aid. This was a dramatic change from the quake of June, 1990, when foreign aid was refused in spite of 50,000 killed and 60,000 injured. More than 60 nations responded to President Khatami's appeal, sending supplies and workers. Only aid from Israel was refused. The United States had broken off diplomatic relations with Iran during the 1980-1981 hostage crisis, dealing with the country only through third parties, but in this situation U.S. officials spoke directly with their Iranian counterparts to arrange aid. U.S. military airplanes brought emergency supplies on December 28, and 80 American doctors and aid workers arrived in Bam on December 30. Noting Iran's new openness, the U.S. government proposed a high-level humanitarian mission to be headed by Senator Elizabeth Dole, a past president of the American Red Cross, but the Iranian government was not ready for this step and "held it in abeyance." Iran accused the United States of trying to turn the situation to its own advantage, although the tone was far less strident than it had been in the past. Eventually, medical care, food, water, temporary shelter, blankets, a sanitation system, and more were provided by Iran and other nations.

CULTURAL HERITAGE. President Khatami promised that Bam would be rebuilt, and in July, 2004, the World Heritage Committee of the United Nations Educational, Scientific, and Cultural Organization (UNESCO) declared Bam a World Heritage site, stating that it represented a historical culture of which Iranians were justifiably proud. With this declaration, UNESCO became the head of the international efforts for the cultural preservation of Bam. Under its direction, experts from Japan began helping to reconstruct the Citadel, a project expected to take fifteen years.

Bam was a trading center as early as 250 B.C.E. and became a pilgrimage site when a Zoroastrian fire temple was built there. After the temple was destroyed, it was replaced in the ninth century C.E. by one of the earliest mosques in Iran, the Jame Mosque. Built on the ancient Silk Road, the old trade route between Europe and Asia, Bam was a convenient place for traders with silk from China or carved ivory and gold baubles from India to bargain with traders bringing fine Roman glass and other goods from the west. Bam became famous for textiles and for garments of silk and cotton. As water became available for farming, Bam also became famous for its dates and other fresh fruit.

Ingenuity allowed the inhabitants to live in a region that can reach 50 degrees Celsius on a hot summer day. Bam is built beside a river that seldom has water, but water is available to those who know how to find it. It comes from deep wells and from underground channels called *qanats*, which were invented in Iran perhaps 3,000 years ago. They are channels built by hand underground to minimize evaporation of the water into the dry desert air. They begin in the aquifer at the base of the mountains many kilometers away. The *qanat* is constructed with only a shallow slope so that water flows nicely, but not so rapidly that it erodes the tunnel. Vertical shafts every 20 or 30 meters provide air as well as access to construct and maintain the *qanat*. Bam has some of the oldest *qanats* in Iran. Before the quake, 126 *qanats* supplied about half of the water used by Bam and its surroundings, but most were damaged in the quake, and 40 percent were severely damaged.

Windcatchers (*badgir*) have been used for more than 1,000 years. The simplest is a vertical shaft from the ceiling of a room to the outside. The top of the shaft has a roof supported by columns or perforated walls. Wind blowing across the top of the shaft will reduce the pressure there and suck the warmest air from the room below. If the room has thick adobe walls that were chilled by the windcatcher drawing in cold night air, the room may remain cool all day. If the windcatcher has a scoop that diverts the wind down its shaft, over a pool of water, and into a room, the air will be chilled by evaporative cooling. It will be even cooler if the windcatcher forces dry air through a *qanat* so that it undergoes evaporative cooling and also draws chilled air from the underground chamber. In fact, if this combination is used to chill a well-insulated building, ice can be harvested in winter and kept in such a building well into the summer.

OUTLOOK FOR THE FUTURE. In an opinion piece for *The Iranian* called "Ready for Future Bams?" on January 3, 2003, Sassan Pejhan writes that as he watched the television coverage of the Bam quake, he could not help but recall previous earthquakes in Iran: Roudbar in 1990, where 50,000 were killed and 60,000 were injured, and the Tabas earthquake in 1978, in which 25,000 were killed. The Tabas quake reminded Pejhan's parents of the 1968 earthquake at Khorasan, where 12,000 were killed, and Pejhan's grandparents were reminded of the earthquake at Salmas, where 4,000 were killed. Pejhan wonders what can break this vicious cycle of tragedy and concern followed by apathy and little progress.

Four days before the Bam quake, a quake of the same magnitude struck California's central coast and killed only 2 people in the town of Paso Robles. On October 23, 2004, a series of quakes, the first of magnitude 6.8 (several times more powerful than the Bam quake), struck northern Japan, killing 35 and injuring 1,300. Simply put, Iran has not invested in building earthquake-resistant structures to the extent that more developed countries have. It is not merely a matter of mud brick construction, since modern buildings in Iran also collapsed. After the quake, Investigators found that fired bricks were often so weak that they disintegrated when struck sharply. Weak bricks had not been fired hot enough or long enough. Had buildings been constructed to the standards required by the Iranian building code, most probably would have survived. It is not simply a matter of money, since Iran has a great deal of oil money but has chosen to spend it elsewhere.

The Ayatollah Ali Khamenei visited Bam three days after the quake and comforted the people by assuring them that the quake was not a punishment from God but instead a test to see if they would remain faithful during difficulties. Too many people have taken this statement to mean that they should not work to prevent future tragedies. In fact, a consensus has been expressed by many writers both inside and outside Iran that a prevalent submissive and fatalistic mindset keeps the people from making necessary changes. Those who are trying to implement steps to make buildings more earthquake-resistant find it difficult to institute change because of these attitudes.

Research shows that adobe homes could be greatly strengthened by using iron straps to tie walls to foundations, floors, ceilings, and roofs. Some horizontal and vertical concrete beams would also greatly strengthen adobe buildings. Covering adobe with a layer of adhesive, fiber-based polymers (quake wrap) has been shown to help. Even placing adobe bricks in sandbags and putting barbed wire between layers of bricks greatly strengthened test buildings. Enforcing building codes is probably the most effective step that could be taken.

Locals complained that money donated by other nations for the rebuilding of Bam was being withheld by the government and that the rebuilding was proceeding too slowly. The government responded that donor nations have been slow to fulfill their pledges. They also pointed out that before rebuilding could be started, it took more than six months to develop a plan for a modern city that would solve some of the problems with the old city. By 2006, although there were still many piles of rubble waiting to be cleared, the rebuilding was well underway, but ensuring that the new buildings are built to code requires constant vigilance.

Charles W. Rogers

FOR FURTHER INFORMATION:

Campi, Giovanni. "The Bam Earthquake: The Tragedy of a Cultural Treasure 'Depicted in the Faces of People.'" *UN Chronicle* 41 (December 1, 2004): 40.

Earthquake Engineering Research Institute. *2003 Bam, Iran, Earthquake Reconnaissance Report.* Oakland, Calif.: Author, 2006.

Ghafory-Ashtiany, Mohsen, et al. *Journal of Seismology and Earthquake Engineering: Special Issue on Bam Earthquake.* Tehran: International Institute of Earthquake Engineering and Seismology, 2004.

Hough, Susan Elizabeth, and Roger G. Bilham. *After the Earth Quakes: Elastic Rebound on an Urban Planet.* New York: Oxford University Press, 2006.

Lawler, Andrew. "Earthquake Allows Rare Glimpse into Bam's Past—and Future." *Science* 303 (March 5, 2004): 1463.

■ 2004: THE INDIAN OCEAN TSUNAMI

EARTHQUAKE AND TSUNAMI

DATE: December 26, 2004

PLACE: 11 countries bordering the Indian Ocean—Thailand, Indonesia, Malaysia, Myanmar, Bangladesh, Sri Lanka, India, the Maldives, the Seychelles, Somalia, and Kenya

MAGNITUDE: 9.3

RESULT: Official death toll of 186,983, later revised upward to 212,000; 42,883 missing; thousands dead from injuries and diseases directly attributable to the tsunami

T sunamis, which seldom occur in the Atlantic and Indian Oceans, are more frequent in the Pacific Ocean, the average depth of which is much greater. However, one minute before 7:00 A.M. on December 26, 2004, the strongest earthquake recorded in the previous 40 years erupted on the floor of the Indian Ocean near the west coast of the Indonesian island of Sumatra.

This quake was originally assigned an magnitude of 9.0 on the Richter scale, but seismologists ultimately determined that the actual magnitude was 9.3. In contrast, the magnitude of the earthquake that leveled much of San Francisco in 1906 measured 7.8 on the Richter scale, and the greatest magnitude ever recorded was 9.5 in the earthquake the struck Chile on May 22, 1960.

Although the earthquake in the Indian Ocean did not immediately produce huge ocean surges, the energy emanating from its epicenter equaled that of more than 23,000 atomic bombs of the sort dropped on Hiroshima, Japan, in 1945. The ocean's surface immediately after the earthquake experienced waves of about 1 foot, which made them virtually undetectable as a tsunami.

As the energy that the earthquake released moved in concentric circles from the epicenter, however, the size of the waves increased dramatically. They moved at speeds in excess of 600 miles an hour, slowing down only when they reached the shallow coastal waters in areas bordering the ocean. As they advanced, the waves created outflows that drained harbors, causing the curious to walk toward receding shorelines, fascinated by what was exposed in the shallow areas.

Almost instantly, without warning, the shoreline was inundated by waves as high as 50 feet that crashed with a force that pulverized everything in their paths. In tsunamis, the tops of the waves travel much faster than the bottoms, which results in a dramatic rising of the sea. The combined speed and weight of the raging water makes human survival unlikely.

The areas affected by the Indian Ocean Tsunami were quite impoverished. Many of their structures, especially those in which natives live, were badly built, making them incapable of resisting the force of such a powerful tsunami. These structures were either flattened or tossed about like matchboxes when the high waves hit.

Because this fearsome tsunami struck the day after Christmas, resorts on the Indian Ocean were booked to capacity with tourists, many from Europe and the United States. In the fishing villages abutting the ocean, many of the men had gone out on their boats, which accounts for the fact that four times more women than men died in the disaster. In addition, one-third of the dead were children. The initial official combined death toll for 11 countries of 186,983 was ultimately revised upward to about 212,000.

THE CAUSES OF THE TSUNAMI. Earthquakes occur when two tectonic plates push against each other to the point that they produce a violent reaction. Such a reaction may build gradually over thousands of years before it produces an earthquake. The section of the earth's crust called the India plate has been sliding at barely perceptible speeds under the Burma plate for millennia. On December 26, 2004, the India plate that was sliding under the Burma plate finally created a rupture about 600 miles long off the coast of the Indonesian island of Sumatra. It displaced the area beneath the water by an estimated 10 yards horizontally and several yards vertically.

The result was that rock measured in trillions of tons was displaced and propelled by water moving at more than 600 miles an hour. It moved along hundreds of miles, causing the worst underwater upheaval since the Great Alaska Earthquake of 1964. Any earthquake that measures more than 6.0 on the Richter scale can be devastating. When the measurement exceeds 9.0, the results are staggering.

The fissure that the quake created filled with seawater, resulting in a huge disruption on the ocean floor. As billions of gallons of water poured into the newly created trench, waves radiated from the long fissure, sending killer concentric waves toward land. When these waves reached landfall, they engulfed everything in their paths with a force so great that little could withstand them.

THE IMMEDIATE AFTERMATH. The destruction the tsunami caused was so widespread and all-encompassing that the engulfed coastal areas resembled war zones. The country hit hardest and first was Indonesia, with Sri Lanka, Thailand, and India suffering severe damage as the waves raced across the Indian Ocean in all directions. Little remained standing along the shore. Bodies dangled from trees or protruded from the great rivers of mud left behind when the waters receded. More people were dead than alive. After the tsunami retreated, the gentler ocean waves washed thousands of bodies to shore.

The poverty of the affected areas prevented them from having the sophisticated advanced tsunami warning systems that are available in more prosperous regions. Had such systems been in place, mass evacuations could have spared thousands of lives. Moving to higher ground saved some who sensed that the tsunami was imminent, but most people did not realize the danger until it was upon them.

Many of those who survived were made numb by the magnitude of the disaster. They wandered about aimlessly amid areas whose only shelters had been washed out to sea or catapulted far into the higher reaches of the terrain that was dotted by the boats, automobiles, trucks, and heavy equipment that the rushing water had tossed like toys and deposited up to 2 miles from where they had originated.

Aftershocks shook the area, causing not only additional damage to the few remaining structures that might have been used to shelter the survivors but also terrifying the stunned people who had managed to escape the original assault. Between December 26 and January 1, 2005, the affected area was shaken by 84 aftershocks whose magnitude ranged from 5.0 to 7.0 on the Richter scale.

Of these aftershocks, 26 were felt on the same day as the major underwater quake that had triggered the tsunami. At least one such aftershock had a magnitude of 7.0, which in itself was sufficient to cause severe damage to inhabited areas. Survivors much in need of shelter were reluctant to enter buildings that they feared would collapse as the aftershocks destabilized the ground beneath them.

In the days immediately following the tsunami, tens of thousands of people needed medical treatment for such problems as open wounds, broken bones, contusions, dysentery, and various endemic diseases. Such assistance was not available to them because the afflicted areas, many of which never had adequate medical facilities, had lost most of their physicians and nurses and had suffered the loss of clinics that vanished beneath the waves.

Help from outside was on its way, but it did not arrive in time to save many of the more critically injured victims of the tsunami. As the survivors were forced to live in intensely crowded conditions, a great danger arose from communicable respiratory diseases, particularly influenza and pneumonia. Conditions were right for mosquitoes to breed, raising the threat of malaria.

In the week following the December 26 disaster, survivors had little to eat. They drank what water they could find at their own risk, as water supplies had been contaminated by raw sewage and decaying bodies. Among the first food shipments to arrive from outside the

A still image from a video shot by British tourists in Phuket, Thailand, on December 26, 2004, as a tsunami breaks on the shore. (AP/Wide World Photos)

stricken area were cases of dried noodles that these had to be prepared by adding boiling water. Unfortunately, many people did not have any means of boiling water, which in most cases was so polluted that bringing it to boiling temperature would not wholly eliminate the dangers that drinking it posed.

FACTORS COMPLICATING RECOVERY. The immediate task facing the survivors was to dispose of the decaying corpses that were quickly deteriorating in the hot, humid climate. Survivors frantically tried to find and identify dead relatives. In the end, many of the dead had to be cremated or buried anonymously in mass graves.

Problems arose because many people in the tsunami's path were Hindu, Buddhist, or Muslim. Muslims prohibit cremation of a dead person's remains, which made it difficult for many of the afflicted communities to employ the most efficient and sanitary way to dispose of bodies. Some efforts were made to photograph every body before it was buried in a mass grave so that survivors might eventually identify their loved ones.

Some of the religions followed by people in the countries struck by the tsunami deny death if a body is not present. Therefore, hordes of people refused to admit that family members had perished because their bodies had not been found. Further, Hindus and Buddhists believe in gods with mercurial temperaments and that natural disasters reflect divine anger. Such beliefs caused many of the survivors to suffer from guilt, which sometimes resulted in passivity and resignation preventing them from facing the realities of the disaster and taking the actions needed to set recovery efforts in motion.

In both India and Indonesia, separatist groups were seeking independent political status, creating additional difficulties. Sometimes such groups interfered with recovery efforts. The devastated city of Banda Atjeh, which lost one-third of its 320,000 inhabitants, had been a stronghold of Muslim extremists who were seeking independence from Indonesia. It was feared that these extremists would do violence to rescuers who came into the area.

Also, Indonesia was slow to accept rescuers because, since the country had gained independence in 1949, it had allowed no foreign military personnel on Indonesian soil. When the Indonesian government finally admitted military personnel from foreign countries, it stipulated that rescuers must be unarmed.

WORLDWIDE RELIEF EFFORTS. All the civilized world was dismayed by the loss of life and property that the tsunami caused. Early reports that suggested casualty rates below 10,000 elicited immediate help and support from a number of nations, but as reports of fatalities zoomed, rapidly increasing offers of help were forthcoming.

On December 28, two days after the tsunami, U.S. president George W. Bush pledged $15 million in relief funds to the stricken nations. By December 31, when heightened casualty reports flooded in, Bush increased that aid to $350 million. By February 10, as the dimensions of the tragedy grew, Bush urged Congress to appropriate $950 million for tsunami relief. Congress passed the requested legislation. Soon after the disaster, President Bush dispatched two American aircraft carriers, the USS *Abraham Lincoln* and the USS *Bonhomme Richard*, to the area to serve as staging grounds for helicopter flights to the places most in need of immediate relief. In many instances, the tsunami had wiped out roads, making access by air the only workable alternative.

Among other major contributors to the relief effort were Japan, with a pledge of $500 million; Australia, with a pledge of $800 million that was later increased to $1.1 billion; the European Union, with a pledge of $675 million; Denmark, with a pledge of $420 million; Germany, with a pledge of $653 million; and Canada, with a pledge of $425 million. Even small countries offered assistance: tiny Monaco, $133 million; Bosnia, $67,000; Cambodia, $40,000; Croatia, $917,000; Belgium, $15.67 million; and Cyprus, $1.3 million.

Private donations, both corporate and personal, came pouring in. When an Indian oncologist living and practicing in Florida set out to raise $100,000 for tsunami relief, he raised twice that amount between December 26 and January 7.

Military personnel arrived from the United States as well as from Australia, Singapore, and a number of European countries. Members of the Australian and Singaporean air forces quickly built air strips in Medan, Indonesia, so that relief planes could land. They flew in large cargo planes filled with food, water, and medical supplies that were then transferred to helicopters for transportation to the areas where they were needed the most.

United Nations Secretary-General Kofi Annan visited the stricken areas of Sri Lanka and pledged food and other necessities to every person who needed them. The United States remembered the dead by flying flags on all public buildings at half-staff in the week following the tsunami. Americans were urged to make donations to relief organizations.

President Bush enlisted the aid of former presidents George H. W. Bush and Bill Clinton to organize fund-raising efforts. Even though Clinton was recovering from recent heart surgery, he plunged into relief activities with characteristic vigor and enthusiasm, as did the 80-year-old Bush. The two visited the affected areas, bringing hope and promises of tangible assistance to community leaders throughout the region.

OUTCOMES. Remarkably, the epidemics many feared would follow the tsunami did not develop. Broken bones mended and torn flesh healed as survivors began to reconstruct their lives and rebuild their communities. On a personal level, most of the people who had lived near the Indian Ocean planned to rebuild in the same areas, as is often the case following such disasters as typhoons, hurricanes, earthquakes, and tsunamis.

As a result of the 2004 Indian Ocean Tsunami, considerable attention is being paid to natural phenomena that seem predictive of impending disaster. Somehow, hundreds of members of a tribe that had inhabited the Andaman and Nicobar Islands off the coast of India for many centuries, through some unexplained sixth sense, foresaw that a tsunami was imminent and moved to higher ground, thereby reducing their casualty rate to zero.

Similarly, few animals were killed by the tsunami. Elephants, water buffalo, dogs, cats, and many species of birds escaped the devastation that wiped out so much of the human population in the places that were their natural habitats. Biologists, meteorologists, and climatologists have engaged in far-reaching studies designed to explain what clues cause animals to sense oncoming natural disasters.

Despite the relative poverty of the areas in which the tsunami struck, efforts are being made to install sophisticated early warning technologies such as those that exist in the Pacific Ocean to protect such vulnerable places as Hawaii and Alaska. When such systems are in place, mass evacuations may virtually eliminate the huge numbers of deaths that marked the Indian Ocean Tsunami.

R. Baird Shuman

FOR FURTHER INFORMATION:

Adamson, Thomas K. *Tsunamis.* Mankato, Minn.: Capstone Press, 2006.

Anderson, Robert Mark. "Wave Files." *Natural History* 115 (February, 2006): 54.

Bernard, E. N. *Developing Tsunami-Resilient Communities: The National Tsunami Hazard Mitigation Program.* Norwell, Mass.: Springer, 2005.

Fang, Mark Bay. "Remembering All the Lost, and Rebuilding." *U.S. News & World Report* 40 (January 9, 2006): 10-11.

Stewart, Gail B. *Catastrophe in Southeastern Asia: The Tsunami of 2004.* Chicago: Gale/Lucent, 2005.

Torres, John Albert. *Disaster in the Indian Ocean: Tsunami 2004.* Hockessin, Del.: Mitchell Lane, 2005.

2005: HURRICANE KATRINA

HURRICANE

DATE: August 25-September 2, 2005
PLACE: South Florida, the Florida Panhandle, coastal Alabama, Mississippi, and Louisiana, particularly New Orleans
CLASSIFICATION: Category 4 at landfall
RESULT: 1,500-2,000 estimated dead, hundreds missing, $75 billion in property damage

Hurricane Katrina was the eleventh named storm of the 2005 hurricane season. Meteorologists have recorded just 5 other hurricanes approaching Katrina's intensity. It was the second most deadly hurricane in U.S. history (after the 1900 Galveston hurricane) and the most costly, devastating coastal areas from south Florida to New Orleans and beyond.

During the 2005 hurricane season, so many named storms developed that names beginning with the letters of the English alphabet were exhausted, necessitating some storms to be assigned letters from the Greek alphabet. The most destructive of the storms of 2005, one of three hurricanes to reach Category 5 at some point, was Hurricane Katrina, which some eyewitnesses called "The Doomsday Storm." It swept slowly across south Florida, classified as a Category 1 storm that deposited heavy rains on the area. When it meandered into the Gulf of Mexico, it gained considerable energy from the 80-degree surface temperatures of the Gulf's waters.

Accelerating quickly, Katrina hit the Florida Panhandle, then continued its ruinous course along the Gulf Coast, first as a Category 3 hurricane but quickly strengthening to a Category 4 and then a Category 5 storm with winds exceeding 155 miles an hour. It made landfall at Buras, Louisiana, some 60 miles southeast of New Orleans, leaving havoc in its wake as its counterclockwise winds moved north. The storm's fury left the Alabama coast and the city of Mobile severely damaged. It wiped out almost totally such Mississippi communities as Pascagoula, Slidell, Biloxi, Gulfport, Pass Christian, and Bay St. Louis before striking New Orleans, most of which lies below sea level.

THE SITUATION IN NEW ORLEANS. Before the hurricane, New Orleans had a population of more than 500,000 people, 23 percent of whom lived below poverty level. On August 28, when New Orleans mayor Ray Nagin issued the order for mandatory evacuation, 100,000 New Orleans residents would not or could not evacuate. Left behind were the elderly, the chronically ill, the impoverished, thousands of helpless children, and those without automobiles or other means of transportation. Some people who could have left refused to abandon beloved pets that they were not permitted to take with them to evacuation centers.

The storm struck at the end of the month when many of the impoverished, living marginally on welfare checks, had exhausted their August payments, leaving them without the wherewithal to afford commercial transportation away from the storm's path. Hardest hit was the poorest section of New Orleans, the Ninth Ward. Even though Katrina flooded and flattened other wards, residents from the more prosperous parts of town could evacuate in advance of the devastation. Hurricanes can be predicted far enough in advance for people to be forewarned in time to escape the storm's deadly course.

Residents of New Orleans await rescue on a roof. (FEMA)

Once the storm hit with full fury on the morning of August 29, New Orleans, a crescent nearly surrounded by water—Lake Pontchartrain, the Mississippi River, the Industrial Canal, the Intercoastal Waterway, and the Gulf of Mexico some 60 miles to the south—began to flood. Many parts of the city are 6 feet below sea level, so the storm surge of more than 20 feet that poured in from the Gulf of Mexico proved devastating.

Nevertheless, Katrina's eye passed southeast of New Orleans. So, although the canals and the Mississippi River raged with great walls of rushing water, the city did not receive the full brunt of the storm. The following day, *The New York Times* reported that New Orleans had a mess to clean up but suggested that the destruction could have been much worse.

Only later was the full extent of the city's problems evident. For decades, New Orleans had been protected from floods by earthenware dams, most of them topped with steel reinforced concrete, or by more modern reinforced concrete barriers that had held through dozens of previous storms. The city also had a well-developed system of pumps that returned standing water from the lowlands to Lake Pontchartrain to control flooding.

By August 30, it became clear that the city's disaster was about to be compounded. The levees, whose underpinnings were compromised by the force of the water pushing against them, began to give way. The Seventeenth Street and London Avenue levees came apart bit by bit, dumping millions of gallons of water, most of it polluted, into the streets of the flooded city. The hurricane had disabled many of the pumping stations, which, even had they been working at top capacity, could not have prevented the agitated waters from engulfing everything in their paths.

Katrina killed many people. In one nursing home, 30 residents died in its aftermath. Mayor Nagin announced immediately after the hurricane that as many as 10,000 might be dead, although a number of agencies soon lowered this figure. Flooded hospitals had to close their doors. Bodies piled up in makeshift morgues: 22 in freezers in the Convention Center, an estimated 1,200 in the St. Gabriel Prison Morgue and its stopgap satellites.

The total number of people killed in all the communities ravaged by Hurricane Katrina has been estimated at between 1,500 and 2,000.

As long as six months afterward, human remains were still being found. Some refugees who were deployed to distant venues returned to New Orleans eight to ten months following the storm to finally identify and claim bodies in the city's morgues.

ORIGINS AND DIMENSIONS. Hurricane Katrina began as Tropical Depression 12 that formed over the Bahamas on August 23, 2005. It advanced to South Florida the following day as a named tropical storm, but by August 25, it was designated a Category 1 hurricane. It inundated much of south Florida, and its 75-mile-an-hour winds caused an estimated $400 million in property damage.

The storm pushed on slowly to the Gulf of Mexico, where, over the Gulf's warm surface waters, it gained considerable speed and intensity, advancing to a Category 3 storm. It increased quickly to a Category 4 and, within hours, to a Category 5. It left substantial wind and water damage in the Florida Panhandle as well as in coastal Alabama.

Some meteorologists consider Katrina the strongest hurricane ever to hit the United States. The breadth of the damage that it caused, which ranged more than 100 miles from its center, makes it unique in the annals of meteorology. Before it ended, Katrina had left behind more than $75 billion in property damage as it moved relentlessly from Florida to Louisiana, making it the costliest hurricane in recorded history.

PREPARING FOR THE HURRICANE. When it became evident on August 26 that the Gulf Coast was in the path of a rapidly developing hurricane, Governor Kathleen Blanco of Louisiana declared a state of emergency. On the same day, she requested that the federal government provide National Guard troops to help meet the emergency. The following day, after Katrina was upgraded to a Category 3 hurricane, Governor Haley Barbour of Mississippi and Governor Bob Riley of Alabama also declared a state of emergency.

On August 27, Governor Blanco asked President George W. Bush to declare a federal state of emergency in her state, making it eligible for federal assistance to supplement the assistance that state and city governments could provide. The White House was slow to declare the requested state of emergency but finally gave the Department of Homeland Security (DHS) and the Federal Emergency Management Agency (FEMA) the authority to respond to the threat that the hurricane posed.

On August 28, at 2 A.M., Katrina was upgraded to a Category 4 hurricane. By dawn, it had been upgraded again, this time to a Category 5, the most severe designation assigned to hurricanes on the Saffir-Simpson scale. On that morning, the *Lafayette Daily Advertiser* ran a story warning that the existing levees in New Orleans probably could not withstand the exigencies of a Category 5 storm. The National Hurricane Center's director, Max Mayfield, echoed this sentiment, warning the White House that the levees had been compromised and speculating on the results of their probable failure.

By 4 P.M. on August 28, the National Weather Service issued an urgent warning that outlined what sort of damage would accompany a Category 4 or 5 hurricane. The agency cautioned that the area might not be habitable for weeks or, possibly, months. It predicted that even well-built homes would suffer wall and roof failure and that the ensuing power outages might last for weeks. Pure water would not be available unless it was imported from outside the hurricane zone.

As the hurricane approached, Mayor Nagin urged people in New Orleans who had not already evacuated to gather at 12 designated pickup points, where they would be collected and transported by bus to the Superdome, which had been stocked with 2.5 million liters of bottled water and 3 million meals ready to eat (MREs). An estimated 25,000 displaced people gathered in the Superdome.

Evacuees were urged to bring food and other supplies with them to last for three days, but many arrived empty-handed. Some remained there considerably beyond three days. The storm peeled off portions of the Superdome's roof, allowing the heavy rains that accompanied the storm to inundate the facility, which had already lost its electrical power and whose overtaxed sanitary facilities were failing rapidly.

Another 25,000 people fled to the New Orleans Convention Center, which was less well equipped than the Superdome to deal with the emergency. Many stayed there for almost a week. Meanwhile, the National Guard asked FEMA to provide 700 buses to help with the evacuation, but only 100 were forthcoming. Some 700 school buses and municipal buses that might have been pressed into service to evacuate the city remained idle.

RESCUE, RECOVERY, AND REHABILITATION. Rescue efforts immediately following the hurricane were blighted by a lack of focus. Local

The town of Gulfport, Mississippi, was devastated by Hurricane Katrina. (FEMA)

and state agencies responded as quickly and efficiently as they could, but the federal government was slow to act. President Bush, vacationing in Texas, was criticized for not coming immediately to the shattered areas to inspect them and to set in motion federal rescue and relief initiatives. Instead, he honored speaking commitments in California and Arizona at a time when the hurricane had virtually obliterated large sections of America's Gulf Coast.

In New Orleans, most members of the city's police force of 1,600 had themselves suffered severe personal losses. The homes of many police officers were destroyed and their family members drowned or injured. A total of 249 New Orleans police officers deserted. Some committed suicide. Nevertheless, contingents of tireless rescuers guided boats through flooded streets, picking up survivors wherever they found them. The water in many sections had completely flooded the second levels of houses, forcing residents to retreat into attics or onto rooftops.

When federal aid finally arrived, its specific priorities were to save lives, to sustain lives, and to execute a comprehensive recovery effort. President Bush appointed former presidents George H. W. Bush and Bill Clinton to lead a private fund-raising program, much like the one that the two had organized in response to the Indian Ocean Tsunami of 2004. The two men worked unceasingly to obtain outside assistance for the recovery effort.

FEMA, faced with monumental challenges, evacuated many homeless survivors. Thousands were transported by bus to Houston, Texas, to be housed temporarily in the Astrodome. FEMA subsidized the transportation and placement for extended periods of many survivors in apartments or hotel rooms throughout the United States.

The agency chartered cruise ships and docked them near New Orleans to provide housing for police officers and firefighters who had lost their homes and for workers who came to the area to assist in relief and recovery efforts. It also spent $400 million on mobile homes, but survivors could not be moved into them until they had been connected to electrical and water lines, which in many cases took weeks. Nine months after the hurricane, 18,000 mobile homes were parked unused in Hope, Arkansas, running up monthly storage charges exceeding $250,000.

In order to give storm victims immediate relief, FEMA issued debit cards that holders could use without delay for purchases. Although most of these cards were obtained legally and used to buy necessities, some of them were procured fraudulently. Some claimants, using phony Social Security numbers and other bogus identification, obtained multiple debit cards and used them to pay for more than $1.4 billion in luxury vacations, season tickets to ballgames, pornography, and, in one case, sex change surgery. In June, 2006, the Department of Homeland Security sent to the Justice Department for possible prosecution the names of more than 7,000 people accused of committing fraud in connection with obtaining and using FEMA debit cards.

Many criticized the botched management of the Katrina recovery effort, but federal agencies learned from their mistakes and performed more efficiently following Hurricanes Rita and Wilma, which struck shortly after Katrina.

THE AFTERMATH. It will take years to repair the damage that Hurricane Katrina left in its wake. Affected coastal areas are rebuilding. Gambling casinos on the Mississippi coast, lifted off their foundations and deposited far from where they initially stood, have been rebuilt and have resumed business.

New Orleans was slow to recover, although the French Quarter, being at the highest elevation in New Orleans, quickly resumed its activities. In June, 2006, the American Library Association held its annual convention in the city, and other such conventions were scheduled. Tourists soon began to trickle in.

Many displaced residents were relocated in distant cities that offered housing and jobs to hurricane refugees. A number of these people opted to remain in their new locations, although large numbers vowed to return to the city that they loved.

After the hurricane, many questioned the wisdom of rebuilding New Orleans. Its location makes it extremely vulnerable when hurricanes strike. The city occupies a huge natural declivity, a virtual tub, 6 feet below sea level and surrounded by water. Moreover, industrial and residential developments have destroyed wetlands that once flourished beside the Mississippi River. Throughout history, these wetlands flooded every year and were built up by the silt that the Mississippi River deposited during the annual floods. Now the wetlands are disappearing at the rate of about 20 square miles a year, decreasing the land available to absorb large quantities of water like those that accompanied Katrina.

The case for restoring New Orleans is an emotional and ultimately political one to which the federal government has responded by giving its assurance that the city will be rebuilt. Whether it is reasonable to rebuild is beside the point. People who have spent their lives where their parents and grandparents lived understandably resist suggestions that they abandon such areas.

A crucial step in the process of rebuilding New Orleans is the immediate restoration of a levee system that will prevent the sort of flooding that Hurricane Katrina caused. The Army Corps of Engineers is building new seawalls deeper and stronger than those that crumbled during Katrina.

Housing has been a continuing problem in post-hurricane New Orleans. In June, 2006, FEMA announced that it would rebuild only 6 of the 10 major public housing projects that had been ravaged by the hurricane and that people who had lived in the buildings that were not to be restored would be given vouchers to provide $1,100 a month as rent subsidies until other arrangements could be found for them in a city with few available rentals.

A FEMA report to Congress in June, 2006, warned that most large cities in the United States are ill-equipped to deal with disasters such as Katrina. Time will tell whether New Orleans can withstand the ravages of another Category 4 or 5 hurricane.

R. Baird Shuman

FOR FURTHER INFORMATION:

Brinkley, Douglas. *The Great Deluge: Hurricane Katrina, New Orleans, and the Mississippi Gulf Coast.* New York: William Morrow, 2006.

Cooper, Christopher, and Robert Block. *Disaster: Hurricane Katrina and the Failure of Homeland Security.* New York: Times Books, 2006.

Dyson, Michael Eric. *Come Hell or High Water: Hurricane Katrina and the Color of Disaster.* New York: Basic Civitas Books, 2006.

Horne, Jed. *Breach of Faith: Hurricane Katrina and the Near Death of a Great American City.* New York: Random House, 2006.

Townsend, Frances Fragos. *The Federal Response to Hurricane Katrina: Lessons Learned.* Washington, D.C.: U.S. Government Printing Office, 2006.

Van Heerden, Ivor, and Mike Bryan. *The Storm: What Went Wrong and Why During Hurricane Katrina—the Inside Story from One Louisiana Scientist.* New York: Viking Press, 2006.

■ 2005: THE KASHMIR EARTHQUAKE

EARTHQUAKE

DATE: October 8, 2005
PLACE: Kashmir and North-West Frontier Province, Pakistan
MAGNITUDE: 7.6
RESULT: More than 90,000 dead; about 106,000 injured; 3.3 million homeless; $5 billion in damage

At 8:50 A.M. Pakistan Standard Time, an earthquake occurred with an epicenter some 60 miles north of the Pakistani capital of Islamabad. It proved to be the biggest natural disaster in the history of Pakistan and also affected the neighboring country of India. The area in which it occurred was extremely mountainous, with very poor lines of communication. It was also split by political boundaries. More significant, the area was overpopulated and very poor, with many makeshift buildings and few medical facilities. The rescue efforts were hampered by these factors, plus the sheer size of the operation needed. Although much international assistance was forthcoming, many areas had to wait weeks for help to arrive. The whole area was expected to need years to recover its infrastructures and to rehouse the displaced.

BACKGROUND. Three background factors governed the enormity of the devastation created by the Kashmir earthquake. The first is geological. The Indian subcontinent, including the countries of India and Pakistan, is separated tectonically from the rest of Asia. The South Asian plate was originally attached to Antarctica some 150 million years ago. It then started drifting northward, and 50 million years ago it slammed into the Eurasian plate, forcing the ground up to form the Himalaya mountain ranges, the highest on earth, including the Hindukush and Karakoram ranges. The plate has continued to move northward at the rate of more than an inch a year.

The result is frequent earth tremors and occasional major earthquakes. The most notable recent quakes have been the Quetta earthquake of 1935 in the Sind Province and the 2001 Gujrat earthquake in India. In the more immediate area, a quake in 1974 with a 6.2 magnitude killed 5,300 people. Although a quake of the magnitude of 7.6 is generally serious, the main factor with the Kasmir earthquake was the shallowness of its hypocenter, which was no more than 16 miles deep.

The second background factor is geographical. The northern areas of Pakistan are extremely mountainous. For example, the Kaghan valley running north of Balakot, one of the towns most affected by the quake, is carved through the mountains, with cliffs up to 1,000 feet towering above it on either side. Even a moderately heavy storm will send landslides crashing over the few dirt roads that hug the mountainsides, requiring army bulldozers to cut a new road out. The area is desperately poor, subsistence living at best on the rocky terraced hillsides, but is seriously overpopulated. Pakistan is a Third World country, despite being a nuclear power, and so provision of medical and educational facilities is basic, often housed in buildings that are below standard. Almost no regulations exist for reinforced buildings in such areas.

Third, the area is divided politically. In 1947 the country of Pakistan was formed out of India for the Indian subcontinent's Muslim population. The mountainous northern region of Kashmir had a Hindu ruler but a largely Muslim population. The result was that the Vale of Kashmir was occupied by Indian forces, the mountainous west and north by Pakistani ones. A cease-fire line was created as a temporary measure, but efforts to resolve the territorial dispute have been thwarted. The dispute has led to several wars, an insurgency movement, and the proliferation of nuclear weapons. The Pakistani part of Kashmir is known as Azad (Free) Kashmir. It is administered separately from Pakistan proper and is even poorer than the neighboring North-West Frontier Province. The epicenter of the quake lay inside the cease-fire line.

IMMEDIATE IMPACT. The earthquake struck at around 9 A.M. Saturday morning. Saturday is a normal working day, so the schools were full of children. However, it was also during the month of fasting, Ramadan, which meant than many people had gotten up before dawn to eat and then gone back to bed for a while. The epicenter was located near the village of Garhi Habibullah, on the border of Azad Kashmir and the North-West Frontier Province, with the quake being felt as far afield as Kabul in Afghanistan, New Delhi in India, and Karachi on the coast of Pakistan.

The Kashmir earthquake caused a 10-story apartment building in Islamabad to collapse. (AP/Wide World Photos)

The immediate effect of the quake was the collapse of many buildings, landslides, and the displacement of rocks and boulders. There were even reports of new waterfalls appearing in the high mountain valleys. A block of flats collapsed in Islamabad, causing immediate panic, and there were similar scenes in Lahore, Pakistan's second largest city. Over the rest of the day, 147 secondary shocks were recorded, 28 with a magnitude between 5 and 6. Also, devastating hail and rainstorms continued throughout that day and into the next. Reports quickly came in of schools and hospitals collapsing, roads blocked, and communications down. It was immediately obvious that

965

the devastation was enormous, though no one had any idea how widespread it was.

What was also obvious in the light of the scope was the inadequacy of the Pakistani government's equipment in the more remote areas. A state of emergency was declared in all the hospitals of Islamabad and its twin city of Rawalpindi, and the army and emergency services were put on full alert.

The first pictures from the region showed the collapsed apartment block in Islamabad and efforts being made to rescue those trapped inside. First estimates were 18,000 killed and 45,000 injured in an area where close to 3 million people lived. The most affected areas appeared to be around Muzaffarabad, the capital of Azad Kashmir; Balakot, at the entrance to the Kaghan Valley; and the Mansehra district. Efforts to reach those places, however, were hampered by blocked roads. Muzaffarabad was reached only late Sunday afternoon by a handful of trucks. It was estimated that 60 to 70 percent of all buildings had collapsed in these places. In Garhi Habibullah, both boys' and girls' high schools had collapsed, crushing students and teachers, as had the hospital. Because of the aftershocks, few people dared to stay in the remaining homes or any other building, preferring to stay out in the pouring rain.

On the Indian side of Kashmir, there was much damage, but not on the scale of that on the Pakistani side. The army took over search-and-rescue operations, the usual practice in both countries, with both armies being well-equipped and well-trained. First estimates put the dead in India at 600. Damage was also reported as far afield as Delhi and Amritsar, and in Gujrat, the site of a major earthquake in 2001, there was panic.

RELIEF EFFORTS. The next day, Pakistan president Pervez Musharraf appealed to the international community for aid. The immediate need was for search-and-rescue teams, heavy-lifting helicopters, medical supplies, tents, and blankets. Pakistan possessed only 34 suitable helicopters. Many countries and groups made immediate pledges, including the World Bank, the United States, the European Union, China, and Russia. By contrast, the Indian government claimed that it needed no assistance and even offered some to its traditional enemy, Pakistan. Various search-and-rescue teams arrived very quickly. They were flown by helicopter to the worst affected areas and pulled people out of the rubble for a number of days. The real challenge, however, was to transport the injured by helicopter to the designated hospitals and to ferry in supplies of food and shelter. In fact, there were never enough helicopters at any time. In addition, the weather conditions were poor and unrelenting, hampering much of this effort.

Where aid did arrive, scenes were often chaotic, as people were desperate to get what they could. By October 12, Pakistan had received $350 million in pledges in answer to the president's appeal and also that of the U.N. aid chief, Nils Egland. Some 20,000 troops had been deployed. U.S. aid slowly began to trickle, and U.S. secretary of state Condoleezza Rice visited. The U.S. government felt it particularly necessary to help, as Pakistan was a vital partner in its war against al-Qaeda. President George W. Bush was also aware of criticism over his slow response to Hurricane Katrina in New Orleans one month before the Kashmir earthquake.

Despite heroic efforts by those on the ground, aid was slow to get through. The voluntary aid agencies had been drained by such disasters as the Indian Ocean tsunami just 10 months before and by ongoing emergencies in Africa. Even during the rescue operation in Kashmir, another hurricane hit Central America. Muslim organizations around the world responded, many starting their own makeshift operations, raising aid and money on a private basis, especially among immigrants in Europe and the United States who still had family in the affected area. Some smaller charities and missions deployed small teams of personnel in the country to help. Always, however, the greatest problem was access to the worst affected areas. In Azad Kashmir, members of the insurgency were often the only ones who could bring help and rescue.

FURTHER IMPACT. Aftershocks continued the rest of October, 2005, those of magnitude 4 or above totaling nearly 1,000, mainly to the northwest of the original epicenter. After a short time, it became clear that many people were dying of injuries that had been left untreated. As more and more remote areas were reached, the scale of this problem became even more evident. Also starvation was becoming a threat, as were the increasingly cold nights in the mountains, where elevations up to 20,000 feet were not uncommon and the winter snows were due to begin soon. Anger against perceived government inadequacies began to rise on both sides of the border in those who had received little or no aid.

By now, estimates of dead were climbing to 38,000, 42,000, and then 47,000, with similar numbers for the injured, with half of those affected being children. These numbers continued to climb over the next few months. The number of homeless stayed at around the 2 million mark. By contrast, the number of injured who were evacuated was put at 6,000 when the total injured was being estimated at 52,000. In Muzaffarabad, a French team of doctors were operating a 6-bed field hospital, an indication of the desperate shortage of medical facilities. In all, it was estimated that 26 hospitals and 600 health clinics had been destroyed. Amputations for gangrenous limbs became increasingly common, as were cases of paralysis. By November, a pneumonia epidemic threatened more lives.

Although Pakistan was the main producer of tents worldwide, the need for additional winterised tents was significant, with 350,000 more tents required. The Pakistan government started plans for refugee camps along the flatter valleys, where people could be more easily reached during the winter. Prime Minister Shaukat Aziz appealed to the mountain people to come to the camps, but they were reluctant, fearing the sense of enclosure in such camps and worrying that their land would be stolen.

Fortunately, the winter did delay somewhat and people came to the camps, only to live a miserable existence there. Possibly up to 1,000 villages had been destroyed.

On the Indian side, 30,000 families had been displaced, though the number of dead and injured remained surprisingly low at 1,360 and 6,266, respectively. Indian prime minister Manmohan Singh visited the area and promised a grant of $2,255 to every family that had suffered death or homelessness. Tents, however, were in as short a supply as over the border, with only 13,000 available out of the 30,000 needed.

One hoped-for effect, a cessation of hostilities between Indian forces and the insurgents, did not happen, and although the cease-fire line was opened briefly, mainly for relief purposes, the overall political tension remained high. In fact, during the relief operations, a female suicide bomber blew herself up near Indian troops and terrorists attacked government buildings in New Delhi.

At the international level, the Pakistani government claimed that money pledged to it came too little and too late. In any case, the scale of the earthquake was unprecedented, and it came in a year of quite unprecedented disasters.

David Barratt

FOR FURTHER INFORMATION:

Ali, M. M. "With Relief Slow to Arrive, Earthquake Death Toll Continues to Rise in Kashmir." *Washington Report on Middle East Affairs* 25, no. 1 (January 1, 2006): 44.

The New York Times, October, 9-29, 2005.

U.S. Congress. Senate. Committee on Foreign Relations. *Pakistan Earthquake: International Response and Impact on U.S. Foreign Policies and Programs.* 109th Congress, 1st session, 2005. Senate Report 109-41.

Walton, Frances. "One Nurse Can Make a Big Difference." *Australian Nursing Journal* 14, no. 2 (August 1, 2006): 15.

■ 2006: The Leyte mudslide

Mudslide

Date: February 17, 2006
Place: Southern Leyte, the Philippines
Result: More than 200 confirmed dead, 1,800 missing and presumed dead; 297 of 300 houses in village of Barangay Guinsaugon destroyed

The tiny village of Saint Bernard in the southern reaches of the Philippine island of Leyte was just coming to life around 9 A.M. on Friday, February 17, 2006. The 246 students in the local school and their 7 teachers had eaten their breakfasts, come to school, and were beginning their daily lessons. About 100 visitors had arrived in the village for a women's group meeting.

Suddenly, the entire town was awash in mud as the mountain behind it collapsed. In some places, the mud reached depths exceeding 30 feet (more than 9 meters) and completely covered an area of 0.5 square mile (1 square kilometer). The mudslide obliterated everything in its path almost instantly.

A slimy muck flowed relentlessly over some 15 other villages near Saint Bernard, completely covering buildings such as Saint Bernard's school, from which just one student and one teacher emerged alive. Everyone else in the school was sucked into the roaring river of roiling mud that completely consumed the village. A police officer watched helplessly as the school, where his wife taught and four of his children were students, disappeared beneath a sea of mud, wiping out his immediate family.

In the neighboring village of Barangay Guinsaugon, just 3 of the town's 300 houses survived the onslaught. Those who were not pulled into the muddy maelstrom watched helplessly as people, pets, livestock, and the town's structures—houses, schools, shops, and official buildings—vanished before their eyes. The irresistible force of the mudflow precluded the possibility of immediate rescue by those who had in some miraculous way escaped the unforgiving vortex of the mudslide.

SOUTHERN LEYTE'S HISTORY OF MUDSLIDES. The mudslide of 2006 was preceded by a number of similar disasters that occurred in the quarter century before this devastating event. In 1991, Ormoc City, on the western coast of Leyte, suffered floods and landslides triggered by a tropical storm that dumped unprecedented rainfall upon the countryside. More than 6,000 people died in these floods and mudslides.

In December, 2003, an additional 133 people died in floods and in the ensuing mudslides in San Francisco in southern Leyte, an area close to where the 2006 mudslide occurred. In December, 2004, Philippine president Gloria Macapagal Arroyo suspended logging operations in geohazardous areas of the Philippines following mudslides that took the lives of 640 Filipinos.

Only 5 days before the mudslide of February 17, 7 road workers died when a landslide engulfed them in Sogod, a town close to Barangay Guinsaugon. The Philippines's Bureau of Mines and Geosciences pointed out the danger areas in a geohazard mapping project that specifically pinpointed the general area in which the February 17 disaster took place. This report, however, did not contain sufficient detailed information about the towns that were under the greatest threat. As recently as 2003, the Philippine government declared more than 80 percent of Leyte to be subject to geological hazards.

In the Philippines, which have long been subjected to the dangers of floods, earthquakes, landslides, cyclones, and other natural catastrophes, it is estimated that more than 34,000 people perished in natural disasters between 1970 and 2000. Between 1990 and 2000, such events are estimated to have disrupted the lives of 35 million people, killing or injuring many.

Although people could have been evacuated from the villages overwhelmed during the February 17 disaster, most of the impoverished villagers could not conceive of how great and imminent the danger of annihilation was. Many of them had no place to which they could flee. Most were reluctant to leave the places in which they earned their scant livings.

During the weeks of February 6 and 13, when the villages near Barangay Guinsaugon had four times the amount of rainfall considered normal for the area in that season, some residents did leave. Not realizing fully how unstable the saturated soil had become, however, many of them ended their evacuation and returned to their homes on February 15 or 16, encouraged because the rains had subsided and the sun had broken through. Some of these villages had ongoing activities planned for the upcoming weekend. The people who lived in them were unwilling to participate in an evacuation that would disrupt their plans.

SOME CAUSES OF THE MUDSLIDE. Several major factors contributed to the disastrous mudslide in southern Leyte on February 17, 2006. Climate change was in part responsible. Unusually heavy rainfalls in the weeks preceding the mudslide—20 inches in one month—were partially the result of La Niña, a climatic condition created by higher-than-usual surface temperatures in the surrounding oceans. The exceptional rainfall accompanying La Niña destabilized the soil significantly.

Overpopulation was another salient factor in creating conditions that made a mudslide likely. Related to this factor is the major deforestation that resulted from clearing land for human occupancy as populations expanded sharply. Leyte is mountainous and is one of the most heavily forested areas in the Philippines, but many of its forests have been sacrificed as residential communities replace forested areas to accommodate the country's burgeoning population.

Another factor related to deforestation is the replacement of native, deep-rooted trees with coconut palms, whose roots are relatively shallow. Trees have provided the area's commercial interests with a ready source of revenue both through selling the timber recovered from the deep-rooted trees that were cut down and through the sale of coconuts, a significant cash crop in the area. Whereas the native trees with their deep roots served to stabilize the soil, the replacement trees afforded little such protection.

Over and above these contributory factors was another one that dates back several decades to the time when considerable mining was done on Leyte. The earth beneath the island is honeycombed with mine shafts and tunnels that were abandoned decades earlier. These tunnels were subject to collapse when the soil became oversaturated.

The mud had already begun to flow when, on the morning of February 17, the affected area was struck by an earthquake so minor that under normal circumstances it would hardly have been noticed by the average person. It had a magnitude of 2.3 on the Richter scale, which is generally considered inconsequential. Given the instability of the waterlogged soil, however, this almost imperceptible tremor was sufficient to collapse abandoned mine shafts, to cause saturated mountains to crumble, and to exacerbate the mudslide that had already begun to exact its fearsome toll.

THE RESCUE EFFORT. Initial rescue efforts were hampered in many places because there were more victims than survivors. The depth of the mud flow was so great that there was little hope of penetrating it. Attempts to do so were discouraged because those trapped by the mud could not have survived beneath it. The instability of the soil was such that rescue attempts presented extreme hazards to anyone undertaking them.

A week before this disaster, when 7 road workers died in a landslide in nearby Sogod, only 3 bodies were retrieved because of the instability of the earth where they had been lost. Now, with thousands of people missing and with many of the survivors suffering physical injury and severe emotional stress, immediate rescue attempts proved futile.

As soon as she learned of the tragedy in southern Leyte, President Arroyo sent military rescue teams and ships from the Philippine coast guard and navy to the area to mount an immediate rescue effort. This effort, however, was impeded by a number of factors: roads blocked by huge boulders, washed out bridges, and deep mud that could swallow up rescuers in an instant. Rescuers also lacked the heavy earth-moving equipment that would possibly have facilitated their efforts, although the mud was so deep and the earth so unstable that heavy equipment might simply have sunk into the quagmire that covered the lost villages.

Much of the world offered the Philippines assistance. Malaysia sent a search and rescue team of sixty people to the area. A Spanish organization, Unidad Canina de Rescate y Salvamento, sent a specialized team of 6 rescuers with 5 trained sniffer dogs to assist in the rescue operation. New Zealand pledged $133,000 toward the rescue effort. South Korea pledged $1 million in aid. Japan sent 27 million pesos to be used in the rescue effort, but only 3 million ever reached the affected area, with the remainder being lost, presumably, to governmental graft.

By nightfall on February 17, the Philippine Red Cross reported that 53 people had been rescued, but close to 2,000 remained unaccounted for. Rescue efforts had to be suspended when night fell because of a lack of lighting and because of the imminent danger of flash floods and further mudslides.

RELIEF EFFORTS. When the mudslide began, the U.S. Navy had two vessels, the USS *Essex* and the USS *Harper's Ferry*, nearby. These ships were diverted immediately to the stricken area. About 6,000 U.S. Army and Marine Corps troops that were in the Philippines to participate in a bilateral training exercise were also pressed into assisting in the relief effort.

The United States distributed $100,000 worth of disaster equipment to the Philippine Red Cross. It followed this contribution with more than half a million dollars that USAID provided for the purchase of food, blankets, mosquito netting, temporary shelters, medical supplies, and water purification tablets and equipment.

Relief also came in the form of contributions from China (about $1 million in cash and materials), Taiwan ($100,000 as well as enough medicine to treat 3,000 people for six weeks), Thailand ($100,000), Australia (about $740,000), and a number of other countries. The United States flew relief planes into the area with emergency trauma kits, flashlights, medicine, rubber boots, and clothing to provide immediate assistance.

THE AFTERMATH. Recovering from a disaster such as the Leyte mudslide is a discouraging process. The root causes of such a disaster are, to a large extent, outside human and governmental control. Such natural causes as La Niña, unusually heavy rainfall, and earthquakes are not preventable.

Contributing factors such as heavy mining in a mudslide area, deforestation, and rapidly expanding populations have taken place over a long enough period that undoing their catastrophic results seems all but impossible. When a disaster such as the mudslide in southern Leyte strikes, the survivors, most of whom are rooted in the area, are usually reluctant to relocate. They tend to rebuild and trust that such disasters will not recur, although the odds do not support this optimistic view.

Only totalitarian governments can forcibly relocate large populations, which would seem a possible remedy for the problems facing southern Leyte. In a democracy such as the Philippines, however, massive mandatory relocation is a virtual impossibility. The government, therefore, has limited options. It can attempt to educate people to the natural dangers of geohazardous areas, but even those who are made aware of such dangers tend to become apathetic over time.

Nevertheless, the government can engage in massive reforestation efforts, which have been launched in the Philippines and should yield some long-term benefits. It can also support programs that offer opportunities for young people to move away from dangerous areas, although family considerations often make such intervention ineffective.

R. Baird Shuman

FOR FURTHER INFORMATION:

Asio, Victor B., and Marlito Jose M. Bande. "Innovative Community-Led Sustainable Forest Resource Conservation and Management in Baybay, Leyte, the Philippines." In *Innovative Communities: People-Centred Approaches to Environmental Management in the Asia-Pacific Region*, edited by Jerry Velasquez. New York: United Nations University Press, 2005.

De Souza, Roger-Mark. "Is the Catastrophic Mudslide in the Philippines Just Another Disaster Story?" *Population Reference Bureau.* http://www.prb.org/Template.cfm?Section=PRB&template=/ContentManagement/ ContentDisplay.cfm&ContentID=13677.

"Mudslides in Philippines; Merciless Heat and Drought in Africa; Greenland Glaciers Melting: Israel and Hamas." *The America's Intelligence Wire,* February 17, 2006.

"Philippine President Suspends Logging After Storms Unleash Mudslides That Kill 640." *The America's Intelligence Wire,* December 5, 2004.

■ GLOSSARY

Acid rain: Rain with higher levels of acidity than normal; the source of the high levels of acidity is polluted air.

Acquired immunodeficiency syndrome (AIDS): A progressive loss of immune function and susceptibility to secondary infections that arises from chronic infection with HIV.

African sleeping sickness: An infectious disease transmitted through the bite of a tsetse fly with symptoms of fever, lymph node swelling, fatigue, and possibly coma and death.

Aftershock: A minor shock following the main tremor of an earthquake.

AIDS. *See* Acquired immunodeficiency syndrome (AIDS)

Airship: A lighter-than-air aircraft that uses hydrogen for buoyancy.

Alluvium: Sediment deposited by flowing water.

Alpine glacier: A small, elongate, usually tongue-shaped glacier commonly occupying a preexisting valley in a mountain range.

Amplitude: Wave height.

Angle of repose: The maximum angle of steepness that a pile of loose material such as sand or rock can assume and remain stable; the angle varies with the size, shape, moisture, and angularity of the material.

Anthrax: An infectious disease caused by a bacterium, with symptoms of external nodules or lesions in the lungs.

Antibiotic: Any substance that destroys or inhibits the growth of microorganisms, especially bacteria.

Antibody: A protein substance produced by white blood cells in response to an antigen; combats bacterial, viral, chemical, or other invasive agents in the body and provides immunity against disease-causing microorganisms.

Aquifer: A water-bearing bed of rock, sand, or gravel, capable of yielding substantial quantities of water to wells or springs.

Arson: The willful or malicious burning of property.

Ash: Fine-grained pyroclastic material less than 2 millimeters in diameter, ejected from an erupting volcano.

Asteroid: A small, rocky body in orbit around the sun; a minor planet.

Asteroid belt: The region between the orbits of Mars and Jupiter, containing the majority of asteroids.

Atmosphere: The five clearly defined regions composed of layers of gases and mixtures of gases, water vapor, and solid and liquid particles, extending up to 483 kilometers above the earth.

Atoll: A tropical island on which a massive coral reef, often ringlike, generally rests on a volcanic base.

Avalanche: Any large mass of snow, ice, rock, soil, or a mixture of these materials that falls, slides, or flows rapidly downslope; velocities may reach in excess of 500 kilometers per hour.

Bacteria: Microscopic single-celled organisms that multiply by means of simple division; bacteria are found everywhere and most are beneficial, with only a few species causing disease.

Base surge: The initial volcanic blast of an ash flow.

Basin: A regionally depressed structure in which sediments accumulate.

Bathymetry: The measurement of water depth at various places in a body of water.

Beaufort scale: A scale from 0 to 12 that measures wind velocity.

Blizzard: A long, severe snowstorm.

Body wave: A seismic wave that propagates interior to a body; there are two kinds—P waves and S waves—that travel through the earth, reflecting and refracting off of the several layered boundaries within the earth.

Bore: A nearly vertical advancing wall of water that may be produced by tides, a tsunami, or a seiche.

Brisance: The shattering or crushing effect of an explosive.

Brushfire: A wildfire.

Bubo: An inflammatory swelling of a lymph gland.

Bubonic plague: A form of plague characterized by the sudden onset of fever, chills, weakness, headache, and buboes in the groin, armpits, or neck.

Caldera: A large, flat-floored volcanic depression that is formed on top of a large, shallow magma chamber during the eruption or withdrawal of magma; calderas are usually tens of kilometers across and can be a kilometer or more in depth.

Calve: To separate a piece from an ice mass.

Cannibalism: The eating of human flesh by human beings.

CD4 cell: A type of white blood cell (helper T cell) that helps other immune cells work together to fight a variety of diseases.

Cholera: A disease marked by severe gastrointestinal symptoms.

Cinder cone: A small volcano composed of cinder or lumps of lava containing many gas bubbles, or vesicles; often the early stage of a stratovolcano.

Cirque: A steep-sided, gentle-floored, semicircular hollow produced by erosion at the head of a glacier high on a mountain peak.

Coal: Dark brown to black rock formed by heat and compression from the accumulation of plant material in swampy environments.

Cold front: The contact between two air masses when a bulge of cold, polar air surges southward into regions of warmer air.

Combustion: An exothermic, self-sustaining, chemical reaction usually involving the oxidation of a fuel by oxygen in the atmosphere and the emission of heat, light, and mechanical energy, such as sound.

Comet: A solar system body, usually in an elongated and randomly oriented orbit, composed of rocky and icy materials that form a flowing head and extended tail when the body nears the sun.

Comet nucleus: The central core of a comet, composed of frozen gases and dust; the source of all cometary activity.

Conduction: Heat transfer between two bodies in direct contact with each other.

Cone: The hill or mountain, more or less conical, surrounding a volcanic vent and created by its ejecta; it is normally surmounted by a crater.

Conflagration: A fire that spreads from building to building through flame spread over some distance, often a portion of a city or a town.

Continental glacier or ice sheet: A glacier of considerable thickness that completely covers a large part of a continent, obscuring the relief of the underlying surface.

Convection: Heat transfer within a fluid.

Cordillera: A long, elevated mountain chain marked by a valley-and-ridge structure.

Core: The spherical, mostly liquid mass located 2,900 kilometers below the earth's surface; a central, solid part is known as the inner core.

Couloir: A mountain-side gorge.

Crater: The circular depression atop a volcanic cone or formed by meteoritic impact.

Creep: The slow, more or less continuous downslope movement of earth material.

Crust: The outermost layer of the earth; the continental crust, composed of dominantly silicon-rich igneous rocks, metamorphic rocks, and sedimentary rocks, is between 30 and 40 kilometers thick, while the oceanic crust, composed of magnesium- and iron-rich rocks such as basalt, is merely 5 kilometers thick.

Cwm: A cirque.

Cyclone: A major tropical storm that originates in the Indian Ocean.

Debris flow: A flowing mass consisting of water and a high concentration of sediment with a wide range of size, from fine muds to coarse gravels.

Deflagration: An explosive reaction that spreads outward as burning materials ignite the materials next to them at a rate slower than the speed of sound.

Deforestation: The process of clearing forests.

Delta: A deposit of sediment, often triangular, formed at a river mouth where the wave action of the sea is low.

Deoxyribonucleic acid (DNA): A protein found in the nucleus of a cell comprising chromosomes that contain the genetic instructions of an organism.

Detonation: An explosive reaction in which a shock wave progressively combusts materials by compressing them when the rate is faster than the speed of sound.

Dew point: The temperature at which a vapor begins to condense.

Dike: A tabular igneous rock body that cuts across the fabric of the solid rocks.

Dilatancy: An increase in volume as a result of rock forming cracks by expansion, pressure, or agitation.

Diphtheria: A highly contagious bacterial infection that usually affects the respiratory system.

DNA. *See* Deoxyribonucleic acid (DNA)

Doppler radar: A radar system that measures velocity (as of wind).

Downburst: A downward outflowing of air and the associated wind shear from a thunderstorm that is especially hazardous to aircraft.

Downdraft: A downward current of air or gas.

Drainage basin: The land area that contributes water to a particular stream; the edge of such a basin is a drainage divide.

Drought: An extended period of below-normal precipitation that is sufficiently long and severe that crops fail and normal water demand cannot be met.

Dust Bowl: The period from 1932 to 1938 in the U.S. Midwest and Southeast during which drought conditions caused much dust to form and drift.

Dust devil: A rotating column of rising air, made visible by the dust it contains; smaller and less destructive than a tornado, it has winds of less than 60 kilometers per hour.

Dust storm: The result of wind erosion, desertification, and physical deterioration of the soil caused by persistent or temporary lack of rainfall and wind gusts.

Earthquake: A sudden release of strain energy in a fault zone as a result of violent motion of a part of the earth along the fault.

Ebola virus: A disease in which the patient experiences fever, muscle pain, blood clots in vital organs, hemorrhaging, shock, kidney failure, and often death.

Ejecta: The material ejected from the crater made by a meteoric impact; also, material thrown out of a volcano during eruption.

El Niño: Part of a gigantic meteorological system called the Southern Oscillation that links the ocean and atmosphere in the Pacific, causing periodic changes in climate.

Elastic waves: Waves that travel through a material because of its ability to recover from an instantaneous elastic deformation.

Encephalitis: Inflammation of the brain.

Enzootic: An infection that is present in an animal community at all times but manifests itself only in a small fraction of instances.

Ephemeral stream: A river or stream that flows briefly in response to nearby rainfall; such streams are common in arid and semiarid regions.

Epicenter: The point on the earth's surface directly above the focus of an earthquake.

Epidemic: A disease that affects a large human population.

Epidemiology: The medical field that studies the distribution of disease among human populations, as well as the factors responsible for this distribution.

Epizootic: An outbreak of disease in which many animals become infected at the same time.

Ergotism: A disease of the central nervous system caused by ingesting the alkaloids (one of which is LSD) of the ergot fungus, *Claviceps purpurea*, which infects rye grain; symptoms include numbness of the extremities, vomiting and diarrhea, dizziness, and delusions and convulsions usually ending in a painful death.

Erosion: The removal of weathered rock and mineral fragments and grains from an area by the action of wind, ice, gravity, or running water.

Eruption: Volcanic activity of such force as to propel significant amounts of magmatic products over the rim of the crater.

Evaporite: A rock largely composed of minerals that have precipitated upon evaporation of seawater or lake water.

Evapotranspiration: The movement of water from the soil to the atmosphere in response to heat, combining transpiration in plants and evaporation.

Exothermic reaction: A reaction in which the new substances produced have less energy than the original substances.

Explosion: Combustion that expands so quickly that the fuel volume cannot shed energy rapidly enough to remain stable.

Extinction: The disappearance of a species or large group of animals or plants.

Extrusion: The emission of magma or lava and the rock so formed onto the earth's surface.

Extrusive rock: Igneous rock that has been erupted onto the surface of the earth.

Eye: The calm central region of a hurricane, composed of a tunnel with strong sides.

Eyewall: The area surrounding the eye, or center, of a hurricane.

Famine: A lack of access to food, the cause of which can be a natural disaster, such as a drought, or a situation created by humans, such as a civil war.

Fault: A fracture or system of fractures across which relative movement of rock bodies has occurred.

Fault drag: The bending of rocks adjacent to a fault.

Fault slip: The direction and amount of relative movement between the two blocks of rock separated by a fault.

Fifty-year-flood: A hypothetical flood whose severity is such that it would occur on average only once in a period of fifty years, which equates to a 2 percent probability each year.

Fire: The process of combustion.

Fireball: A very large and bright meteor that often explodes with fragments falling to the ground as meteorites; sometimes called a bolide.

Firebrand: A piece of burning material that is carried by convective forces, such as wind, from one location to another.

Firestorm: A large, usually stationary fire characterized by very high temperatures, in which the central column of rising, heated air induces strong inward winds that supply oxygen to the fire.

Flash floods: Floods that begin very quickly and last only a short time.

Flash point: The minimum temperature at which vapors above a volatile substance ignite in air when exposed to flame.

Flood: The result of a river overflowing its banks and spreading out over the bordering floodplain; defined in terms of the volume of water moving past a given point in the stream channel per unit of time (cubic feet per second).

Floodplain: The relatively flat valley floor on either side of a river which may be partly or wholly occupied by water during a flood.

Flow rate: The amount of water that passes a reference point in a specific amount of time, measured in liters per second.

Flu. *See* Influenza

Fluvial: Of or related to streams and their actions.

Focus: The region within the earth from which earthquake waves emanate; also called the hypocenter.

Foehn: A warm, dry wind blowing in the valleys of a mountain.

Fog: Dense water vapor, reducing visibility to less than 0.6 mile (1 kilometer), that occurs when the temperature of any surface falls below the dew point of the air directly above it.

Freeze: The occurrence of abnormally low temperatures for an extended period of time over a region.

Fresh water: Water with less than 0.2 percent dissolved salts, such as is found in most streams, rivers, and lakes.

Front: The boundary between two dissimilar air masses.

Fuel: A material that will burn.

Fujita scale: A rating scale that examines structural damage to assess the wind speed of a tornado.

Fumarole: A vent that emits only gases.

Glacier: An accumulation of ice that flows viscously as a result of its own weight; a glacier forms when snowfall accumulates and re-crystallizes into a granular snow (firn, or névé), which becomes compacted and converted into solid, interlocking glacial ice.

Graben: A roughly symmetrical crustal depression formed by the lowering of a crustal block between two normal faults that slope toward each other.

Graupel: Soft hail.

Groundwater: Water that is located beneath the surface of the earth in interconnected pores.

Hail: Precipitation consisting of layers of ice and snow in the form of small balls.

Harmonic tremor: A movement or shaking of the ground accompanying volcanic eruptions.

Hawaiian eruption: A low intensity volcanic eruption (VEI values of 0 or 1) characterized by a calm outpouring of low viscosity, low silicon lava.

Headwater: The source of a stream.

Heat Index: A scale that measures how hot it feels when the relative humidity is factored into the actual air temperature.

Heat wave: The occurrence of abnormally high air temperatures for an extended period of time over a region, destroying crops, damaging infrastructures, and sometimes causing both animal and human deaths.

HIV. *See* Human immunodeficiency virus (HIV)

Host: A living animal or plant giving lodgment to a parasite.

Hot spot: A zone of hot, upwelling rock that is rooted in the earth's upper mantle; as plates of the earth's crust and lithosphere glide over a mantle plume, a trail of hot spot volcanoes is formed and the earth's surface bulges upward in a dome several hundred kilometers wide by 1 kilometer high. Also called a mantle plume.

Human immunodeficiency virus (HIV): A retrovirus that makes the immune system weak by destroying CD4 cells, causing the body to be susceptible to infection; the virus that causes AIDS.

Hundred-year-flood: A hypothetical flood whose severity is such that it would occur on average only once in a period of one hundred years, which equates to a 1 percent probability each year.

Hurricane: A severe tropical storm with winds exceeding 119 kilometers per hour that originates in tropical regions; the term "hurricane" is sometimes used only for storms originating in the Atlantic Ocean, with "typhoon" used for those originating in the Pacific Ocean and "cyclone" used for those originating in the Indian Ocean.

Hydrocarbon: An organic compound composed of carbon and hydrogen often occurring in petroleum, natural gas, coal, and bitumens.

Hyperthermia: Excessively high body temperature.

Hypocenter: The central underground location of an earth tremor; also called the focus.

Hypothermia: Excessively low body temperature.

Ice storm: Rain falling from an above-freezing layer of upper air to a layer of below-freezing air on or near the earth's surface, coating everything with a layer of ice called glaze.

Iceberg: An ice mass, originating from a glacier, that typically floats in an ocean.

Ignimbrite: An igneous rock deposited from a hot, mobile, ground-hugging cloud of ash and pumice.

Immune system: The body system that is responsible for fighting off infectious disease.

Impact crater: A depression, usually circular, in a planetary surface, caused by the high-speed impact of rocky debris or comet nuclei.

Influenza: Any one of a group of serious respiratory disease caused by viruses.

Intensity: An arbitrary measure of an earthquake's effect on people and buildings, based on the modified Mercalli scale.

Island arc: A curved chain of volcanic islands, generally located a few hundred kilometers from a trench where active subduction of one oceanic plate under another is occurring.

Jet stream: A narrow current of high-speed winds in the upper atmosphere.

K/T boundary: The thin clay layer that lies between the rocks of the Cretaceous geological period and the rocks of the following Tertiary period.

La Niña: The part of the Southern Oscillation that brings cold water to the South American coasts, which makes easterly trade winds stronger, the waters of the Pacific off South America colder, and ocean temperatures in the western equatorial Pacific warmer than normal.

Lahar: A mudflow composed chiefly of volcanic debris on the flanks of a volcano.

Landslide: A general term that applies to any downslope movement of materials; landslides include avalanches, earthflows, mudflows, rockfalls, and slumps.

Lava: The fluid rock issued from a volcano or fissure and the solidified rock it forms when it cools.

Lava tube: A cavern structure formed by the draining out of liquid lava in a pahoehoe (basaltic rock) flow.

Legionnaires' disease: An acute bacterial pneumonia caused by a bacterial infection, with symptoms of fever, chills, and muscle pain; also called legionellosis.

Levee: A dikelike structure, usually made of compacted earth and reinforced with other materials, that is designed to contain the stream flow in its natural channel.

Lightning: A high-voltage electrical spark which occurs most often when a cloud attempts to balance the differences between positive and negative charges within itself.

Limestone: A common sedimentary rock containing the mineral calcite; the calcite originated from fossil shells of marine plants and animals or by precipitation directly from seawater.

Liquefaction: The loss in cohesiveness of water-saturated soil as a result of ground shaking caused by an earthquake.

Low: An area of low barometric pressure.

Lymphocyte: A white blood cell that produces antibodies.

Macrophage: A tissue cell that protects the body from infection.

Magma: Molten silicate liquid plus any crystals, rock inclusions, or gases trapped therein.

Magnitude: A measure of the amount of energy released by an earthquake, based on the relation between the logarithm of ground motion at the detecting instrument and its distance from the epicenter.

Mantle: The portion of the earth's interior extending from about 60 kilometers in depth to 2,900 kilometers; it is composed of relatively high-density minerals that consist primarily of silicates.

Mantle plume: Hot spot.

Marine: Referring to a seawater, ocean environment.

Meteor: A bright streak of light in the sky, sometimes called a shooting star, produced by a meteoroid entering the earth's atmosphere at high speed and heating to incandescence.

Meteor shower: A meteor display caused by comet dust particles burning up in the upper atmosphere during the annual passage of earth through a cometary wake or debris field.

Meteoric water: Surface water that infiltrates porous and fractured crustal rocks; the same as groundwater.

Meteorite: The remnant of an interplanetary body that survives a fall through the earth's atmosphere and reaches the ground.

Meteoroid: A natural, solid object traveling through interplanetary space.

Meteorology: The study of weather.

Modified Mercalli scale: A means of calculating the intensity of shaking at the surface of the earth.

Monsoon: A seasonal pattern of wind at boundaries between warm ocean bodies and landmasses.

Mudflow: Both the process and the landform characterized by very fluid movement of fine-grained soil with a high (sometimes more than 50 percent) water content.

Nuée ardente: A hot cloud of rock fragments, ash, and gases that suddenly and explosively erupt from some volcanoes and flow rapidly down their slopes.

Orography: A branch of physical geography that deals with mountains.

Oxidant: A substance that combines another substance with oxygen.

Oxidation: A chemical reaction in which an oxidizing agent and a reducing agent combine to form a product with less energy than the original materials.

Ozone: A gas containing three atoms of oxygen; it is highly concentrated in a zone of the stratosphere.

P wave: A type of seismic wave generated at the focus of an earthquake, traveling 6-8 kilometers per second, with a push-pull vibratory motion parallel to the direction of propagation; P stands for "primary," as P waves are the fastest and first to arrive at a seismic station.

Palmer Drought Index (PDI): Defines drought as the period of time, generally measured in months or years, when the actual moisture supply at a specified location is always below the climatically anticipated or appropriate supply of moisture.

Pandemic: A disease occurring over a wide geographic area.

PDI. *See* Palmer Drought Index (PDI)

Peléan eruption: A volcanic eruption often considered a subclass of Vulcanian eruption, in which nuées ardentes often cause the collapse or explosion of a volcanic dome sitting over the vent.

Photochemical smog: Smog caused by the action of solar ultraviolet radiation on an atmosphere polluted with hydrocarbons and nitrogen oxides from automobile exhaust.

Phreatic eruption: An eruption in which water plays a major role; also called hydrovolcanic.

Plague: An infection transmitted by fleas, which may prove fatal if left untreated.

Plate tectonics: The theory that the outer surface of the earth consists of large moving plates that interact to produce seismic, volcanic, and orogenic activity.

Plinian eruption: The most explosive and rare of the volcanic eruptions of historic record, having VEI values of 4 to 6; they spew an abundance of ash into the stratosphere.

Pneumonic plague: A form of plague, limited to humans, which directly transmits the infection via infected aerosol droplets from a person with a lung infection.

Point-release avalanche: A loose snow avalanche caused by a cohesionless snow layer resting on a slope steeper than its angle of repose.

Poliomyelitis: A viral illness that may cause meningitis and permanent paralysis; it can be prevented through immunization.

Pollution: A condition in which air, soil, or water contains substances that make it hazardous for human use.

Precipice: A steep or overhanging area of earth or rock.

Primary explosives: Fuels that explode when ignited by a nonexplosive source.

Pumice: A vesicular glassy rock commonly having the composition of rhyolite; a common constituent of silica-rich explosive volcanic eruptions.

Pyroclastic fall: The settling of debris under the influence of gravity from an explosively generated plume of material.

Pyroclastic flow: A highly heated mixture of volcanic gases and ash that travels down the flanks of a volcano.

Pyroclastic rocks: Rocks formed in the process of volcanic ejection and composed of fragments of ash, rock, and glass.

Pyrolysis: The process of breaking a substance down through the application of heat into its constituent elements before it can be oxidized.

Quarantine: A state of enforced isolation designed to prevent the spread of disease.

Radiant heat transfer: Heat transfer by electromagnetic waves across distances.

Recurrence interval: The average time interval, expressed in number of years, between occurrences of a flood of a given or greater magnitude than others in a measured series of floods.

Ribonucleic acid (RNA): The material contained in the core of many viruses that is responsible for directing the replication of the virus inside the host cell.

Richter scale: The scale, devised by Charles F. Richter, used for measuring the magnitude of earthquakes.

Rift valley: A region of extensional deformation in which the central block has dropped down in relation to the two adjacent blocks.

Right-lateral strike-slip: Sideways motion along a steep fault in which the block of the earth's crust across the fault from the observer appears to be displaced to the right; left-slip faults are displaced to the left.

Ring of Fire: The ring of earthquake zones and volcanoes in the Pacific Ocean.

RNA. *See* Ribonucleic acid

Rock: A naturally occurring, consolidated material of one or more minerals.

Rockfall: A relatively free-falling movement of rock material from a cliff or steep slope.

Runoff: The total amount of water flowing in a stream, including overland flow, return flow, interflow, and base flow.

S wave: The secondary seismic wave, traveling more slowly than the P wave and consisting of elastic vibrations transverse to the direction of travel; S waves cannot propagate in a liquid medium.

Saltation: The process of small particles being lifted off the surface, traveling 10 to 15 times the height to which they are lifted, then spinning downward with sufficient force to dislodge other soil particles and break down earth clods.

Sandstorm: A dust storm that results from dislodging larger, heavier particles of soil and rock; sandstorms tend to occur in conjunction with desert cyclones.

Scarp: A steep cliff or slope created by rapid movement along a fault.

Seiche: An oscillation in a partially enclosed body of water such as a bay or estuary.

Seismic: Pertaining to an earthquake.

Seismic belt: A region of relatively high seismicity, globally distributed; seismic belts mark regions of plate interactions.

Seismic waves: Elastic oscillatory disturbances spreading outward from an earthquake or human-made explosion; they provide the most important data about the earth's interior.

Seismicity: The occurrence of earthquakes, which is expressed as a function of location and time.

Seismogram: An image of earthquake wave vibrations recorded on paper, photographic film, or a video screen.

Seismograph: An instrument used for recording the motions of the earth's surface, caused by seismic waves, as a function of time.

Seismology: The application of the physics of elastic wave transmission and reflection to subsurface rock geometry.

Shallow-focus earthquake: An earthquake having a focus less than 60 kilometers below the surface.

Shear: A stress that forces two contiguous parts of an object apart in a direction parallel to their plane of contact, as opposed to a stretching, compressing, or twisting force; also called shear stress.

Shield volcano: A volcano in the shape of a flattened dome, broad and low, built by flows of very fluid basaltic lava.

Shock wave: A compressional wave formed when a body undergoes a hypervelocity impact; it produces abrupt changes in pressure, temperature, density, and velocity in the target material as it passes through.

Sinkhole: A hole or depression in the landscape, produced by dissolving bedrock; sinkholes can range in size from a few meters across and deep to kilometers wide and hundreds of meters deep.

Slab avalanche: An avalanche in which a large slab of the snow layer is released.

Sleet: Frozen or partly frozen rain.

Slump: A term that applies to the rotational slippage of material and the mass of material actually moved; the mass has component parts called scarp, failure plane, head, foot, toe, and blocks; the toe may grade downslope in a flow.

Smallpox: A highly contagious viral disease with symptoms of fever, cough, and a rash; it has been eradicated worldwide.

Smog: Air pollution in the form of haze, which can be sulfurous or photochemical in origin.

Solfatara: A volcanic vent that emits hot vapors and sulfurous gases.

Spillway: A broad reinforced channel near the top of the dam, designed to allow rising waters to escape the reservoir without overtopping the dam.

Squall line: A line of vigorous thunderstorms created by a cold downdraft with rain, which spreads out ahead of a fast-moving cold front.

Storm surge: A general rise above normal water level, resulting from a hurricane or other severe coastal storm.

Stratovolcano: A volcano constructed of layers of lava and pyroclastic rock; also called a composite volcano.

Stress: The force per unit area acting at any point within a solid body such as rock, calculated from a knowledge of force and area.

Strike-slip fault: A fault across which the relative movement is mainly lateral.

Strombolian eruption: A weakly explosive volcanic eruption (VEI values of 1 or 2) that usually begins with the volcano tossing out molten debris to form cinders and clots of liquid that solidify in the air to fall as bombs.

Subduction zone: A region where a plate, generally oceanic lithosphere, sinks beneath another plate into the mantle.

Sulfurous smog: Smog caused by the mixture of particulate matter and sulfurous compounds in the atmosphere when coal is burned.

Syncline: A folded structure created when rocks are bent downward; the limbs of the fold dip toward one another, and the youngest rocks are exposed in the middle of the fold.

Syncytium: A multinucleate mass of protoplasm resulting from fusion of cells.

Syphilis: A sexually transmitted disease that causes widespread tissue destruction and, potentially, death if left untreated by penicillin.

T lymphocytes: Small white blood cells that kill host cells infected by bacteria or viruses or that produce a chemical compound which mediates the destruction of the host cells.

T-test: A statistical test used especially in testing hypotheses about means of normal distributions when the standard deviations are unknown.

Tectonic plates: Segments that comprise the crust (either oceanic or continental crust) and a portion of the earth's mantle beneath it

Tectonics: The study of the processes that formed the structural features of the earth's crust; it usually addresses the creation and movement of immense crustal plates.

Teleseism: An earthquake recorded at great epicentral distances.

Tephra: All pyroclastic materials blown out of a volcanic vent, from dust to large chunks.

Thermocline: A layer within a water body, characterized by a rapid change in temperature.

Thunder: A loud sound resulting from the heating of air surrounding a lightning bolt, which causes a very rapid expansion of air that moves at supersonic speeds and forms shock waves.

Tidal wave: The popular but inaccurate term for a tsunami.

Torino Impact Hazard Scale: A scale dealing with the perceived probability of an asteroid or comet hitting Earth.

Tornado: A violent rotating column of air extending downward from a thunderhead cloud and having the appearance of a funnel, rope, or column.

Tornado Alley: An area of the United States where tornadoes are common, extending from Texas northward to Nebraska.

Trade winds: Winds in the tropics that blow from the subtropical highs to the equatorial low.

Transform fault: A fault connecting offset segments of an ocean ridge along which two plates slide past each other.

Trench: A long and narrow deep trough on the sea floor that forms where the ocean floor is pulled downward because of plate subduction.

Triage: Quick evaluation of victims before administering emergency assistance; victims are grouped according to those likely to survive without immediate treatment, those likely to survive only with immediate treatment, and those unlikely to survive even with emergency treatment.

Tropical storm: A severe storm with winds ranging from 45 to 120 kilometers per hour.

Tsunami: A seismic sea wave created by an undersea earthquake, a violent volcanic eruption, or a landslide at sea.

Tuff: A general term for all consolidated pyroclastic rocks.

Twenty-year-flood: A hypothetical flood whose severity is such that it would occur on average only once in a period of twenty years, which equates to a 5 percent probability each year.

Typhoid fever: A particular disease syndrome most often associated with infection by *Salmonella typhi* but occasionally caused by other types of salmonella bacteria.

Typhoon: A major tropical storm that originates in the Pacific Ocean.

Typhus: An acute infectious disease caused by rickettsiae, microorganisms that are smaller than bacteria but larger than viruses.

Ultra-Plinian eruption: A highly explosive volcanic eruption (VEI values of 7 and 8); none has occurred in recorded history.

Vaccine: A preparation of killed microorganisms or living organisms that is administered to produce or artificially increase immunity to a particular disease.

VEI. *See* Volcanic Explosivity Index (VEI)

Vent: A break or tear on the side of a mountain through which magma and pressure can escape.

Vesiculation: The process of water being released from magma and boiling to form bubbles.

Vigra: Precipitation that falls from clouds and evaporates before reaching the ground.

Viscosity: A substance's ability to flow; the lower the viscosity, the greater the ability to flow.

Volcanic earthquakes: Small-magnitude earthquakes that occur at relatively shallow depths beneath active or potentially active volcanoes.

Volcanic Explosivity Index (VEI): A scale from 0 to 8 that classifies the intensity of volcanic eruptions.

Volcanic rocks: Igneous rocks formed at the surface of the earth.

Volcanic tremor: A long, continuous vibration, detected only at active volcanoes.

Volcano: A vent at the earth's surface in which gases, rocks, and magma erupt and build a more or less cone-shaped mountain.

Vulcanian eruption: An explosive volcanic eruption (VEI values ranging from 2 to 4) in which the magma is viscous, there are few lava flows, and thick liquid clots are shot far into the air.

Watershed: A region bounded by a divide and draining to a particular body of water.

Waterspout: A tornado occurring over water.

Whiteout: A blizzard that severely reduces visibility.

Wildfire: An outdoor fire, occurring in forests, grasslands, or farms, that is caused either by an act of nature, such as a lightning strike, or by human actions; also called a brushfire.

Wind gust: A localized difference in atmospheric pressure caused by frontal weather changes.

Wind shear: Radical shift in wind speed and direction.

Yellow fever: An acute viral infection of the liver, kidneys, and heart muscle with such symptoms as fever, muscle pain, vomiting of blood, and jaundiced (yellow) skin.

Zoonosis: An animal disease that can also be transferred to humans.

■ TIME LINE

2 billion B.C.E.: An asteroid impact at Vredefort, South Africa, produces a 186-mile-diameter crater, the largest known on Earth.

1.85 billion B.C.E.: An asteroid impact at Sudbury, Ontario, Canada, produces a 155-mile-diameter crater. Groundwater, upwelling through fractured rocks, eventually produces one of the world's richest nickel deposits.

65 million B.C.E.: A 6.2-mile-diameter asteroid produces a 112-mile-diameter crater on the Yucatán Peninsula. The associated environmental disaster causes most of the species then living, including the dinosaurs, to become extinct.

49,000 B.C.E.: The impact of a huge nickel-iron boulder forms the Barringer meteorite crater in Arizona.

5000 B.C.E.: Crater Lake, Oregon, erupts, sending pyroclastic flows as far as 37 miles (60 kilometers) from the vent; 25 cubic miles of material are erupted as a caldera forms from the collapse of the mountaintop.

c. 3500 B.C.E.: The first known references of famine are recorded in Egypt.

c. 1470 B.C.E.: Thera erupts in the Aegean Sea, possibly causing the disappearance of the Minoan civilization on Crete and leading to stories of the lost "continent" of Atlantis.

11th century B.C.E.: Biblical passage Samuel I tells of the Philistine plague, a pestilence outbreak that occurred after the capture of the Ark of the Covenant.

7th century B.C.E.: Assyrian pestilence slays 185,000 Assyrians, forcing King Sennacherib to retreat from Judah without capturing Jerusalem.

600-500 B.C.E.: Perhaps the first recorded tornado is the "whirlwind" mentioned in Ezekiel 2:4 and 2 Kings 2:11 of the Old Testament.

451 B.C.E.: The Roman pestilence, an unidentified disease but probably anthrax, kills a large portion of the slave population and some in the citizenry and prevents the Aequians of Latium from attacking Rome.

436 B.C.E.: Thousands of Romans prefer drowning in the Tiber to starvation during a severe famine.

430 B.C.E.: The mysterious Plague of Athens early in the Peloponnesian War against Sparta results in about 30,000 dead.

387 B.C.E.: According the records of Livy, a series of 11 epidemics strikes Rome through the end of the republic.

250-243 B.C.E.: "Hunpox," or perhaps smallpox, strikes China.

218 B.C.E.: Hannibal loses 20,000 men, 2,000 horses, and several elephants in a huge avalanche near Col de la Traversette in the Italian Alps.

48 B.C.E.: Epidemic, flood, and famine occur in China.

64 C.E.: Much of the city burns during the Great Fire of Rome.

August 24, 79 C.E.: Vesuvius erupts, burying Pompeii and Herculaneum.

May 29, 526: The Antioch earthquake in Syria (now Turkey), estimated at magnitude 9.0, kills 250,000.

542-543: Plague of Justinian is the first pandemic of bubonic plague that devastates Africa, Asia Minor, and Europe. The first year the plague kills 300,000 in Constantinople; the infection resurfaces repeatedly over the next half century.

585-587: The Japanese smallpox epidemic, probably the country's first documented episode of the disease, infects peasants and nobility alike. Because it occurs after the acceptance of Buddhism, it is believed to be a punishment from the Shinto gods and results in the burning of temples and attacks on Buddhist nuns and priests.

917-918: Famine strikes northern India as uncounted thousands die.

1064-1072: Egypt faces starvation as the Nile fails to flood for seven consecutive years.

October 17, 1091: The earliest British tornado for which there is an authentic record hits London, killing 2 and demolishing 600 houses.

12th and 13th centuries: Air pollution in London is caused by extensive burning of coal.

1200-1202: A severe famine across Egypt kills more than 100,000; widespread cannibalism is reported.

1228: Flooding in Holland results in at least 100,000 deaths.

1235: An estimated 20,000 inhabitants of London die of starvation.

1270-1350: A prolonged drought in the U.S. Southwest destroys Anasazi Indian culture.

1273: A law passes in London to restrict the burning of soft coal in an attempt to improve air quality in the area.

1306: England's Parliament issues a proclamation requiring citizens to burn wood instead of coal in order to improve local air quality.

1315-1317: Central Europe, struck by excessive rains, experiences crop failures and famine.

1320-1352: Europe is stricken by the Black Death (bubonic plague), claiming over 40 million lives.

1333: The Arno River floods Venice, with a level of up to 14 feet (4.2 meters).

1333-1337: Famine strikes China, and millions die of starvation.

1347-1380: The Black Death kills an estimated 25 million in Asia. A reported two-thirds of the population in China succumbs.

1478: About 60 soldiers of the Duke of Milan are killed by an avalanche while crossing the mountains near Saint Gotthard Pass in the Italian Alps.

1494-1495: A syphilis epidemic strikes the French army in Naples and is considered the first appearance of this venereal infection in Europe.

1507: Hispaniola smallpox is the first recorded epidemic in the New World, representing the first wave of diseases that eventually depopulate America of most of its native inhabitants. In the next two centuries, the population plunges by an estimated 80 percent.

1512: A landslide causes a lake to overflow, killing more than 600 in Biasco, the Alps.

1520-1521: About 2 to 5 million die in the Aztec Empire when they contract smallpox during the Spanish conquest and colonization of Mexico.

January 23, 1556: 830,000 people die in Shaanxi, China, the greatest death toll from an earthquake to date.

1557: Severe cold and excessive rain causes famine in the Volga region of Russia.

1585-1587: A severe drought destroys the Roanoke colonies of English settlers in Virginia.

1588: A major storm destroys the Spanish Armada, which is seeking to escape the English navy under Sir Francis Drake.

September, 1618: Two villages are destroyed by landslides, and 2,427 are reported dead in Chiavenna Valley, Italy.

September, 1618: An avalanche kills 1,500 inhabitants of Plurs, Switzerland.

August 15, 1635: A colonial hurricane strikes Massachusetts and Rhode Island coastal settlements.

1642: More than 300,000 people die in China from flooding.

1643-1653: Europe experiences its severest winters after the Ice Age.

March, 1657: The Meireki Fire destroys Edo (now Tokyo), Japan, killing more than 100,000 people.

1665-1666: Very hot summers in London exacerbate the last plague epidemic.

1666: In the Great Fire of London, about 436 acres of the city burn, eliminating the Great Plague.

March 11, 1669: Sicily's Mount Etna begins a series of devastating eruptions that will result in more than 20,000 dead and 14 villages destroyed, including the seaside town of Catania, Italy.

1679: Fire burns portions of the city of Boston.

1680: Scientist Isaac Newton notes that the comet of 1680 passes less than 621,400 miles (1 million kilometers) from the Sun and deduces that its nucleus must be solid in order to survive.

1689: A series of avalanches kills more than 300 residents in Saas, Switzerland, and surrounding communities.

1690: Siberia experiences extreme heat, probably due to southerly winds; at this time, Europe is abnormally cold.

1692: An earthquake and tsunamis in Port Royal, Jamaica, kill 3,000.

1703: 5,000 die in tsunamis in Honshū, Japan, following a large earthquake.

1707: A 38-foot-high tsunami kills 30,000 in Japan.

January, 1718: The town of Leukerbad, Switzerland, is destroyed by two avalanches that leave more than 55 dead and many residents seriously injured.

1718-1719: Great heat and drought affect most of Europe during the summers of these years.

September 27, 1727: A hurricane strikes the New England coast.

1741: Following volcanic eruptions, 30-foot waves in Japan cause 1,400 deaths.

September 15 and October 1, 1752: Two hurricanes strike South and North Carolina.

November 1, 1755: An earthquake on All Saints' Day kills worshipers in Lisbon, Portugal, in the collapse of stone cathedrals or in the accompanying tsunamis; as many as 50,000 perish.

December 25, 1758: The first predicted return of Halley's comet is observed.

1769: Drought-induced famine kills millions in the Bengal region of India.

1769: 1,000 tons of gunpowder stored in the state arsenal at Brescia, Italy, explode when struck by lightning. One-sixth of the city is destroyed, and 3,000 people are killed.

September 8-9, 1769: The Atlantic coast of North America, from the Carolinas to New England, is hit by a hurricane.

1783: A tsunami in Italy kills 30,000.

June 8, 1783-February 7, 1784: The Laki fissure eruption in Iceland produces the largest lava flow in recorded history, with major climatic effects. Benjamin Franklin speculates on its connection to a cold winter in Paris the following year.

October 22-23, 1783: A hurricane strikes the Atlantic coast, from the Carolinas to New England.

1786: The people of Paris make bell-ringing during thunderstorms illegal. The ringing of church bells was believed to prevent lightning strikes but often proved fatal to ringers.

1788: New Orleans burns.

July 13, 1788: A severe hailstorm damages French wheat crops.

1794-1803: Scientists prove that meteorites do fall from the sky.

September, 1806: Portions of Rossberg Peak collapse, destroying 4 villages and killing 800 people in Goldau Valley, Switzerland.

December 16, 1811; January 23 and February 7, 1812: In the sparsely settled region of New Madrid, Missouri, the largest historic earthquakes in North America to date rearrange the Mississippi River and form Reelfoot Lake.

1812: Moscow is set on fire by troops of Napoleon I.

1814: Washington, D.C. is burned by occupying British troops.

April 5, 1815: The dramatic explosion of Tambora, 248.6 miles (400 kilometers) east of Java, the largest volcanic event in modern history, produces atmospheric and climatic effects for the next two years. Frosts occur every month in New England during 1816, the Year Without a Summer.

June 3, 1816: The steamboat *Washington* explodes on the Ohio River.

May, 1817: The steamboat *Constitution* explodes on the Mississippi River.

1842: Most of the city of Hamburg, Germany, burns, leaving 100 dead.

1845: Moist, southerly winds and a hot summer provide the perfect growing conditions for the potato blight fungus, resulting in the Irish Potato Famine.

1845-1849: Ireland's potato famine leads to the deaths of over 1 million and the emigration of more than 1 million Irish.

Early October, 1846: An early blizzard in the Sierra Nevada traps the Donner Party.

May 4, 1850: Fire burns large portions of the city of San Francisco.

May 3-4, 1851: San Francisco again experiences large fires; 30 die.

December 24, 1851: The Library of Congress is burned.

April 3, 1856: 4,000 are killed on the Greek island of Rhodes when lightning strikes a church where gunpowder is stored.

August 13, 1856: A hurricane striking Last Island, Louisiana, results in a death toll of 137.

January 9, 1857: The San Andreas fault at Fort Tejon, California, in the northwest corner of Los Angeles County, ruptures dramatically. Trees snap off near the ground, landslides occur, and buildings collapse into rubble.

1861: Earth passes through the tail of the Great Comet of 1861 with no measurable effects.

April 27, 1865: 1,500 die in the explosion of the steamboat *Sultana* on the Mississippi River.

January 23, 1867: The East River in New York City freezes.

1868: Tsunamis in Chile and Hawaii claim more than 25,000 lives.

October 8, 1871: The Great Peshtigo Fire affects a large area in northern Wisconsin; 1,200 are killed, and 2 billion trees are burned.

October 8-10, 1871: The Great Chicago Fire leaves 250 dead and causes $200 million in damage.

November 9-10, 1872: The Great Boston Fire kills 13, destroys 776 buildings, and causes $75 million in damage.

December, 1873: An air pollution event in London kills between 270 and 700 people.

1876-1878: Drought strikes India, leaving about 5 million dead.

1876-1879: China experiences a drought that leaves 10 million or more dead.

August 13-October 29, 1878: The Great Yellow Fever Epidemic results in over 100,000 cases and 20,000 deaths, particularly in Memphis, Tennessee.

February, 1880: Approximately 1,000 people die in London from an air pollution event.

September 8, 1880: A mine explosion at the Seaham Colliery in Sunderland, England, kills 164.

January 19, 1883: 357 die in fog-related collision of steamers *Cimbria* and *Sultan* near Borkum Island off the German coast.

August 26, 1883: A cataclysmic eruption of Krakatau, an island in Indonesia, is heard 2,968 miles away. Many die as pyroclastic flows race over pumice rafts floating on the surface of the sea; many more die from a tsunami.

1887: The Yellow River floods, covering over 50,000 square miles of the North China Plain. Over 900,000 people die from the floodwaters and an additional 2 to 4 million die afterward due to flood-related causes.

1887-1896: Droughts drive out many early settlers on the Great Plains.

March 11-14, 1888: The Great Blizzard of 1888 strikes the eastern United States; 400 die.

April 17, 1889: The first teleseism is recorded in Potsdam, Germany, of an earthquake on that date in Japan.

May 31, 1889: A dam bursts upstream from Johnstown, Pennsylvania, and the floodwaters kill over 2,200 people.

1890: The Federal Weather Bureau is created.

1892-1894: A cholera pandemic leaves millions dead but confirms the theory that the disease is caused by bacteria in contaminated water.

July, 1892: St. Gervais and La Fayet, Swiss resorts, are destroyed when a huge avalanche speeds down Mont Blanc, killing 140 residents and tourists.

December, 1892: A smog episode kills 1,000 people in London.

1896: As many as 27,000 die after tsunamis hit Sanriku, Japan.

May 27, 1896: The Great Cyclone of 1896, an F4 tornado, hits St. Louis, Missouri, leaving 306 dead and 2,500 injured and destroying or damaging 7,500 buildings as well as riverboats and railroads.

1898: A hurricane warning network is established in the West Indies.

1899: The failure of monsoons in India results in many deaths.

1900: The first quantitative measurements of peak current in lightning strikes are conducted.

September 8, 1900: A hurricane in Galveston, Texas, leads to the highest death toll from a hurricane to date, from the ensuing storm surge.

1900-1915: "Typhoid Mary" Mallon, a cook, spreads typhoid fever to more than 50 people, causing at least 3 deaths.

1901: Transatlantic wireless radio sends first signal to receiver in St. John's, Newfoundland.

1902: Willis H. Carrier designs the first system to control the temperature of air.

May 8, 1902: Pelée, on the northern end of the island of Martinique in the Caribbean, sends violent pyroclastic flows into the city of St. Pierre, killing all but 2 of the 30,000 inhabitants.

April, 1903: A 0.5-mile section of Turtle Mountain near Frank, Alberta, slides down the mountain, killing 70 people in the town.

1906: The term "air-conditioning" is used for the first time, by an engineer named Stuart W. Cramer.

April 18, 1906: The San Andreas fault slips 20 feet near San Francisco in a magnitude 8.3 earthquake. Much of the city is severely damaged, and a firestorm starts when cinders escape a damaged chimney, leveling the city.

June 30, 1908: A huge boulder or a small comet explodes over Tunguska, Siberia, causing widespread destruction.

December 28, 1908: The Messina earthquake kills 120,000 and destroys or severely damages numerous communities in Italy.

November 13, 1909: A fire breaks out in the Cherry Mine in Illinois, trapping and killing 259 miners.

1910: Wildfires rage throughout the U.S. West in the most destructive fire year in U.S. history to date.

1910: American geologist H. F. Reid publishes a report on the 1906 San Francisco earthquake, outlining his theory of elastic rebound.

March, 1910: An avalanche sweeps through the train station in Wellington, Washington State, destroying 3 snowbound passenger trains and killing 96.

1910-1915: First in a series of recurring droughts affects the Sahel region in Africa.

1911: The Yangtze River in China floods, killing more 100,000 people.

March 25, 1911: The Triangle Shirtwaist Factory fire occurs in New York City; 145 employees, mostly young girls, die.

June 6, 1912: Katmai erupts in Alaska with an ash flow that produces the Valley of Ten Thousand Smokes.

April 28, 1914: An explosion in the Eccles Mine in West Virginia leaves 181 dead.

May 29, 1914: More than 1,000 drown in the sinking of the Canadian liner *Empress of Ireland* following its collision with Norwegian freighter *Storstad* in heavy fog on the St. Lawrence River.

1916: The Great Polio Epidemic affects 26 states, particularly New York, prompting quarantines and resulting in 27,000 reported cases and at least 7,000 deaths.

June 30, 1916: Canada's most lethal twister to date kills 28 in Regina, Saskatchewan.

December, 1916: Heavy snows result in avalanches that kill more than 10,000 Italian and Austrian soldiers located in the Tirol section of the Italian-Austrian Alps.

1917: The first photographic record of the spectrum from lightning using a spectroscope is made.

December 6, 1917: Munitions ships in Halifax, Nova Scotia, harbor explode and burn; 2,000 die.

1918: In Nasatch National Forest, Utah, 504 sheep are killed by a lightning strike.

1918-1920: The Great Flu Pandemic sweeps the globe, killing 30 to 40 million, perhaps the largest single biological event in human history.

1920: Arizona's Barringer Crater is the first Earth feature recognized to have been caused by a meteorite impact.

December, 1920: An earthquake shears off unstable cliffs in Gansu Province, China, destroying 10 cities and killing 200,000.

1921-1922: Famine strikes the Soviet Union, which pleads for international aid; Western assistance saves millions, but several million die.

September 1, 1923: 143,000 people die as a result of the Great Kwanto Earthquake, centered in Sagami Bay, Japan.

1925: First radio signal to warn of fog is sent to ships on the Great Lakes.

1925: The U.S. Weather Bureau applies sensors to airplane wings to record atmospheric conditions.

March 18, 1925: The Great Tri-State Tornado, the United States' worst tornado disaster to date, occurs when a 219-mile-long twister destroys entire towns along its path through Missouri, Illinois, and Indiana, causing 689 deaths, more than 2,000 injuries, and $16-18 million in damage.

July 10, 1926: Explosions triggered by lightning at an ammunition dump in New Jersey kill 21 people, blasting debris 5 miles.

September 15-22, 1926: The Great Miami Hurricane strikes Florida and the Gulf states, resulting in 243 dead.

1927: French scientists produce the radiosonde, an instrument package designed to measure pressure, temperature, and humidity during balloon ascents and radio the information back to earth.

1927: Extensive flooding of the Mississippi River results in 313 deaths.

March 12, 1928: The St. Francis Dam collapses in Southern California, leading to about 450 deaths.

September 10-16, 1928: A Category 4 storm, the San Felipe, or Lake Okeechobee, hurricane claims over 4,000 lives in the Caribbean and Florida.

1929: American scientist Robert H. Goddard launches a rocket carrying an instrument package that includes a barometer, a thermometer, and a camera.

Early 1930's: Charles Richter, working with Beno Gutenberg at the Seismological Laboratory of the California Institute of Technology, develops the Richter scale.

December, 1930: A thick fog settles in the industrialized area along the Meuse River in Belgium and is trapped for three days; thousands of people become ill and 60 die.

1932-1934: Communist collectivization schemes in the Soviet Union precipitate famine; an estimated 5 million die.

1933: 3,000 are killed by tsunamis in Sanriku, Japan.

December 23, 1933: Two trains collide in fog near Paris, killing 230.

1932-1937: Extensive droughts in the southern Great Plains destroy many farms, creating the Dust Bowl, in the worst drought in more than three hundred years in the United States. Between 15,000 and 20,000 die.

May 6, 1937: The German zeppelin *Hindenburg* explodes into a massive fireball as it tries to land in Lakehurst, New Jersey, killing 36.

1938: Chinese soldiers are ordered to destroy the levees of the Yellow River in order to create a flood to stop the advance of Japanese troops. It works, but at a terrible cost to the Chinese people; more than 1 million die.

September 21, 1938: The Great New England Hurricane of 1938 causes high winds, flooding, and a storm surge that leave 680 dead, more than 1,700 injured, and $400 million in damage.

1939: Flooding of the Yellow River kills over 200,000 people.

November 28, 1942: The Cocoanut Grove nightclub burns in Boston, killing 491.

1943: A major smog episode in Los Angeles leads local officials to begin to look at regulations to reduce air pollution.

February 20, 1943: Paricutín comes into existence in a cultivated field in Mexico. The eruption of this volcano continues for nine years.

July, 1943: Hamburg, Germany, is destroyed, mostly by incendiary bombs; 60,000-100,000 are killed.

July 17, 1944: Two ammunition ships in Port Chicago, California, explode, killing 300.

December 17-18, 1944: A typhoon in the Philippine Sea kills 790.

1945: Radar is used for tracking civilian traffic in ships and planes.

1945: A large section of the Oregon forest ignites in the third in a series of wildfires known as the Tillamook burn.

February 13, 1945: 25,000 die in the destruction of Dresden by incendiary bombs.

March 9, 1945: Incendiary bombs destroy 25 percent of Tokyo.

1946: The Aleutian tsunami creates 32-foot-high waves in Hilo, Hawaii, causing 159 deaths there.

1946: 2,000 die in Honshū, Japan, after an earthquake spawns tsunamis.

1947: Honshū Island, Japan, is hit by floods that kill more than 1,900 people.

March 25, 1947: A mine explosion in Centralia, Illinois, kills 111.

April 16, 1947: The French vessel *Grandcamp* explodes in Texas City, Texas, killing 581.

September 4-21, 1947: A hurricane impacts the Gulf states, leaving over 50 dead.

March 25, 1948: Air Force officers Ernest Fawbush and Robert Miller issue the first tornado watch in the United States, but it is for military use only.

December, 1948: Smog accumulates over Donora, Pennsylvania, and is trapped in the valley of the Monongahela River for four days, resulting in 18 deaths above the average number for that time period.

November, 1949: Smog forms in Berkeley, California, from the exhaust of automobiles being driven into the area for a football game.

January, 1951: A series of avalanches leaves 240 dead; the village of Vals, Switzerland, is completely destroyed.

March 17, 1952: The U.S. Weather Bureau issues the first tornado watch to the American public.

December 5-9, 1952: A dense fog develops over London, mixes with smoke, and remains stagnant for five days, leading to 4,000 deaths above the average number for that time interval.

1953: The system of naming hurricanes is adopted.

1953: Smog accumulates in New York City, causing at least 200 deaths.

February 1, 1953: A massive flood in the North Sea kills 1,853 in the Netherlands, Great Britain, and Belgium.

May 11, 1953: A tornado destroys much of downtown Waco, Texas, leaving 114 dead and 1,097 injured.

June 8, 1953: A tornado devastates parts of Flint, Michigan, killing 120 and injuring 847.

June 9, 1953: The worst tornado to date to strike the northeastern United States plows a path greater than a half-mile wide through Worcester, Massachusetts; 94 people are killed, 1,288 are injured, and more than 4,000 buildings are damaged or destroyed.

January, 1954: In one of the worst avalanches in Austrian history, 145 people are killed over a 10-mile area.

October 12-18, 1954: Hurricane Hazel strikes the Atlantic coast, causing 411 deaths and $1 billion in damage.

1956: A severe smog episode in London leads to the deaths of 1,000 people.

March 30, 1956: The volcano Bezymianny in Russia erupts with a violent lateral blast, stripping trees of their bark 18.6 miles (30 kilometers) away.

July 25-26, 1956: The Italian liner *Andrea Doria* sinks after being struck by a Swedish vessel in fog.

November, 1956: At least 46 people die in a smog episode in New York City.

June 27-30, 1957: More than 500 die when Hurricane Audrey hits the Louisiana and Texas coastlines.

1958: H. Jeffreys and K. E. Bullen publish seismic travel time curves establishing the detailed, spherically symmetrical model of the earth.

1959: The first meteorological experiment is conducted on a satellite platform.

1959: Hurricane rains and an earthquake combined with a series of massive landslides bury the 800 residents of Minatitlan, Mexico, and kill another 4,200 in surrounding communities.

November 1, 1959: More than 2,000 people die in floods in western Mexico.

1959-1962: As many as 30 million die in Communist China as a result of the Great Leap Forward famine.

May 22, 1960: A large earthquake, measuring 8.5, strikes off the coast of Chile, making the earth reverberate for several weeks. For the first time, scientists are able to determine many of the resonant modes of oscillation of the earth.

September 6-12, 1960: The Atlantic coast's Hurricane Donna results in 168 dead and almost $2 billion in damage.

October, 1960: Bangladesh floods kill a total of 10,000 people.

1960-1990: Repeated droughts occur in the Sahel, east Africa, and southern Africa.

1962: Over 700 people die in a smog event in London.

1962: Melting snow rushes down the second-highest peak in South America at speeds in excess of 100 miles per hour, killing around 4,000 in Peru.

February 17, 1962: Major storms blanket Germany; 343 are killed.

December, 1962: 60 people die from smog in Osaka, Japan.

1963: The first quantitative temperature estimates are made for individual lightning strikes.

1963: Lightning strikes a Boeing 707 over Elkton, Maryland, killing all 81 persons on board. This is the first verified instance of a lightning-induced airplane crash.

January-February, 1963: Smog kills up to 400 people in New York City.

October 9, 1963: A landslide caused by an earthquake destroys the Vaiont Dam, drowning almost 3,000 residents of Belluno, Italy.

November, 1963: Grand Rivière du Nord, Haiti, is devastated by landslides brought about by tropical downpours; an estimated 500 tourists and residents are killed.

1964: Earthquakes and rains cause landslides near Niigata, Japan, killing 108, injuring 223, and leaving more than 40,000 homeless.

1964: 195-foot waves engulf Kodiak, Alaska, after the Good Friday earthquake; 131 die.

March 27, 1964: The Good Friday earthquake near Anchorage, Alaska, with a magnitude of 8.6, causes extensive damage near the southern coast of Alaska and generates tsunamis that damage vessels and marinas along the western coast of the United States.

April 11, 1965: The Palm Sunday Outbreak of around 50 tornadoes kills 271, injures more than 3,100, and causes more than $200 million in damages in Illinois, Indiana, Iowa, Michigan, Ohio, and Wisconsin.

1966: A four-day smog event in New York City results in the deaths of 80 people; Governor Nelson A. Rockefeller declares a state of emergency.

January 29-31, 1966: The worst blizzard in seventy years strikes the eastern United States.

June 8, 1966: The first $100 million tornado in the United States cuts a path through Topeka, Kansas, killing 16 and destroying more than 800 homes and much of the Washburn University campus.

October 21, 1966: A slag heap near Aberfan, Wales, collapses and kills 147 people, including 116 children.

November 3-4, 1966: Flooding in Florence, Italy, destroys many works of art.

January 24-March 21, 1967: Flooding in eastern Brazil takes 1,250 lives.

1967-1969: The Biafran civil war in Nigeria leads to the deaths of 1.5 million Biafrans because of starvation.

1968: More than 1,000 are killed in Bihar and Assam, West Bengal, by floods and landslides.

July 21-August 15, 1968: Flooding in Gujarat State in India results in 1,000 deaths.

October 7, 1968: Floods in northeastern India claim 780 lives.

1968-1974: The Sahel drought leads to famine; international aid limits deaths to about a half million.

January, 1969: Torrential rains lasting more than a week trigger mudslides that kill 95 and cause more than $138 million in damage in Southern California.

August 15-18, 1969: Hurricane Camille rages across the southern United States; 258 die.

1970's: Severe smog conditions are recognized in many Chinese cities; death rates as high as 3,500 people per year are reported in some areas in 1979.

January 3, 1970: The fall of the Lost City, Oklahoma, meteorite is photographed, and its orbit is later traced back to the asteroids.

April, 1970: A hospital in Sallanches, France, is destroyed by an avalanche that kills 70, most of them children.

May 11, 1970: A powerful tornado twists the frame of a twenty-story office building as it plows through downtown Lubbock, Texas, killing 26 and injuring more than 1,500. This tornado initiates a new interest in tornado studies, including Theodore Fujita's development of a tornado rating scale.

May 31, 1970: The magnitude 7.7 Ancash earthquake in northern Peru leaves 70,000 dead, 140,000 injured, and 500,000 homeless.

November 12-13, 1970: The Bhola cyclone strikes the Ganges Delta and East Pakistan (now Bangladesh), killing at least 300,000 people.

1971: An earthquake unleashes a huge avalanche of snow and ice, killing 600 and destroying Chungar, Peru, and surrounding villages.

February 9, 1971: In the first serious earthquake to strike a densely populated area in the United States since 1906, a moderate (magnitude 6.6) earthquake centered in Sylmar, California, causes $1 billion in damage.

1972: A heat wave affects Russia and Finland.

February 4-11, 1972: Heavy snow falls on Iran; 1,000 perish.

June 9, 1972: Heavy rainfall over Rapid City, South Dakota, causes an upstream dam to fail and release floodwaters; 238 people lose their lives.

June 21-23, 1972: 122 die during Hurricane Agnes.

July, 1972: Landslides caused by torrential rains kill 370 persons and cause $472 million in property damage throughout Japan.

August 10, 1972: A house-sized rock forms a brilliant fireball as it hurtles through Earth's atmosphere and back into space.

January, 1973: During an eruption on Heimaey Island, Iceland, the flow of lava is controlled by cooling it with water from fire hoses.

January 10, 1973: South America's worst tornado to date destroys parts of San Justo, Argentina; 50 people are killed.

July 31, 1973: A Delta Airlines jet crashes while attempting to land at Boston's Logan International Airport in fog; 89 die.

1974: A landslide in Huancavelica, Peru, creates a natural dam on the Mantaro River, forcing the evacuation of 9,000 living in the area and killing an estimated 300.

April 3-4, 1974: In the Jumbo Outbreak, 148 tornadoes, including 6 rated F5, kill 316 and injure almost 5,500 in 11 midwestern and southern states; an additional 8 deaths occur in Canada. Hardest hit communities include Xenia, Ohio, with 35 deaths and 1,150 injured, and Brandenburg, Kentucky, with 31 deaths and 250 injured.

December 1-2, 1974: Nineteen inches of snow falls on Detroit in the worst snowstorm in eighty-eight years.

December 23, 1975: A single lightning strike in Umtrali, Rhodesia (now Zimbabwe), kills 21 people.

1975-1976: Heat waves are recorded in Denmark and the Netherlands.

1975-1979: Khmer Rouge policies of genocide provoke famine in Cambodia; more than 1 million die of starvation.

February 4, 1976: A slip over a 124-mile stretch of the Motagua fault in Guatemala kills 23,000.

July 21-August 4, 1976: 221 American Legion veterans contract a mysterious type of pneumonia at a hotel in Philadelphia, and 29 of them die; the media names the illness "Legionnaires' disease."

July 28, 1976: The magnitude 8.0 Tangshan earthquake in northeastern China kills an estimated 250,000 people and seriously injures 160,000 more; almost the entire city of 1.1 million people is destroyed.

July 31, 1976: A flash flood rushes down Big Thompson Canyon, Colorado, sweeping 139 people to their deaths.

September 1-October 24, 1976: An Ebola virus epidemic in Zaire kills 280 people and proves one of the deadliest diseases of the late twentieth century.

January 28-29 and March 10-12, 1977: Blizzards ravage the Midwest; Buffalo reports 160 inches of snow.

March 27, 1977: Two airliners collide in fog in Tenerife, Canary Islands; 583 die.

1977-1978: The western United States undergoes a drought.

January 25-26, 1978: A major snowstorm strikes the midwestern United States, with 31 inches of snow and 18-foot drifts.

February 5-7, 1978: The worst blizzard in the history of New England strikes the Northeast; eastern Massachusetts receives 50 inches of snow, and winds reach 110 miles per hour.

January 12-14, 1979: Blizzards in the Midwest yield 20 inches of snow, with temperatures at −20 degrees Fahrenheit; 100 die.

February 18-19, 1979: Snow blankets the District of Columbia.

September 7-14, 1979: Hurricane Frederic strikes the Gulf Coast states, causing $1.7 billion in damage.

1980: A heat wave in Texas produces forty-two consecutive days above 100 degrees Fahrenheit.

March 1-2, 1980: The mid-Atlantic region experiences a blizzard.

May 18, 1980: Mount St. Helens, in Washington State, erupts with a directed blast to the north, moving pyroclastic flows at velocities of 328 to 984 feet (100 to 300 meters) per second (nearly the speed of sound).

June, 1980: Luis Alvarez and others at the University of California at Berkeley publish an article in *Science* presenting the hypothesis that an asteroid impact caused the extinction of the dinosaurs.

November 21, 1980: A fire in the MGM Grand Hotel in Las Vegas kills 84.

1980's-1990's: Reports of increase of deadly air pollution conditions in Eastern Europe, Mexico, and China.

1981: U.S. epidemic reported by U.S. Centers for Disease Control in June and given the name acquired immunodeficiency syndrome (AIDS). In some regions of Africa the infection touches 90 percent of the population and poses a constant pandemic threat.

July, 1981: Over 1,300 people die in the flooding of Sichuan, Hubei Province, China.

1982: Thirteen students and teachers are killed by an avalanche in Salzburg, Austria.

March 28-April 4, 1982: El Chichón, an "extinct" volcano in Mexico, erupts violently, killing 2,000, injuring hundreds, destroying villages, and ruining over 100 square miles of farmland.

1982-1983: Droughts affect Brazil and northern India.

June, 1982-August, 1983: A destructive El Niño episode is held responsible for more than 2,000 deaths and $13 billion in damage and introduces the public to this Pacific Ocean weather phenomenon.

February 5-28, 1984: A series of snowstorms strikes Colorado and Utah.

March 29, 1984: A snowstorm covers much of the East Coast.

June 9, 1984: Europe's worst tornado to date kills over 400 and injures 213 in Belyanitsky, Ivanovo, and Balino, Russia.

1984-1985: Drought in Ethiopia, the Sahel, and southern Africa endangers more than 20 million Africans, but extensive international aid helps to mitigate the suffering.

September 19, 1985: A magnitude 8.1 earthquake near Mexico City kills 10,000 people, injures 30,000, and causes billions of dollars worth of damage.

November 13, 1985: Mudflows from the eruption of the Nevado del Ruiz, in Colombia, kill at least 23,000 people.

March, 1986: The nucleus of Halley's comet is photographed.

April 25-26, 1986: 32 are killed when a nuclear reactor at Chernobyl, Russia, explodes.

August 21, 1986: After building up from volcanic emanations, carbon dioxide escapes from Lake Nyos, Cameroon, killing more than 1,700 people.

1986-1988: Many farmers in the U.S. Midwest are driven out of business by a drought.

September, 1987: Mudslides wipe out entire sections of the Villa Tina area of Medellín, Colombia, killing 183 residents and leaving 500 missing.

May-October, 1988: Fires affect some 1.2 million acres in Yellowstone National Park and other western forests.

July 6, 1988: The explosion of Piper Alpha oil rig in the North Sea kills 167.

September 12-17, 1988: Hurricane Gilbert kills 260 in the Caribbean and Mexico.

December 7, 1988: The Leninakan earthquake in Armenia leaves 60,000 dead, 15,000 injured, and 500,000 homeless; it destroys 450,000 buildings, including thousands of historical monuments, and causes $30 billion in damage.

April 26, 1989: The world's deadliest tornado to date occurs in Bangladesh when a twister slashes a 50-mile-wide path north of Dhaka; about 1,300 people are killed, more than 12,000 are injured, and almost 80,000 are left homeless.

September 13-22, 1989: 75 die as Hurricane Hugo strikes the Caribbean, then South Carolina.

October 17, 1989: An earthquake in the Santa Cruz Mountains, in the vicinity of Loma Prieta, California, kills 67 and produces more than $5 billion worth of damage in the San Francisco-Oakland area.

1990: The United Nations' Intergovernmental Panel on Climate Change (IPCC) predicts that, if unchecked, greenhouse gases and carbon dioxide emissions produced by human activity could raise world surface temperatures by 0.25 degree Celsius per decade in the twenty-first century.

1990's: National Oceanographic and Atmospheric Administration (NOAA) polar-orbiting and geostationary satellites employ advanced microwave sounding units for improved storm intensity estimates. Weather satellites view entire storm systems, sense conditions of the ocean, measure temperatures at different altitudes, and provide humidity profiles of the atmosphere, as well as surface winds.

April 10, 1991: 138 die in crash of ferry *Moby Prince* and oil tanker *Agip Abruzzo* in Italy.

April 30, 1991: A cyclone hits Bangladesh and kills over 131,000.

June, 1991: Pinatubo erupts in the Phillipines after having been dormant for four hundred years.

September, 3, 1991: A chicken-processing plant in North Carolina burns, killing 25 workers.

October 19-21, 1991: Wildfires burn much of Oakland Hills, California; 25 die.

August 22-26, 1992: Hurricane Andrew strikes southern Florida, leaving 50 dead and $26 billion in damage.

October 9, 1992: A meteorite smashes the rear end of a 1980 Chevy Malibu automobile in Peekskill, New York.

1992-1994: Civil war sparks famine in Somalia, where hundreds of thousands die before international efforts restore food supplies.

April 19, 1993: A cult compound in Waco, Texas, is destroyed by fire; 80 people die.

June-August, 1993: Largest recorded floods of the Mississippi River occur; 52 people die, over $18 billion in damage is inflicted, and more than 20 million acres are flooded.

January 17, 1994: A moderate earthquake, with a magnitude of 6.7, strikes the northern edge of the Los Angeles basin near Northridge, California. There are 57 deaths, and damage is estimated at $20 billion.

June, 1994: An earthquake in the Huila region of Colombia causes avalanches and mudslides that leave 13,000 residents homeless, 2,000 trapped, and 1,000 dead.

July, 1994: The impact of the fragmented Comet Shoemaker-Levy 9 on Jupiter is widely observed.

July 4-10, 1994: A Glenwood Springs, Colorado, forest fire kills 14 firefighters.

August, 1994: A severe heat wave and drought parches Japan.

1995: The IPCC predicts carbon dioxide and greenhouse emissions to raise Earth's surface temperature between 0.8 and 3.5 degrees Celsius within one hundred years.

January 17, 1995: The most costly natural disaster to date occurs when an earthquake strikes Kobe, Japan. The death toll exceeds 5,500, injuries require 37,000 people to seek medical attention, and damage is estimated at $50 billion.

April-May, 1995: An outbreak of Ebola virus in Kitwit, Zaire, leaves 245 dead.

July, 1995: A heat wave in the midwestern United States kills almost 500 people in Chicago alone, as well as 4,000 cattle.

November, 1995: A series of avalanches kills 43 climbers in Nepal.

January 7, 1996: The East Coast is hit by another big snowstorm.

May 10-11, 1996: A sudden and intense blizzard on Mount Everest, Earth's highest peak, traps climbers, killing 9 and leaving 4 others with severe frostbite.

May 13, 1996: A large tornado levels several towns near Tangail, Bangladesh; more than 1,000 are dead and 34,000 are injured, with 100,000 left homeless.

July 5-15, 1996: Hurricane Bertha hits the Caribbean and the Atlantic coast; winds exceed 100 miles per hour.

September-November, 1996: Eruption of lava beneath a glacier in the Grimsvötn Caldera, Iceland, melts huge quantities of ice, producing major flooding.

March, 1997: A park geologist and a volunteer are killed by an avalanche while working on a project to monitor Yellowstone National Park geothermal features.

April 1, 1997: The April Fool's storm strikes the Northeast.

April 15, 1997: A fire at a tent city outside Mecca, Saudi Arabia, costs 300 lives.

May 27, 1997: An F5 tornado hits Jarrell, Texas; 27 are dead, 8 are injured, and 44 homes are damaged or destroyed.

June 25, 1997: On the Caribbean island of Montserrat, 19 people die and 8,000 are evacuated when the Soufrière Hills volcano erupts.

November 3, 1997: Typhoon Linda kills more than 1,100 in Vietnam.

1998: Three avalanches in southeastern British Columbia, Canada, leave 8 dead and injured.

1998: A drought destroys crops in the southern Midwest and causes ecological damage on the East Coast.

January 5-12, 1998: A major ice storm covers northeastern Canada.

January-March, 1998: Large forest fires burn in Indonesia, sickening thousands; 234 die in a Garuda Indonesia plane crash caused by poor visibility from smoke.

June 8, 1998: A Kansas grain elevator explodes, killing 6.

June 9, 1998: A cyclone hits the Indian state of Gujarat; more than 1,300 are killed.

July, 1998: A heat wave hits the southwestern and northeastern United States; daytime temperatures in Texas hit 110 degrees Fahrenheit, with forty-one days of above-100-degree weather, causing huge crop losses and 144 deaths.

July, 1998: Worldwide, July is determined to be the hottest month in history to date.

July 17, 1998: Waves created by an undersea landslide caused by an earthquake kill 2,000 in Papua New Guinea.

August, 1998: The village of Malpa, India, is destroyed by boulders and mud, leaving 202 dead; only 18 survive.

August, 1998: India reaches 124 degrees Fahrenheit; 3,000 people die in the worst heat wave there in fifty years.

August, 1998: As a result of summer heat, 50 people die in Cyprus, and 30 die in Greece and Italy; grapes die on vines.

August, 1998: In Germany, record heat produces severe smog, and cars lacking antipollution devices are banned.

September 16-29, 1998: 400 die when Hurricane Georges strikes in the Caribbean, then the Gulf Coast; winds exceed 130 miles per hour.

October 27, 1998: Hurricane Mitch hits Central America; the death toll exceeds 11,000.

1999: A major drought strikes the U.S. Southeast, the Atlantic coast, and New England.

1999: 7 die in an epidemic of encephalitis in New England and New York.

1999: A tsunami and earthquake at the island of Vanuatu kills 10, injures more than 100, and leaves thousands homeless.

February, 1999: The Galtür avalanche in Austria kills 38 and traps 2,000.

February 11, 1999: Cyclone Rona strikes Queensland, Australia; 1,800 are left homeless.

May 3, 1999: Part of the Oklahoma Tornado Outbreak, one of the most expensive tornadoes in U.S. history destroys nearly 2,500 homes and kills 49 in Oklahoma City and its suburbs; damage estimates approach $1.5 billion.

August 17, 1999: More than 17,000 die when a magnitude 7.4 quake strikes İzmit, Turkey.

February-March, 2000: Severe flooding in Mozambique, caused by five weeks of rain followed by Cyclone Eline, kills 800 people and 20,000 cattle.

2001: A tsunami in Peru leaves 26 dead and 70 missing.

October 4-9, 2001: Hurricane Iris kills 31 and does $150 million in property damage in Belize.

2002: A severe, long-term drought begins in Australia. Urban areas begin to feel its effects by 2006, as major cities pass heavy restrictions on water usage and Perth constructs a desalination plant.

January 17, 2002: The Nyiragongo volcano erupts in the Democratic Republic of Congo, sending lava flows into the city of Goma; 147 die and 500,000 are displaced.

November, 2002-July, 2003: A virulent atypical pneumonia, dubbed severe acute respiratory syndrome (SARS), spreads quickly through China and then internationally, infecting at least 8,422 victims and causing 916 known deaths.

May 15, 2003: A researcher is able to insert probes called "turtles" into an F4 tornado to measure its pressure.

July-August, 2003: A heat wave grips all of Europe, especially France, Italy, Spain, and Portugal; as many as 40,000 die from heat-related causes, and drought and wildfires follow.

September 18, 2003: Category 5 Hurricane Isabel makes landfall south of Cape Hatteras, North Carolina, leaving 53 dead and property damage of $3.37 million.

October 21-November 4, 2003: Warm winds fuel at least 12 wildfires that burn simultaneously across Southern California; 22 die, 80,000 are displaced, and 3,500 homes are destroyed.

December 26, 2003: An earthquake in Bam, Iran, kills more than 26,000 and leaves 75,000 homeless.

2004: Four Category 5 storms—Charley, Frances, Ivan, and Jeanne—make landfall in the United States, the most in a hurricane season since 1963.

April 22, 2004: In Ryongchon, North Korea, a train carrying flammable cargo explodes at the railway station, killing 54 people and injuring 1,249.

December 26, 2004: A massive tsunami strikes 11 nations bordering the Indian Ocean, leaving at least 212,000 dead and almost 43,000 missing.

January 20-24, 2005: A heavy blizzard blankets New England with snow up to 40 inches in some places, shutting down Logan International Airport in Boston.

August 25-September 2, 2005: Hurricane Katrina kills 1,500-2,000 people in Louisiana, Mississippi, Alabama, and Florida and leaves hundreds missing; property damage is estimated at $75 billion. The levees protecting New Orleans are breached, and the city is completely flooded. Two other powerful hurricanes, Rita and Wilma, hit the Gulf Coast shortly afterward.

October 8, 2005: A powerful earthquake rocks Kashmir in Pakistan. More than 90,000 are dead and about 106,000 are injured; 3.3 million people are made homeless, and the damage is estimated at $5 billion.

December, 2005: In Tehran, Iran, businesses and schools close because of severe smog conditions; hundreds of people are taken to the hospital.

February 17, 2006: A mudslide buries 16 villages on the island of Leyte in the Philippines; more than 200 are confirmed dead, and 1,800 are missing.

May 26, 2006: A 6.3 magnitude earthquake in Java, Indonesia, kills more than 6,000 people, injures nearly 40,000, and leaves 1.5 million homeless.

January 12-16, 2007: A freezing winter storm moves across the United States causing extensive power outages and 65 related deaths, many of them in Oklahoma.

February 2, 2007: A tornado outbreak in central Florida kills 20 people; it is the first event to be measured by the Enhanced Fujita Scale, which factors in storm damage.

■ BIBLIOGRAPHY

AVALANCHES

Armstrong, Betsy R., Knox Williams, and Richard L. Armstrong. *The Avalanche Book*. Rev. and updated ed. Golden, Colo.: Fulcrum, 1992.

Cupp, D. "Avalanche: Winter's White Death." *National Geographic* 162 (September, 1982): 280-305.

CyberSpace Avalanche Center. http://www.avalanche-center.org/.

Ferguson, Sue, and Edward R. LaChapelle. *The ABCs of Avalanche Safety*. 3d ed. Seattle: Mountaineers Books, 2003.

Fredston, Jill. *Snowstruck: In the Grip of Avalanches*. Orlando, Fla.: Harcourt, 2005.

Graydon, E. *Mountaineering: The Freedom of the Hill*. Seattle: Mountaineers Books, 1992.

Jenkins, McKay. *The White Death: Tragedy and Heroism in an Avalanche Zone*. New York: Random House, 2000.

Logan, Nick, and Dale Atkins. *The Snowy Torrents: Avalanche Accidents in the United States, 1980-86*. Denver: Colorado Geological Survey, Department of Natural Resources, 1996.

Mears, Arthur I. *Avalanche Forecasting Methods, Highway 550*. Denver: Colorado Department of Transportation, 1996.

National Research Council Panel on Snow Avalanches. *Snow Avalanche Hazards and Mitigation in the United States*. Washington, D.C.: National Academy Press, 1990.

National Snow and Ice Data Center. *Avalanche Awareness*. http://nsidc.org/snow/avalanche/

Parfit, M. "Living with Natural Hazards." *National Geographic* 194 (July, 1998): 2-39.

Rosen, Michael J. *Avalanche*. Cambridge, Mass.: Candlewick Press, 1998.

USDA Forest Service. *Snow Avalanche: General Rules for Avoiding and Surviving Snow Avalanches*. Portland, Oreg.: USDA Forest Service, Pacific North West Region, 1982.

BLIZZARDS, FREEZES, ICE STORMS, AND HAIL

Allaby, Michael. *Dangerous Weather: Blizzards.* Rev. ed. New York: Facts On File, 2003.

Annual Frequency of Hailstorms in the United States. http://www.nhoem.state.nh.us/mitigation/fig%203-17.htm.

Battan, Louis J. *Weather in Your Life.* New York: W. H. Freeman, 1983.

Christian, Spencer, and Tom Biracree. *Spencer Christian's Weather Book.* New York: Prentice-Hall, 1993.

Eagleman, Joe R. *Severe and Unusual Weather.* 2d ed. Lenexa, Kans.: Trimedia, 1990.

Erikson, Jon. *Violent Storms.* Blue Ridge Summit, Pa.: Tab, 1988.

Gokhale, Narayan. *Hailstorms and Hailstone Growth.* Albany: State University of New York Press, 1975.

Laskin, David. *The Children's Blizzard.* New York: HarperCollins, 2004.

Ludlum, David M. *National Audubon Society Field Guide to North American Weather.* New York: Alfred A. Knopf, 1997.

_____. *The Weather Factor.* Boston: Houghton Mifflin, 1984.

Lyons, Walter A. *The Handy Weather Answer Book.* Detroit: Visible Ink Press, 1997.

Moore, Gene. *Hail Storms.* http://www.chaseday.com/hail.htm.

Murphy, Jim. *Blizzard! The Storm That Changed America.* New York: Scholastic Press, 2000.

DISASTER RELIEF

Comerio, Mary C. *Disaster Hits Home: New Policy for Urban Housing Recovery.* Berkeley: University of California Press, 1998.

H. John Heinz III Center for Science, Economics, and the Environment. *Human Links to Coastal Disasters.* Washington, D.C.: Author, 2002.

Haas, J. Eugene, et al., eds. *Reconstruction Following Disaster.* Cambridge: Massachusetts Institute of Technology Press, 1977.

Landesman, Linda Young. *Public Health Management of Disasters: The Practice Guide.* Washington, D.C.: American Public Health Association, 2005.

Leaning, Jennifer, Susan M. Briggs, and Lincoln C. Chen, eds. *Humanitarian Crises: The Medical and Public Health Response.* Cambridge, Mass.: Harvard University Press, 1999.

Redmond, Anthony D., et al., eds. *ABC of Conflict and Disaster.* Malden, Mass.: BMJ Books, 2006.

Rosenfeld, Lawrence B., et al. *When Their World Falls Apart: Helping Families and Children Manage the Effects of Disasters.* Washington, D.C.: NASW Press, 2005.

DROUGHTS

Allaby, Michael. *Droughts.* Rev. ed. New York: Facts On File, 2003.

Andryszewski, Tricia. *The Dust Bowl: Disaster on the Plains.* Brookfield, Conn.: Milbrook Press, 1994.

Benson, Charlotte, and Edward Clay. *The Impact of Drought on Sub-Saharan African Economies: A Preliminary Examination.* Washington, D.C.: World Bank, 1998.

Berk, Richard A., et al. *Water Shortage: Lessons in Conservation from the Great California Drought, 1976-1977.* Cambridge, Mass.: Abt Books, 1981.

Bryson, Reid A., and Thomas J. Murray. *Climates of Hunger.* Madison: University of Wisconsin, 1977.

Dixon, Lloyd S., Nancy Y. Moore, and Ellen M. Pint. *Drought Management Policies and Economic Effects in Urban Areas of California, 1987-92.* Santa Monica, Calif.: Rand, 1996.

Dolan, Edward F. *Drought: The Past, Present, and Future Enemy.* New York: Franklin Watts, 1990.

Frederiksen, Harald D. *Drought Planning and Water Resources: Implications in Water Resources Management.* Washington, D.C.: World Bank, 1992.

Garcia, Rolando V., and Pierre Spitz. *Drought and Man: The Roots of Catastrophe.* Vol. 3. New York: Pergamon Press, 1986.

Riggio, Robert P., George W. Bomar, and Thomas I. Larkin. *Texas Drought: Its Recent History, 1931-1985.* Austin: Texas Water Commission, 1987.

Riney-Kehrberg, Pamela. *Rooted in Dust: Surviving Drought and Depression in Southwestern Kansas.* Lawrence: University Press of Kansas, 1993.

Rosenberg, Norman J., ed. *North American Droughts.* Boulder, Colo.: Westview Press, 1978.

Shindo, Charles J. *Dust Bowl Migrants in the American Imagination.* Lawrence: University Press of Kansas, 1997.

Wilhite, Donald A., ed. *Drought and Water Crises: Science, Technology, and Management Issues.* Boca Raton, Fla.: Taylor & Francis, 2005.

Wilhite, Donald A., and William E. Easterling, eds., with Deborah A. Wood. *Planning for Drought: Toward a Reduction of Societal Vulnerability.* Boulder, Colo.: Westview Press, 1987.

DUST STORMS AND SANDSTORMS

Morales, Chister, ed. *Saharan Dust: Mobilization, Transport, Deposition.* Chichester, England: John Wiley & Sons, 1979.

Pewe, Troy L., ed. *Desert Dust: Origin, Characteristics, and Effect on Man.* Boulder, Colo.: Geological Society of America, 1981.

Shindo, Charles J. *Dust Bowl Migrants in the American Imagination.* Lawrence: University Press of Kansas, 1997.

Stallings, Frank L. *Black Sunday: The Great Dust Storm of April 14, 1935.* Austin, Tex.: Eakin Press, 2001.

Sundar, Christopher A., et al. *Radiative Effects of Aerosols Generated from Biomass Burning, Dust Storms, and Forest Fires.* Washington, D.C.: National Aeronautics and Space Administration, 1996.

Tannehill, Ivan Ray. *Drought: Its Causes and Effects.* Princeton, N.J.: Princeton University Press, 1947.

Worster, Donald. *Dust Bowl: The Southern Plains in the 1930's.* 25th anniversary ed. New York: Oxford University Press, 2004.

EARTHQUAKES

Bagnell, Norma Hayes. *On Shaky Ground: The New Madrid Earthquakes of 1811-1812.* Columbia: University of Missouri Press, 1996.

Bolin, Robert. *The Northridge Earthquake: Vulnerability and Disaster.* New York: Routledge, 1998.

Bolt, Bruce A. *Earthquakes.* 5th ed. New York: W. H. Freeman, 2006.

Brooks, Charles B. *Disaster at Lisbon: The Great Earthquake of 1755.* Long Beach, Calif.: Shangton Longley Press, 1994.

Brumbaugh, David S. *Earthquakes, Science, and Society.* Upper Saddle River, N.J.: Prentice Hall, 1999.

Coch, Nicholas K. "Earthquake Hazards." In *Geohazards: Natural and Human.* Englewood Cliffs, N.J.: Prentice Hall, 1995.

Cohen, Stan. *8.6: The Great Alaska Earthquake March 27, 1964.* Missoula, Mont.: Pictorial Histories, 1995.

Collier, Michael. *A Land in Motion: California's San Andreas Fault.* Berkeley: University of California Press, 1999.

Colvard, Elizabeth M., and James Rogers. *Facing the Great Disaster: How the Men and Women of the U.S. Geological Survey Responded to the 1906 "San Francisco Earthquake."* Reston, Va.: U.S. Geological Survey, 2006.

Fradkin, Philip L. *Magnitude 8: Earthquakes and Life Along the San Andreas Fault.* New York: Henry Holt, 1998.

Hadfield, Peter. *Sixty Seconds That Will Change the World: The Coming Tokyo Earthquake.* Boston: Charles E. Tuttle, 1991.

Hammer, Joshua. *Yokohama Burning: The Deadly 1923 Earthquake and Fire That Helped Forge the Path to World War II.* New York: Free Press, 2006.

Heppenheimer, T. A. *The Coming Quake: Science and Trembling on the California Earthquake Frontier.* New York: Times Books, 1988.

Hough, Susan Elizabeth, and Roger G. Bilham. *After the Earth Quakes: Elastic Rebound on an Urban Planet.* New York: Oxford University Press, 2006.

Housner, George W., and He Duxin, eds. *The Great Tangshan Earthquake of 1976.* Pasadena, Calif.: California Institute of Technology, 2004.

Keller, Edward A., and Nicholas Pinter. *Active Tectonics: Earthquakes, Uplift, and Landscape.* 2d ed. Upper Saddle River, N.J.: Prentice Hall, 2002.

Kimball, Virginia. *Earthquake Ready.* Rev. ed. Malibu, Calif.: Roundtable, 1992.

Kurzman, Dan. *Disaster! The Great San Francisco Earthquake and Fire of 1906.* New York: William Morrow, 2001.

Levy, Matthys, and Mario Salvador. *Why the Earth Quakes: The Story of Earthquakes and Volcanoes.* New York: W. W. Norton, 1995.

Lundgren, Lawrence W. "Earthquake Hazards." In *Environmental Geology.* 2d ed. Upper Saddle River, N.J.: Prentice Hall, 1999.

Murck, Barbara W., Brian Skinner, and Stephen C. Porter. *Dangerous Earth: An Introduction to Geologic Hazards.* New York: John Wiley & Sons, 1997.

Page, Jake, and Charles Officer. *The Big One: The Earthquake That Rocked Early America and Helped Create a Science.* Boston: Houghton Mifflin, 2004.

Poniatowska, Elena. *Nothing, Nobody: The Voices of the Mexico City Earthquake.* Philadelphia: Temple University Press, 1995.

Reti, Irene, ed. *The Loma Prieta Earthquake of October 17, 1989.* Santa Cruz: University of California, Santa Cruz, 2006.

Sieh, Kerry, and Simon Le Vay. *The Earth in Turmoil: Earthquakes, Volcanoes, and Their Impact on Humankind.* New York: W. H. Freeman, 1998.

Stewart, David, and Ray Knox. *The Earthquake America Forgot: 2,000 Temblors in Five Months.* Marble Hill, Mo.: Guttenberg-Richter, 1995.

Verluise, Pierre. *Armenia in Crisis: The 1988 Earthquake.* Translated by Levon Chorbajian. Detroit: Wayne State University Press, 1995.

Winchester, Simon. *A Crack in the Edge of the World: America and the Great California Earthquake of 1906.* New York: HarperCollins, 2005.

Zeilinga de Boer, Jelle, and Donald Theodore Sanders. *Earthquakes in Human History: The Far-Reaching Effects of Seismic Disruptions.* Princeton, N.J.: Princeton University Press, 2005.

EL NIÑO

Allan, Rob, Janette Lindesay, and David Parker. *El Niño Southern Oscillation and Climatic Variability.* Collingwood, Australia: CSIRO, 1997.

Arnold, Caroline. *El Niño: Stormy Weather for People and Wildlife.* New York: Clarion, 1998.

Babkina, A. M., ed. *El Niño: Overview and Bibliography.* Hauppauge, N.Y.: Nova Science, 2003.

D'Aleo, Joseph S. *The Oryx Resource Guide to El Niño and La Niña.* Westport, Conn.: Oryx Press, 2002.

Diaz, Henry F., and Vera Markgraf, eds. *El Niño: Historical and Paleoclimatic Aspects of the Southern Oscillation.* New York: Cambridge University Press, 1992.

Fagan, Brian. "El Niños That Shook the World." In *Floods, Famines, and Emperors: El Niño and the Fate of Civilization.* New York: Basic Books, 1999.

Glantz, Michael H. *Currents of Change: El Niño's Impact on Climate and Society.* New York: Cambridge University Press, 1996.

Lyons, Walter A. *The Handy Weather Answer Book.* Detroit: Visible Ink Press, 1997.

Nash, J. Madeleine. *El Niño: Unlocking the Secrets of the Master Weather-Maker.* New York: Warner Books, 2002.

Philander, S. George. *Is the Temperature Rising? The Uncertain Science of Global Warming.* Princeton, N.J.: Princeton University Press, 1998.

_____. *Our Affair with El Niño: How We Transformed an Enchanting Peruvian Current into a Global Climate Hazard.* Princeton, N.J.: Princeton University Press, 2004.

EPIDEMICS

Barnett, Tony, and Alan Whiteside. *AIDS in the Twenty-first Century: Disease and Globalization.* 2d ed. New York: Palgrave Macmillan, 2006.

Barry, John M. *The Great Influenza: The Epic Story of the Deadliest Plague in History.* New York: Viking, 2004.

Benedictow, Ole J. *The Black Death, 1346-1353: The Complete History.* Rochester, N.Y.: Boydell Press, 2006.

Bollet, Alfred J. *Plagues and Poxes: The Impact of Human History on Epidemic Disease.* New York: Demos, 2004.

Byrne, Joseph P. *The Black Death.* Westport, Conn.: Greenwood Press, 2004.

Crosby, Alfred W. *America's Forgotten Pandemic: The Influenza of 1918.* 2d ed. New York: Cambridge University Press, 2003.

Crosby, Molly Caldwell. *The American Plague: The Untold Story of Yellow Fever, the Epidemic That Shaped Our History.* New York: Berkley, 2006.

Diamond, Jared. *Guns, Germs, and Steel: The Fates of Human Societies.* New York: W. W. Norton, 1997.

Evans, Alfred S., and Philip S. Brachman. *Bacterial Infections of Humans: Epidemiology and Control.* 3d ed. New York: Plenum Medical Book Company, 1998.

Farrell, Jeanette. *Invisible Enemies: Stories of Infectious Disease.* 2d and rev. ed. New York: Farrar, Straus and Giroux, 2005.

Gehlbach, Stephen H. *American Plagues: Lessons from Our Battles with Disease.* New York: McGraw-Hill Medical, 2005.

Glynn, Ian, and Jenifer Glynn. *The Life and Death of Smallpox.* New York: Cambridge University Press, 2004.

Graf, Mercedes. *Quarantine: The Story of Typhoid Mary.* New York: Vantage Press, 1998.

Hays, J. N. *The Burdens of Disease: Epidemics and Human Response in*

Western History. New Brunswick, N.J.: Rutgers University Press, 1998.

Karlen, Arno. *Man and Microbes: Disease and Plagues in History and Modern Times*. New York: Putnam, 1995.

Kelly, John. *The Great Mortality: An Intimate History of the Black Death, the Most Devastating Plague of All Time*. New York: HarperCollins, 2005.

Kleinman, Arthur, and James L. Watson, eds. *SARS in China: Prelude to Pandemic?* Stanford, Calif.: Stanford University Press, 2006.

Kolata, Gina. *Flu: The Story of the Great Influenza Pandemic of 1918 and the Search for the Virus That Caused It*. New York: Simon & Schuster, 2001.

Levy, Elinor, and Mark Fischetti. *The New Killer Diseases: How the Alarming Evolution of Mutant Germs Threatens Us All*. New York: Crown, 2003.

McNeill, William H. *Plagues and Peoples*. New York: Anchor Press/ Doubleday, 1998.

Moote, A. Lloyd, and Dorothy C. Moote. *The Great Plague: The Story of London's Most Deadly Year*. Baltimore: Johns Hopkins University Press, 2004.

Oldstone, Michael B. A. *Viruses, Plagues, and History*. New York: Oxford University Press, 1998.

Orent, Wendy. *Plague: The Mysterious Past and Terrifying Future of the World's Most Dangerous Disease*. New York: Free Press, 2004.

Oshinsky, David M. *Polio: An American Story*. New York: Oxford University Press, 2005.

Pierce, John R., and Jim Writer. *Yellow Jack: How Yellow Fever Ravaged America and Walter Reed Discovered Its Deadly Secrets*. Hoboken, N.J.: John Wiley & Sons, 2005.

Preston, Richard. *The Hot Zone*. New York: Random House, 1994.

Regis, Ed. *Virus Ground Zero: Stalking the Killer Viruses with the Centers for Disease Control*. New York: Pocket Books, 1996.

Shader, Laurel. *Legionnaire's Disease*. Philadelphia: Chelsea House, 2006.

Smith, Tara C. *Ebola*. Philadelphia: Chelsea House, 2006.

FAMINES

Aaseng, Nathan. *Ending World Hunger.* New York: Franklin Watts, 1991.

Bartoletti, Susan Campbell. *Black Potatoes: The Story of the Great Irish Famine, 1845-1850.* Boston: Houghton Mifflin, 2001.

Becker, Jasper. *Hungry Ghosts: Mao's Secret Famine.* New York: Henry Holt, 1998.

Cuny, Frederick C. *Famine, Conflict and Response: A Basic Guide.* West Hartford, Conn.: Kumarian Press, 1999.

Curtis, Donald, Michael Hubbard, and Andrew Shepherd. *Preventing Famine: Policies and Prospects for Africa.* London: Routledge, 1988.

DeRose, Laurie Fields. *Who's Hungry? And How Do We Know? Food Shortage, Poverty, and Deprivation.* New York: United Nations University Press, 1998.

Donnelly, James S., Jr. *The Great Irish Potato Famine.* Phoenix Mill, Gloucestershire, England: Sutton, 2001.

Field, John Osgood, ed. *The Challenge of Famine: Recent Experience, Lessons Learned.* West Hartford, Conn.: Kumarian Press, 1993.

Golkin, Arline T. *Famine, a Heritage of Hunger: A Guide to Issues and References.* Claremont, Calif.: Regina Books, 1987.

Jordan, William C. *The Great Famine: Northern Europe in the Early Fourteenth Century.* Princeton, N.J.: Princeton University Press, 1996.

Kutzner, Patricia L. *World Hunger: A Reference Handbook.* Santa Barbara, Calif.: ABC-Clio, 1991.

Sen, Amartya Kumar. *Poverty and Famines: An Essay on Entitlement and Deprivation.* Oxford, England: Clarendon Press, 1981.

Varnis, Stephen. *Reluctant Aid or Aiding the Reluctant: U.S. Food Aid Policy and Ethiopian Famine Relief.* New Brunswick, N.J.: Transaction, 1990.

Von Braun, Joachim, Tesfaye Teklu, and Patrick Webb. *Famine in Africa: Causes, Responses, and Prevention.* Baltimore: Johns Hopkins University Press, 1999.

Webb, Patrick, and Joachim von Braun. *Famine and Food Security in Ethiopia: Lessons for Africa.* New York: John Wiley, 1994.

Woodham-Smith, Cecil, and Charles Woodham. *The Great Hunger: Ireland, 1846-1849.* New York: Penguin, 1995.

FIRES

Balcavage, Dynise. *The Great Chicago Fire.* Philadelphia: Chelsea House, 2002.

Bales, Richard F. *The Great Chicago Fire and the Myth of Mrs. O'Leary's Cow.* Jefferson, N.C.: McFarland, 2002.

Branigan, Francis. *Building Construction for the Fire Service.* Quincy, Mass.: National Fire Protection Association, 1992.

Carrier, Jim. *Summer of Fire: The Great Yellowstone Fires of 1988.* Salt Lake City: Gibbs-Smith, 1989.

Cote, Arthur, ed. *Fire Protection Handbook.* 19th ed. Quincy, Mass.: National Fire Protection Association, 2003.

Cottrell, William H., Jr. *The Book of Fire.* 2d ed. Missoula, Mont.: Mountain Press, 2004.

Gess, Denise, and William Lutz. *Firestorm at Peshtigo: A Town, Its People, and the Deadliest Fire in American History.* New York: Henry Holt, 2002.

Hanson, Neil. *The Great Fire of London: In That Apocalyptic Year, 1666.* Hoboken, N.J.: John Wiley & Sons, 2002.

Krauss, Erich. *Wall of Flame: The Heroic Battle to Save Southern California.* Hoboken, N.J.: John Wiley & Sons, 2006.

Lyons, Paul Robert. *Fire in America!* Boston: National Fire Protection Association, 1976.

Murphy, Jim. *The Great Fire.* New York: Scholastic, 1995.

Porter, Stephen. *The Great Fire of London.* Phoenix Mill, Gloucestershire, England: Sutton, 2002.

Pyne, Stephen J. *World Fire: The Culture of Fire on Earth.* Seattle: University of Washington Press, 1995.

Sammarco, Anthony Mitchell. *The Great Boston Fire of 1872.* Dover, N.H.: Arcadia, 1997.

Soddens, Betty. *Michigan on Fire.* Thunder Bay, Ontario: Thunder Bay Press, 1998.

Sullivan, Margaret. *Firestorm! The Story of the 1991 East Bay Fire in Berkeley.* Berkeley, Calif.: City of Berkeley, 1993.

Tebeau, Mark. *Eating Smoke: Fire in Urban America, 1800-1950.* Baltimore: Johns Hopkins University Press, 2003.

Tinniswood, Adrian. *By Permission of Heaven: The Story of the Great Fire of London.* New York: Riverhead Books, 2004.

FLOODS

Beyer, Jacqueline L. "Human Response to Floods." In *Perspectives on Water,* edited by David H. Spiedel, Lon C. Ruedisili, and Allen F. Agnew. New York: Oxford University Press, 1988.

Changnon, Stanley, ed. *The Great Flood of 1993: Causes, Impacts, and Responses.* Boulder, Colo.: Westview Press, 1996.

Dunne, Thomas, and Luna B. Leopold. *Water in Environmental Planning.* New York: W. H. Freeman, 1978.

Dzurik, Andrew A. *Water Resources Planning.* 2d ed. New York: Rowman & Littlefield, 1996.

Evans, T. William. *Though the Mountains May Fall: The Story of the Great Johnstown Flood of 1889.* New York: Writers Club Press, 2002.

Hornberger, George M., Jeffrey P. Raffensberger, Patricia L. Wilberg, and Keith N. Eshleman. *Elements of Physical Hydrology.* Baltimore: Johns Hopkins University Press, 1998.

Johnson, Willis Fletcher. *History of the Johnstown Flood.* Reprint. Westminster, Md.: Heritage Books, 2001.

Jones, J. A. A. *Global Hydrology.* Essex, England: Longman, 1997.

Martini, I. Peter, Victor R. Baker, and Guillermina Garzón, eds. *Flood and Megaflood Processes and Deposits: Recent and Ancient Examples.* Malden, Mass.: Blackwell Science, 2002.

Myers, Mary Fran, and Gilbert F. White. "The Challenge of the Mississippi Floods." In *Environmental Management,* edited by Lewis Owen and Tim Unwin. Malden, Mass.: Blackwell, 1997.

National Weather Service. *The Great Flood of 1993.* National Disaster Survey Report. Washington, D.C.: National Oceanic and Atmospheric Administration, 1994.

Nunis, Doyce B., Jr., ed. *The Saint Francis Dam Disaster Revisited.* Los Angeles: Historical Society of Southern California, 2002.

O'Connor, Jim E., and John E. Costa. *The World's Largest Floods, Past and Present: Their Causes and Magnitudes.* Reston, Va.: U.S. Geological Survey, 2004.

Pielke, Roger A., Jr. *Midwest Flood of 1993: Weather, Climate, and Societal Impacts.* Boulder, Colo.: National Center for Atmospheric Research, 1996.

Pollard, Michael. *North Sea Surge: The Story of the East Coast Floods of 1953.* Suffolk, England: Terence Dalton, 1978.

Strahler, Alan, and Arthur Strahler. *Introducing Physical Geography.* 4th ed. Hoboken, N.J.: John Wiley & Sons, 2006.

HURRICANES

Barnes, Jay. *Florida's Hurricane History.* Chapel Hill: University of North Carolina Press, 1998.

————. *North Carolina's Hurricane History.* Rev. ed. Chapel Hill: University of North Carolina Press, 1998.

Brinkley, Douglas. *The Great Deluge: Hurricane Katrina, New Orleans, and the Mississippi Gulf Coast.* New York: William Morrow, 2006.

Burns, Cherie. *The Great Hurricane—1938.* New York: Atlantic Monthly Press, 2005.

Carrier, Jim. *The Ship and the Storm: Hurricane Mitch and the Loss of the "Fantome."* New York: McGraw-Hill, 2002.

Emanuel, Kerry. *Divine Wind: The History and Science of Hurricanes.* New York: Oxford University Press, 2005.

Greene, Casey Edward, and Shelly Henley Kelly, eds. *Through a Night of Horrors: Voices from the 1900 Galveston Storm.* College Station: Texas A&M University Press, 2000.

Hearn, Philip D. *Hurricane Camille: Monster Storm of the Gulf Coast.* Jackson: University Press of Mississippi, 2004.

Horne, Jed. *Breach of Faith: Hurricane Katrina and the Near Death of a Great American City.* New York: Random House, 2006.

Kleinberg, Eliot. *Black Cloud: The Great Florida Hurricane of 1928.* New York: Carroll & Graf, 2003.

Larson, Erik. *Isaac's Storm: A Man, a Time, and the Deadliest Hurricane in History.* New York: Crown, 1999.

Longshore, David. *Encyclopedia of Hurricanes, Typhoons, and Cyclones.* New York: Facts On File, 1998.

Pielke, R. A., Jr., and R. A. Pielke, Sr. *Hurricanes: Their Nature and Impacts on Society.* New York: John Wiley & Sons, 1997.

Provenzo, Eugene F., Jr., and Asterie Baker Provenzo. *In the Eye of Hurricane Andrew.* Gainesville: University Press of Florida, 2002.

Scotti, R. A. *Sudden Sea: The Great Hurricane of 1938.* Boston: Little, Brown, 2003.

Sheets, Bob, and Jack Williams. *Hurricane Watch: Forecasting the Deadliest Storms on Earth.* New York: Vintage, 2001.

Simon, Seymour. *Hurricanes.* New York: HarperCollins, 2003.

Williams, John M., and Iver W. Duedall. *Florida Hurricanes and Tropical Storms, 1871-2001.* Gainesville: University of Florida Press, 2002.

Zebrowski, Ernest, and Judith A. Howard. *Category 5: The Story of Camille, Lessons Unlearned from America's Most Violent Hurricane.* Ann Arbor: University of Michigan Press, 2005.

LANDSLIDES, MUDSLIDES, AND ROCKSLIDES

Bloom, Arthur L. "Mass Wasting and Hillslopes." In *Geomorphology: A Systematic Analysis of Late Cenozoic Landforms.* 3d ed. Upper Saddle River, N.J.: Prentice Hall, 1998.

Bryant, Edward A. *Natural Hazards.* 2d ed. Cambridge, England: Cambridge University Press, 2005.

Cooke, R. U., and J. C. Doornkamp. *Geomorphology in Environmental Management.* Oxford, England: Clarendon Press, 1990.

Easterbrook, Don J. *Surface Processes and Landforms.* 2d ed. Upper Saddle River, N.J.: Prentice-Hall, 1999.

Landslides . . . Unsafe at Any Speed. http://www.anaheim-landslide.com/unsafe.htm.

Larson, Robert A., and James E. Slosson. *Storm-Induced Geologic Hazards: Case Histories from the 1992-1993 Winter in Southern California and Arizona.* Boulder, Colo.: Geological Society of America, 1997.

Lee, Fitzhugh T., Jack K. Odum, and John D. Lee. *Rockfalls and Debris Avalanches in the Smugglers Notch Area, Vermont.* Washington, D.C.: U.S. Government Printing Office, 1994.

Mears, Arthur I. *Debris-Flow Hazard Analysis and Mitigation: An Example from Glenwood Springs, Colorado.* Denver: Colorado Geological Survey, Department of Natural Resources, 1977.

Plummer, Charles C., David McGeary, and Diane H. Carlson. *Physical Geology.* 11th ed. Boston: McGraw-Hill Higher Education, 2007.

Ritter, Dale F., R. Craig Kochel, and Jerry R. Miller. *Process Geomorphology.* 4th ed. Dubuque, Iowa: Wm. C. Brown, 2002.

Schultz, Arthur P., and Randall W. Jibson. *Landslide Processes of the Eastern United States and Puerto Rico.* Boulder, Colo.: Geological Society of America, 1989.

Voight, Barry, ed. *Rockslides and Avalanches.* New York: Elsevier Scientific, 1978-1979.

LIGHTNING STRIKES

Dennis, Jerry. *It's Raining Frogs and Fishes: Four Seasons of Natural Phenomena and Oddities of the Sky.* New York: HarperCollins, 1992.

Gardner, Robert L., ed. *Lightning Electromagnetics.* New York: Hemisphere, 1990.

Rakov, Vladimir A., and Martin A. Uman. *Lightning: Physics and Effects.* New York: Cambridge University Press, 2003.

Renner, Jeff. *Lightning Strikes: Staying Safe Under Stormy Skies.* Seattle: Mountaineers Books, 2002.

Salanave, Leon E. *Lightning and Its Spectrum.* Tuscon: University of Arizona Press, 1980.

Uman, Martin A. *The Lightning Discharge.* Mineola, N.Y.: Dover, 2001.

Williams, Jack. *The Weather Book.* 2d rev. ed. New York: Vintage Books, 1997.

METEORITES AND COMETS

Burke, John G. *Cosmic Debris: Meteorites in History.* Berkeley: University of California Press, 1986.

Chapman, Clark R., and David Morrison. *Cosmic Catastrophes.* New York: Plenum Press, 1989.

Cox, Donald W., and James H. Chestek. *Doomsday Asteroid: Can We Survive?* Amherst, N.Y.: Prometheus Books, 1996.

Lewis, John S. *Comet and Asteroid Impact Hazards on a Populated Earth: Computer Modeling.* San Diego, Calif.: Academic, 2000.

_____. *Rain of Iron and Ice: The Very Real Threat of Comet and Asteroid Bombardment.* Reading, Mass.: Addison-Wesley, 1996.

Sagan, Carl, and Ann Druyan. *Comet.* New York: Random House, 1985.

Steel, Duncan. *Rogue Asteroids and Doomsday Comets: The Search for the Million Megaton Menace That Threatens Life on Earth.* New York: John Wiley & Sons, 1995.

Verma, Surendra. *The Tunguska Fireball: Solving One of the Great Mysteries of the 20th Century.* Cambridge, England: Icon Books, 2006.

Verschuur, Gerrit L. *Impact! The Threat of Comets and Asteroids.* New York: Oxford University Press, 1996.

Zanda, Brigitte, and Monica Rotaru, eds. *Meteorites: Their Impact on Science and History.* Translated by Roger Hewins. New York: Cambridge University Press, 2001.

NATURAL DISASTERS—VARIOUS

Bryant, Edward A. *Natural Hazards.* 2d ed. Cambridge, England: Cambridge University Press, 2005.

Cleary, Margot Keam. *Great Disasters of the Twentieth Century.* New York: Gallery Books, 1990.

Erickson, Jon. *Quakes, Eruptions, and Other Geologic Cataclysms: Revealing the Earth's Hazards.* Rev. ed. New York: Facts On File, 2001.

Frank, Beryl. *Great Disasters of the World.* New York: Galahad Books, 1981.

McCall, G. J. H., D. J. C. Laming, and S. C. Scott. *Geohazards: Natural and Man-Made.* New York: Chapman and Hall, 1992.

Nash, Jay Robert. *Darkest Hours.* Chicago: Nelson-Hall, 1976.

Robinson, Andrew. *Earthshock: Hurricanes, Volcanoes, Tornadoes, and Other Forces of Nature.* Rev. ed. New York: Thames and Hudson, 2002.

Rosenfield, Jeffrey. *Eye of the Storm: Inside the World's Deadliest Hurricanes, Tornadoes, and Blizzards.* New York: Basic Books, 2003.

Tufty, Barbara. *1001 Questions Answered About Hurricanes, Tornadoes, and Other Natural Air Disasters.* Rev. ed. New York: Dover, 1987.

SAFETY GUIDES

Adams, Christopher R. *Building Better Warning Partnerships: National Weather Service Emergency Management Forum.* Upland, Pa.: Diane, 1997.

Daffern, Tony. *Avalanche Safety: For Skiers and Climbers.* Seattle: Mountaineers Books, 1999.

Leonard, Barry, ed. *Automated Local Flood Warning Systems Handbook.* Upland, Pa.: Diane, 1998.

Palm, Risa, and John Carroll. *Illusions of Safety: Culture and Earthquake Hazard Response in California and Japan.* Boulder, Colo.: Westview Press, 1997.

Stringfield, William H. *Emergency Planning and Management: Ensuring Your Company's Survival in the Event of a Disaster.* Rockville, Md.: Government Institutes, 1999.

SMOG

Allaby, Michael. *Fog, Smog, and Poisoned Rain.* New York: Facts On File, 2003.

Benarde, Melvin A. *Our Precarious Habitat.* New York: John Wiley & Sons, 1989.

Elsom, Derek M. *Atmospheric Pollution: A Global Problem.* Cambridge, Mass.: Blackwell Scientific, 1992.

Environmental Protection Agency. *Smog—Who Does It Hurt? What You Need to Know About Ozone and Your Health.* Washington, D.C.: Author, 1999.

Graedel, T. E., and Paul J. Crutzen. *Atmospheric Change: An Earth System Perspective.* New York: W. H. Freeman, 1993.

Group Against Smog and Pollution (GASP). http://www.gasp-pgh .org/.

Keller, Edward A. *Environmental Geology.* 8th ed. Upper Saddle River, N.J.: Prentice Hall, 2000.

Soroos, Marvin S. *The Endangered Atmosphere.* Columbia: University of South Carolina Press, 1997.

Wise, William. *Killer Smog: The World's Worst Air Pollution Disaster.* New York: Ballantine, 1970.

TORNADOES

Akin, Wallace E. *The Forgotten Storm: The Great Tri-State Tornado of 1925.* Guilford, Conn.: Lyons Press, 2004.

Ball, Jacqueline A. *Tornado! The 1974 Super Outbreak.* New York: Bearport, 2005.

Bluestein, Howard. *Tornado Alley: Monster Storms of the Great Plains.* New York: Oxford University Press, 1999.

Bradford, Marlene. *Scanning the Skies: A History of Tornado Forecasting.* Norman: University of Oklahoma Press, 2001.

Butler, William S., ed. *Tornado: A Look Back at Louisville's Dark Day, April 3, 1974.* Louisville, Ky.: Butler Books, 2004.

Church, Christopher, Donald Burgess, Charles Doswell, and Robert Davies-Jones, eds. *The Tornado: Its Structure, Dynamics, Prediction, and Hazards.* Washington, D.C.: American Geophysical Union, 1993.

Curzon, Julian, comp. and ed. *The Great Cyclone at St. Louis and East St. Louis, May 27, 1896: Being a Full History of the Most Terrifying and Destructive Tornado in the History of the World.* 1896. Reprint. Carbondale: Southern Illinois University Press, 1997.

Eagleman, Joe R. "The Strongest Storm on Earth." In *Severe and Unusual Weather.* Lenexa, Kans.: Trimedia, 1990.

Felknor, Peter E. *The Tri-State Tornado.* Ames: Iowa State University Press, 1992.

Grazulis, Thomas P. *Significant Tornadoes: 1680-1991.* St. Johnsbury, Vt.: Environmental Films, 1993.

_____. *Significant Tornadoes Update, 1992-1995.* St. Johnsbury, Vt.: Environmental Films, 1997.

_____. *The Tornado: Nature's Ultimate Windstorm.* Norman: University of Oklahoma Press, 2003.

Lane, Frank. *The Violent Earth.* Topsfield, Mass.: Salem House, 1986.

Ludlum, David. *Early American Tornadoes: 1586-1870.* Boston: American Meteorological Society, 1970.

Weems, John Edward. *The Tornado.* College Station: Texas A&M University Press, 1991.

Whipple, A. B. "Thunderstorms and Their Progeny." In *Storm.* Alexandria, Va.: Time-Life Books, 1982.

TSUNAMIS

Adamson, Thomas K. *Tsunamis.* Mankato, Minn.: Capstone Press, 2006.

Bernard, E. N. *Developing Tsunami-Resilient Communities: The National Tsunami Hazard Mitigation Program.* Norwell, Mass.: Springer, 2005.

Dudley, Walter C., and Scott C. S. Stone. *The Tsunami of 1946 and 1960 and the Devastation of Hilo Town.* Marceline, Mo.: Walsworth, 2000.

Karwoski, Gail Langer. *Tsunami: The True Story of an April Fools' Day Disaster.* Plain City, Ohio: Darby Creek, 2006.

Lander, James F., and Patricia A. Lockridge. *United States Tsunamis, 1690-1988.* Boulder, Colo.: National Geophysical Data Center, 1989.

Lockridge, Patricia A., and Ronald H. Smith. *Tsunamis in the Pacific Basin, 1900-1983.* Boulder, Colo.: National Geophysical Data Center and World Data Center A for Solid Earth Geophysics, 1984.

Myles, Douglas. *The Great Waves.* New York: McGraw-Hill, 1985.

Robinson, Andrew. "Floods, Dambursts, and Tsunamis." In *Earthshock: Hurricanes, Volcanoes, Tornadoes, and Other Forces of Nature.* Rev. ed. New York: Thames and Hudson, 2002.

Satake, Kenji, ed. *Tsunamis: Case Studies and Recent Developments.* Springer, 2006.

Solovev, Sergei, and Chan Nam Go. *Catalogue of Tsunamis on the East-*

ern Shore of the Pacific Ocean. Sidney, B.C.: Institute of Ocean Sciences, Department of Fisheries and Oceans, 1984.

————. *Catalogue of Tsunamis on the Western Shore of the Pacific Ocean.* Sidney, B.C.: Institute of Ocean Sciences, Department of Fisheries and Oceans, 1984.

Stewart, Gail B. *Catastrophe in Southeastern Asia: The Tsunami of 2004.* Chicago: Gale/Lucent, 2005.

Torres, John Albert. *Disaster in the Indian Ocean, Tsunami 2004.* Hockessin, Del.: Mitchell Lane, 2005.

VOLCANIC ERUPTIONS

Bardintzeff, Jacques-Marie, and Alexander R. McBirney. *Volcanology.* 2d ed. Sudbury, Mass.: Jones and Bartlett, 2000.

Bonaccorso, Alessandro, et al., eds. *Mt. Etna: Volcano Laboratory.* Washington, D.C.: American Geophysical Union, 2004.

Bullard, Fred M. *Volcanoes of the Earth.* 2d rev. ed. Austin: University of Texas Press, 1984.

Carson, Rob. *Mount St. Helens: The Eruption and Recovery of a Volcano.* Seattle: Sasquatch Books, 2000.

Chester, David. *Volcanoes and Society.* New York: Routledge, Chapman and Hall, 1993.

Davison, Phil. *Volcano in Paradise: The True Story of the Montserrat Eruptions.* London: Methuen, 2003.

De Carolis, Ernesto, and Giovanni Patricelli. *Vesuvius, A.D. 79: The Destruction of Pompeii and Herculaneum.* Los Angeles: J. Paul Getty Museum, 2003.

Decker, Robert, and Barbara Decker. *Volcanoes.* 4th ed. New York: W. H. Freeman, 2006.

Druit, T.H., and B. P. Kokelaar, eds. *The Eruption of Soufrière Hills Volcano, Montserrat, from 1995 to 1999.* London: Geological Society, 2002.

Fisher, Richard V. *Out of the Crater: Chronicles of a Volcanologist.* Princeton, N.J.: Princeton University Press, 1999.

Fisher, Richard V., Grant Heiken, and Jeffrey B. Hulen. *Volcanoes: Crucibles of Change.* Princeton, N.J.: Princeton University Press, 1997.

Fouqué, Ferdinand. *Santorini and Its Eruptions.* Translated by Alexander R. McBirney. Baltimore: Johns Hopkins University Press, 1998.

Francis, Peter, and Clive Oppenheimer. *Volcanoes.* 2d ed. New York: Oxford University Press, 2004.

Morgan, Peter. *Fire Mountain: How One Man Survived the World's Worst Volcanic Disaster.* London: Bloomsbury, 2003.

Newhall, Christopher G., James W. Hendley II, and Peter H. Stauffer. *The Cataclysmic 1991 Eruption of Mount Pinatubo, Philippines.* Vancouver, Wash.: U.S. Geological Survey, 1997.

Rosi, Mauro, et al. *Volcanoes.* Buffalo, N.Y.: Firefly Books, 2003.

Scarth, Alwyn. *La Catastrophe: The Eruption of Mount Pelee, the Worst Volcanic Eruption of the Twentieth Century.* New York: Oxford University Press, 2002.

_____. *Volcanoes: An Introduction.* College Station: Texas A&M University Press, 1994.

_____. *Vulcan's Fury: Man Against the Volcano.* New ed. New Haven, Conn.: Yale University Press, 2001.

Sigurdsson, Haraldur, ed. *Encyclopedia of Volcanoes.* San Diego, Calif.: Academic, 2000.

Simkin, Tom, and Richard S. Fiske, eds. *Krakatau, 1883: The Volcanic Eruption and Its Effects.* Washington, D.C.: Smithsonian Institution Press, 1983.

Sparks, R. S. J., et al. *Volcanic Plumes.* New York: John Wiley & Sons, 1997.

Stommel, Henry, and Elizabeth Stommel. *Volcano Weather: The Story of 1816, the Year Without a Summer.* Newport, R.I.: Seven Seas Press, 1983.

Sutherland, Lin. *The Volcanic Earth: Volcanoes and Plate Tectonics, Past, Present, and Future.* Sydney: University of New South Wales Press, 1995.

Tilling, Robert I., Lyn Topinka, and Donald A. Swanson. *Eruptions of Mount St. Helens: Past, Present, and Future.* Reston, Va.: U.S. Department of the Interior, U.S. Geological Survey, 1990.

Winchester, Simon. *Krakatoa: The Day the World Exploded, August 27, 1883.* New York: HarperCollins, 2003.

Wohletz, Kenneth, and Grant Heiken. *Volcanology and Geothermal Energy.* Berkeley: University of California Press, 1992.

Zebrowski, Ernest. *The Last Days of St. Pierre: The Volcanic Disaster That Claimed 30,000 Lives.* New Brunswick, N.J.: Rutgers University Press, 2002.

Zeilinga de Boer, Jelle, and Donald Theodore Sanders. *Volcanoes in Human History: The Far-Reaching Effects of Major Eruptions.* Princeton, N.J.: Princeton University Press, 2002.

WIND GUSTS

Freier, George D. *Weather Proverbs: How 600 Proverbs, Sayings, and Poems Accurately Explain Our Weather.* Tucson, Ariz.: Fisher Books, 1992.

Kimble, George H. T. *Our American Weather.* New York: McGraw Hill, 1955.

National Aeronautics and Space Administration. *Making the Skies Safe from Windshear.* http://www.nasa.gov/centers/langley/news/factsheets/Windshear.html.

National Transportation Safety Board. http://www.ntsb.gov/ntsb/query.asp.

Palmén, E., and C. W. Newton. *Atmospheric Circulation Systems: Their Structure and Physical Interpretation.* New York: Academic Press, 1969.

Wood, Richard A., ed. *The Weather Almanac: A Reference Guide to Weather, Climate, and Related Issues in the United States and Its Key Cities.* 11th ed. Detroit: Thompson/Gale, 2004.

■ ORGANIZATIONS AND AGENCIES

AMERICA OXFORD COMMITTEE FOR FAMINE RELIEF (OXFAM)
Headquarters:
Oxfam America
226 Causeway Street, 5th Floor
Boston, MA 02114
Ph.: (800) 77-OXFAM
Fax: (617) 728-2594
Policy and Advocacy Office:
Oxfam America
1100 15th Street NW, Suite 600
Washington, DC 20005
Fax: (202) 496-1190
E-mail: info@oxfamamerica.org
Web site: http://www.oxfamamerica.org
Creates solutions to hunger, poverty, and social injustice around the
world. Provides emergency aid when disaster strikes, assisting refu-
gees and survivors of natural disasters.

AMERICAN FRIENDS SERVICE COMMITTEE (AFSC)
1501 Cherry Street
Philadelphia, PA 19102
Ph.: (215) 241-7000, (888) 588-2372 (donations)
Fax: (215) 241-7275
E-mail: afscinfo@afsc.org
Web site: http://www.afsc.org
A Quaker organization that focuses on issues related to economic
and social justice in the United States, Africa, Asia, Latin America,
and the Middle East.

AMERICAN JEWISH JOINT DISTRIBUTION COMMITTEE
E-mail: info@jdc.org
Web site: http://www.jdc.org
Sponsors programs of relief, rescue, and reconstruction to Jews af-
fected by natural and human-made disasters around the world.

AMERICAN RED CROSS DISASTER RELIEF FUND
2025 E Street NW
Washington, DC 20006
Ph.: (202) 303-4498, (800) REDCROSS (donations)
Web site: http://www.redcross.org
Provides relief to victims of disasters and helps people prevent, prepare for, and respond to emergencies.

AMERICARES FOUNDATION
88 Hamilton Avenue
Stamford, CT 06902
Ph.: (800) 486-HELP
Web site: http://www.americares.org
Dispenses emergency medicines, medical supplies, and nutritional items to victims of disasters, famine, and war to over 130 countries worldwide. Supports long-term health care programs.

BAPTIST WORLD ALLIANCE
405 North Washington Street
Falls Church, VA 22046
Ph.: (703) 790-8980
Fax: (703) 893-5160
E-mail: bwa@bwanet.org
Web site: http://www.bwanet.org/bwaid
Supports refugees and victims of famine and natural disasters. Feeds the starving and malnourished, especially in countries suffering from drought and food shortages.

BROTHER'S BROTHER FOUNDATION
1200 Galveston Avenue
Pittsburgh, PA 15233
Ph.: (412) 321-3160
Fax: (412) 321-3325
E-mail: mail@brothersbrother.org
Web site: http://www.brothersbrother.org
Links America's vast medical resources to global health care needs. Provides immunizations and donates medical supplies and equipment, seed, other agricultural inputs, and educational materials to needy countries across the globe.

CARIBBEAN DISASTER EMERGENCY RESPONSE AGENCY (CDERA)
Building #1 Manor Lodge
Lodge Hill, St. Michael
Barbados
Ph.: (246) 425-0386
Fax: (246) 425-8854
E-mail: cdera@caribsurf.com
Web site: http://www.cdera.org
Coordinates regional disaster management activities within 16 coun-
tries. Mobilizes and arranges disaster relief from governmental
and nongovernmental organizations for affected participating
countries. Aims for response to, recovery from, rebuilding from,
and prevention of natural disasters.

CATHOLIC RELIEF SERVICES
Information:
209 West Fayette Street
Baltimore, MD 21201
Ph.: (410) 625-2220, (800) 235-2772
Fax: (410) 685-1635
Web site: http://www.catholicrelief.org
Donations:
P.O. Box 17090
Baltimore, Maryland 21203-7090
Ph.: (888) 277-7575 (M-F), (800) 736-3467 (evenings/weekends)
Gives assistance based on need to people affected by natural disasters
in more than 80 countries around the world.

CHRISTIAN RELIEF SERVICES
2550 Huntington Avenue, Suite 200
Alexandria, VA 22303
Ph.: (703) 317-9086, (800) 33-RELIEF
E-mail: info@christianrelief.org
Web site: http://www.christianrelief.org
Collaborates with grass-roots charitable groups, churches, and hu-
man service agencies to help those in need in their own communi-
ties. Enables people to help themselves.

COOPERATIVE FOR AMERICAN RELIEF TO EVERYWHERE (CARE)

151 Ellis Street NE
Atlanta, GA 30303
Ph.: (404) 681-2552
Fax: (404) 589-2651
E-mail: info@care.org
Web site: http://www.care.org
Reaches tens of millions of people whose lives are devastated by humanitarian emergencies each year in more than 60 countries. Provides food, water, shelter, and health care to survivors of natural disasters and armed conflicts.

DIRECT RELIEF INTERNATIONAL

27 S. La Patera Lane
Santa Barbara, CA 93117
Ph.: (805) 964-4767
Fax: (805) 681-4838
E-mail: info@directrelief.org
Web site: http://www.directrelief.org
A nonprofit, nonsectarian medical relief organization that provides medical support with new and used medical equipment, pharmaceuticals, and supplies to over three thousand charitable health facilities worldwide. Distributes product contributions from manufacturers, hospitals, and health clinics.

DISASTER PREPAREDNESS AND EMERGENCY RESPONSE ASSOCIATION INTERNATIONAL (DERA)

Information:
P.O. Box 280795
Denver, CO 80228
E-mail: dera@disasters.org
Web site: http://www.disasters.org
Donations:
P.O. Box 797
Longmont, CO 80502
Assists communities in disaster preparedness, response, and recovery. Links professionals, volunteers, and organizations in all phases of emergency preparedness and management.

Do Unto Others (DUO)
21 Tamal Vista Boulevard, Suite 209
Corte Madera, CA 94925
Ph.: (800) 934-9755
Web site: http://www.duo.org
Responds to human-made and natural disasters wherever they occur in the world. Works to ease the suffering of people affected by war, natural disaster, famine, and epidemics.

Doctors Without Borders
Information:
333 7th Avenue, 2d Floor
New York, NY 10001-5004
Ph.: (212) 679-6800
Fax: (212) 679-7016
Web site: http://www.dwb.org
Donations:
Doctors Without Borders USA
P.O. Box 5030
Hagerstown, MD 21741-5030
Ph.: (888) 392-0392
The world's largest independent international medical relief agency, aiding victims of armed conflict, epidemics, and natural and human-made disasters in over 80 countries. Provides primary health care, performs surgery, vaccinates children, operates emergency nutrition and sanitation programs, and trains local medical staff. Also known as Médecins Sans Frontières (MSF).

Farm Service Agency (FSA)
U.S. Department of Agriculture
Farm Service Agency
Public Affairs Staff
1400 Independence Avenue SW
STOP 0506
Washington, DC 20250-0506
Web site: http://www.fsa.usda.gov/fsa
An agency of the United States Department of Agriculture (USDA). Offers assistance to farmers and ranchers suffering from droughts,

floods, freezes, tornadoes, or other natural disasters. Shares the cost of rehabilitating farmlands damaged by natural disaster and provides emergency water assistance. Programs include the Non-insured Crop Disaster Assistance Program (NAP), Emergency Loan (EM) Assistance, and Emergency Haying and Grazing Assistance.

FEDERAL EMERGENCY MANAGEMENT AGENCY (FEMA)
500 C. Street SW
Washington, DC 20472
Ph.: (800) 621-FEMA to apply for disaster assistance
Web site: http://www.fema.gov
An independent agency of the federal government founded in 1979. Helps millions of Americans face disaster and its terrifying consequences. Aims to reduce loss of life and property and protect the U.S. infrastructure from all types of hazards through a comprehensive, risk-based, emergency management program of mitigation, preparedness, response, and recovery.

FRIENDS OF THE WORLD FOOD PROGRAM (FWFP)
1819 L Street NW, Suite 400
Washington, DC 20036
Ph.: (202) 530-1694
Fax: (202) 530-1698
E-mail: info@friendsofwfp.org
Web site: http://www.friendsofwfp.org
Supports the World Food Program (WFP), which provides food aid to areas facing food deficits caused by human-made and natural disasters and helps more than 86 million people in 82 countries.

GLOBAL IMPACT
66 Canal Center Plaza, Suite 310
Alexandria, VA 22314
Ph.: (703) 717-5200, (800) 638-4620
Fax: (703) 717-5215
Web site: http://www.charity.org
A coalition of America's leading international relief and development organizations. Helps people who suffer from hunger, poverty, disease, or natural disasters.

INTERNATIONAL AID
17011 W. Hickory Street
Spring Lake, MI 49456-9712
Ph.: (616) 846-7490, (800) 968-7490, (800) 251-2502 (donations)
Fax: (616) 846-3842
Web site: http://www.internationalaid.org
Provides medicines, medical supplies, food, blankets, and other tangible resources to local groups caring for people in over 170 countries affected by natural disasters. Partners with local and national
churches and agencies that provide distribution, logistical support, and on-site administration for overseas relief efforts.

**INTERNATIONAL FEDERATION OF RED CROSS AND RED
CRESCENT SOCIETIES**
P.O. Box 372
CH-1211 Geneva 19
Switzerland
Ph.: (+41 22) 730 42 22
Fax: (+41 22) 733 03 95
Web site: http://www.ifrc.org
The Red Crescent is used in place of the Red Cross in many Islamic
countries. Provides humanitarian relief to people affected by di-
sasters or other emergencies and development assistance to em-
power vulnerable people to become more self-sufficient in 176
countries.

INTERNATIONAL MEDICAL CORPS (IMC)
1919 Santa Monica Boulevard, Suite 300
Santa Monica, CA 90404
Ph.: (310) 826-7800, (800) 481-4462 (donations)
Fax: (310) 442-6622
E-mail: imc@imcworldwide.org
Web site: http://www.imcworldwide.org
Responds rapidly to emerging epidemics, purchases vaccines and
emergency medical supplies to vaccinate children against disease
and prevent thousands of needless deaths. Rehabilitates health
posts in remote areas in 16 countries.

LUTHERAN WORLD RELIEF
Information:
700 Light Street
Baltimore, MD 21230
Ph.: (410) 230-2800
Fax: (410) 230-2882
E-mail: lwr@lwr.org
Web site: http://www.lwr.org
Donations:
P.O. Box 17061
Baltimore, MD 21298-9832
Ph.: (800) LWR-LWR2
Offers health care, food, water, and other relief supplies around the
  world. Works to improve harvests, health, and education in some
  50 countries.

MAP INTERNATIONAL
2200 Glynco Parkway
P.O. Box 215000
Brunswick, GA 31521-5000
Ph.: (800) 225-8550
Web site: http://www.map.org
Provides essential medicines, works for the prevention and eradica-
  tion of disease, and promotes community health development
  worldwide.

MERCY CORPS
Information:
Dept W
3015 SW 1st Avenue
Portland, OR 97201
Ph.: (800) 292-3355
Fax: (503) 796-6844
Web site: http://www.mercycorps.org
Donations:
Dept W
P.O. Box 2669
Portland OR 97208

Ph.: (888) 256-1900

Works to alleviate suffering caused by drought and famine. Provides food, shelter, health care, and economic opportunity to more than 3 million people in 68 countries, sending emergency goods and material aid.

NATIONAL RELIEF NETWORK
P.O. Box 125
Greenville, MI 48838-0125
Ph.: (616) 225-2525, (866) 286-5868
Fax: (616) 225-1934
E-mail: info@nrn.org
Web site: http://www.nrn.org

Brings large numbers of volunteers to areas struck by natural disasters for as long as it takes to bring help to each and every family in need.

NAZARENE DISASTER RESPONSE USA
Information:
Ph.: (888) 256-5886
E-mail: ndr@ncmi.org
Web site: http://www.ncm.org/min_ndr.aspx
Donations:
General Treasurer
Church of the Nazarene
6401 The Paseo
Kansas City, MO 64131-1213

Provides disaster relief to victims in the United States.

UNITARIAN UNIVERSALIST SERVICE COMMITTEE (UUSC)
130 Prospect Street
Cambridge, MA 02139
Ph.: (617) 868-6600, (800) 388-3920
Fax: (617) 868-7102
Web site: http://www.uusc.org

A nonsectarian organization that promotes human rights and social justice in the United States, South and Southeast Asia, Central Africa, Latin America, and the Caribbean. Provides financial and technical support when disasters strike impoverished areas.

UNITED NATIONS OFFICE FOR THE COORDINATION OF HUMANITARIAN AFFAIRS (OCHA)
Office for the Coordination of Humanitarian Affairs
United Nations Secretariat
S-3600
New York, NY 10017
Ph.: (212) 963-1234
Fax: (212) 963-1013
Web site: http://ochaonline.un.org
Provides information on emergencies and natural disasters collected from over 170 sources. Coordinates emergency response primarily through the Inter-Agency Standing Committee (IASC), with the participation of humanitarian partners such as the Red Cross.

U.S. AGENCY FOR INTERNATIONAL DEVELOPMENT (USAID)
Information Center
U.S. Agency for International Development
Ronald Reagan Building
Washington, DC 20523-1000
Ph.: (202) 712-4810, (202) 712-0000
Fax: (202) 216-3524
Web site: http://www.usaid.gov
A federal government agency that implements America's foreign economic and humanitarian assistance programs. The principal U.S. agency to extend assistance to countries recovering from disaster.

U.S. COMMITTEE FOR UNICEF
333 East 38th Street
New York, NY 10016
Ph.: (212) 686-5522, (800) 4UNICEF
Fax: (212) 779-1670
Web site: http://www.unicefusa.org
Raises money for UNICEF, which works in more than 160 countries and territories providing health care, clean water, improved nutrition, and education to millions of children in Africa, Asia, Central and Eastern Europe, Latin America, and the Middle East. Promotes the survival, protection, and development of children worldwide.

WORLD ASSOCIATION FOR DISASTER AND EMERGENCY MEDICINE (WADEM)
P.O. Box 55158
Madison, WI 53705-8958
Ph.: (608) 263-2069
Fax: (608) 265-3037
E-mail: wadem@medicine.wisc.edu
Web site: http://wadem.medicine.wisc.edu
Promotes the worldwide development and improvement of emergency and disaster medicine. Helps people affected by medical emergencies and national and international disasters.

WORLD CONCERN
International Headquarters
19303 Fremont Avenue North
Seattle, Washington 98133
Ph.: (206) 546-7201, (800) 755-5022
Fax: (206) 546-7269
E-mail: info@worldconcern.org
Web site: http://www.worldconcern.org
Provides food relief and life skill enrichment to impoverished families worldwide. Offers emergency relief, rehabilitation, and long-term development.

WORLD HEALTH ORGANIZATION (WHO)
Avenue Appia 20
1211 Geneva 27
Switzerland
Ph: (+41 22) 791 21 11
Fax: (+41 22) 791 3111
E-mail: info@who.int
Web site: http://www.who.int
Promotes technical cooperation for health among nations, carries out programs to control and eradicate disease, and cooperates with governments in strengthening national health programs. Develops and transfers appropriate health technology, information, and standards and strives to improve the quality of human life. A specialized agency of the United Nations with 191 member countries.

WORLD RELIEF

7 East Baltimore St

Baltimore, MD 21202

Ph.: (443) 451-1900

E-mail: worldrelief@wr.org

Web site: http://www.wr.org

Provides quick, effective assistance to the most vulnerable victims of earthquakes, hurricanes, drought, or war. Combats poverty and disease to keep children healthy. Part of the World Evangelical Fellowship.

WORLD VISION

Headquarters:

34834 Weyerhaeuser Way South

Federal Way, WA 98001

Ph.: (888) 511-6548

E-mail: info@worldvision.org

Web site: http://www.worldvision.org

Mailing address:

P.O. Box 9716, Dept. W

Federal Way, WA 98063-9716

Serves the world's poor and displaced by providing programs that help save lives, bring hope, and restore dignity.

Lauren Mitchell

INDEXES

■ CATEGORY LIST

HURRICANES, TYPHOONS, AND CYCLONES
Hurricanes, Typhoons, and Cyclones (overview)
1900: The Galveston hurricane, Texas
1926: The Great Miami Hurricane
1928: The San Felipe hurricane, Florida and the Caribbean
1938: The Great New England Hurricane of 1938
1957: Hurricane Audrey
1969: Hurricane Camille
1970: The Bhola cyclone, East Pakistan
1989: Hurricane Hugo
1992: Hurricane Andrew
1998: Hurricane Mitch
2005: Hurricane Katrina

ICE STORMS. *See* **BLIZZARDS, FREEZES, ICE STORMS, AND HAIL**

ICEBERGS AND GLACIERS
Icebergs and Glaciers (overview)

LANDSLIDES, MUDSLIDES, AND ROCKSLIDES
Landslides, Mudslides, and Rockslides (overview)
1963: The Vaiont Dam Disaster, Italy
1966: The Aberfan Disaster, Wales
2006: The Leyte mudslide, Philippines

LIGHTNING STRIKES
Lightning Strikes (overview)

METEORITES AND COMETS
Meteorites and Comets (overview)
c. 65,000,000 B.C.E.: Yucatán crater, Atlantic Ocean
1908: The Tunguska event, Siberia

MUDSLIDES. *See* **LANDSLIDES, MUDSLIDES, AND ROCKSLIDES**

ROCKSLIDES. *See* **LANDSLIDES, MUDSLIDES, AND ROCKSLIDES**

SANDSTORMS. *See* **DUST STORMS AND SANDSTORMS**

■ GEOGRAPHICAL LIST

AFRICA. *See also individual countries*
1984: Africa famine
2004: The Indian Ocean Tsunami

ALABAMA
2005: Hurricane Katrina

ALASKA
1964: The Great Alaska Earthquake

ARMENIA
1988: The Leninakan earthquake

ASIA. *See also individual countries*
2002: SARS epidemic
2004: The Indian Ocean Tsunami

ATLANTIC OCEAN
c. 65,000,000 B.C.E.: Yucatán crater
1953: The North Sea Flood of 1953

AUSTRIA
1999: The Galtür avalanche

BAHAMAS
1992: Hurricane Andrew

BANGLADESH. *See also* **EAST PAKISTAN**
2004: The Indian Ocean Tsunami

BELGIUM
1953: The North Sea Flood of 1953

CALIFORNIA
1906: The Great San Francisco Earthquake

1928: St. Francis Dam collapse
1989: The Loma Prieta earthquake
1991: The Oakland Hills Fire
1994: The Northridge earthquake
2003: The Fire Siege of 2003

CAMEROON
1986: The Lake Nyos Disaster

CANADA
1914: *Empress of Ireland* sinking
1974: The Jumbo Outbreak
2002: SARS epidemic

CARIBBEAN
1692: The Port Royal earthquake, Jamaica
1902: Pelée eruption, Martinique
1928: The San Felipe hurricane
1989: Hurricane Hugo
1992: Hurricane Andrew
1997: Soufrière Hills eruption, Montserrat

CENTRAL AMERICA. *See also individual countries*
1998: Hurricane Mitch

CHINA
1959: The Great Leap Forward Famine
1976: The Tangshan earthquake
2002: SARS epidemic

EAST PAKISTAN
1970: The Bhola cyclone

EGYPT
1200: Egypt famine

ENGLAND
1665: The Great Plague of London

1666: The Great Fire of London
1880: The Seaham Colliery Disaster
1952: The Great London Smog

ETHIOPIA
1984: Africa famine

EUROPE. *See also individual countries*
1320: The Black Death
2003: Europe heat wave

FLORIDA
1926: The Great Miami Hurricane
1928: The San Felipe hurricane
1992: Hurricane Andrew
2005: Hurricane Katrina

FRANCE
2003: Europe heat wave

GREAT BRITAIN. *See also* **ENGLAND; IRELAND; WALES**
1953: The North Sea Flood of 1953

GREAT PLAINS, U.S.
1932: The Dust Bowl

GREECE
430 B.C.E.: The Plague of Athens

HAWAII
1946: The Aleutian tsunami

HONG KONG
2002: SARS epidemic

ICELAND
1783: Laki eruption

IDAHO
1988: Yellowstone National Park fires

ILLINOIS
1871: The Great Chicago Fire
1909: The Cherry Mine Disaster
1925: The Great Tri-State Tornado
1995: Chicago heat wave

INDIA
2004: The Indian Ocean Tsunami
2005: The Kashmir earthquake

INDIAN OCEAN
2004: The Indian Ocean Tsunami

INDIANA
1925: The Great Tri-State Tornado

INDONESIA
1815: Tambora eruption
1883: Krakatau eruption
2004: The Indian Ocean Tsunami

IRAN
2003: The Bam earthquake

IRELAND
1845: The Great Irish Famine

ITALY
64 C.E.: The Great Fire of Rome
79: Vesuvius eruption
1669: Etna eruption
1908: The Messina earthquake
1963: The Vaiont Dam Disaster

JAMAICA
1692: The Port Royal earthquake

JAPAN
1657: The Meireki Fire
1923: The Great Kwanto Earthquake
1995: The Kobe earthquake

KENYA
2004: The Indian Ocean Tsunami

LOUISIANA
1957: Hurricane Audrey
1992: Hurricane Andrew
2005: Hurricane Katrina

MARTINIQUE
1902: Pelée eruption

MASSACHUSETTS
1872: The Great Boston Fire

MEDITERRANEAN
c. 1470 B.C.E.: Thera eruption, Aegean Sea
1669: Etna eruption, Sicily

MEXICO
1520: Aztec Empire smallpox epidemic
1982: El Chichón eruption
1985: The Mexico City earthquake

MIDWEST, U.S.
1965: The Palm Sunday Outbreak
1974: The Jumbo Outbreak

MISSISSIPPI
2005: Hurricane Katrina

MISSISSIPPI RIVER
1993: The Great Mississippi River Flood of 1993

MISSOURI
1811: New Madrid earthquakes
1896: The Great Cyclone of 1896, St. Louis
1925: The Great Tri-State Tornado

MONTANA
1988: Yellowstone National Park fires

MONTSERRAT
1997: Soufrière Hills eruption

NEPAL
1996: The Mount Everest Disaster

NETHERLANDS
1953: The North Sea Flood of 1953

NEW ENGLAND
1888: The Great Blizzard of 1888
1938: The Great New England Hurricane of 1938

NEW JERSEY
1937: The *Hindenburg* Disaster

NEW YORK
1900: Typhoid Mary

NORTH CAROLINA
1989: Hurricane Hugo

NORTH SEA
1953: The North Sea Flood of 1953

OKLAHOMA
1999: The Oklahoma Tornado Outbreak

L

PACIFIC OCEAN
1982: Pacific Ocean El Niño

PAKISTAN
2005: The Kashmir earthquake

PAPUA NEW GUINEA
1998: Papua New Guinea tsunami

PENNSYLVANIA
1889: The Johnstown Flood
1976: Legionnaires' disease, Philadelphia

PERU
1970: The Ancash earthquake

PHILIPPINES
1991: Pinatubo eruption
2006: The Leyte mudslide

PORTUGAL
1755: The Lisbon earthquake

RUSSIA
1908: The Tunguska event

SIBERIA
1908: The Tunguska event

SOUTH, U.S.
1974: The Jumbo Outbreak

SOUTH CAROLINA
1989: Hurricane Hugo

SRI LANKA
2004: The Indian Ocean Tsunami

SUDAN
1976: Ebola outbreaks
1984: Africa famine

SYRIA
526: The Antioch earthquake

TENNESSEE
1878: The Great Yellow Fever Epidemic, Memphis

TEXAS
1900: The Galveston hurricane
1947: The Texas City Disaster
1957: Hurricane Audrey
1997: The Jarrell tornado

THAILAND
2004: The Indian Ocean Tsunami

TURKEY
1999: The İzmit earthquake

UNITED STATES. *See also individual states and regions*
1916: The Great Polio Epidemic
1932: The Dust Bowl, Great Plains
1938: The Great New England Hurricane of 1938
1965: The Palm Sunday Outbreak
1974: The Jumbo Outbreak

WALES
1966: The Aberfan Disaster

WASHINGTON STATE
1980: Mount St. Helens eruption

WEST INDIES
1902: Pelée eruption, Martinique
1928: The San Felipe hurricane

1992: Hurricane Andrew
1997: Soufrière Hills eruption, Montserrat

WEST VIRGINIA
1914: The Eccles Mine Disaster

WISCONSIN
1871: The Great Peshtigo Fire

WORLDWIDE
1892: Cholera pandemic
1918: The Great Flu Pandemic
1980: AIDS pandemic

WYOMING
1988: Yellowstone National Park fires

ZAIRE
1976: Ebola outbreaks
1995: Ebola outbreak

INDEX

Texas City, Texas, 97, 620-626
Thailand tsunamis, 948
Thera, 301-305
Thermals, 18
Thermocline, 67
Thíra, 301
Third-degree burns, 121
Third World, 109
3TC, 726
Thucydides, 306
Thunder, 204, 207
Thunderheads, 19
Thunderstones, 223
Thunderstorms, 18, 204, 240, 290
Tidal bores, 253
Tidal waves, 253
Tiltmeters, 198, 281
Titanic, 187
Tjiringin, Indonesia, 455
TNT, 94
Toc, Mount, 650
Tokyo; earthquakes, 566, 571; fires, 350
Toledo, Ohio, 660
Topples, 192
Topsoil, 599
Torino Impact Hazard Scale, 216
Tornado Alley, 242
Tornadoes, 171, 237-252, 485, 573, 659, 694, 820, 873, 903; forecasting, 243, 248-249; warnings, 243, 250; watches, 243, 250
Toronto epidemics, 925
Trade winds, 67
Trains, 154
Transform faults, 54, 513
Translational slides, 191
Trash fires, 116
Triage, 58

Triangle Shirtwaist Factory, 124
Tropical Atmosphere-Ocean (TAO) array, 70
Tropical storms, 169
Truman, Harry, 735
Tsunamis, 253-268, 283, 376-377, 382, 453, 458, 528, 566, 615, 652, 885, 946; fluvial, 397
Tunguska event, 218, 524-526
Turkey earthquakes, 328, 909
Twenty-year-flood, 131
Twisters. *See* Tornadoes
Typhoid fever, 82, 501
Typhoid Mary, 501-504
Typhoons, 165-182
Typhus, 82

■ **U**

Ultra-Plinian eruptions, 276
United Nations, 106
United States. *See* individual states and regions
United States Forest Service, 733
United States Geological Survey, 805
Unzen, 272
Updrafts, 18
Upslope fog, 148
Urbani, Carlo, 924
U.S. Army Corps of Engineers, 140
USFS. *See* United States Forest Service
USGS. *See* United States Geological Survey

■ **V**

Vaccination, 83
Vaiont Dam, Italy, 145, 194, 648-651